DAILY LIFE IN

THE SOVIET
UNION

The Greenwood Press "Daily Life Through History" Series

DAILY LIFE IN

THE SOVIET UNION

KATHERINE B. EATON

The Greenwood Press "Daily Life Through History" Series

GREENWOOD PRESS
Westport, Connecticut • London

Library of Congress Cataloguing-in-Publication Data

Eaton, Katherine Bliss.
    Daily life in the Soviet Union / Katherine B. Eaton.
        p. cm. — (The Greenwood Press "Daily life through history" series,
    ISSN 1080–4749)
    Includes index.
    ISBN 0–313–31628–7 (alk. paper)
    1. Soviet Union—Social life and customs. 2. Soviet Union—History. I. Title.
    II. Series.
    DK266.4.E17   2004
    947.084—dc22   2004012486

British Library Cataloguing in Publication Data is available.

Library of Congress Catalog Card Number: 2004012486
ISBN: 0–313–31628–7
ISSN: 1080–4749

First published in 2004

Greenwood Press, 88 Post Road West, Westport, CT 06881
An imprint of Greenwood Publishing Group, Inc.
www.greenwood.com

Printed in the United States of America

The paper used in this book complies with the
Permanent Paper Standard issued by the National
Information Standards Organization (Z39.48–1984).

10 9 8 7 6 5 4 3 2 1

Copyright Acknowledgments

The author and publisher gratefully acknowledge permission for use of the
following:

Extracts from Katherine Bliss Eaton, ed. *Enemies of the People: The Destruction of
Literary, Theater, and Film Arts in the Soviet Union in the 1930s.* Evanston, IL: Northwestern University Press, 2002, and Victor Terras, translator.

Copyright © 2001 from *Censorship: A World Encyclopedia* by Derek Jones. Reproduced by permission of Routledge/Taylor & Francis Books, Inc.

Recipe for Russian Kulich courtesy of Fleischmann's Yeast, a division of Burns
Philp Food, Inc.

Every reasonable effort has been made to trace the owners of copyright materials
in this book, but in some instances this has proven impossible. The author and
publisher will be glad to receive information leading to more complete acknowledgments in subsequent printings of the book and in the meantime extend their
apologies for any omissions.

For Henry, Stephen, and Jonathan Eaton

There are secrets galore in the Soviet Union, but the principal and most carefully guarded state secret is the daily life of the Soviet people.

—*Vladimir Voinovich*

contents

preface

The idea of "daily life" implies an orderly routine in a stable environment, the ability to go about one's business confident that life is reasonably predictable, that the ground rules of one's society and upbringing will hold and not suddenly, horribly, evaporate. The Soviet period, which lasted 73 years, was a time of repeated seismic shifts in people's everyday lives. Add to that the sheer size of the Soviet empire, with its scores of ethnic groups, nationalities, cultures, and languages; its variety of religions; and the wide gaps in the lifestyles of different social classes. How, in a book on "daily life," do we include mass starvation, terror, war deaths, executions, and imprisonment of innocent people for decades on end, among all social classes and nationalities? At the same time, millions of people lived out their lives relatively undisturbed; millions more survived terrors and kept on going, perhaps even finding joy in their existence.

In this book I have focused on the day-to-day experiences of average people, mainly those who lived and worked in Russia's cities and on farms. But I have not ignored other regions. Similarly, although this book is not about USSR concentration camps or dispossessed families, no chapter overlooks the dark side of Soviet existence. For many Soviet citizens, terror was a distant backdrop against which they played out their ordinary lives, but for many others, it was the very fabric of life itself.

In describing the conditions of Soviet reality, whether ghastly or humdrum, I found works of literature especially useful. Because artists so trenchantly communicate the texture of life, I have frequently drawn upon the words of fine Soviet authors to illustrate a point. In most cases, those words were banned from publication in their time.

acknowledgments

I appreciate the assistance of the Greenwood editors who worked with me on various manuscript drafts: Barbara Rader, Kevin Ohe, and Michael Hermann. Thanks also to the copyeditor, Barbara Juhas Walsh, for her excellent work and thanks to the staff at Impressions. It helped a lot to participate in the University of Illinois Russian and East European Center's Summer Research Lab for two weeks in the summers. The rest of the time, I made heavy use of the library facilities at the University of North Texas, including Interlibrary Loan. With the help of Library of Congress Prints and Photographs Division librarians, I was able to find many fine pictures, and in that regard I want to particularly mention Marilyn Ibach, who quickly found answers to my questions. Special thanks to Cyndi Lewis. Above all my husband, Henry Eaton, was the biggest help because he read and edited each chapter. I benefited from his expert knowledge of Russian and Soviet history and editing skill. Any defects remaining in the final version are my responsibility.

A Note on Transliteration

In transliterating the sounds of Russian from the Cyrillic to the Roman alphabet, I have generally followed the systems (I and II) outlined by J. Thomas Shaw in *The Transliteration of Modern Russian for English-Language Publications* (Madison: University of Wisconsin Press, 1967). However, I made exceptions, especially where certain spellings that do not follow Shaw's system would look more familiar or be less confusing to readers.

Brief chronology of Russia and the Soviet Union in the Twentieth century

1898   Formation of the Marxist Russian Social Democratic Labor Party (RSDLP or SDs).

1901–02   Formation of Socialist Revolutionary Party (SRs); terrorist section of SRs devoted to assassination of government officials.

1903   RSDLP split: Bolsheviks under Vladimir I. Lenin, Mensheviks under Yuly Martov.

1905   Revolution: Bloody Sunday (Jan. 9 [old style]); massive strikes; Nicholas II issues October Manifesto (Oct. 17 [old style]) establishing elected legislative assembly, the Duma.

1906–11   Prime Minister Pyotr Stolypin intensifies police actions against anti-tsarists and introduces a promising program of major agricultural reforms. In 1911 Stolypin is assassinated by a double (police/revolutionary) agent.

1914–18   World War I.

1917   February Revolution (March 8–16 [new style]); two popular assemblies form themselves by March 12–14 (new style): Provisional Government (which grew out of the Duma) and Petrograd Soviet of Workers' and Soldiers' Deputies (soon composed mainly of SRs, Mensheviks, and Bolsheviks); Nicholas II abdicates (March 2 [old style]/15 [new style]); Bolsheviks overthrow Provisional Government and seize power (October 24–25 [old style]/ November 6–7 [new style]).

1918	Constituent Assembly (elected in November 1917, SRs dominate) meets once on January 18–19 and is then dissolved by Bolsheviks; Nicholas II and family executed on July 17.
1918–20	Civil War between Reds (mainly Bolsheviks), who called their war policy "War Communism," and Whites (widely different political groups joined to fight Bolsheviks); United States, Britain, France, and Japan assist Whites.
1921	Kronstadt Revolt in March crushed by Bolsheviks; end of War Communism; great famine of 1921–22.
1921–29	New Economic Policy (NEP), door partly opened to private enterprise.
1920s	Stalin situates himself in top Party committees; elected General Secretary of Party in 1922.
1922	USSR (Union of Soviet Socialist Republics) founded on December 30.
1922–24	Lenin impaired by three strokes (May 1922–March 1923); dies January 21, 1924.
1924–29	Stalin outmaneuvers other leading Bolsheviks in struggle for political power.
1926	Family Code (October): eased divorce restraints but expanded rights to alimony, child support, and property obtained while married.
1928–32	First of the Five-Year Plans begins economic, especially industrial, revolution in USSR.
1929	National celebration of Stalin's 50th birthday on December 21 launches cult of personality; Stalin ends NEP and demands all-out collectivization of agriculture and liquidation of *kulaks* (prosperous peasants).
1930	Collectivization begins in January.
1932–33	Great famine, especially in Ukraine.
1934	Leningrad Party leader Sergey Kirov assassinated (December 1); pretext for mass police terror.
1936–38	Stalin destroys the party of Lenin: orders "trials," convictions, and execution of leading Bolsheviks: first Moscow trial, August 1936; second trial, January 1937; third trial, March 1938.
1937–38	Thousands of military officers, including top commanders, arrested and executed.

1939   Nazi Germany–USSR sign nonaggression pact and secretly agree to a partition of Eastern Europe; German invasion of Poland (from September 1) begins World War II; USSR invades eastern Poland (from September 17).

1939–40   USSR–Finland "Winter War."

1940   USSR annexes Baltic states (Estonia, Latvia, and Lithuania).

1941–45   World War II, known to Russians as the Great Fatherland War. German invasion of USSR begins on June 22, 1941.

1942–43   Soviet victory at Battle of Stalingrad (August–February) is one of war's turning points.

1943   Karachais and Kalmyks deported to the east in November–December.

1944   Chechens, Ingush, Balkars, Crimean Tatars, Ukrainians, and Byelorussians deported eastward.

1945   Soviet forces invade Germany in January, enter Berlin in April; Germany surrenders May 8.

1946–49   Soviet takeover of east-central Europe; police repression grows; cooling toward West; nuclear power and guided ballistic missiles developed; A-bomb tested (September 1949).

1953   Stalin's death (March 5) ends police action against alleged Jewish "doctors' plot"; top Party leaders jockey for power; H-bomb tested (August); Nikita Khrushchev elected First Secretary of Central Committee (September).

1953–54   Rehabilitation of police terror victims and return of Gulag prisoners begins; signs of cultural thaw—Ilya Ehrenburg publishes novel *The Thaw* (1954)—but heavy-handed censorship and persecution of dissident writers continues.

1956   Twentieth Party Congress (February 14–25); Khrushchev delivers "secret" speech accusing Stalin of crimes; Hungarian revolt suppressed by Soviet troops (October–November).

1957   *Sputnik* launched (October 4).

1959   Underground press (*samizdat*, self-publishing) appears.

1961   Yuri Gagarin, aboard *Vostok*, becomes first man launched into space.

1962   Cuban missile crisis in October; Solzhenitsyn's *One Day in the Life of Ivan Denisovich*, depicting Gulag prison life, published in November with Khrushchev's blessing (but author deported from USSR in 1974 after publication of his longer exposé, *Gulag Archipelago,* in Paris).

1964   Central Committee replaces Khrushchev (1894–1971) with Leonid Brezhnev (1906–82).

1968   Soviet troops invade Czechoslovakia; in Moscow, demonstrators against invasion are arrested and prosecuted.

1979   Soviet invasion of Afghanistan in December.

1982–85   Deaths of aged leaders quickly follow one another: Brezhnev, Andropov, Chernenko.

1985   Mikhail Gorbachev replaces Chernenko as First Secretary (March 11); advocates *glasnost'* (openness), *perestroika* (reconstruction), and democratic political reform.

1986   Disorders in Georgia (Soviet troops kill demonstrators); Chernobyl disaster (April 26) not reported for several days despite Gorbachev's promise of glasnost.

1989   USSR Congress of People's Deputies elected, some in democratic elections; Gorbachev announces USSR will leave Afghanistan; workers' strikes; Lithuanian national movement grows.

1990   Russian Federation begins to pull away from USSR as Boris Yeltsin and others move to establish their own parties; Gorbachev elected USSR president.

1991   Yeltsin elected president of the Russian Federation in June; in August Yeltsin foils attempt of hard right to overthrow Gorbachev; Yeltsin's actions put him in the spotlight of favorable public attention.

1991   Independence movements grow; Soviet forces kill 14 in Vilnius (Lithuania); six republics declare independence in October; recognition that the rest of the 15 republics are independent and the USSR dissolved comes with the formation of the Commonwealth of Independent States (CIS) on December 21; Gorbachev resigns on December 25; USSR formally dissolved on December 31.

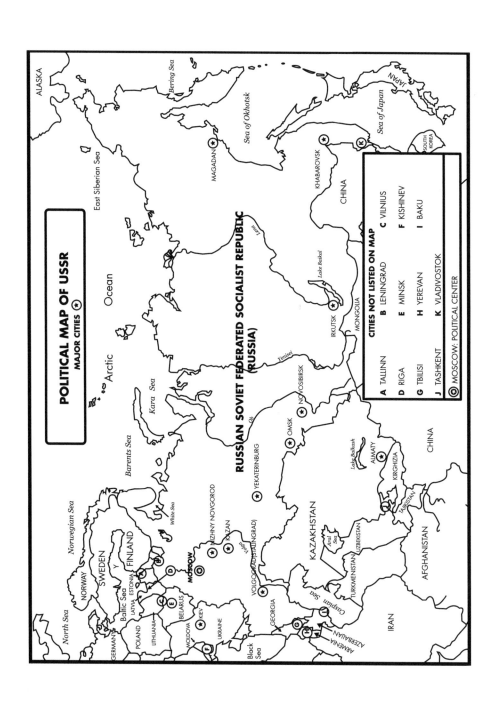

POLITICAL MAP OF USSR
MAJOR CITIES ✹

RUSSIAN SOVIET FEDERATED SOCIALIST REPUBLIC (RUSSIA)

CITIES NOT LISTED ON MAP

A TALLINN	B LENINGRAD	C VILNIUS
D RIGA	E MINSK	F KISHINEV
G TBILISI	H YEREVAN	I BAKU
J TASHKENT	K VLADIVOSTOK	

◉ MOSCOW: POLITICAL CENTER

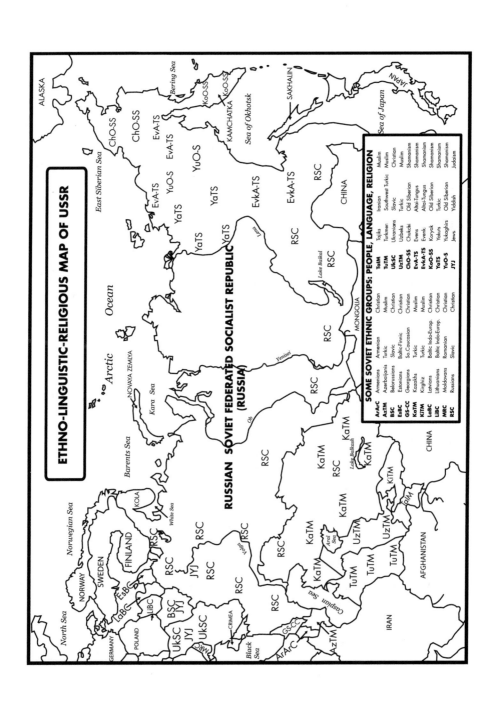

ETHNO-LINGUISTIC-RELIGIOUS MAP OF USSR

RUSSIAN SOVIET FEDERATED SOCIALIST REPUBLIC (RUSSIA)

SOME SOVIET ETHNIC GROUPS: PEOPLE, LANGUAGE, RELIGION						
ArArC	Armenians	Armenian	Christian	**TaM**	Tajiks	Iranian	Muslim
AzTM	Azerbaijanis	Turkic	Muslim	**TuTM**	Turkmen	Southwest Turkic	Muslim
BSC	Belorussians	Slavic	Christian	**UkSC**	Ukranians	Slavic	Christian
EsBC	Estonians	Baltic-Finnic	Christian	**UzTM**	Uzbeks	Turkic	Muslim
GS-CC	Georgians	So-Caucasian	Christian	**ChO-SS**	Chukchi	Old Siberian	Shamanism
KaTM	Kazakhs	Turkic	Muslim	**EvA-TS**	Evenk	Altai-Tungus	Shamanism
KiTM	Kirghiz	Turkic	Muslim	**EvkA-TS**	Evenk	Altai-Tungus	Shamanism
LaBC	Latvians	Baltic Indo-Europ.	Christian	**KoO-SS**	Koryak	Old Siberian	Shamanism
LiBC	Lithuanians	Baltic Indo-Europ.	Christian	**YaTS**	Yakuts	Turkic	Shamanism
MRC	Moldovans	Romanian	Christian	**YuO-S**	Yukoghirs	Old Siberian	Shamanism
RSC	Russians	Slavic	Christian	**JYJ**	Jews	Yiddish	Judaism

I

The soviet union, 1917–1991

The Russian revolutions of 1917 appeared to open the way for a great experiment in democracy and social justice. In March a popular uprising overthrew the monarchy, and in November its successor, the Provisional Government, was swept aside by the Bolsheviks. These events occurred in the midst of World War I, a devastating war for Russia, one that revealed how misguided and indecisive was the last tsar, Nicholas II. Looking beyond the immediate for the deeper causes of the 1917 upheavals, we should keep in mind the impact on Russians of political thought and revolutions in the West as well as the long history of oppression in their country, punctuated at times by explosions of public anger and violence.

THE REVOLUTION OF FEBRUARY/MARCH 1917[1]

On August 2, 1914, a large crowd gathered in St. Petersburg before the Winter Palace to greet Tsar Nicholas II and the declaration of war against Germany with wave after wave of hurrahs. During the next two years, however, popular enthusiasm gave way to grief and frustration over the great number of combat casualties and woefully inadequate support Russian soldiers got from the home front. Finally, in a mood quite different from when the war started, people gathered in the streets to openly demonstrate their grievances. In the extraordinarily cold winter of 1916–1917, residents of the capital, Petrograd,[2] as in other cities, began to experience severe shortages, especially of bread and of fuel used for heating and cooking and for powering industry. The problem was not so much a scarcity of these things as it was government ineptitude in organizing transports of supplies into the city. Factories were forced to shut down, and anxious residents emptied bakery shelves. On March 7 and 8 the streets of Petrograd became crowded with locked-out or striking workers, women trying to find bakeries with bread to sell or out in recognition of International Women's Day (March 8), and soldiers, themselves cold and hungry, afraid of being sent to the front and reluctant to shoot into the unruly crowds. Day by day the size and aggressiveness of the crowds grew.

A critical turning point occurred Sunday to Monday, March 11 and 12. Soldiers fired on and killed some demonstrators on Sunday. That night troops of the Pavlovsky Regiment, many of them recently conscripted peasant men and boys, discussed the killings and voted to disobey their officers if ordered, the next day, to do the same. Other units began joining the Pavlovsky Regiment on Monday, and by evening that day most of the tens of thousands of troops stationed in Petrograd had mutinied.

Relatively little blood was shed in toppling the irresolute Nicholas, who was away from the capital during the crisis and failed to understand how serious the disturbances were. Events passed him by. The two political institutions that replaced his government were being established even before he resigned (March 15, 1917). There was the Provisional Government, made up of leading members of the disbanded Duma (legislature), who pledged to serve briefly until a constituent assembly, chosen in a broadly inclusive democratic election, could create a new constitution and legitimate government. The Provisional Government advocated the supremacy of law and the guarantee of individual and civil liberties and moved quickly to free political prisoners and abolish capital punishment. However, it failed to resolve two issues about which Russians were very concerned; it refused to redistribute land to peasants (small farmers and agricultural workers) and continued the disastrous war against Germany and Austria.

Arising in Petrograd, literally beside the Provisional Government, in the same building and during the same days (Taurida Palace, March 12–14), was the Petrograd Soviet (or Council) of Workers' and Soldiers' Deputies. Hundreds of workers and soldiers crowded into the halls and rooms of the palace. At first, well-known leftist Duma representatives, in particular, Mensheviks (members of a wing of the Russian Social Democratic Labor Party), were elected to the Soviet's top positions. Over the next few weeks, however, as other socialist leaders surfaced, shedding their anonymity or returning from prison or exile, the leadership came to reflect the importance of three socialist parties: Socialist Revolutionaries (SRs), Mensheviks, and Bolsheviks. SRs claimed to speak for the Russian peasants; the latter two were Marxist parties whose members had, until 1903, belonged to a single Russian Social Democratic Labor Party (RSDLP). Between the March and November revolutions the Provisional Government and Petrograd Soviet existed as dual powers in an uneasy alliance, the one acting as government, the other as guardian of the revolution.

THE BOLSHEVIK COUP OF OCTOBER–NOVEMBER 1917

It was Vladimir Lenin (V. I. Ulyanov, 1870–1924) who, in 1903, insisted on splitting the RSDLP into Bolsheviks and Mensheviks over differences in political strategy. Many social democrats in both groups opposed the breakup, but Lenin would not retreat from his decision. Such determination was characteristic—time and again, even against strong opposition within his own Bolshevik faction, he prevailed. Intelligent, well-grounded in Marxism, and keenly observant and pragmatic, this political bulldog, once he returned to Russia (April 16, 1917) from exile in Switzerland, immediately began moving the Bolsheviks toward taking political power. The success of this move, however, was not only a matter of his leadership. The Provisional Government, troubled by one crisis after another, with its ministers being changed every few weeks, could hardly build public confidence in its ability to govern. Furthermore, despite its commitment to and the urgency of creating a popular government, it delayed election of a constitutional convention until November. By election time the Bolsheviks had already taken over. For their part, many members of the Petrograd Soviet, despite or because of the Soviet's popularity, were reluctant to take over the government and assume responsibility for resolving nearly insurmountable problems.

Lenin had no such reluctance, and on November 6–7, 1917 (October 24–25, Old Style), after weeks of his urging, the Bolsheviks finally overthrew the Provisional Government, against relatively little resistance and without much bloodshed. Late on the evening of November 7, the Second All-Russian Congress of Soviets met for its opening session. Leon Trotsky (Lev Davidovich Bronstein, 1877–1940), chairman of the Petrograd Soviet, told the delegates what had just happened and, backed by a majority in the congress of Bolsheviks and some SRs, took over the convention. He ridiculed a proposal to have the Bolsheviks join with other democratic parties in forming a government. Many Menshevik and SR delegates walked out. The next day Lenin was received by the delegates with tremendous enthusiasm. He proclaimed the beginning of the construction of socialism and introduced three decrees: one to end the war, another to abolish private property, and a third to create a new government. The name of this government was Council of People's Commissars, and every commissar was to be a Bolshevik: Lenin, chairman; Trotsky, foreign affairs; Aleksei Rykov (1881–1938), internal affairs; Joseph Stalin (Iosif V. Dzhugashvili, 1879–1953), nationalities; and so on. All was done in the name of the Soviet. Thus, at the start, a transparent fiction was created that the Congress of Soviets, rather than the Bolsheviks, was the governing power. In fact, there was to be no democracy and only some temporary sharing of power with sympathetic SRs and Mensheviks. Election of delegates to the Constituent Assembly began in late November, three weeks after the Bolshevik victory. Despite some efforts by Lenin's Party to bend the election their way, SRs got 40 percent of the vote and 53 percent of the delegates. The Bolsheviks were a distant second with 24 percent of the vote and (with a small number of supporting Left SRs) 30 percent of the delegates. The disappointed Lenin permitted the assembly to have only one meeting, its opening session, which he attended, January 18–19, 1918.

One year after the great March upheaval toppled the monarchy, the Seventh Party Congress of the RSDLP Bolsheviks (March 6–8, 1918) changed its name to the Russian Communist Party (Bolshevik) and ratified the Treaty of Brest-Litovsk, ending war with Germany. A vast territory and tens of millions of persons were signed over to the Germans, who were now so close to Petrograd that the government moved itself to Moscow. To overcome strong opposition to the treaty among Communist leaders, Lenin had threatened to resign from the Party. Outside the Party, resistance to the treaty turned violent. Left SRs, having failed to persuade the Soviet government to reject the Brest Treaty, broke their political alliance with the Communists by assassinating German ambassador Mirbach (July 6, 1918), hoping that action would lead to a renewal of war. On August 30, Lenin himself was shot and seriously wounded.

Peasant-oriented SRs, who had won the most democratic election in Russia's history by a wide margin, had good reason to resent the Communist Party, which denied them all but marginal political power. SR membership in Soviet Congresses and in the central executive committees of these congresses, described by Lenin himself as the supreme governing institutions, came to mean little, dominated as they were by the "workers' dictatorship," namely the Communist Party and its own executive committees. Only because the Communists faced a host of enemies in the summer of 1918 did they delay (until 1922) ridding their government of remaining Mensheviks and SRs.

CIVIL WAR AND WAR COMMUNISM, 1918–1921

The Provisional Government made a number of bungling attempts to stifle the Bolsheviks in the summer of 1917. Perhaps the Party's reaction against such efforts, as much as anything else, spurred it to action in the coup of November 6–7. That takeover, followed by the Bolsheviks' high-handed treatment of other socialist parties, dissolution of the Constituent Assembly, the Brest Treaty, the reckless use of terror against alleged enemies, and murder of the royal family on July 16–17, 1918, helped bring together a varied group of opponents to the Communist regime. There were the so-called Whites: monarchists, constitutional democrats, SRs, former tsarist officials, officers, soldiers, and Cossacks; a pro-Allied Czechoslovak Legion, stuck in Russia as a result of the Brest Treaty; and thousands of troops from several Allied countries, including Japan, Great Britain, France, and the United States. Furthermore, various nationalities, taking advantage of war and revolution, began separating themselves from the former Russian empire: Finland, the Baltic states (Estonia, Latvia, and Lithuania), and Poland succeeded in becoming independent; Ukraine, Byelorussia, the Transcaucasus (Georgia, Azerbaijan, and Armenia), and several other groups in the south of European Russia and in Central Asia only succeeded, more or less, in becoming short-lived republics.

War Communism is a phrase used to define the aggressive and even brutal actions taken by the Reds, or Communists, from 1918 to 1921, to defeat Whites and secessionists, overcome the countless problems caused by the severely diminished economy, and begin the socialist transformation of Russian society. Political divisions among the Whites was their great weakness; the only thread that held them all together was opposition to the Reds. They differed over basic issues: the best form of government, land reform, and questions of self-determination for ethnic or

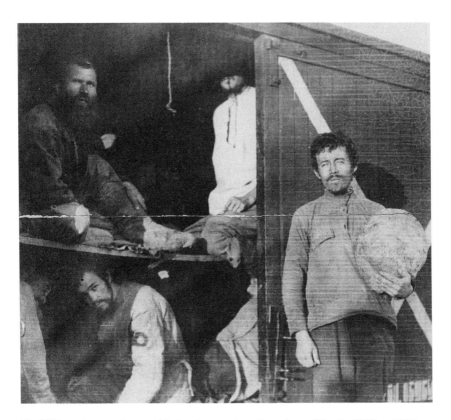

Civil War prisoners jammed into a boxcar, two tiers deep. Siberia, 1919 or 1920. Reproduced from the Collections of the Library of Congress, LC-USZ62-91460.

national minorities. The Reds fought from inside a great circle and with a more unified command than the Whites, whose forces were spread out around the perimeter. Great savagery characterized fighting on both sides of the Civil War.

The Communists' heaviest blows fell on Whites and peasants. Separated by Germans or Ukrainians or Whites from much of the best grain-producing areas of the Ukraine and southern Russia and desperate for food, the Reds stripped grain from peasants, sometimes paying low fixed prices, sometimes paying nothing. They created committees of poor peasants or gangs of armed workers and peasants to make war on so-called kulaks (*kulaki,* "wealthy" peasants) and to purge villages of whatever grain they could find. Peasants who could not keep their grain hidden often ceased producing more than was needed to feed themselves. But the Reds confiscated even small stores of grain and seed reserved for the next planting. This conflict in the countryside, where peasants sometimes violently resisted attempts to take their food, resembled the disaster that occurred 10 years later when the state set out to collectivize agriculture. On both occasions millions of peasants starved. A notable difference between the two disasters is that the Soviet government admitted foreign agencies (most importantly the American Relief Administration under the direction of Herbert Hoover) into Russia to provide relief during the famine of 1920–1922, whereas a decade later, in 1932–1933, the Soviet government refused even to acknowledge the more devastating famine of those years.

THE NEW ECONOMIC POLICY, 1921–1928

The Whites lost the Civil War, but final defeat of the peasants was delayed. Early in 1921, in the midst of peasant disturbances and unrest among industrial workers, Lenin and the Communist Party were shocked by a rebellion of sailors at the Kronstadt Island naval base located in the Gulf of Finland about 20 miles west of Petrograd. Kronstadt sailors were angered by the indiscriminate and extremely repressive measures taken by the Party against groups and individuals, including Communists, not under its firm control. They demanded that the political arena be opened to all leftist factions, political prisoners be freed, industrial workers (proletarians) be allowed to organize their own unions, and peasants have control over the land they farmed. This attack signaled a great danger for the Party. The mutiny came from what had been, only three years before, a center of Communist strength and came at a time of great suffering in villages and cities across the land. The sailors' disillusionment, anger, and appeals for democratic change were bound to attract widespread sympathy from peasants and workers.

The Party met the challenge in two ways. First, the rebels were smashed in a short, bloody campaign. Second, in order to address the desperate

The railroad yards at a station north of Petrograd (later Leningrad), 1919–1920. Two peasant women are bringing up a load of wood to fuel the locomotive of a train loaded with relief supplies from the American Red Cross. Reproduced from the Collections of the Library of Congress, LC-USZ62-76103.

Famine in Russia, 1921. Pallbearers are carrying the bodies of two infants.
Reproduced from the Collections of the Library of Congress, LC-USZ62-95141.

economic needs of the people and thus take some steam out of the public's resentment, Lenin abandoned War Communism and introduced a New Economic Policy (NEP). He presented his plan to the 10th Party Congress March 8–16, 1921, at the very time the battle between Red forces and Kronstadt sailors was raging. NEP was a retreat from attempts to bulldoze Russia, especially the peasants, into a Party-dominated socialist order. It was, like the Brest-Litovsk Treaty, three years before, strongly opposed by some Communist leaders. They saw NEP as a step backward, or worse, a permanent retreat, toward capitalism. Forced requisitions from peasants were replaced by a graduated tax in kind, representing a much smaller amount of produce than that taken under War Communism. Furthermore, peasants were allowed to treat the land they cultivated as their own and to sell what they harvested, after taxes, on the open market. Expectations that NEP would immediately bring about an upswing in agricultural production were dashed by the overwhelming crop failures and famine of 1921–1922. However, during the disaster further measures were taken to stimulate both the production and marketing of farm produce. NEP also provided for the existence of small private commercial or industrial operations, enterprises with 20 or fewer workers.

Lenin's retreat proved to be quite successful. For some seven years, beginning in 1914, Russia had been devastated by war, revolution, civil

Refugees from civil war–torn and famished European Russia fled to Siberia, and then sought to protect themselves from the cold by living in dugout shelters. This photo was taken around 1924. Reproduced from the Collections of the Library of Congress, LC-USZ62-29421.

war, and famine. Out of the ruins of these disasters and over the next seven NEP years (1921–1928), agricultural production was substantially raised and industrial production was restored to the levels of 1914. Still, the picture of economic recovery was not rosy in every respect. Agricultural production on a per capita basis lagged behind 1914 outputs due to the growth of the peasant population. Another reason farm production did not reach higher levels was that peasants received low prices for their produce relative to the high prices they had to pay for manufactured goods. Seen from the peasants' point of view, this was an imbalance that took away one of their chief incentives (availability of consumer goods they could afford) to grow more than they could themselves consume. As a result they tended to cut back on what they could send to the market. Despite shortcomings, NEP was an island of relative calm and prosperity in a sea of troubles that stormed over Russia and the Soviet Union from the beginning of one world war to the end of another (1914–1945). During periods of severe hardship that followed NEP, some people looked back on it as a kind of golden age. But among the highest Party leaders it was a most contentious matter. Some saw it as a convenient way to advance the Soviet economy, milking the revived peasant economy to pay for industrialization. To others it was a policy that betrayed communism and the 1917

A despairing, famine-stricken Russian family, 1921. Reproduced from the Collections of the Library of Congress, LC-USZ62-096999.

Bolshevik Revolution and only served the interests of those who remained capitalists at heart.

Lenin died on January 21, 1924. More than a year earlier, in December 1922, the already seriously ill Lenin wrote about his fear of a split in the Party because of friction between two of the most important leaders, Stalin and Trotsky. He described Trotsky as the most able member of the Central Committee and questioned Stalin's ability to use his great power wisely. He faulted Stalin especially for what he believed was his tactless handling of the Georgian desire for national independence.[3] On January 4, 1923, in response to a telephone call in which Stalin insulted Lenin's wife, Krupskaya, Lenin wrote that because of Stalin's rudeness he ought to be removed from his post as Secretary-General of the Party, an action that, he pointed out, would also reduce the likelihood of a split in the Central Committee.

Even if Lenin had lived longer and succeeded in ousting Stalin, it is most unlikely that non-Russian nationalities would have been allowed to govern themselves. The Moscow-dominated Union of Soviet Socialist Republics (USSR), or Soviet Union, was being formed during the last several months of Lenin's life. The First All-Union Congress of Soviets of the USSR was held at the end of December 1922; the Second Congress met on January 31, 1924, 10 days after Lenin's death, and ratified the first constitution of the USSR.[4] One of the fictions of the new law was the right of republics to secede from the Union.

More important politically than the organization of law and government was the reshaping of the real agency of power and policy, the Communist Party. While Lenin lived he was the principal figure in a small and elite group, the Communist Party Central Committee (CPCC). After the October–November Revolution the Party expanded the number of its members and officials in order to keep up with its widening responsibilities and to extend its control over every important aspect of the emerging Soviet state. The CPCC itself grew, making it an increasingly clumsy policy-making body. And so, over several months, as the need arose, top leaders refashioned and transformed the Party hierarchy. The Central Committee continued to exist, but its executive power was transferred into three agencies. At the summit was the Political Bureau, or Politburo (called Presidium from 1952 to 1966), already functioning for several weeks before it was formally recognized in March 1919. It did not represent a change from the former command nucleus, including among its small membership Lenin, Trotsky, and Stalin. To see that policies of the Politburo were carried out, an Organization Bureau, or Orgburo, was created in January 1919. The third powerful agency to emerge was the expanded secretariat of the Central Committee.

During the 1920s the Communist Party of the Soviet Union (CPSU) and government of the Union of Soviet Socialist Republics (USSR) were pretty much given their final and legal institutional structures, and Stalin's ascendancy settled the question of supreme political power. As for the great communist experiment in equality and democracy, for many the dream was still alive in the 20s, but clear-sighted proponents of these ideals saw their hopes fade. To protect the Party, any means became justified: police terror, summary trials and executions, suppression of open debate, and so on. The "dictatorship of the proletariat" remained a fiction, a convenient phrase for defending the Party's actions, even against the workers themselves. For example, though no one doubted that alcoholism was a blight on the toiling masses, the Party, at the beginning of 1923, legalized the production and sale of vodka and, taking a page from tsarist times, revived a very profitable state-run liquor monopoly. Public discussion of key issues was tolerated less and less. Even at the highest levels open debate was severely restricted when, at the same 10th Party Congress of March 1921 that introduced NEP, a resolution was passed forbidding Party factions. What should a loyal but outspoken critic do? Take as advice, perhaps, the words of poet Vladimir Mayakovsky, and smother his own voice.

During the NEP years, Soviet politics was far removed from the lives of most people, some 80 percent of whom were peasants. From the low point of 1921–1922 peasants increased their production rather substantially each year until 1927–1928. The upward trend was helped along at first by good weather conditions in 1922 and the marketing incentives introduced at the beginning of NEP. Other liberalizing policies followed. Generally these were intended to get the state out of the peasant's way, to eliminate or ease rules and penalties that held peasants back from expanding production and that restricted their use of leased land, for example, or of hired labor. Some Party leaders, like Nikolay Bukharin (1888–1938) and Alexey Rykov, believed that, for the time being, even kulaks, progressive and prosperous peasants who worked their own farms, benefited the state, adding to its wealth and showing the way to advanced methods of farming. Other signs of improvement in rural life, besides increased production, were the introduction in many villages of electricity and the teaching of reading and writing. There were also many signs of backwardness and resistance to change. Most Soviet peasants in the 1920s lived not much differently than their parents or grandparents. According to the imperial census of 1897 approximately 75 percent of peasants 10 to 49 years of age were illiterate; according to the Soviet census of 1926 the figure was still about 50 percent.[5] The religious calendar as well as demands of planting and harvesting still determined the rhythm of village life. Communal farming, with fields divided into multiple strips assigned to various local households, remained in practice, and peasants preferred that village affairs be organized by their own commune (*mir*) rather than by the local government council or soviet. As in the past, peasants distilled and drank a good deal of home-brewed hard liquor. Violence, drunkenness, and holidays commonly went together.

THE STALIN REVOLUTION, 1928–1941

Stalin and Trotsky were the main contenders for Lenin's mantle, but all the top figures became embroiled in the successionist conflict. Stalin, the victor, humbled one old Party comrade after another and then, in a bizarre and terrifying display of power and arrogance, had them tried on false charges of treason and executed. Spectacular though they were, the show trials and executions of Old Bolsheviks were a small chapter in the "Great Terror," which had a direct and devastating effect on millions of Soviet citizens—they were killed outright, deliberately starved to death, forcibly exiled from their native lands, or banished into the oblivion of prison labor camps. The crime was vast. It is difficult to believe that the waves of fear and violence that spread out from Stalin did not in some way touch every citizen. Tens of millions were victims, and the number of perpetrators, from Stalin down to camp guards and civilian informers, was also large. No one, except the paranoid leader himself, was safe; even the highest police officials and military commanders were destroyed at the master's whim.

"The Terror" accompanied, and played an important role in, another vast enterprise, an economic revolution that transformed agriculture and made the Soviet Union a great industrial power. Society was marshaled for the great effort and was itself profoundly changed during the political and economic upheavals. Marriage and family, initially disparaged as bourgeois institutions, regained respectability; education was vigorously advanced; all forms of public information, including art, were turned into propaganda; prisons supplied armies of labor slaves; forests were cut down; great quantities of ore were dug out of the earth; millions of tons of iron flowed out of the mills; huge concrete and steel dams were raised up to harness the power of rivers; electrical power was extended ever deeper into backwater areas; and large cities and industrial complexes grew up overnight. The pace was breathtaking, and the cost in human misery immense.

After Lenin, Trotsky was the most likely person to dislodge Stalin, but, though he was the Secretary-General's strongest critic, he seems to have underestimated his enemy and been unwilling to undertake, or ill prepared for, a drawn-out political battle. A few days before Lenin's death, Trotsky left Moscow because of ill health, and remained away during the funeral. Stalin took full advantage of the occasion to draw attention to himself as the great leader's heir. Furthermore, Stalin allied himself against Trotsky with two other prominent Old Bolsheviks, Grigory Zinoviev (b. Apfelbaum, 1882–1936) and Lev Kamenev (b. Rosenfeld, 1883–1936), the more easily since Trotsky had attacked them for trying to scuttle Lenin's plan in 1917 for overthrowing the Provisional Government. Regarding Lenin's anti-Stalin letters, Trotsky made no use of them when they were presented to Party leaders in May 1924. He did not seek to have them presented, as Lenin wanted, to a Party congress, or even the much smaller Central Committee. On the contrary, in 1925 he diminished the importance of these epistolary bombs when he publicly discredited what he must have known were quite accurate extracts from them published in the West.[6]

After Lenin's death, Stalin, firmly anchored in the main branches of the Party hierarchy, steadily increased his power at the expense of other old-guard leaders. An important advantage for him was that these leaders were divided among themselves over a number of burning issues: whether, in their own "dictatorship of the proletariat," workers should be given the power to manage their own affairs; how to counteract the swelling Party and government bureaucracy; whether to pursue world revolution or consolidate socialism at home; whether to continue NEP or sacrifice it and the wishes of peasants to a regimented and painfully rapid industrialization. Stalin played these factions against one another but seemed himself to rise above their quarrels. In 1925 he was already in a position to discredit and demote his competitors. Over the next five years one Party leader after another—Trotsky, Zinoviev, Kamenev, Bukharin, Rykov, Tomsky—was brought to his knees, dropped from the Politburo, and stripped of his offices. Some were expelled from the Central Committee and even from the Party. Stalin elevated his own supporters into the vacancies. When the dictator's 50th birthday was celebrated on December 21, 1929, the slogan for the occasion was "Stalin is Lenin today."

After 1926 peasants slowed their grain production. Why should they grow more than they could consume or sell on the private market, when the state paid so little for their grain and the finished goods they wanted to buy were overpriced and often poorly manufactured? The problem was not, however, only a matter of prices and incentives. Grain production in the late 1920s was affected by bad weather. It also suffered because areas farmed by individual peasants were growing smaller; the reason for this was that although the total sown area was no longer expanding, as had occurred earlier in the decade, the peasant population and number of peasant households continued to grow. Serious grain shortages occurred in 1927 and 1928. What were Stalin and the Party to do? How could the Soviet Union become industrialized without grain to feed the cities and for export? Before 1917 large private estates had been Russia's most effective commercial producers, but of course, they no longer existed.

Stalin dominated the 15th Party Congress of December 1927, Trotsky and Zinoviev having just been expelled from the Party in November. During the congress, Kamenev (despite a speech in which he humbled himself before the delegates) and 121 other opponents of the Secretary-General, members of the so-called Left Opposition, were also expelled.

In January 1928, the same month Trotsky was exiled to Central Asia, Stalin visited the Urals and western Siberia, where, on his own authority, he ordered that peasants who were holding back be forced to sell their grain to the state or face imprisonment and confiscation of their property. This rough treatment, aimed especially at better-off peasants, seemed to be in line with those who wanted to push stridently in the direction of socialism, namely, the Left Opposition, which Stalin had just crushed. Despite criticism, now from the right, Stalin pressed on, cautiously at first, then with savage momentum, toward industrialization and the subjugation of agriculture to that end. In August 1928 he accepted the five-year plan (1929–1933) of the State Planning Agency (*Gosplan*, established in 1921), which proposed modest growth, but later in the year he began attacking the economically moderate right.

In 1929 the way was cleared for a radical transformation of Soviet life. In April the Party decided on a faster-paced five-year plan than originally conceived and a more aggressive attack against religion. It also purged itself of members who, during the past eight years, had openly opposed Stalin. It was in April that Bukharin, leader of the moderate right, which was against a radical departure from NEP, was stripped of important Party offices by the Central Committee. In November he was expelled from the Politburo. Meanwhile, forced requisitions and collectivization were stepped up. In December, a few days after the gala celebration of his 50th birthday on the 21st, Stalin announced the end of NEP and called for the liquidation of kulaks.

Although the institution varied, for most peasants collectivization meant pooling their land, equipment, livestock, and labor into a collective farm (*kolkhoz*) that they managed together. This was the lesser evil, the other, preferred by the Party, being a state farm (*sovkhoz*), operated like a factory by bosses and hired workers. The revised, accelerated five-year plan of spring 1929 had called for 15 percent of agriculture to be collectivized by 1933. At the beginning of 1930 the Party decided first to have the process nearly completed by 1933 and then to have the task finished within months. Some peasants, in particular those without much property, joined voluntarily, but most had to be bullied into collectives by Party or government agencies, including armed police and soldiers. Many reluctant peasants were sent to labor camps, and often those who violently resisted were shot. During the 1927–1937 decade the number of collectivized peasant households rose from about 195,000 to 18,500,000, from about 1 percent to 93 percent of all peasant households.[7]

What were the circumstances that moved forward this remarkable and extremely painful transformation of Soviet agriculture and radically changed Soviet society? In part the answer lies in the ascendancy of Stalin, who apparently had no regard for others except as they furthered or hindered his goals. The failure of the state's grain procurement program is also important. Satisfying as it must have been for Stalin to rise above other Party leaders (who considered themselves better suited to lead), this failure left him in command of a stagnant economy without the means of promoting rapid industrial growth. What path would Stalin take? No one, perhaps not even the leader himself, anticipated how quickly and thoroughly people would be regimented, with what speed and magnitude society would be collectivized and industrialized, and how great would be the human cost—millions killed and millions more imprisoned.

The show trials of the 1930s were presaged in the summer of 1928 when 53 mining technicians, directors, and engineers, of the south Russian district of Shakhty in Ukraine, were tried in Moscow for being "wreckers." Except that defendants were not former Party leaders, most elements of the later trials were present in the Shakhty case: a theatrically staged public trial of coerced defendants falsely charged with being employed by foreign intelligence services. Some defendants confessed and five were executed. The purpose of the trial was to convince citizens they were under attack from outside and within, and so prepare them for the hard measures they were about to endure in defending and strengthening the Soviet Union against its enemies.

Collectivization was massively enforced during the early weeks of 1930. Laws permitting the hiring of labor or leasing of land were revoked. Kulaks and their families were targeted for deportation. Their property— land, livestock, buildings, and equipment—went to collectives and were used as enticements to encourage poor peasants to join kolkhozes and sovkhozes (Russian, *kolkhozy, sovkhozy*). Some kulaks committed suicide or killed their families and themselves rather than face the loss of all they owned and then deportation. Many peasants slaughtered their farm animals rather than turn them over to the collectives. Some attacked city workers and officials sent out to the villages as *kolkhoz* organizers.

Because the upheaval threatened to seriously disrupt spring planting, Stalin called a temporary halt to collectivization. He did this by having *Pravda*, the Party newspaper, publish his article, "Dizziness from Success" (March 2, 1930). In it he blamed workers and rural officials who were directly involved in forcing peasants into collectives with being overzealous. In fact, their all-out effort was precisely what the great leader had demanded of them. Assured now that joining was voluntary, millions of peasants withdrew from collectives. But theirs was a momentary reprieve. Voluntarism was a fiction and private farming had become a dead end. Any peasant who persisted in farming privately and prospered in the face of state restrictions and penalties was bound to suffer the consequences of being labeled a kulak. In the fall of 1930 forced collectivizing was resumed. As an enticement and concession to private initiative, each household entering a collective was permitted to have a small garden plot and a few animals of its own. About half of all peasant households, some 13 million, were collectivized by the spring of 1931.[8]

Collectivization directly affected the great majority of Soviet peoples. Millions perished—they were killed outright, died during deportation or in exile, died in prison labor camps (*gulag*), or starved to death. The greatest killer was the famine of 1932–1934. During the two years before the famine, grain production had been down, partly the result of drought. This downturn was mitigated somewhat by the reduced need to feed animals, much of the livestock population having recently been slaughtered. Still, low productivity on the new collective farms, continued high procurements and export of grain (even as people starved), official denial of famine, and rejection of relief offers from abroad spelled disaster. Some five million persons perished, most of them in Ukraine.

Industrialization was the favored partner with collectivization in the great economic transformation of the 1930s, destined to ride the back of agriculture to extraordinary heights. As in the first five-year plan for agriculture, planned increases in industrial production were revised upward again and again, and the allotted time for reaching the heightened goals shortened. "Five Years in Four" became the motto of the first industrial five-year plan. In 1938 rural output was about where it had been 10 years earlier. During the same decade, mining and industrial production soared. This was especially true in the production of electricity and the basic materials of heavy industry: oil, coal, iron, and steel. During the first three five-year plans (1928–1941, the last shortened by war) Soviet workers more than tripled industrial production. The output of chemicals and electric power rose several times in this span of years. In its magnitude and speed the rise of Soviet industry outpaced even the great industrial revolutions of nineteenth-century Europe and America. This would have been a most extraordinary achievement even in the best of times. In fact, it occurred during a world depression, the rising threat of war, and a campaign of terror that often swept away scientists, engineers, technicians,

The "Stalin" Metallurgical Plant in Kuznetsk, 1955; pig iron leaving the blast furnace. This photo embodies the Soviet government's push toward rapid industrialization, an economic goal achieved at great human cost. Reproduced from the Collections of the Library of Congress, Lot 7403 #3.

and managers. Working men and women made extraordinary efforts in the face of many difficulties, both within the workplace and outside of it: lack of skills, unfamiliarity with foreign-made machinery, long hours, dangerous working conditions, tiny living quarters, and poor-quality consumer goods to buy with declining real wages. Workers who excelled were rewarded with higher pay, better goods, better housing, and the like.

While industrialization and collectivization were transforming the Soviet economy, a third quite extraordinary event occurred that, like the other two, cascaded down from Stalin through the whole society. This was the Great Terror. It had two most spectacular features. One was the trial of the Party elite, a staged tragedy in which dozens of one-time revolutionary comrades of Lenin were publicly humiliated and destroyed. The other was a purge of top military officers. Between Lenin's death in 1924 and 1930 Stalin managed to cut down, from their high places, all other Party leaders who might have competed with him for power. Their public prosecution, however, did not begin until 1936, by which time the Party had considerable experience in show trials. Like the Shakhty case noted previously, these trials pretended to expose "wreckers," those responsible for one or another of the breakdowns that plagued the rapidly changing economy.

On December 1, 1934, Sergei Kirov (b. 1888) was murdered. He had headed the Party in Leningrad, had been a member of the Politburo since 1930, and was popular among Communist leaders, favored by some of them to replace Stalin as Secretary-General. Stalin probably ordered the assassination. It rid him of a challenger and served as a convenient pretext to launch a campaign to destroy all other potential challengers. Before the end of December the killer and 13 alleged accomplices were tried and executed. Within weeks accusations of conspiracy in the murder began to spread. A multitude of alleged conspirators were accused of being linked to Zinoviev and Trotsky, of spying for Germany and Japan, of wanting to kill Stalin and destroy the USSR. In three public trials (August 1936, January 1937, and March 1938) 54 Old Bolsheviks and Henry Yagoda, former chief of the secret police, or NKVD, confessed to these crimes, were found guilty, and all but a few executed. Shortly after the second trial the Central Committee became reluctant to expand the purge. Over the next several months Stalin had most members of the committee executed. Between the summers of 1937 and 1938 most top military commanders and many lower-ranking officers were arrested and shot. *Yezhovshchina,* a word that identified the terror, was named after Nikolay Yezhov, who replaced the purged Yagoda as head of the NKVD in September 1936. Like his predecessor, he too was replaced and executed. At the height of the terror, from the beginning of 1935 to the end of 1938, millions of persons were being arrested and sent into the burgeoning NKVD prison labor camp system, where many died as a result of inadequacies of all kinds, exhaustion, exposure, illness, or a combination of afflictions.

Almost anyone could be picked up—artists, scientists, teachers and professors, Party members, government officials, factory managers and engineers, colleagues, friends, spouses. Compliance and silence were no guarantees of safety, but people who criticized the regime asked for trouble. When the poet Osip Mandelstam recited his poem critical of Stalin, the man with "cockroach mustaches," his friends knew he had invited death. Outstanding cultural leaders and scholars were forced to betray others, ally themselves with the Stalinist line, become the underlings of sycophants, or be destroyed. One of the most striking cases was that of

Trofim Lysenko, who gained the leader's favor and ruled over the biological sciences and agronomy. He demanded that biologists accept the principle of the inheritance of acquired characteristics. This being so, Stalin could work a biological as well as a social miracle on humanity.

Like Tsar Ivan the Terrible (ruler 1533–1584) Stalin carried out a cruel and destructive war on his own subjects. Why the Soviet leader slowed the terror is as much a puzzle as why he began it. Perhaps he had achieved what he wanted: dominance so complete that his underlings tried not only to carry out his wishes, but to anticipate them. Collectivization was nearly complete, the USSR had become an industrial giant, the old Party had been destroyed, those who might have contemplated opposing him had been purged, and prison camps were full. Perhaps threats from outside the Soviet Union, the dangers of war, now attracted his attention.

Soviet foreign policy followed two tracks. On one was the Comintern, or Communist International (1919–1943), which tried to promote revolutions around the world through foreign communist parties. On the other was the People's Commissariat of International Affairs, which conducted a more conventional relationship with other countries. Although the tracks seemed at times to run in contrary directions, negotiating with and trying to overthrow the same government, their destination was the same, to advance the interests of the USSR. In 1935, worried about the rise of Nazism, the Soviet Union agreed to join France against Germany should that country attack Czechoslovakia. At about the same time the Comintern introduced a popular front policy, urging communists to join with other groups against fascism. Neither fascism nor Germany were stopped.

Fascism rolled on: Italy invaded Ethiopia (1935); German troops moved into the Rhineland (1936); Germany and Italy joined Japan in an Anti-Comintern Pact (1936–1937); Germany annexed Austria in 1938 and in the same year France and Britain gave in to Hitler's takeover of the Czech Sudetenland; Soviet-supported antifascists were defeated in the Spanish Civil War (1936–1939), and in 1939 Germany grabbed the rest of Czechoslovakia. Also in 1939 Japanese troops threatened along the Manchurian-Mongolian border. Western democracies not only failed to stand up against Hitler, but he preempted their offers of alliance with the USSR as well. On August 23, 1939, Germany and the USSR signed a nonaggression pact and, in anticipation of the impending German invasion of Poland, agreed secretly to divide the territories between them into spheres of interest. Germany began the invasion of Poland from the west on September 1, 1939, Britain and France declared war on Germany on the 3rd, and Soviet forces invaded Poland from the east on the 17th.

The agreement helped clear the way for Germany's aggressive designs: the USSR would not contest the invasion of Poland, Germany would be supplied with much-needed raw materials and, secure against a war in the east, be free to throw the great weight of its military forces against western Europe. On its side the Soviet Union moved quickly to benefit from the pact. Within a month of invading Poland it forced Estonia, Latvia, and Lithuania into "mutual assistance" agreements that permitted the stationing of Soviet troops in those countries. Finland rejected demands for territorial concessions and was attacked by the USSR on November 29, 1939. For three and a half months the Finns held out, losing but suffering many fewer casualties than they inflicted. This "Winter War" likely reinforced Hitler's contempt for Soviet weakness. In June 1940 the Soviets annexed their last two "spheres," Bessarabia and Northern Bukovina, from Romania. During the same month Germany completed its lightning conquest of France. Who would be the next victim? In July 1940, about the time the Soviet Union was digesting the Baltic states (turning them into union republics), Hitler was talking about his own appetite for a spring 1941 invasion of the USSR.

WORLD WAR II AND POSTWAR STALINISM, 1941–1953

The code name for the attack was Operation Barbarossa. It commenced on Sunday morning, June 22, 1941, along a front that reached from the Baltic Sea to the Black Sea. For some three years German troops fought in the Soviet Union. It was an immensely costly campaign. Notable among its horrors was the systematic mass extermination of innocent Jews by *Einsatzgruppen,* special Nazi mobile killing units, which followed in the wake of advancing Axis forces.

Each side committed momentous blunders. Despite clear evidence of German preparations, Stalin refused to ready his military for the attack. Hitler's forces swept forward practically unhindered, destroying ground and air defenses, driving before them a multitude of civilians and soldiers, killing, wounding, and capturing millions. Stalin was petrified. Hours passed before Soviet troops were ordered to fight back. As for the Germans, delay of the invasion, originally set to begin in mid-May, holdups of the *Wehrmacht* (German armed forces) at Kiev and Smolensk, and the onset of an early Russian winter meant that German soldiers had to contend with extreme cold weather. Exalted by the early successes of his armies and unprepared for stiff resistance from the Red Army, Hitler spread his forces, driving them toward Leningrad and Moscow, and across the mineral- and grain-rich south. The campaigns failed. Besieged Leningraders held out, starving and freezing, for two and a half years. The advance on Moscow cost the Red Army dearly, and in mid-November the city itself came under attack, but tenacious defense, heavy German losses, freezing temperatures, and lack of reserves stopped the attackers. In early December Soviet troops began a counteroffensive.

Most successful was the German drive across Ukraine and south Russia. However, at Stalingrad, during the winter of 1942–1943, Soviet soldiers encircled General von Paulus's Sixth Army of some 100,000 soldiers

Parents find the body of their murdered son in Kerch, Eastern Crimea. This photo was probably taken in 1942, after the Germans captured the city. Reproduced by permission of British Information Services and from the Collections of the Library of Congress, Lot 11640-B.

and forced it to surrender. It was a turning point in the war. The Wehrmacht did launch one more major offensive in the USSR, in midsummer 1943, but it was countered by seasoned Soviet troops, superior in number and arms. Especially in the south (Ukraine, Crimea, lower Volga, northern Caucasus) Germans might have taken advantage of anti-Soviet or anti-Russian feelings. Instead they were contemptuous of, and brutal toward, the conquered peoples. Of the more than three million Soviet POWs captured early in the war, some, at least (perhaps many), were willing to fight with Germany against the Stalin regime. Rather than cultivate and show some regard for these feelings, the Germans treated their captives with

Soviet residents watching German war prisoners being escorted though a village, past homes they had burned, around 1942–1943. Reproduced by permission of British Information Services and from the Collections of the Library of Congress, LC-USZ62-72772.

extreme cruelty. Several hundred were deliberately murdered in the first test on humans of the poison gas hydrogen cyanide (Zyklon-B), used to exterminate Jews at Auschwitz.

Soviet war losses were immense, far greater even than Germany's. More than 20 million soldiers and civilians were killed. Jews in particular had been systematically hunted down and murdered. Two of the greatest single massacres of the Holocaust were carried out in September and October 1941 in or near the cities of Kiev and Odessa by Germans and Romanians. The Soviet government itself targeted certain ethnic groups for murder or deportation. Most of the many thousands of Poles rounded up during the Soviet occupation of Poland in 1939 were sent to Central Asia or Siberia, but several thousand Polish military officers were executed by security police, probably in 1940. Four thousand, four hundred and forty-three of these victims were unearthed near Smolensk in a place called Katyn Forest. Late in 1944 Polish fighters in Warsaw rose up against German occupiers, expecting support from the approaching Red Army. The Soviet units held up, however, waiting nearby for weeks while the uprising was crushed. In these ways Stalin eliminated potential opponents to his plans to Sovietize Poland. Some ethnic groups were accused of collaboration with the enemy and deported. Volga Germans at the beginning of the war and others later (Crimean Tatars, Kalmyks, Ingush, Karachay, Chechens, Balkars) were violently uprooted from their homelands and those who survived planted in Kazakhstan, Central Asia, or Siberia.

After the war's end Stalin told the victorious and hopeful Soviet people that they must bend to the hard tasks of reconstruction. A new five-year plan (1946–1950) with a 1930s emphasis on heavy industry called for Herculean efforts and sacrifices. These burdens were not lightened by financial help from outside. United States Lend-Lease ended, Stalin turned down Marshall Plan aid, and the possibility of foreign loans diminished as the cold war grew. The screws of repression, eased during the war, were again tightened. Returning POWs and other repatriates were regarded as spies—some were shot, others sent to the gulag. The value of rubles saved during the war by industrious peasants, working their private plots, was practically wiped out by a currency devaluation. Rural life continued to be hard and often dreary. Private plots were made smaller, earnings remained meager, and collectives merged into bigger collectives. Young men went to the cities if they could, leaving farms largely populated by the elderly, children, and women. Crowded cities grew more crowded. Food, housing, and every other necessity were in short supply. Residents were constantly on the lookout and foraging for any useful thing.

In contrast to the Soviet people, bent down by deprivation and heavy work, the Soviet state emerged from the war stronger than any other European country and one of the two great world powers. Except for Finland, Imperial Russia was nearly reassembled, the restored parts incorporated into the USSR or, in the case of Poland, overrun by Soviet military forces.

In fact, the Red Army overran all the countries of central Europe and by the end of the 1940s had turned them (Poland, Czechoslovakia, Romania, Hungary, Bulgaria, and eastern Germany) into satellite states, ruled by communist governments under Moscow's supervision. Communist parties independent of Moscow took over Yugoslavia and Albania. The most notable among postwar communist victories occurred in China, where Mao Tse-tung's forces overthrew the Kuomintang government of Chiang Kai-shek. Thus, all within a decade, the two great powers of the Eurasian continent, Japan and Germany, were crushed, and on their wreckage arose two new communist leviathans, every bit as hostile to Western liberal traditions as the fascist states had been.

As the USSR pressed its advantages and consolidated its hold over Eastern Europe, the West, especially the United States, began to take measures to prevent further expansion. President Truman announced in 1947 his government's willingness to assist countries trying to preserve their independence. Aid that year to Greece and Turkey may have prevented communist takeovers there. The Truman Doctrine and then the containment theory came to identify Western responses to Soviet expansionist moves, and the cold war to describe the general conflict. Moscow and Washington, D.C., did not directly shoot at each other but were drawn onto opposite sides of a number of threatening or deadly confrontations. Tens of thousands of U.S. soldiers died fighting Soviet-supported Koreans and Vietnamese, who died by the hundreds of thousands. Nuclear weapons added to these conflicts an ever-present threat of world annihilation. The USSR first tested an atomic bomb in 1949 and a hydrogen bomb in 1953.

The cold war had a powerful and negative effect on the lives of Soviet citizens. It was used to justify or explain nearly every hardship: the underfunding of agriculture and consumer goods in favor of heavy industry and military spending, constant police surveillance and disregard for justice, the vast prison labor system, wholesale spoliation of the environment, and so on.

The 19th Party Congress was held in October 1952. It approved the new five-year plan (1951–1955), which, like the others, emphasized heavy industry. During the congress Stalin increased membership in the top executive branches of the Party: the Presidium (Politburo merged with the Orgburo), the Secretariat, and the Central Committee—enough additional members to replace all the established (since the late 1930s) officers. The great leader, it seems, was preparing another purge. In satellite countries Party leaders were already being arrested and tried for being more or less disloyal, for advancing the interests, for example, of Zionists, Titoists, and imperialists. This time, however, besides Party officials, Stalin had Jews in his sights.

An anti-Jewish campaign promised to have wide popular support. One of the things that the revolutions of 1917 had not interrupted was the strong current of anti-Semitism. Even destruction of some two million Soviet Jews during the war had not erased the hatreds. One of the worst among a number of Stalin's anti-Jewish actions was the execution in 1952 of members of the Jewish Antifascist Committee, a wartime organization of prominent Soviet citizens who had appealed successfully to American Jews for their financial support of the Soviet war effort. In January 1953 nine prominent doctors, most of them Jews, were arrested. They were charged with murdering high Party officials and forced by torture to confess their guilt. Widely publicized, the "doctors' plot" set in motion waves of accusations against Jews, doctors in particular.

REFORM AND REACTION, 1953–1991

Stalin died on March 5, 1953. Immediately a struggle commenced between those who wanted to continue, more or less, the policies of the great leader and those who wanted basic changes. That the conservatives would eventually lose was not clear until the very end.

After Stalin the problem for conservatives was not preventing change but keeping it within certain bounds. Even this was a most difficult task. Having been saved by Stalin's death from being purged, were they likely to favor another strongman rule? Could they continue to sacrifice the needs of agriculture and desires of consumers to industry and arms? Could they depend on terror to whip productivity out of workers and peasants? Could they continue to smash down non-Russian minorities or keep nationalism in the republics and satellites from exploding?

Within weeks of Stalin's death the Party and government began to reverse some of his policies. The "doctors' plot" was dismissed as a hoax and the seven surviving defendants released (two had died under torture). People were promised more food and consumer goods in the near future. In the topmost political arena, the contest for power became less tangled after the arrest and execution of Lavrenty Beria, chief of the security police since 1938 and a main contender. Following Beria's elimination, organized by Nikita Khrushchev (1894–1971) and carried out by the military (July 1953), the security police agency was investigated and discovered to have committed an array of horrific crimes, many of them against the Party itself. As a result the powerful agency was now put more securely under Party control. In line with the investigation, several hundred prisoners (out of several hundred thousand) were freed. The people's response to these events, their hopeful expectations about the future and questions about the recent past, became the subject of a number of writings. The title of one of these, Ilya Ehrenburg's novel, *The Thaw* (1954), was the name popularly given to the times, the mid-1950s.

Khrushchev succeeded Stalin as Party leader, although, excepting Beria, other prominent figures, including potential contenders, retained high offices. It was not what some called "collective leadership" but was a step in that direction. Khrushchev's immediate forebears were serfs, peasants, and coal miners. The sorry harvest of 1953, his promise to make dramatic improvements in food production, and his quick actions in this regard got the attention of other leaders. He raised state procurement prices and lowered taxes on private plots. In 1954 he introduced a plan to add tens of millions of acres of northern Khazakstan and southwestern Siberia to the growing of grain. At first these "virgin lands" were blessed with adequate rainfall and grain production rose substantially, as did Khrushchev's political stock.

At the 20th Party Congress of February 1956 Khrushchev spoke at length about Stalin's viciousness, arrogance, faulty leadership, and crimes. He denounced the purge trials of perfectly loyal Bolsheviks, convicted on fictional evidence and tortured-out confessions. Though he did not mention the worst crimes, including the deliberate starvation of millions of peasants, the speech stunned the delegates, not only for what was said, but also because it was said at all. Khrushchev delivered his "secret speech" at a special closed session on the last day of the congress, which had begun, more than two weeks before, with praises for the great leader. Some members of the Presidium had strongly opposed the speech, especially those who had been closest to Stalin. Why did Khrushchev do this? Perhaps he wanted to show that, despite his own complicity, he was repelled by Stalin's monstrous deeds, or expected to wound other leaders whose hands were even bloodier than his, or saw the need to denounce Stalin's reign of terror, especially because of his close connection to it, in order to take a different course. Whatever the reasons, the speech began the destruction of the Stalin icon and called into question the communist regime he personified. Khrushchev again attacked Stalin in 1961 at the 22nd Congress, which voted to remove Stalin's body from Lenin's tomb. Stalin's name began to be removed from public places. Stalingrad, site of the Soviet Union's greatest military victory, was renamed Volgograd. A great blow was delivered with the publication, authorized by Khrushchev himself, of Aleksandr Solzhenitsyn's novel about the prison labor camps, *One Day in the Life of Ivan Denisovich* (1962). Among the characters, innocent victims of Stalin's crimes, are the very best of men, "without whom," taking a passage from Solzhenitsyn's *Matryona's Home*, "no village can stand. Nor any city. Nor our whole land."[9]

The 22nd Congress planned to transform the USSR over the next 20 years into a socialist society rivaling the United States in wealth and productivity, despite the fact that the rate of agricultural production had been slipping since 1957. Khrushchev had tried to prevent the slowdown with various reorganizing, pricing, and carrot-stick schemes, anything but heavy capital investment. Drought greatly diminished output in the "virgin lands," and wind erosion of the loosened dry topsoil resulted in an ecological disaster. Khrushchev had boasted of ever richer harvests and so much feed corn that the Soviet Union would soon pass the United States in the production of meat and dairy foods. Reality was something quite different. In 1963 the government was forced to import several million tons of grain.

In foreign affairs as in agriculture Khrushchev failed more than he succeeded. He rejected the domineering, belligerent manner of Stalin and was determined to deal with the world, including Soviet satellites, in a more conventional and accommodating way. He helped end the Korean War (1950–1953), tried to undo bad relations that had existed between Stalin and Josip Broz Tito (dictator of Yugoslavia), and agreed with Western leaders to a general withdrawal of allied troops from Austria. At the 20th Party Congress (1956) he suggested that the USSR could coexist with the capitalist world and, having Tito's Yugoslavia in mind, accepted the fact that there were "different roads to socialism." Khrushchev's widely known "secret speech" against Stalin at the same congress and his idea about "different roads" encouraged reformers in Soviet satellites to try to free themselves from Moscow's controls. His remarks had a direct bearing on riots that year in Poland and Hungary.

In Poland, disclosures of corruption and brutality in its secret police pushed popular discontent to the surface. Some factory workers were killed in battles with police and soldiers. Near the point of sending in Soviet troops and setting off a catastrophic escalation, Khrushchev agreed to a number of concessions. Among them was the acceptance of Wladyslaw Gomulka as the new Polish leader, though he had been imprisoned as a "Titoist" under Stalin. In general, Moscow accepted in principle Poland's right to find its own path to socialism without Soviet interference. Meanwhile, spurred by the Polish example, people in Budapest took to the streets. Their anger had been fired up by the Stalinist-like tyranny of Matyas Rakosi. Following his demotion by Moscow and under the reform leadership of Imre Nagy, Hungary began moving quickly and radically toward independence and away from a strictly socialist polity. This time the Soviet government responded with tanks and troops, moving on Budapest, killing and wounding thousands of defenders while suffering several hundred casualties to its own forces. In the aftermath of the uprising, tens of thousands of Hungarians fled westward or were arrested and deported to the Soviet Union. Imre Nagy was executed in June 1958.

Outside the Soviet Eastern European sphere, Khrushchev's government encountered other serious problems. Soviet-Chinese relations appeared to be caught in a maelstrom. Wherever the common interest of the two countries touched, whether the concerns were important or petty, there was disagreement. From Mao's perspective the USSR was mistaken in rejecting Stalinism and accommodating itself to the West. He wanted to develop nuclear weapons; Khrushchev agreed to limit testing. Soviet technicians were expelled from China, Chinese students from the Soviet Union. China raised old border issues with the USSR; Moscow supported India in that country's border disputes with China. One serious consequence of the quarrel was to favor defense spending over much-needed domestic programs.

Mao was right about Khrushchev's intentions to draw closer to, and ease tensions with, the West. But Khrushchev's efforts in this regard resulted in some spectacular failures. In 1959 he was warmly received by the United States and looked forward to a return visit from Eisenhower and a summit meeting with the president. However, these prospects collapsed after a U.S. spy plane was shot down over the Soviet Union. Failure to force Western powers out of Berlin also got much public attention, especially the 1948–1949 blockade, thwarted by a great airlift of supplies into the city, and the building of the Berlin Wall in 1961, closing off the Soviet sector. The wall itself became a symbol of failure, a sign that people wanted to get out of the communist East. Most remarkable was Khrushchev's decision in 1962 to put nuclear missiles in Cuba. The United States responded with a naval blockade of the island, raising the threat of war between the two superpowers. Khrushchev's removal of the missiles was greeted with much relief around the world and led to efforts by Washington and Moscow to guard against such confrontations in the future. Chinese leaders condemned the retreat.

Khrushchev the reformer, for all his shortcomings and failures, aimed to better the lives of Soviet peoples and did so in a number of ways. Attacking Stalin and investigating the security police and reining in its power eased people's fears and directly and almost immediately began the rehabilitation of millions of political prisoners and other innocent persons. Arbitrary arrest and imprisonment did not end but began to give way to lawful procedures. People's standard of living improved. Millions of apartments were built, poorly constructed but greatly appreciated by new occupants. He paid special attention to the lives of peasants, who still represented about half the population in the 1950s and remained at the bottom of the economic ladder. Grain procurement prices were raised, taxes on private plots reduced, and peasants' financial security and mobility (inside the country) improved. In his last years, however, agrarian production and reform were slowed or reversed because of natural disasters, underfunding, and faulty quick fixes. This reversal was compounded by a slowdown in industrial production. Incomes leveled off or declined and the high expectations raised by the First Secretary's early successes and blustering promises came to a disappointing end.

In June 1957, while Khrushchev was in Helsinki, most members of the Presidium, who regarded his reforms as irresponsible and dangerous, decided to remove him from office. (Mikhail Gorbachev, the last Soviet reformer, would face the same sort of challenge for much the same reasons in 1991.) Khrushchev returned to Moscow, where the Presidium demanded his resignation, whereupon he quickly rounded up the Party Central Committee, which had the power to elect and remove the First Secretary. With its blessing, he removed his chief opponents from the Presidium and replaced them with his supporters. Seven years later, in October 1964, the tables were turned. The less popular Khrushchev, no longer backed by the military and security police and ridiculed for his outlandish behavior and crazy schemes, was opposed by the Presidium, and this time the Central Committee forced him to resign.

After Khrushchev's "resignation" the Soviet Union was ruled by a group of Party/government leaders representing various other powerful agencies: military, security police, and industry. By 1971 Leonid Brezhnev (1906–1982) emerged from the pack as chief Party secretary and head of the Politburo. Politically, the Brezhnev years (1964–1982) were a retreat from the anti-Stalinism, active reforming, and limited openness of the Khrushchev decade. Reasons for dissent grew apace with escalating social miseries, the failure of economic half measures, ecological disasters, and so on. Airing out problems, expressing ideas different from the Party line, or discussing crimes of the Stalin past were not tolerated. At the same time, the Brezhnev government restored Stalin's image as the great leader and revived his repressive methods. Nevertheless, though threatened with an array of terrible punishments, from hard labor in Siberian prisons to "treatments" in mental hospitals, dissenters got their messages out; sometimes they were published abroad, sometimes under the noses of KGB agents in underground publications.

The economy continued to slump. In industry, reforms that would loosen the grip (power) of central planners and give greater freedom (responsibility) to factory managers were resisted by both planners and managers. A very promising producing-for-profit experiment, begun under Khrushchev in a small corner of the textile industry, was abandoned. The rate of industrial growth declined and planned increases usually fell short, often considerably short, of goals. In agriculture, private plots continued to produce a significant portion of the total output of meat, dairy products, and vegetables, and Brezhnev had the good sense to permit their expansion. In other areas agriculture suffered for the same old reasons. Collectives, combined to make huge agrarian factories with hundreds of workers and thousands of acres, failed to keep up with the needs of a growing population. Heavy defense spending meant reduced investments in agriculture. Rubles that could have gone to agriculture went to buy grain from abroad, millions of tons of it during Brezhnev's last years. Living standards were not much improved, consumer goods (despite more of them) disappointed the public's needs or wants, and housing was generally dilapidated and inadequate. People's health suffered from increases in alcoholism, drug use, air and water pollution, and violent crimes, as well as a slowdown in health-care funding. The country's vital signs revealed how serious the problems were in the 1960s and 1970s—life expectancy got shorter and infant mortality began to rise.

Foreign affairs for the Brezhnev government were a minefield. Strained relations with China in the 1960s erupted in fighting along the border. Long-disputed territory taken by Russia was the immediate issue. Behind that were ideological differences that had arisen during the Khrushchev years, and the claim by Chinese communists that their country rather than the USSR should bear the socialist standard for the third world. While the Soviets struggled against their Chinese comrades they appeared to grow friendly toward capitalist America. This warming, called détente, began about 1969 as the Soviet invasion of Czechoslovakia receded from people's concerns and the United States began to negotiate a withdrawal from Vietnam. The two powers worked on a Strategic Arms Limitation Treaty (SALT I), which they signed in May 1972. Further agreements followed, on limiting weapons and, in Helsinki in 1975, on European boundaries; on the exchange of goods, technology, and culture; and on respecting human rights. This last accord gave human rights advocates in the Soviet Union a legal platform from which to protest the government's repressive measures. Included in the accord was a provision on the right of people to travel and was meant to address the USSR's restrictions on the emigration of Soviet Jews.

In December 1979 détente collapsed with the Soviet invasion of Afghanistan, an effort to shore up a faltering communist government and extend its power southward between south Asia and the Middle East. Afghan guerrillas suffered heavy casualties and millions of civilians fled to Pakistan, but Soviet forces never secured mountainous regions and were continually harassed, taking many casualties themselves. In February 1989 the USSR pulled its last troops out of the disastrous war, which had added substantially to military spending and weakened Soviet influence in Asia, especially among Muslims. The United States, besides cutting off exports of technology and grain to the USSR, began to strengthen its own presence in Asia. It was an opportunity to promote closer ties with China, a policy already being moved along since President Nixon's visit to Peking in 1972.

Brezhnev was faced with two major challenges to Soviet authority from the satellites. A strong jolt of resistance occurred in Czechoslovakia in 1968. In January of that year the reform-minded Alexander Dubček became leader of the Czechoslovakian Communist Party, encouraging discussions about topics that had been on people's minds for some time, such as free press and multiparty government. Dubček did away with censorship, began to improve his country's relations with the West, and did not heed warnings from Moscow to bring an end to the "Prague Spring." Finally, on August 21, 1968, Soviet military units, supported by other satellite member countries of the Warsaw Pact (organized in 1955), invaded and quickly took over the country. The second jolt came from Poland. Living standards there had gone up in the 1970s as a result of an industrial boom based partly on Western credits in the form of technology. In the second half of the decade industry was not ready to pay for itself, payments came due on the credits, and the economy collapsed. But people's expectations remained high. Mixed in with frustrations over high prices and shortages, especially of food, was anger at the Polish Communist Party's deference to Moscow. A hike in food prices set off strikes across the country in August 1980. Workers drew support from the Church, students, intellectuals, and peasants. Out of these strikes crystallized "Solidarity," an independent (of state and party) trade union movement. Within months membership in autonomous unions numbered in the millions. Workers wanted political as well as economic changes, among them free elections and an end to censorship. Their actions got the sympathetic attention of workers and reformers in the other satellites. What was Brezhnev to do? Military intervention would likely be resisted, and the Soviet Union was already engaged in the Afghan war. Allow Poland to cut its ties with Moscow, and the other satellites would surely try to follow. In the end the conflict was put on hold. In December 1981 Polish General Jaruzelski, with or without Moscow's orders, took over the government and imposed martial law. Solidarity went into hibernation, the economy did not get fixed, and resentment remained high.

In the Soviet Union resentment was given a public voice in the writings of dissenters. Though not likely to be murdered, they still faced the possibility of heavy punishments—imprisonment in Siberian labor camps or in mental hospitals, for example. They made their views known by having their writings published in the West or as *samizdat* (self-published) manuscripts, distributed in typed or mimeographed form. The best-known case, one that set in motion a widening protest movement, involved Andrey Sinyavsky and Yuly Daniel, who published their writings under pseudonyms from 1956 to 1965. They were publicly tried in 1966 for slandering the Soviet Union in works printed abroad. Sinyavsky was sentenced to seven years and Daniel to five years at hard labor. Alexander Ginzburg, Yury Galanskov, and two others, who made a thorough record of the trial, a copy of which was published in the West, were also tried and harshly punished. Pavel Litvinov was tried and punished for publishing his account of the latter trial. Several hundred persons publicly protested the illegal trial of Ginzburg, Galanskov, and others. In 1968 *The Chronicle of Current Events* began self-publishing accounts of violations of law by the state. Among dissenters was the world-renowned physicist Andrey Sakharov, founder of the Human Rights Committee in 1970, and the novelist Solzhenitsyn, whose account of Soviet concentration camps, *The Gulag Archipelago*, began to come out abroad in 1974. Both were exiled, Sakharov to the city of Gorky and Solzhenitsyn out of the country. Dissent concerned, among other things, ethnic and religious persecution, anti-Semitism, suppression of national aspirations, Russification, invasions of Czechoslovakia and Afghanistan, and violations of rights guaranteed by the Soviet constitution or Helsinki accords.

Brezhnev died at age 76 in November 1982. His elderly successors were Yuri Andropov, who died in 1984, and Konstantin Chernenko, who died the following year. The aging Brezhnev was ill during his last months, and both successors were also in poor health. They continued the war in Afghanistan and did little to raise the economy from its depression, or to warm relations with China or the United States. Chernenko's death was announced on March 11, 1985. He was succeeded by the relatively young and vigorous Mikhail Gorbachev (b. 1931).

The new First Secretary brought his supporters into top Party and government posts. He was well educated, determined, and optimistic. He wanted to change for the better the lives of Soviet people. Against him were a legion of problems, not least of which was how to bring about change and not be swept away himself. Some serious economic ills needed immediate attention. Other urgent problems, such as poor public health and environmental pollution, would require sustained Herculean efforts to repair. But how could the government, burdened with debt and strapped with heavy military spending, find anything approaching the funds necessary to fix even one of the most serious problems?

Gorbachev believed that constructive criticism was essential, that problems had to be exposed to be corrected: *glasnost'* (openness) before *perestroika* (reconstruction). Gorbachev freed from exile the outspoken human rights advocate Andrey Sakharov. On the other hand, he failed an early glasnost test himself in April 1986 after a near meltdown at the Chernobyl nuclear plant by waiting 18 days, days critical to the health of many people, before announcing the accident. Openness meant giving Stalin's crimes even greater exposure and rehabilitating more of his victims, but there were dangers in opening up everything. If the Stalin-Hitler pact of August 1939 was criminal, then the claim of Baltic peoples that their states were illegally taken by the Soviet Union had merit since, as part of the agreement, the two dictators divided up parts of Eastern Europe between them and Stalin's part of the loot included the Baltic states. And how would Poles react to information that Soviet, not German, units had rounded up and executed more than fifteen thousand Polish officers, professors, journalists, doctors, and others?

Economic reforms were critical to any restructuring program, but Gorbachev made little headway here. He wanted central planners to provide only general guidelines, leaving managers of enterprises to work out the details of their operations. State subsidies and price-fixing would stop. Unprofitable factories would die. In agriculture the First Secretary promoted leasing arrangements whereby groups or families could farm land outside the collectives. However, collective agriculture remained dominant. There were quick fixes and half measures such as importing consumer goods. When the state attempted to reduce its alcohol production, it lost much revenue to illegal private brewing. Growth rates in industry and agriculture remained depressed while government spending continued to grow.

There was much to reveal in the Gorbachev years of openness. Able now to report on the state of things, the media began to uncover shocking facts about the poverty and brutality of life in the Soviet Union. Women especially were vulnerable, likely to suffer from abusive drunken husbands and hard, dirty, dangerous work. Many women had two full-time jobs: factory and home. Reports on the environment revealed extraordinary cases of damage. The Aral Sea, for example, was rapidly drying up because water that once flowed into it was being siphoned off for agriculture and industry. Even a deliberate scheme to get rid of the sea could hardly have reduced it faster. As the water receded it left great expanses of exposed seabed laden with noxious chemicals ready to be wind-borne into the atmosphere.

While the economy languished, Gorbachev altered the course of Soviet foreign policy. He met cordially with presidents Reagan and Bush. Their talks centered on arms control, and they came to substantial agreements. Détente during the Brezhnev years had been a temporary accommodation with the enemy. Gorbachev pursued genuinely friendly relations with the West and rejected an attitude of belligerency in the conduct of Soviet foreign policy. The Politburo decided to pull out of Afghanistan in 1987 and did so in February 1989. Late that same year when Eastern European satellites began to break away, Gorbachev did not intervene. These were convincing signs of his commitment to peace and good relations with the West. In that pivotal year of 1989 Gorbachev visited China, a first step in overcoming decades of hostility between the two communist powers. These were extraordinary events, marking an important change in world politics, but they were grounded in quite practical considerations. Its huge military budget and other spending related to the cold war prevented the Soviet Union from providing desperately needed funds to industry, agriculture, health care, education, and housing construction. Gorbachev had to assume the USSR could reduce its military spending, deal with the United States in good faith, and not be attacked. He made clear that the Soviet Union would no longer fight for dominance in the third world. The Afghanistan war, which seriously troubled relations between the superpowers and which the Kremlin decided was a losing cause anyway, was expensive and not suitable to the new policy. Eastern Europe was no longer to be thought of as a corridor for invasion from the West.

A strike movement in Poland in 1988 persuaded Communists there to begin talks with Solidarity leaders and other influential groups. Elections the following year returned to Parliament a minority of Polish Communists. Gorbachev did not send in paratroops and tanks; he advised the comrades to join the government. This was a signal that the USSR would not try to crush movements toward independence in central Europe. All at once the Soviet empire began to unravel. In the West even experts on Soviet history and politics were amazed at the collapse. Quite different images mark the end of Moscow's rule over the satellites: in Berlin the dismantling of a wall (November 1989); in Romania the murder-execution of dictator Nicolai Ceaușescu and his wife, Elena (December 1989). At the same time the satellite shell was peeling away, the core itself, the USSR, was beginning to break up. In December 1987 Gorbachev appointed a Russian instead of a Kazakh to head the Party in Kazakhstan. Protests over the appointment turned into violent anti-Russian demonstrations. In February 1988 fighting occurred between Azerbaijani and Armenians. The conflict was driven by nationalistic, ethnic, and religious feelings, and the two Soviet republics fought each other like independent states. In the late 1980s Baltic peoples began protesting the Nazi-Soviet pact and secret (spheres of interest) protocol of 1939 and Soviet annexations of 1940. In 1989 nationalist demonstrations took place in the Baltic states. In Tbilisi, capital of Georgia, Soviet troops brutally put down a nationalist demonstration, killing a number of participants and adding fire to the separatist cause. Perhaps the overwhelming political and economic problems of the years 1988–1991 prevented Gorbachev from giving the nationalist and separatist movements his sufficient attention. In 1990 Soviet republics in the Baltic and Caucasus began to act as independent states. Under the leadership of Boris Yeltsin, once the Communist Party chief of Moscow, even the Russian Republic began to distance itself from the USSR.

As individual republics grew stronger, Gorbachev, the Party, and Soviet government lost standing. His power and popularity waning, Gorbachev, trying to find a way to preserve his power, shifted his support first to Yeltsin and other radical reformers and then to the conservatives. In January 1991 he demonstrated his realignment by threatening to smash Lithuanian separatism. In fact, some Lithuanians were killed in a clash with KGB troops in the capital of Vilnius. Yeltsin flew to Lithuania to protest Gorbachev's action. In April Gorbachev moved back toward the left, meeting with Yeltsin and leaders of other republics to replace the Soviet Union with a federation of independent states. In June Yeltsin was elected President of the Russian Republic, which made him the most prominent leader in a swirl of emerging independent states.

The anticlimax of the disintegration of the Soviet Union was a desperate effort by a group of conservative Party leaders, who called themselves the Committee for the State of Emergency, to restore the Party and government and themselves to power. On August 19, 1991, the day before former republics were scheduled to sign away the USSR, the Committee had Gorbachev arrested, announced he was ill, and claimed they were taking over the government. The coup was badly managed by unpopular men who had not secured the backing of military or KGB troops. Opposed by the popular Yeltsin, the coup lasted three days. On December 1, 1991, Ukrainians voted themselves independent and on the 8th Russia, Belarus (formerly Byelorussia), and Ukraine formed the Commonwealth of Independent States (CIS). Except for Georgia and the Baltic states, all the former republics had joined the CIS by the end of December. On December 25, 1991, the USSR formally ceased to be.

NOTES

1. The Russian (or Julian) calendar of 1914 was 13 days behind the Gregorian calendar used in the West. Dates in this text correspond to the Gregorian calendar. Thus, Nicholas's announcement of Russia's declaration of war against Germany occurred on August 2, 1914 (July 20, 1914, according to the Russian/Julian calendar). At the beginning of February 1918 the difference was resolved when the Bolsheviks converted to the Gregorian calendar: February 1 (Old Style) became February 14 (New Style).

2. The city was known as St. Petersburg before 1914 and again after 1991, Petrograd from 1914 to 1924, and Leningrad from 1924 to 1991.

3. Robert Tucker, editor, *The Lenin Anthology* (New York: Norton, 1975), 719–21.

4. The first Soviet constitution, of the Russian Soviet Federated Socialist Republic (RSFSR), was promulgated on July 10, 1918; the second, on January 31, 1924, formally recognized the USSR (four republics: RSFSR, Ukrainian SSR, Byelorussian SSR, Transcaucasian SFSR); the third on December 6, 1936 recognized nine republics: RSFSR, Ukraine, Byelorussia, Turkmenistan, Uzbekistan, Tajikistan, Georgia, Azerbaijan, Armenia; the fourth on October 7, 1977 recognized 15 republics: RSFSR, Byelorussia, Ukraine, Estonia, Latvia, Lithuania, Moldavia (later Moldova), Georgia, Azerbaijan, Armenia, Kazakhstan, Turkmenistan, Uzbekistan, Tajikistan, and Kyrgyzstan.

5. J. W. Leasure and R. A. Lewis, *Population Changes in Russia and the USSR,* Social Science Monograph Series vol. 1, no. 2 (San Diego: San Diego State College Press, 1966), 35.

6. Leonard Schapiro, *The Communist Party of the Soviet Union,* 2nd ed. (New York: Vintage, 1971), 287, 300–301.

7. Lazar Volin, *A Century of Russian Agriculture. From Alexander II to Khrushchev* (Cambridge, MA: Harvard University Press, 1970), 211.

8. Volin, 211.

9. Aleksandr Solzhenitsyn, *Matryona's Home,* in *The Norton Anthology of World Masterpieces,* ed. Maynard Mack et al., expanded edition, vol. 2 (New York: W. W. Norton, 1995), 2331.

2

ethnic groups and nationalities[1]

"Russian Empire" refers to a place and a time—the nearly two centuries, from 1721 when Peter the Great was awarded the title "Emperor of All Russia" by his Senate to the end of Emperor Nicholas II's reign in 1917. However, the process of empire building was already well advanced in Russia by the reign of Peter, though he raised the empire to the status of world power, and did not end following the abdication of Nicholas, who ushered in the most cruel chapter of its history (1914–1953), a generation of wars, revolutions, famines, and political terror. One of the striking things about Soviet history is that near the end of this cataclysmic time, Russian/Soviet imperialism reached farthest, achieved its fullest power, and exhibited its greatest influence on world affairs. Dozens of formerly independent states or peoples who had suffered under the heel of the imperial government in St. Petersburg were now dominated by the Soviet government in Moscow. The lives of Soviet peoples were more or less transformed and brought into a general cultural mainstream by central planners and Party bosses. There were benefits in this arrangement, especially for those at the very bottom of the social order. However, when the empire began to crumble in the late 1980s, people in the satellite countries and Soviet republics clearly showed their nonallegiance to Moscow by running for the exits.

The collapse of the USSR meant independence for six satellites, controlled by Moscow since the late 1940s (*Poland, Czechoslovakia, East Germany, Hungary, Romania,* and *Bulgaria*) and independence for the 15 Soviet republics. These republics, which together made up the USSR, were as follows: *Russia,*

At the winter pastures for livestock at the Voroshilov Kolkhoz (Uzbek USSR), 1955. Reproduced from the Collections of the Library of Congress, Lot 7401 #24.

or the RSFSR (Russian Soviet Federated Socialist Republic, also referred to as the Russian Federation), larger than all the other union republics together; the Baltic states, annexed by Russia in the eighteenth century (*Estonia* and *Latvia* in 1721, *Lithuania* in 1795), freed as a result of the revolutionary upheavals of 1917–1920, but annexed by Stalin in the summer of 1940, a move sanctioned by a secret "sphere of interest" division of east central Europe made at the time of the Molotov-Ribbentrop Pact of August 23, 1939; *Moldavia* (or Bessarabia), taken by Russia in 1812, granted to Romania in 1918, and grabbed by the USSR in June 1940 in accordance with the same 1939 Soviet-Nazi secret agreement; the two East Slavic nations that share much the same historical and cultural heritage as Russia—*Ukraine* and *Byelorussia;* the three Caucasian republics—*Georgia* and *Armenia,* whose histories as states go back to pre-Christian times, and neighboring *Azerbaijan;* and finally, five central Asian republics: *Kazakhstan, Uzbekistan, Turkmenistan, Kyrgyzstan,* and *Tajikistan,* comprising a territory most of which was conquered by Russia in the latter half of the nineteenth century.

Each former satellite and Soviet republic is populated by several or dozens of different ethnic groups, and these are further separated by various circumstances into subethnic populations; the Russian Federation alone has hundreds of such groupings. To write even briefly about each one would require volumes.

In some parts of the Russian/Soviet empire indigenous peoples became minorities as Russians moved in. In a few places Russians came to far outnumber local peoples, for example, accounting for about 70 percent of the populations in the Buryat and Karelia Autonomous Republics (ARs), according to the 1979 census. Some groups were uprooted and transplanted. This was true especially during the Stalin dictatorship (1928–1953), when hundreds of thousands of people were driven from their home territories to distant places. The Crimean Tatars and Volga Germans, for example, were deported en masse and scattered into western Siberia and Central Asia. The intrusion of Russians, Ukrainians, and Byelorussians into non-Slavic cultures and the rooting out and scattering of peoples tended to homogenize Soviet society, but nothing was more important in creating a general sameness than the great leap forward that transformed the USSR from a predominantly farming into a largely industrial and urban society. The most far-flung groups, from arctic hunters to central Asian herders, shared, more or less, in these changes so that their lives came to have common features. On the other hand, not all human activities and beliefs were pressed into the same mold. Much as the government pushed for uniformity, the Soviet Union remained a community of many contrasts (see Tables 1 and 2).

The two main ethnic populations—East Slavs (Russians, Ukrainians, and Byelorussians) and Turkic/Muslims—together made up about 80 percent of the empire's population in 1897 and nearly 90 percent in 1959[2] (see Table 3).

Table 1
Populations—USSR Republics in 1989

USSR Republic	Population
Armenia SSR:	3,288,000
Azerbaijan SSR:	7,038,000
Byelorussia SSR:	10,200,000
Estonia SSR:	1,573,000
Georgia SSR:	5,443,000
Kazakhstan SSR:	16,536,000
Kyrgyzstan SSR:	4,290,000
Latvia SSR:	2,680,000
Lithuania SSR:	3,690,000
Moldavia SSR:	4,338,000
RSFSR:	147,386,000
Tajikistan SSR:	5,109,000
Turkmenistan SSR:	3,534,000
Ukraine SSR:	51,707,000
Uzbekistan SSR:	19,905,000
Total:	287,000,000

The census figures in Table 3 reveal a noticeable increase in both the number and relative strength of Russians. At the same time, Ukrainian and Turkic/Muslim populations grew sufficiently in number to hold steady as a percentage of the whole.

After 1959, however, the census records present quite a different picture. In the 1960s the death rate among East Slavs, which had been falling, began to rise (for reasons noted in chapter 8, "Health Care and Health Problems"), while birthrates continued to go down. For the two major Slavic republics (RSFSR and Ukraine) this meant a sharp decline in population growth between 1960 and 1980. In Muslim republics the trends were similar but much less pronounced so that they remained far ahead of Slavic republics in growth rates.[3]

Western regions of the Russian Empire were, for a time, home to the largest population of Jews in the world. The decline in their number began with an emigration movement in the late nineteenth century, spurred by waves of violent anti-Jewish persecution following the assassination of Tsar Alexander II in 1881. Then, during World War II, hundreds of thousands of Soviet Jews were destroyed by the Nazis and their Romanian allies. Between 1897 and 1959 the Jewish population shrank by more than half, from about 5 million to 2.3 million. The further decline in their

Table 2
Largest USSR Nationalities in 1989

Nationality (language)	(% of total)
Russian (Slavic)	145,155,000 (50.6)
Ukranian (Slavic)	44,186,000 (15.4)
Uzbek (Turkic)	16,698,000 (5.8)
Byelorussian (Slavic)	10,036,000 (3.5)
Kazakh (Turkic)	8,136,000 (2.8)
Tatar (Turkic)	6,921,000 (2.4)
Azerbaijan (Turkic)	6,770,000 (2.4)
Armenian (Armenian)	4,623,000 (1.6)
Tajik (Iranian)	4,215,000 (1.5)
Georgian (Caucasian)	3,981,000 (1.4)
Moldovan (Romanian)	3,352,000 (1.2)
Lithuanian (Baltic)	3,067,000 (1.1)

Sources: Anatoly Khazanov, *After the USSR: Ethnicity, Nationalism, and Politics in the Commonwealth of Independent States* (Madison: University of Wisconsin Press, 1995), 247, 268–71; Roger Caratini, ed., *Dictionnaire des nationalités et des minorités U.R.S.S.* (Paris: Larousse, 1990), 236–37; *Encyclopedia Britannica 1991 Book of the Year*, 720–21.

Table 3
Censuses

	1897	1959
Totals:	126 million	209 million
Russians	56 million (44%)	114 million (55%)
Ukrainians	22 million (18%)	37 million (18%)
Byelorussians	6 million (5%)	8 million (4%)
Muslims	14 million (11%)	23 million (11%)

numbers in the 1970s and 80s was the result of emigration, mostly to the new state of Israel.

Though it is possible to talk about the different peoples of the Soviet Union (Russians, Jews, Uzbeks, etc.) as if each were a single community, tied together by a more or less common history and culture, it is unlikely that any of them were ever ethnically uniform. During the Soviet era each was composed of some or many groups, clearly distinguished one from another by important aspect(s) of their lives: linguistic, religious, social, economic, and so on.

One of the world's most culturally diverse regions exists in the relatively small, confined mountainous Caucasus area between the Caspian and Black seas, on the border between Asia and Europe. The republics of Armenia, Azerbaijan, and Georgia occupy much of the area, but hundreds of ethnic and subethnic groups, indigenous and foreign, live there also. Azerbaijani, for example, based on their language and the fact that they call or have called themselves Turk and Azeri Turk, are a Turkic people, but different Azeri communities have been heavily influenced by neighboring Caucasians and Iranians. Foreign residents also influenced their culture. In 1979, besides Azeri, who accounted for 78 percent (4.7 million of 6.0 million) of the republic's population, there were almost a half million each of Russians and Armenians, some 205,000 Daghestani, and several thousand each of Jews, Tatars, Ukrainians, Georgians, and others. However, as populations go, Azerbaijan is much less complex and has many fewer pieces in its ethnic puzzle than neighboring Georgia.

Ethnic diversity also characterizes peoples who are spread thinly over the Siberian vastness. In 1989 some 30,000 Evenki lived and worked in a 1.8-million-square-mile area of central and eastern Siberia. Perhaps they were once a single group, but even before the Soviet era they constituted three distinct communities: sedentary coastal fishers and hunters on the Sea of Okhotsk, reindeer herders in the north, and cattle and horse raisers in the south. Because they have been so widely dispersed, often isolated from other Evenki, they speak many different dialects of their Tungus mother language and have taken on some of the language and habits of their closest non-Evenki neighbors (Yakut, Koriak, Chukchi, and Buryat). Evenki are closely related, historically and linguistically, to the Even, who also occupy vast reaches of northeastern Siberia and are divided into sedentary coastal hunters/fishers and reindeer herders and are also distinguished by a number of different dialects.

One of the things that set people apart was standard of living, and one indicator of the economic, social, and cultural "advancement" of one group over another was urbanization. Between 1939 and 1989 the urban population of the USSR rose from 32 percent to 66 percent of the total. As noted elsewhere in these chapters, compared to the lives of hunters, herders, and farmers, life in cities, especially big cities, usually meant better jobs, housing, schools, health care, public transportation, stores, entertainment, and so on. There were relatively small groups who were mainly city dwellers (e.g., Jews and Gypsies), but the largest number, by far, of urbanized Soviet people were Russians.[4] During the Soviet period Russians came to occupy the high ground of urban life and living standards, followed by Baltic peoples; at or near the bottom were central Asians, Azerbaijani, and Moldavians. In 1959 in the Russian Republic (RSFSR) 55 percent of Russians lived in cities; among Russians living in other republics 74 percent were city dwellers. In 1970 Jews, Georgians, Armenians, Russians, Latvians, Estonians, and Ossetians were the most educated and labor-skilled ethnic groups. The least educated and labor skilled were the Chechen-Ingush people on the northern slopes of the Caucasus Mountains. Central Asians also ranked low in these two categories. The "less advanced" central Asian families had about three times more children per family than the "more advanced" western ethnic groups.[5]

A few examples from the USSR's many ethnic groups will show how remarkably diverse they were, and also how distant from the Russian/ Soviet mainstream. Native peoples who inhabit Russia's north are thinly spread along its great expanse, 4,000 miles from the Kola Peninsula in the west to the Chukchi Peninsula in the East. Two bands of vegetation stretch across the region. Northernmost is the tundra, where soils and weather support lichens, mosses, and some stunted trees and shrubs. To the south where trees first appear is the boundary between tundra and taiga, the world's largest conifer forest, which in eastern Siberia extends from the tundra to the China border. Over the centuries northern natives have accommodated themselves to the short, cool summers and long, very cold winters and made the land, rivers, lakes, and seas yield a living, sometimes an abundance. These natives have been exploited by Russian tsars and fur merchants and reformed by Soviet officials, who usually regarded them as old-fashioned and their traditions as barriers to progress. During the Soviet period the traditional life of every one of these northern peoples was changed. Wooden houses replaced tents; airplanes and snowmobiles substituted for reindeer sleds; schools, hospitals, and medical clinics were established; bread, potatoes, and canned vegetables became staples. During the Stalin revolution relatively free-ranging hunters and nomadic herders were reigned into collectives. At the same time the land and water were carelessly exploited by lumber and extraction industries. Religion was discouraged, and in Soviet schools students were weaned away from their native languages.

The Even are an indigenous people of northeastern Siberia who numbered about 17,200 in 1989, up from 12,500 in 1979. Their main occupation for centuries has been reindeer herding. Hunting and fishing are also important, though less so than in the past, and some Even are settled permanently on the Sea of Okhotsk coast, where they pursue these occupations. Because of the perilous circumstances of life in the sparsely peopled taiga and tundra, they developed vital traditions for establishing ties and encouraging cooperation within and among clans, including exogamy (requiring marriage into another clan), communal sharing of a hunter's catch, and community aid for those in distress. They and their herds, numbering several hundreds or thousands of animals, ranged over a territory the size of Western Europe. Reindeer provided food, hide for clothing and tent cover, and transportation. Following long-established custom, men usually engaged in caring for animals, hunting, and making tools or weapons. Women gathered edible roots, berries, and nuts and prepared food—the meat, blood, bone marrow, and organs (including eyeballs) of

the reindeer. Women also prepared hides and fashioned them into clothing and shoes, set up and maintained the conical lightweight and easily
portable tent house, and cared for children. Nomadic herders supplemented their main diet of reindeer flesh with fish and wild game, while
those settled along the coast mainly consumed fish, especially salmon,
and seal meat.

There are several dialects of their mother language, a branch of Tungus,
but most Even learned to speak Russian or Yakut as a first language. Russians began to exert a strong and negative influence on the peoples of eastern Siberia in the seventeenth century, when they overcame native
resistance and introduced, besides smallpox and other deadly diseases,
large quantities of vodka and a fur-extortion scheme that resulted in a serious thinning out of game animals. As a result of this exploitative and
deadly invasion the number of Even and their quality of life declined.

Under Russian influence, some Even exchanged their ancient shamanist-
animist religion for, or mixed it with, Eastern Orthodoxy. At the beginning
of the Soviet era, however, animism and shamanism were still alive. Spirits
filled the Even world, spirits of mountains and rivers as well as animals
and ancestors. Bears were particularly important as spiritual beings, likewise fire and the hearth. Shamans (medicine men and women) were mete-
orologists, tribal historians, carriers of tradition, and guides for herdsmen
and hunters. They knew how to properly address spirits with words,
dance, and drumming, and they had the power to connect humans with
the spiritual realm, protect them against evil, and heal the sick (humans
and animals) or help souls pass from life.

During the Soviet era these beliefs and practices were much diminished
under official antireligious pressures. Shamanism was discouraged, even
banned, but its practice continued throughout the 1930s and later in many
places.[6] In the 1920s Soviet reformers, besides trying to eradicate religion,
discouraged the nomadic ways of the Even and other northern peoples in
favor of what they considered an economically and culturally advanced
sedentary life. But the great transformation came during the Stalin revolution of the 1930s, when settled hunters and fishers as well as reindeer
nomads were collectivized and their land subjected to a massive and
destructive intrusion of logging and mining. Most Even came to be settled
in permanent wood houses, though former nomadic herdsmen continued
to take their animals out on foraging expeditions.

Even society was organized into clans of blood-related members. The
basic household unit was the nuclear family. When a son married, the
bride was usually added to the husband's household until the couple set
up their own house. Arranged marriage was the rule in the early twentieth century but disappeared under the Soviets. Just as in marriage, pregnancy and child bearing were surrounded by an array of rituals intended
to bring about a good outcome. For expectant mothers they were meant
not only to satisfy spirits but also to ensure such things as cleanliness and

proper diet. Also required was the presence of an older, experienced woman to care for the mother-to-be and instruct first-timers on birthing and child care. Protective rules were especially strict from the beginning of labor—at which time jars and other sealed objects in the house were opened, a symbolic green light for the child to come out—until a few days after delivery. Many of the rituals, taboos, and other elaborate preparations associated with marriage and birthing fell away during the Soviet era.

Traditional care of the sick included the administration of certain medicinal plant and animal parts and shamanistic rituals to deal with good and evil spirits. These traditional practices gave way, though not entirely, to "modern" methods during the twentieth century. However, self-reliance and traditional curative practices remained vital throughout the Soviet period, given the isolated circumstances of many clans and the sparsity of clinics and hospitals in the north.

The Soviet government was first to provide the Even with comprehensive schooling. But this too was a mixed blessing. Many children were sent to boarding schools far from home, where they learned Russian and were encouraged to forget their native language. In this way public education drew students away from their families and culture, and even disparaged the life of the older generations as shallow and backward.

Closely related to the Even in culture and history are the Evenki, who share with them vast reaches of central and eastern Siberia. In 1989 the Evenki numbered some 30,000 persons. In almost every respect they experienced, under imperial and Soviet regimes, the same changes to traditional ways as their Even kin. In the north they were reindeer herders and hunters, on the Okhotsk Sea coast settled hunters and fishers. In the south, however, they turned to farming and raising horses and cattle and became assimilated with the Russians and Buryats in that area. Evenki, like their Even cousins, have a rich folklore, and poets memorized epic folktales that sometimes required several evenings in the retelling. Other kinds of entertainment included sporting events (e.g., reindeer races, footraces, wrestling, and archery), and festivities and rituals surrounded the killing, dressing, cooking, and eating of a bear. Images and calls of the crow were important in such ceremonies to convince the bear's spirit that the crow was responsible for killing it. Evenki life was seriously disrupted by Russian and Soviet incursions. Environmental damage was severe, forced collectivizations in the 1930s and later disrupted the lives of hunters and herders, poverty and alcoholism grew, and Soviet education cut or weakened ties between students and their ancestral traditions. Only in the 1980s was there some success in reversing this destructive process.[7]

The far northeast corner of Siberia is home to the Chukchi, who numbered about 15,200 according to the census of 1989. Their isolation from the civilized world is suggested by the fact that a Chukchi alphabet was not created until 1931. The earliest (seventeenth century) reports about them distinguished between nomadic reindeer herders and settled coastal hunters. Eskimos on both sides of the Bering Strait are among their closest neighbors, and each has had a strong influence on the other's culture. Linguistically Chukchi are linked with Eskimos and other Paleo-Asiatic peoples, especially the Koriaks, who live to the southwest on the Kamchatka Peninsula. To the west nomadic Chukchi herdsmen made contact with the Even, among others. Judging by the 1979 census the Chukchi and their immediate neighbors numbered about 50,000 persons in an area about twice as large as the Ukraine, which then had a population of 50,000,000.

Because of their isolation (10 time zones east of Moscow), resistance to outside authority (especially efforts of the tsarist government to conquer them in the mid-eighteenth century), the bitterly cold and windy climate, and what to foreigners appeared to be a barren environment, the Chukchi were among the least exploited and latest colonized Siberian peoples. Contacts with Russian fur traders and American whalers introduced them to new things (guns, iron pots, whisky, vodka, etc.), but until the 1930s they continued to live pretty much according to their old ways. During the Soviet era they were the last to receive books, radios, and electricity.

Chukchi reindeer herders lived in camps consisting of a few families. When their herds needed new pastures of reindeer moss they struck their large cone-shaped, deer-hide-covered tents and moved on. In the nineteenth century, coastal hunters who had lived in semi-subterranean sod or earthen houses adopted the same kind of tent. What reindeer were to herders, sea mammals were to the coastal settlers, supplying them with hides, meat, and oil. Walrus and whale were hunted by kayak or whaleboat in the summer and seals by foot in winter.

Chukchi men were occupied with herding and hunting, women with household chores, child care, curing hides, and, with the men, gathering firewood and edible plants. Polygamy was not unusual, and families tended to be patriarchal, large, and extended. Men came first: they often beat their wives and were served first with the choicest portions at meals. In funeral rituals dead men received gifts of tobacco and weapons, women tools for sewing and dressing skins. Neither premarital sex nor unwed motherhood was condemned, and it was not uncommon for male friends to occasionally share wives with one another. Soviet governments did much to get rid of the worst abuses against Chukchi women and raise their status.

At the beginning of the Soviet era Chukchi religion centered on men and women shaman healers who, in private homes or in public, made contact with ancestral or animal spirits on behalf of the living. Shamans would enter the spiritual realm in a trance, accompanied by tambourine playing, chanting or singing, drumming, animal or bird calls, and dancing. Soviet officials attacked shamans as medical as well as religious frauds. However, Soviet health care itself was hardly adequate, failing to overcome various endemic ills like "Arctic hysteria...[characterized by] sudden fits of rage, depression, or violence"; or imported diseases against which the Chukchi had no immunity; or tuberculosis and alcoholism, which were chronic maladies.

Important seasonal events—winter solstice, calving or slaughter of reindeer, walrus or whale hunts—were marked by celebrations, including music, dance, song, and blanket tossing. On such occasions herdsmen sacrificed a reindeer and used its blood to mark the celebrants and their sleds. For coastal dwellers the successful killing of a whale occasioned a festival. Contests at such gatherings included footraces and reindeer- or dog-sled races. Another favorite amusement was listening to storytellers recount battles between the Chukchi and neighboring tribes; or stories about creation; or legends about animals, evil spirits, and fabulous shamans.

Sharing with others was an important virtue, and rules of hospitality required giving food and shelter to those in need, including strangers, orphans, and widows. Elders deserved respect, and traditionally, when they became incapacitated by old age or ill health, their request to be killed had to be honored.

In the 1930s Soviet officials began forcing collectivization on the Chukchi; coast dwellers (which included Eskimos) were more easily moved than nomadic herders, most of whom continued their private operations in the vast inland tundra until the 1950s. Meanwhile, the state established prison labor camps, mining operations, and military bases, all of which scarred and polluted the environment. Hunting became intensive, mechanized, and wasteful, sharply reducing the number of sea mammals in coastal waters and leading to the demise of small coastal communities of Eskimos and Chukchi, whose economy had been based on hunting walrus and whales. Air and land machines replaced dog and reindeer sleds, and wooden houses or concrete apartments with radios and televisions replaced tents.

Soviet education had the same beneficial and negative impact on the Chukchi as on other people of Siberia's north. Fewer than 1 percent of Chukchi were literate in 1926, about the time Soviet schools began to be set up for them. Illiteracy was soon wiped out, but the removal of children to distant boarding schools, where Russian/Soviet culture was deliberately promoted over the beliefs and practices of the students' own people, created a gulf between them and the traditions of their parents. The movement of Russians into northeastern Siberia during the Soviet period and the rise of cities there also gave momentum to Russification. At the same time native sea-mammal hunters were being shunted aside, some of them into poverty and alcoholism; their children were moving into the ranks of Soviet workers and officials. According to the 1979 census Chukchi, Eskimo, and other indigenous peoples were greatly outnumbered by outsiders, and while most local elders spoke only their native languages, many of their children were bilingual (knowing Russian and their native language) and many of their grandchildren knew only Russian.[8]

Nina Uvarova was born in 1914 in the tundra of the northern Kamchatka Peninsula. She was a Koriak. Like their closely related Chukchi neighbors to the north, the Koriak were settled coastal hunters or nomadic reindeer herders, and from the 1920s and 30s they experienced the same wrenching changes under Soviet rule. Nina lived for a time in the tundra, where her father herded reindeer and taught his daughter the skills of hunting and reindeer husbandry. When Nina's mother died, the father married her younger sister, who neglected to train the stepdaughter in the womanly arts of tanning animal hides and sewing. Nina was married at 13 to a lad who had been brought to her camp to work for three years in order to prove himself a worthy husband. When the couple moved away she received her share of the family herd, which she joined to his. About the mid-1930s Nina began having children. The first five died soon after being born, the last three victims of a "'big disease.'" In 1937 Nina's husband, in response to an official notice (which he could not read), traveled to the town of Telichiki. After two years without word from him, he returned from being imprisoned as an "enemy of the people."

At some point, probably as a result of collectivization, Nina, her husband, and other reindeer herders were moved to the coast. Nina's first surviving child was Maksim, born in 1942 and drowned at sea in 1972. Between 1948 and 1963 Nina had eight more children, four of whom survived. The need to care for them kept her from drinking, though many in the community were heavy drinkers and her husband encouraged her to join in. She recounted with pride that her son Ivan (b. 1960) killed his first seal at age 10 and that his father prepared a big celebration for the occasion. Her pride must have come in part from seeing Ivan preparing to be a hunter as boys did in the old days, when people "'were strong,' she said, 'not weak like today.'"

Soviet officials closed her village and forced its residents to leave. "'We told them that we would not go,' she said, 'but they did not care and just took us.'" She faulted Russians for not understanding the way her people lived and was especially upset by the estrangement of the children.

They took our children away and locked them into the boarding schools...and we could not look after them.... Today it makes me sad that I cannot talk with some of my children and grandchildren. They don't understand our language anymore, and they tell me things I don't understand. They never ask me anything. They don't listen to what I have to say.[9]

CENTRAL ASIA

At the other (southwestern) corner of Siberia from the Chukchi Peninsula is the Republic of Kazakhstan. It was the second largest Soviet republic (in land area) after the RSFSR: 1.1 and 6.6 million square miles, respectively. To the east it borders China and to the west it extends beyond the Ural River into Europe. To the north it has a long border with Russia. To the south it shares common borders with three central Asian republics—Turkmenistan, Uzbekistan, and Kyrgyzstan, with whose local peoples the Kazakhs share a common Turkic language and Muslim religion. Most of the country in the north is treeless grassy plains that fade into desert toward the south and into mountains to the southeast. Except in the mountain areas, precipitation amounts run from slight in the north to extremely little in the hot deserts of the south. Windiness in the region further reduces the land's moisture and in late summer and fall creates large dust storms. According to the 1989 census Kazakhs in the USSR numbered 8.1 million. Among the 16.5 million people in the Kazakhstan republic 6.5 million were Kazakhs, and 6.2 million were Russians; Ukrainians and Germans numbered almost a million each.

Kazakh culture, anchored in a nomadic livestock economy, was well established by the 1860s when it came under the domination of the Russian empire. At that time, however, livestock raising was beginning to be challenged by agriculture, rapidly expanding under the plows of Russian peasants who were immigrating in large numbers and taking over much of the best crop (and grazing) land.

During the 1930s Kazakhs were among the most devastated ethnic groups in the USSR. Hundreds of thousands either perished during collectivization, the campaign to destroy so-called kulaks, and the great famine of 1931–1932, or emigrated to the south or east. Among draconian measures was the determined effort of Soviet officials to force nomad herders into settled collectives. Between 1926 and 1937 the Kazakh population declined 28 percent. World War II saw another surge of Russians, as well as Ukrainians and others, enter the republic in their retreat before German invaders. A third great incursion took place in the 1950s as a wave of agricultural laborers came in to cultivate millions of acres of "virgin land," a scheme implemented by Khrushchev to greatly boost grain production and also solidify his hold on power. Early big harvests, however, gave way to reduced yields caused by inadequate rainfall and exhausted and eroded soils. The vast project also delivered another blow to the traditional livestock economy.

Most Kazakhs continued to live in the countryside during the great urban-industrial transformation of the Soviet Union. The 1989 census tells us that 57 percent of Kazakhstan's population lived in cities—77 percent of the Russian and 38 percent of the Kazakh population did so. In the capital Alma-Ata the ratio of Russians to Kazakhs was almost 3 to 1. For many Kazakh families rural life had serious drawbacks: no indoor plumbing, a scarcity of water, little or no public transportation, and subpar health care. In some rural areas people's health was seriously threatened due to environmental contamination, especially radiation from weapons testing in the north and east and, in the southwest, windblown chemicals picked up from the exposed basin of the rapidly evaporating Aral Sea. Rural schools were usually inferior to those in cities. Regarding education in general, the Kazakh language was second to Russian for school instruction. In the republic's secondary schools in 1990 the language of instruction for 32 percent of students was Kazakh, but in special secondary and higher schools only 11 percent received their instruction in Kazakh, compared to 89 percent in Russian.[10]

In the countryside most Kazakhs lived in large collective and state farms, growing grains (spring wheat in particular), cotton, and cattle. Collective farming tended to be at the lower-income end of the economy and in the late Soviet years was troubled by unemployment brought on by the high growth rate of the Kazakh population and the abundance of youth. Rural households had three or four children on average; the norm for apartment-dwelling urban families was two.

Nomadic herding, the principal economy until the 1930s, was greatly reduced during the drive to collectivize agriculture. Still, some families continued to move their horses, sheep, and goats from pasture to pasture. Camels carried their houses, the traditional centuries-old, easily portable yurts—round, felt-covered, pole-reinforced, dome-shaped structures. Milk from all these animals was a main source of nourishment; horse and mutton were the favorite meats. *Shubat,* sour camel milk, was the drink of choice in some areas. *Kumis,* the fermented national drink, is made from mares' milk. The horse occupies a central place in Kazakh culture, being an indispensable feature of nomadic life on the steppe. The best horses and most skilled riders continue to be greatly admired.[11]

Life and its changing circumstances in twentieth-century Uzbekistan parallel what happened in Soviet Kazakhstan: collectivization of agriculture, immobilizing of nomads, and urbanization. Like their neighbors to the north, most Uzbeks lived and continue to live in the countryside in relatively poor circumstances. Central planners singled them out to produce cotton, just as Kazakh farmers had been targeted for wheat production. In both cases the imprudent, all-out drive to generate big yields had severe negative effects on the environment. The heavy application of insecticides, herbicides, and chemical fertilizers undermined the health of many cotton farmers, and the irrigation of cotton fields, achieved by drawing off water that would otherwise flow into the Aral Sea, has caused the sea to shrink and left bare a vast dry basin of toxic-infused soil ready to be swept by the wind into the air and into people's lungs. A striking difference between the two peoples is demographic. Kazakhs and Uzbeks each numbered 4 million in 1926; by 1989 their populations were 8.1 and 16.7 million, respectively, making Uzbekistan the third-largest Soviet republic. Another difference was the relatively small number of Russians in Uzbekistan; in 1989 they made up only 8.3 percent of the whole population, and though almost all of them lived in cities they were still an urban minority. In the capital, Tashkent, they made up 34 percent and Uzbeks 44 percent of the population.[12]

The remarkable growth of the Uzbek population, especially during the last three decades of the Soviet era (this in spite of very high rates of infant mortality), created serious unemployment problems and put great pressure on public services. The tradition of large families (seven or more children is not unusual) has not readily yielded to family planning. Likewise, efforts by Soviet officials, especially outsiders, to free Uzbek women from what both liberals and Marxists saw as their inferior and degraded status met with stubborn, and more or less successful, defiance.

Almost everywhere in Soviet Asia such efforts, legal and practical, led mainly by secular Russian officials, made only limited headway against age-old discriminations. At issue in Uzbekistan and other central Asian republics (but not limited to these areas) were polygyny, bride-price, seclusion, forced marriage, the marriage of girls (in their early teens or younger), and forced wearing of a veil. Laws against such practices and attempts to enforce them were usually evaded: by ignoring the law, because local indigenous officials preferred not to make trouble for friends and family; bribery; the ruling of Muslim judges who trumped Soviet law with Islamic law; the manufacture of fake documents (e.g., showing girls to be older than they were); and so on. Reform efforts also met with violent attacks against Uzbek women activists, including rape and murder.[13] More cases of flagrant discrimination or crimes against women were undoubtedly hidden than reported, but in most homes women probably embraced or endured their traditional roles. Such customary roles were preserved in many homes out of respect for elders and by the fact that three or four generations lived together.

Various customs surrounded one of the most important celebrations—marriage. The groom's family paid a bride-price, and the bride's family provided their daughter with a dowry; both usually represented generous investments. Lavish ceremonies and festivities were also likely to be expensive. Newlyweds usually satisfied past and present rules by sealing their marriage with both religious (Sunni Muslim) and civil declarations. Ordinarily the bride went to live in her husband's home, where she was expected to do a good deal of housework. Her new family might have been quite large, including other young married couples with children. For many married women the burden of work was very heavy because, under the Soviet drive to boost production, they were pressed to find employment in industry or agriculture while at home their duties were not diminished.[14]

Ethnic minorities in the USSR were sometimes close to, and sometimes far removed from, the culture and history of people in whose territories they lived. The hundreds of thousands of Uzbeks and Kazakhs who lived in each other's neighboring republics were Turkic speakers, Sunni Muslims, and in other ways lived much alike. Tens of thousands of Crimean Tatars also lived and still live in Kazakhstan and Uzbekistan and are mostly Turkic and Sunni Muslim. However, they are reluctant guests, having become residents of Central Asia only when their whole community was moved there in a massive, brutal deportation in 1944. In 1946 the Soviet government reclassified the surviving deportees as Tatars, lumping them with other Tatar groups and doing away with their literary language. Moscow also eliminated the Crimean ASSR (Autonomous Soviet Socialist Republic), making it part of the RSFSR in 1946 and then transferring the territory to the Ukraine in 1954. Only after 45 years of persistent efforts by Crimean Tatars to be sent home did Moscow at last, in 1989, begin a major program of return.

A brief note here on the Tatars: having first arrived in Europe in the thirteenth century among the Mongol invaders, they fell under Ottoman influence and most became Turkic speakers and Muslim. In the USSR the Crimean Tatars were only one of three major groups that made up part of a large and quite diverse Tatar population, mostly urban and spread across the entire Soviet empire. The other two groups are the Kazan (or Volga) Tatars, who occupy the middle Volga region around the city of Kazan, and Lithuanian Tatars, descendants of warriors employed in the thirteenth and fourteenth centuries by the Grand Duchy of Lithuania to fight the Teutonic Knights and who are now living in Lithuania, Byelorussia, and Poland.[15]

Besides Crimean Tatars, Central Asia and western Siberia were also dumping grounds for tens of thousands of Soviet Germans. Their ancestors came in two migrations: into what are now the Baltic states when the Teutonic Knights overran that area in the thirteenth century, and into the Ukraine and lower Volga basin following the invitation of the German-born Catherine II in 1762–1763. Near the beginning of World War II Volga Germans were deported to the east. At about the same time the Volga German republic (ASSR) and German schools were eliminated. Most surviving Baltic and Ukrainian Germans retreated with the Wehrmacht near war's end. The deportation of 1941 involved more than half a million persons, and to these were added many who had retreated to Germany near the end of the war but were later returned to the Soviet Union. Like the Crimean Tatars they lost their own territory, but unlike them the Germans, Lutherans for the most part, were not related by language or religion to their new neighbors, whether in Kazakhstan or elsewhere in Siberia and Central Asia. The breakup of communities and deportations made the Germans an outcast minority. Perhaps this helps explain their rather rapid assimilation since World War II. This assimilation was especially pronounced among Russian and Ukrainian populations and in cities. Increasingly in the twentieth century older Germans spoke German and their grandchildren only Russian. From the mid-1950s Soviet Germans regained their citizenship and had restraints on language instruction and religion lifted. From 1970 there has been a stream of Soviet German emigrants to Germany.[16]

NOTES

1. I have consulted the following useful general sources: Timothy Gall, ed., *Worldmark Encyclopedia of Cultures and Daily Life,* 4 vols. (Cleveland, OH: Eastward Publications, 1998), vol. 3, *Asia and Oceania,* and vol. 4, *Europe;* P. Friedrich and N. Diamond, eds., *Russia and Eurasia/China,* vol. 6, *Encyclopedia of World Cultures,* 10 vols., ed. David Levinson (New York: G. K. Hall / London: Prentice Hall International, 1994); Melvin and Carol Ember, eds., *Countries and their Cultures,* 4 vols. (New York: Macmillan, 2001); Roger Caratini, ed., *Dictionnaire des nationalités et des minorités U.R.S.S.* (Paris: Larousse, 1990); Archie Brown et al., eds., *The Cambridge Encyclopedia of Russia and the Former Soviet Union* (Cambridge, UK: Cambridge University Press, 1994); Ronald Wixman, *The Peoples of the USSR: An Ethnographic Handbook* (Armonk, NY: M. E. Sharpe, 1984); Victor Kozlov, *The Peoples of the Soviet Union,* trans. P. Tiffern (Bloomington: Indiana University Press, 1988).

2. Ralph Clem, "The Ethnic Dimension of the Soviet Union, Part 1," in *Contemporary Soviet Society,* ed. Jerry Pankhurst and Michael Sacks (New York: Praeger, 1980), 23–29; Kozlov, *Peoples of Soviet Union,* 2–4, 21–26, 247–48.

3. Kozlov, *Peoples of Soviet Union,* 122–23.

4. Caratini, *Dictionnaire,* 249.

5. Kozlov, *Peoples of Soviet Union,* 57; Clem, "Ethnic Dimension," 23–29.

6. Wixman, *Peoples of USSR,* 65; James Forsyth, *A History of the Peoples of Siberia: Russia's North Asian Colony, 1581–1990* (Cambridge, England: Cambridge University Press, 1992), 267, 287–90.

7. Wixman, *Peoples of USSR,* 65–66; Gall, *Worldmark,* vol. 4, 141–53; Levinson, *Encyclopedia of World Cultures,* vol. 6, 115–24; Forsyth, *History,* 249–53, 290–95, 311–15, 381–87.

8. Forsyth, *History,* 338–40, 367–69; Gall, *Worldmark,* vol. 4, 100–104.

9. Petra Rethmann, *Tundra Passages: Gender and History in the Russian Far East* (University Park: Pennsylvania State University Press, 2001), 71–79.

10. Khazanov, *After the USSR,* 249, 257, 259, 261.

11. Wixman, *Peoples of USSR,* 98–99; Gall, *Worldmark,* vol. 3, 384–88; *World Cultures,* vol. 6, 172–83.

12. Khazanov, *After the USSR,* 258–61.

13. Douglas Northrop, "Subversion and Resistance in Soviet Uzbek Family Law," *Slavic Review* 60, no. 1 (spring 2001): 115–39.

14. Levinson, *Encyclopedia of World Cultures,* vol. 6, 395–98; Gall, *Worldmark,* vol. 3, 796–801.

15. Wixman, *Peoples of USSR,* 53–54; Levinson, *Encyclopedia of World Cultures,* vol. 6, 91–95.

16. Wixman, *Peoples of USSR,* 72–73; Levinson, *Encyclopedia of World Cultures,* vol. 6, 137–40; Brown et al., *Cambridge Encyclopedia,* 75.

3

Government and Law

OVERVIEW

The Communist Party created the Soviet government. One of Lenin's first actions after the Bolsheviks took power in 1917 was to set up a governing council of ministers, called commissars, of which he was chairman. All were Party members. This structure remained essentially unchanged during the history of the USSR. Top Party officials held top government positions. Important policies were handed down from the highest Party authorities: the Secretariat and its secretary-general (called First Secretary, 1953–1966), Politburo, and Central Committee. Thus a tiny group of men were the sole source of legislation, and state institutions existed to carry out their decisions. Moreover, very many regulations that directly affected people's lives were fashioned not by any legislative process but by decrees, put in place or withdrawn as the leaders willed.

The constitutions of the USSR recognized freedoms of speech, religion, the press, and assembly (as long as all these served to "strengthen socialist reality") and proclaimed the inviolability of the home. However, through its police powers, the regime dictated if, when, and to what extent people could enjoy their promised civil liberties. In May 1970, when police, without a warrant, forced their way into the home of biologist Zhores Medvedev, he reminded them that they were barging into "a private apartment," but the police sergeant retorted, "It belongs to the State.... and the police have the right to enter any apartment."[1] Any activities the authorities interpreted as undermining their own power were labeled seditious and the offenders punished, often harshly. Persecution of ordinary people was most severe in the Stalin era, but anyone at any time could be turned into a political criminal, because all crimes could be interpreted as crimes against the state: grand and petty theft, negligence in the workplace, arson, attempts to emigrate or publish abroad, and so on. Under Stalin, millions of people who had not committed any crimes were "repressed" and "liquidated." Against such injustices the public had no legal recourse given that the Soviet constitution did not provide people adequate means to enforce constitutional rights through the courts. The secret police had wide authority to interrogate, torture, judge, and punish alleged criminals. Stalin's secret police (NKVD) was the only governmental agency independent of the Party. All other Soviet organizations were subordinate to the Party, but the NKVD chief reported directly to Stalin.[2]

After Stalin's death, the Party leadership decided to rein in the power of the secret police, though the agency remained a vigorous and useful means of control. Through its own apparatus as well as through its militia (ordinary police) subdivisions and informants, the political police never ceased to watch, harass, and intrude on the private lives of Soviet citizens. The rest of the repressive process was left to a judicial system heavily weighted against defendants. Russian prosecutors could (and still can) overturn a court's decision.[3]

THE COURT SYSTEM FROM 1922

The lowest court, which heard most trials, was called the People's Court; it consisted of two lay "assessors," chosen from the general population, and a professional judge. The judge and assessors listened to the prosecutor's and defense attorney's arguments during the trial, determined guilt or innocence, and pronounced sentence. Between the People's Court at the bottom and Supreme Court at the top were territorial, regional, and republic courts, which heard appeals from lower courts. Even though the Supreme Court was the highest court in the land, it had little real authority; it could neither decide whether laws were constitutional, interpret laws, nor throw laws out.[4]

Most law enforcement and judicial workers, including militia, judges, procurators (who were assigned to oversee government agencies to make sure they acted within the law),[5] and detectives, were poorly paid and, in the early years of the Union, likely to be poorly educated, sometimes even illiterate. Professional training for these officials was gradually upgraded, but the best trained among them tended to be concentrated in the larger cities. Their low pay undoubtedly contributed to widespread unprofessional behavior such as accepting bribes in money and consumer goods, and public drunkenness.[6]

Defense lawyers enjoyed a peculiar situation in Soviet life because they were not state employees and did not belong to a government-supported trade union. Instead, the union they were required to join was the relatively independent, self-supporting College of Advocates, about half of whose membership were women, which suggests the lowly status of the profession in the eyes of the government. The state could dictate the expulsion of a member for political reasons, and if that happened it was the end of an attorney's career. Although the government severely capped the fees that defense attorneys could charge clients, nearly all advocates accepted additional money under the table, especially in criminal cases. By accepting extra payments, a hardworking, talented lawyer could become prosperous. An ordinary criminal or client in a civil case was free to choose any defense lawyer from any part of the Soviet Union. Political prisoners, however, had to select from a list of attorneys approved by the secret police; non-Party lawyers were rarely allowed access to political prisoners. In a civil case, lawyers could assist clients from the beginning of a case to its end, but in a criminal matter, attorneys could not consult with clients until the state's preliminary investigation was finished. A client conferring with his attorney in a law office would most likely find himself in a shabby, airless, dimly lit, overcrowded room with no privacy. Not until the late 1970s and early 1980s did the government begin to allot Moscow lawyers more comfortable facilities and even private space for lawyer-client meetings. Under Stalin, defense counsel was not allowed for those accused of espionage, sabotage, or terrorism, and with the exception of show trials, such defendants were tried behind closed doors. To the end of the Soviet period, the outcome of trials of dissidents was determined by Party policy rather than evidence.[7]

Comrades' courts, composed of workers, peasants, or both, were established on all farms, in factories, and in larger apartment complexes. Their main purpose was to control and prevent work-related misbehavior such as drunkenness on the job, lateness, and negligence by shaming the worker in front of family, friends, neighbors, and coworkers. Comrades' courts could also look into neighborhood and family problems. Punishments ranged from a small fine to a recommendation that the defendant be fired.[8]

COMMUNIST PARTY STRUCTURE

The Party was structured like a pyramid. At its base were the local "cells," or PPOs (primary Party organizations) attached to workplaces. A PPO might have as few as three members or (in the case of large industrial enterprises) hundreds. The PPO met once a month; its members were expected to recruit new members, carry out educational work, strive tirelessly for quality control in their workplaces, and in general promote Party loyalty and uphold the Party moral code. The next step up the pyramid was the city or county congress, composed of the local PPOs. That congress was subordinate to the provincial congress. The next level in the hierarchy was the Party

Congress for the individual republic. The peak of the pyramid was the All-Union Party Congress, which met annually until 1925. After that year it convened less regularly, with a 13-year gap between the 18th and 19th congresses (1939, 1952). After Stalin died, it met at least every five years; the most famous was the first post-Stalin congress, the 20th Party Congress (1956), in which the new Party chief, Nikita Khrushchev, in a "secret" speech vigorously condemned some of Stalin's crimes. The last Party Congress, the 28th, was held in 1990. The Party Congress had the appearance of representative government, but its main function was to rubber-stamp policies that had been fashioned at the highest levels.[9]

ELECTORAL PROCESS WITHIN THE PARTY

At each step up the pyramid, Party members elected representatives to the next higher level; those remaining below were expected to be subservient to orders from above. The most important local Party officials were not elected by representatives, however. They were directly appointed by the Central Committee. Delegates to the Party Congress chose members and candidate-members of the Central Committee. A candidate-member could not vote but might be selected as a full member when a place became vacant. The Central Committee was composed of Party leaders. In 1919, the Central Committee created out of itself three new committees: the Political Bureau, or Politburo (from 1952 to 1966 called the Presidium); the Organizational Bureau, or Orgburo (to 1952); and the Secretariat, chosen by Politburo members.[10]

The Politburo, the Party's highest policy-making and executive body, consisted of the most powerful members of the Party and was presided over by the secretary-general. Behind closed doors, it dealt with the nation's most pressing problems and created Party policies. The Orgburo met three times a week and reported to the Central Committee every two weeks. At first, it had as its responsibility the organizational and secretarial work of the Party. Stalin, the only one among the first Orgburo members to also be a member of the Politburo, made the Orgburo into his own power base. Through its powerful subcommittee of Records and Assignments, the Secretariat directly and indirectly controlled all important Party appointments and supervised the whole Party network, a responsibility that Stalin, who was also on this committee, was able to assign to himself. Records and Assignments transmitted the Central Committee's orders to all lower Party organizations and determined whether those orders were carried out.[11]

PARTY MEMBERSHIP

The number of Party members varied but was never more than about 10 percent of the population and consisted mostly of Russian male professionals. Not everyone who applied was accepted; not everyone wanted to belong. Party dues were assessed on a sliding scale depending on a member's income. Once admitted to the Party, members were expected to adhere to "Party discipline," which meant faithfully and unquestioningly carrying out directives handed down from above. From the 1920s to Stalin's death, members accused of defying Party policy faced expulsion from the Party, often followed by unemployment, arrest, imprisonment, and, during Stalin's reign, execution. Although the consequences of expulsion were not so dire after Stalin, being forced out of the Party could still result in the loss of important special privileges (travel, vacation, shopping, and health care), unemployment, and other deprivations. In any case, since the Party or its secretary-general controlled the police as well as all other aspects of government and law, everyone, member or not, submitted to Party dictates.[12]

SOVIET CONSTITUTIONS

This first constitution of the Soviet Union proclaimed the sovereignty, equality, and independence of each constituent republic (see chapter 1) and, theoretically, gave republics the right to secede. In reality, Stalin was already moving quickly to stamp out any independence movements within the non-Russian republics. People who lived in the constituent republics were citizens of the Union rather than of individual republics. As in the pre-Soviet (RSFSR) constitution of July 1918, one worker's vote equaled five peasants' votes, while certain classes of citizens such as priests, nobles, and businesspeople, called "exploiters," were denied the vote and civil rights altogether. The all-powerful Communist (Bolshevik) Party was not mentioned. Another omnipresent source of hardcore power not mentioned in the pre-Soviet constitution was the Vecheka—the secret police— but the 1924 constitution specifically provided for a centralized secret police agency (by that time known by its initials, OGPU). In addition to the secret police, the Union of Soviet Socialist Republics controlled defense, foreign relations, the economy, transportation, communications, education, public health, and the justice system. Everything else was left to the republics. There was no secret ballot. Direct elections occurred only locally—each next higher soviet (district, province, republic, union)—was elected by the level just below it. The constitution also guaranteed freedom of speech, a pleasure that nevertheless remained unknown in the Soviet Union.[13]

The 1924 Constitution

Adoption of the 1936 constitution, rich with declarations of universal voting rights and other basic liberties, coincided with one of the worst periods of terror in the Soviet Union. In June 1936, high Party officials, who would soon be shot as traitors, completed a draft of the new fundamental law. Its first chapter declared the USSR to be a "socialist state of workers and peasants," and that the land, with its mineral wealth, waters, and forests; factories and mines; rail, water, and air transport facilities;

Constitution of 1936 (the "Stalin Constitution") banks; means of communication; large state-organized agricultural enterprises (state farms, machine and tractor stations, etc.); as well as municipal enterprises and the bulk of dwelling houses in the cities and industrial localities are state property—that is, they belonged to the whole people.[14]

Some land was designated as the permanent "socialist property" of collective and cooperative farms. This property included "livestock, buildings, implements, and output." Each peasant family could privately farm a small plot of land and possess a limited number of livestock and small tools. All citizens had the right to own and inherit "articles of household and…personal use and convenience," and a home.

The 1936 constitution also declared that all citizens had the right to education and gender equality, including equal pay for equal work and fully paid maternity leave (paternity leave was not mentioned); to a "wide network of maternity homes, nurseries, and kindergartens"; to "rest and leisure"; to employment; and to financial support in old age and illness. Like civil liberties, these prerogatives in reality depended on the wishes and interests of Party authorities. Neither a republic nor an individual could challenge a law or the lack of an entitlement on the grounds that a constitutional right was being violated. Laws were often passed that conflicted with citizens' rights, or rights were trampled without any legal formalities. People with complaints could appeal to procurators or pursue other channels of appeal, and they might get satisfaction, if the grievance did not conflict with Party policy. Although the constitution proclaimed an independent judiciary, all judges were in the Party's service. People caught in Stalin's net had no effective legal recourses. Some wrote letters of protest directly to him, the very perpetrator of their misery. Political prisoners were usually tried under special procedures designed to quickly process a predetermined sentence.[15]

The Stalin constitution guaranteed a right of asylum for persecuted foreigners, but this too was an empty promise for hundreds of devoted communists and other European antifascists who fled to the Soviet Union only to be arrested as spies during Stalin's regime. Many of them were executed or died from the effects of their imprisonment. When she arrived at Moscow's Butyrki prison in 1939, Yevgenia Ginzburg was thrown into a cell with women communists from Germany, Italy, and China. One of the German women had been tortured by, and escaped from, the Gestapo, only to be arrested in Russia and tortured again.[16]

The 1977 constitutional document did not make any significant changes from the two previous Soviet constitutions. The dictatorship of the Party was reasserted. Citizens were guaranteed equality and basic human rights, with the proviso that they were not free to harm other citizens or

the state. The Party, this constitution declared, would be
the only judge of whether such state and individual
rights had been infringed.[17]

STRUCTURE OF THE SOVIET GOVERNMENT

Governmental structure paralleled that of the Party. Generally, the
higher one's place in the Party, the higher one's place in the national government (USSR), and by the mid-1920s, only Party members held top jobs
in the governments of individual republics.[18]

The 1924 constitution allowed citizens to directly elect soviet members
only on a local level, but after 1936, federal, republic, and local governments were composed of directly elected soviets. Nominations for office
had to be approved by the Party, although not all nominees were members. The highest governmental body that people could vote for directly
was the Supreme Soviet, which was divided into two chambers, the Soviet
of the Union and the Soviet of Nationalities, each with around 600
deputies. Soviet Union deputies were elected directly by all voters,
whereas deputies of the Soviet of Nationalities were elected by voters of
the relevant nationalities. These two soviets, which met briefly twice a
year, elected the standing committees and members of the Presidium of
the Supreme Soviet (before 1936 called the Central Executive Committee).
The Presidium made laws, issued decrees, and elected the Council of Ministers (from 1917 to 1946 called the Council of People's Commissars, or
Sovnarkom), which was the main executive body of the Soviet government. A 1988 amendment to the 1977 constitution created the Congress of
People's Deputies as the highest legislative and executive body. The Congress, whose members had been elected in the first multicandidate (but
not multiparty) election since early Soviet times, first met in May 1989 and
reorganized the Supreme Soviet.[19]

ELECTORAL PROCEDURES FOR GOVERNMENT
OFFICES

The constitution of 1936 laid down election principles for the whole
USSR. It provided for a secret ballot and universal one-person, one-vote
suffrage. All Soviet citizens from age 18 were eligible to vote; any citizen
23 or over could be elected a deputy of the Supreme Soviet, since its members were elected directly, by secret ballot. After 1958 only the mentally ill
were denied the vote, but from the 1960s, this group came to include political troublemakers who were identified as mentally ill and imprisoned in
"special psychiatric hospitals." Voting took place on a Sunday from
six A.M. to midnight. Theoretically, Soviet voters were to follow a procedure familiar to U.S. voters. They were to be given a ballot with multiple
candidates for each office, enter a booth, cross out names of all candidates

except the ones they wanted to vote for, emerge from the booth, and drop their ballot into the ballot box. In fact, the ballot presented only one candidate for each office—there was nothing for Soviet voters to cross out and no particular reason to step inside a voting booth. All they were really expected to do was take a ballot and drop it into the box. If someone actually did go inside the booth, perhaps to cross out a name and write in another, a poll watcher would infer that the voter did not approve of the Party's choice. There could be serious repercussions. Despite the fact that election results were never in doubt, the voter turnout rate was usually close to 100 percent, a fact Soviet leaders pointed to with pride as evidence of an enthusiastic, participatory grassroots democracy. In reality, just as local Party officials would observe who entered a voting booth, they would also know who did not show up at the polling place. It took courage to walk into a voting booth or stay home on election day.[20]

POLICE

The Soviet version of ordinary law enforcement, as opposed to the secret police, was the militia, founded in 1918. This police force was the state authority people came in contact with most often. Operating with the help of millions of unpaid volunteers, numerous informants, and military auxiliaries, the militia was subordinate to and fully cooperative with the secret

Ordinary Police

police. Among their many duties, militiamen issued internal and foreign passports; registered citizens and foreigners; kept track, through their registration system, of where people lived and where they moved to; traced missing persons and draft evaders; located child support and alimony deadbeats; and supervised people sentenced to internal exile, certain categories of released jail and camp prisoners, juvenile delinquents, and orphanages. The militia was also responsible for traffic control and other matters relating to the registration, inspection, and regulation of motor vehicles, including driver education and granting of drivers' licenses. Additionally, like police everywhere, the militia was expected to maintain order, for example, during parades and other public events.

In matters of public health, policemen were supposed to enforce health and sanitation codes and quarantine and track people with infectious diseases, including venereal diseases. They were expected to intervene in cases of family violence. Like their American counterparts, they often feared for their own safety when they had to wade into a family dispute. Because the USSR was poor in social service agencies, and because militiamen had such a wide mandate to maintain order, they were sometimes called "social workers with sticks."

Policemen were responsible for gun control. Private citizens and institutions could own hunting weapons if they had police permission and registered their guns at the local station house. The militia could confiscate weapons and ammunition from people who showed signs of dangerously irresponsible behavior. As with gun control laws in the United States and other countries, enforcement was not always successful. Toward the end of the Soviet era, many guns stolen from the military helped stock the armories of various ethnic guerrilla fighters and terrorists.

Not only firearms and cars were required to have licenses. Almost to the very last days of the Soviet Union, people were expected to register type-writers, printing presses, and photographic equipment with the militia. As information technology grew, so did the regime's efforts to stem the flow of news. Fax machines, computers, copiers, and old-fashioned type-writers were hunted down like fugitives and taken into custody if found.

In addition, the militia granted residency permits and administered internal passports (see later section) and the registration of hotel guests. When citizens wanted permission to travel abroad or emigrate, the secret police made the decisions and the militia did the necessary paperwork. These day-to-day cops on the beat were also empowered to carry weapons, make arrests, and enter and search homes.[21]

Although the agency's name changed several times, the basic functions of the Soviet secret, or political, police remained the same: to watch, mon-itor, arrest, and suppress by any means all suspected enemies of the regime. The Soviet secret police became the world's largest domestic and foreign intelligence service. Frequently its methods turned inward, devouring its own agents and even its own bosses: three of its chiefs, Genrikh Yagoda (1891–1938), Nikolai Yezhov   **Secret Police** (1895–1940), and Lavrenty Beria (1899–1953) were exe-cuted by the government they had bloodily served.

From the revolutionary era through the Stalin period, the domestic branch of the secret police also had wide powers to interrogate, try, con-vict, sentence, and execute. The first political police, called Cheka—earlier Vecheka (short for Extraordinary Commission to Combat Counter-revolution, Sabotage, and Speculation)—was formed in 1917. Originally intended as a temporary agency to be disbanded when the Bolsheviks' power was secure, the Cheka specialized in terror against civilians and uncovering political opposition. From 1917 to 1921 it executed many thousands and sent thousands more to prisons and slave labor camps. As Bolshevik power encroached into new territories so did the power of the Cheka, with the result that local branches were established throughout the RSFSR. In 1922 the GPU (State Political Administration) replaced and suc-ceeded the Cheka, continuing its work.

Decrees issued in August and October 1922 gave the GPU power to exile, imprison, and even execute certain kinds of criminals, including people the GPU judged to be "counterrevolutionaries." In 1922, Lenin wrote, "The law should not abolish terror: to promise that would be self-delusion or deception." A law of November 15, 1923, set up a central Party agency, OGPU (Unified State Political Administration) to direct the work of GPU branches in the various Union republics. OGPU was given its own trial court, called the Judicial Collegium, which sentenced people accused of being counterrevolutionaries, spies, and terrorists.[22]

OGPU took over the GPU's function as censor of printed matter, plays, and films. The system of slave labor camps or gulags (Central Camps Administration) that had existed since 1918 was brought under OGPU authority, as people continued to be executed or sent to the camps for political reasons. The secret police constructed networks of unpaid local police helpers, called "rural executives" and "brigades for assisting the militia." It provided the police machinery for show trials and the massive repression and deportation of millions of peasants after the collectivization drive began in 1929.[23] In 1934 all police agencies in the republics came under the direct control of the Moscow organization (by then known as NKVD, People's Commissariat of Internal Affairs, which had absorbed OGPU). The NKVD became Stalin's direct instrument of repression and terror, answerable to no one but Stalin. Under him, the efficient machinery of repression was fine-tuned.

The NKVD and its successors (MGB and KGB, Ministry of State Security and Commissariat of State Security, respectively), besides administering spy and counterspy networks, prisons, and slave labor camps, at one time or another were in charge (directly or through various branches of the militia) of recording births, deaths, marriages, and divorces; of administering the fire and forest guards, highways and auto transport, weights and measures, railway construction, wartime rationing, and mass deportations of Soviet nationalities (1941–1944); and arresting and executing Red Army soldiers who tried to retreat from the front lines. Until the final days of the Soviet Union, the secret police had huge military forces at its disposal.

PASSPORTS AND RESIDENCE PERMITS

The tsars had tried to control people's movement within the Empire by requiring them to carry "internal passports." This practice was at first renounced by the Bolsheviks as an insult to people's right **The Passport** to travel freely inside their own country. But in December **Law** 1932, in an effort to keep hungry collective farmers from abandoning their farms to seek work in urban areas, as well as to track criminals, potential criminals, and politically "undesirable elements," the regime reintroduced the internal passport. This document was issued to citizens aged 16 and up who worked in cities or were residents of workers' settlements, state farms, or construction sites. The passport showed name, age, nationality, permanent residence (which was normally the only place one was allowed to live), place of employment, and such additional information as previous convictions and failure to pay child support. Passports were reviewed every five years. This gave police the opportunity to keep their records up-to-date and renew, or not, the official stamp that allowed a citizen to continue living in his or her place of residence. In 1937, after having served a three-year sentence of exile (for writing a satirical poem about Stalin), Osip Mandelstam discovered that over 70 cities, including Moscow, where he and his wife owned their apartment, were closed to him because he was a "convicted person." When she went to a Moscow militia station to have her residence permit renewed, Nadezhda Mandelstam was informed that as the wife of a convicted person, she also had no right to live in that city. A secret police informer was given their apartment, and they were once again forced to abandon the city to scratch a living and find shelter as best they could.[24]

Because the government wanted to keep its collective farmworkers down on the farm, until 1976 *kolkhozniki* were denied passports and so were often tied to their farms, much as serfs had been bound to the land under the tsars. When passports were first distributed, many people who were not farmers but were labeled as socially or politically undesirable were also denied the documents, swelling the crowds of those streaming out of cities with no place to go and nothing to eat because, as passportless beings, their ration cards were confiscated and they could not keep their jobs. Only the elderly, the infirm, and children under 16 were allowed to be unemployed residents of cities. Farmers who attempted to leave their farms without special permission from the *kolkhoz* (collective farm) director, or overstayed their allowed leave time, faced steep fines with criminal sentences for repeaters. A farmer who did travel might well have to sleep in train stations since hotels were not allowed to accommodate passportless citizens. Only a *kolkhoznik* who was planning to marry someone from another farm could legally move from one *kolkhoz* to another without official permission from both kolkhozes. Even after collective farmers were finally granted the right to passports, their documents had secret codes which signaled authorities that they belonged to a *kolkhoz*. On the other hand, the intelligentsia, and white- and blue-collar workers, were a more privileged class, free to travel (inside the country) as long as they notified the militia at their departure and arrival points, if they planned to stay more than three days.[25]

Whether farm or city dweller, people who ignored passport and travel registration laws did so at their peril. Those who were in political trouble and ordinary criminal offenders had to be especially careful about violating travel regulations, for fear of being sent (or sent back) to the gulag. Soviet citizens knew they must carry their passports with them always because militiamen had the right to order people to show their documents any time, anywhere, even raiding apartment complexes and dormitories to catch people who were illegal aliens in their own land.[26] The Soviet government tried to persuade its citizenry that mandatory internal passports were a privilege and a healthy part of daily life. When (non-*kolkhoz*) youths turned 16, they received their first passport in a kind of coming-of-age ceremony organized by the militia; proud parents often had dinner parties to celebrate the occasion. When people died, their passports had to be returned to the militia. The internal passport system remained in effect until the end of the USSR.

People who wanted to move from one city or region to another had to get permission from the passport branch of the militia, and permission was not granted automatically. Sometimes spouses from different cities were denied permission to reside together, and kinfolk were sometimes barred from moving in with an aged or ill relative who needed their help. Without the necessary residency permit, people could be denied or lose jobs. Major cities in the Soviet Union, including Moscow, Leningrad, and Kiev, were closed to new residents. In housing as in other areas of life, there were, in addition to published laws, decrees that remained unpublished, even secret, but had the same force as published laws. These unpublished rules determined which cities and areas of the USSR people could move to. Up to the very end, the militia, following unpublished regulations, would not give residence permission to nationalities deported in the 1940s who tried to go back to their native countries, or to Russian and Armenian refugees from massacres in the Caucasus who hoped for a safe haven in Moscow.[27]

Residence Permits

People also had to get permission from their local militia officer to change homes within cities, and just as in other types of residence change, permission could be denied. In cases in which the person who wanted to change residence did not belong to a proscribed group, such as refugees or deported nationalities, the decision to grant or not grant a permit was made by a local militiaman. In that circumstance, bribery was a definite possibility, and often the only hope. Even though passport and residency registration laws were strict, people were always attempting to circumvent them, despite the threat of fines and more serious criminal penalties. Soviet citizens from rural areas, provinces, and republics kept attempting to fashion a better life for themselves in the Soviet Union's large central cities. For example, an estimated million people lived illegally in Moscow at any given time, and other millions resided illegally elsewhere in the USSR. Most went unpunished, but there could be severe penalties for those who were caught repeatedly. In this way, the passport and residency laws had the effect of criminalizing otherwise normal, law-abiding citizens who happened to have been born where they did not want to live. Millions of others did not succeed in living where they chose. The militia's job of regulating people's movements within such a huge empire was made easier by the willing collaboration of much of the civilian population, including local housing councils, apartment building managers, neighbors, and volunteer helpers. Not until the early 1990s were some people, with the help of their lawyers, able to go to court and overturn militiamen's decisions to deny them residence permits. Nevertheless, residency permits outlived the Soviet Union, as did the phenomenon of "closed cities."

Closed or secret cities (known by the acronym ZATO) were scattered across the Soviet Union. Identified only by code names, they did not appear on any Soviet maps or atlases. No foreigners were allowed to enter. Even residents needed special permission to leave or host visitors (including close relatives) from outside the city. The millions who dwelled within their walls and barbed wire enjoyed a much higher standard of living and endured many more restrictions than ordinary Soviet citizens. Run by the military and the secret police, these hidden cities housed scientists, their families, and the support staff needed to live comfortably while developing nuclear weapons of mass destruction.

COMMON WAYS IN WHICH POLITICAL REPRESSIONS WERE CARRIED OUT

Torture of prisoners in order to obtain confessions was usual under Stalin, and a conviction could be obtained solely on the basis of a confession if it was a political case. Helped by the vague, elastic wording of the Criminal Code, any action could be politicized as a crime against the state, including failure to bring in a good harvest. A law of August 7, 1932, made theft of public property, including collective farm property, subject to penalties ranging from 10 years' imprisonment to death. This law was aimed mainly at peasants, who could be prosecuted under it even for petty thefts of grain. Capital punishment was abolished a number of times but always quickly restored. It was done away with and restored in 1920, was abolished in 1947 but reinstated in 1950 for "traitors to the country, spies, and subversive-diversionists" because Stalin had a particular group of "enemies" he wanted shot. After Stalin, the death penalty remained and could be enforced not only for vaguely defined political crimes and violent crimes against people, but, according to a decree of 1961, also for various kinds of economic transgressions, such as large-scale theft and embezzlement, black marketeering, counterfeiting, and "speculation" (privately buying and reselling items for profit).[28]

It was common for people who were to be arrested on political charges to be accused in the state-controlled media before any formal charges were brought. Especially under Stalin, the soon-to-be-arrested might first learn of his or her crime from reading the **Trial by Media** newspaper. The political show trials of the 1920s and 1930s, with their predetermined outcomes, were given widespread local and national press coverage, as were show trials for ordinary crimes. The latter kind of trial was held in factories and villages in order to teach the masses that crime does not pay. The practice of whipping up public sentiment against the accused was reformed somewhat after Stalin, but the media were still used in political cases to persuade the public that the defendant was guilty. For example, the writers Andrey Sinyavsky and Yuly Daniel were arrested in 1965 for having published their banned books outside the Soviet Union. In advance of the trial, Soviet radio announced that "their punishment would certainly have the backing of the Soviet public." Also before the trial began, Soviet readers unable to acquire the banned books could find out what they were missing by reading the negative, nearly hysterical newspaper descriptions of their content. In contrast, the media were not allowed to report on the preliminary investigation or trial of people suspected of ordinary (nonpolitical) crimes, even in sensational murder cases.[29]

According to decrees issued in 1934 and 1936, people accused of "counterrevolutionary activities" could be barred from their own trial, were not entitled to a lawyer, and could not appeal a death sentence. These decrees were repealed in 1956. An amendment to the Criminal Code of 1934 stipulated that if a Soviet citizen was convicted of treason, espionage, or certain other "anti-Soviet activities," relatives who knew about but failed to report such activities could be punished for the same offense. According to that law, even relatives who did not know about the accused's crime could be sent to Siberia for five years. Post-Stalin, there was no penalty for family members who were unaware of the crime, and if a political offender's property was confiscated, relatives were allowed to stay in the offender's house or apartment for a while.[30]

During the 1930s Great Terror, the Military Collegium of the Supreme Court was one of the main bodies that tried and sentenced political prisoners after the accused had confessed. The trial and sentencing usually occurred within a few minutes.

Trying and Convicting a Person Accused of a Political Crime

This military tribunal processed tens of thousands of cases in this summary way; the majority resulted in death sentences. The accused was required to be present at a trial before the Collegium, but not a defense attorney, a prosecutor, or witnesses.[31]

Until Stalin's death, however, most political cases were not dealt with by courts, especially if evidence against the accused was flimsy or nonexistent. In such cases, it was especially convenient to bar the defendant, defense attorney, and witnesses from the proceedings, so in 1934, the Special Board of the NKVD was set up. The Special Board, which operated to the end of the Stalin era, consisted of high officials in the NKVD and the prosecutor-general of the USSR. After being tried in absentia, prisoners were informed of their sentences at a time and in a manner convenient to those running the prison. In addition, the Special Board could, and usually did, prolong the imprisonment of a convict who had served the original sentence. Because most prisoners not sentenced to death were sent to slave labor camps, this system provided the Soviet economy with a huge supply of cheap, easily replaceable workers for mines, construction, and land-clearing projects in the harsh climates of the far north and Central Asia. Court-sentenced prisoners, by comparison, had a better chance of being released after serving their time. Besides the charges of counter-revolution, espionage, and sabotage that became so common in the 1920s, 30s, and 40s, the Special Board frequently sent a "member of the family of a traitor to the Fatherland" or a "wife of a traitor to the Fatherland" to the gulag; these "crimes" generally carried minimum sentences of 5 to 10 years, with the ever-present possibility of rearrest at any time after the sentence was served. Ilya Ehrenburg called the children of such convicts "special orphans."[32]

In 1935 a new sentencing body emerged from the Special Board and coexisted with it. An order of the NKVD gave the powers of the Special Board to *troiki* (singular, *troika*), committees of three officials, which included at least one NKVD officer. *Troiki* had the power to pass the same sentences as the Special Board. Even though court proceedings for politicals were formalities, with sentences usually determined before arrest, and Special Board proceedings were yet more summary, thousands of prisoners were shipped to concentration camps in Siberia or Central Asia or otherwise uprooted from their homes for up to five years without being granted any kind of courtroom hearing. The *troiki* had only to affix the label "socially dangerous element" and the accused was en route to the gulag. In 1937 Stalin handed down a special decree for a new kind of *troika* that was allowed to give death sentences and that often consisted of two rather than three judges. These *troiki* were set up in all parts of the USSR. As with the Special Board, the defendant was not present at the "trial."[33]

Executions could also be carried out by "special order" from Moscow, and during the period of the Great Terror, such orders were transmitted to secret police chiefs in various far-flung cities demanding the mass execution of tens of thousands of "enemies of the people." The authorities customarily covered up a victim's fate by withholding information, refusing to issue a death certificate, or issuing one with false information about the date and cause of death. Lying to relatives about the sentence was common under Stalin and was done in a strangely ritualized manner: "ten years without the right of correspondence with confiscation of personal possessions" meant the victim had been executed. Under Stalin, the length of sentences imposed on political prisoners was related to the date of arrest. In the early 1930s, political offenders generally did not get more than 5 years. Under the secret police chief, Yezhov, that sentence was increased to 10 years, and under his successor, Beria, it was more likely to be 20 to 25 years. The cruel boxcar journey to the gulag, which could last a month, coupled with the extraordinarily harsh conditions of life in the camps, made it difficult for inmates to survive even 5 years, let alone 10 or 20. From 1937 to the end of 1938, at least 1.33 million people were arrested on political charges and sentenced to concentration camps or execution. Politicals whose imprisonment was almost over, or who had served their sentences and been released, might suddenly have the sentence lengthened or be arbitrarily rearrested. In 1937, Nadezhda Mandelstam and her convicted husband, the poet Osip Mandelstam, were afraid to allow themselves to be joyful when the time for his freedom approached. "We knew only too well that the length of your sentence was a matter of chance rather than of law—[it depended] on how your luck ran."[34]

During the Stalin period, when an execution of a political prisoner was about to occur in one of the larger prisons, several wardens and a secret police officer appeared at the condemned person's cell to take him away. The condemned might have time to say good-bye to cellmates and give them personal property such as clothing. At Moscow's Lubyanka prison, the condemned person was taken to one of the rooms off the corridors in the basement, where he took off his clothes and put on **Executions** white underwear. He was then brought to a special cell equipped with a tarpaulin rug to stand on and shot in the back of the head. The tarpaulin was removed for cleaning. A doctor signed a death certificate, which was placed in the prisoner's file but usually not disclosed to relatives. The body was carried off, perhaps to be cremated before burial in an unmarked mass grave. Mass arrests subsided in the post-Stalin era, but political dissent and debate; freedom to emigrate, travel, and publish abroad; free economic enterprise; and free artistic expression remained strictly forbidden.[35]

FAMILY LAW

Before the revolution, marriages and divorces were the responsibility of the religious denomination the parties belonged to, whether Russian Orthodox, Muslim, Roman Catholic, Baptist, Lutheran, Jewish, Buddhist, or some other. Problems concerning marriage or divorce were handled by religious officials, and the state accepted their decisions. After the revolution, the new government rejected the authority of church officials in all aspects of daily life. According to the Family Code of 1918, two people who lived together and considered themselves husband and wife were legally married. The couple had the option of officially recording their marriage at a local Registry Office, which is what most chose to do. This informal approach was preserved in the Family Code of 1926.[36]

After July 1944 marriages had to be registered to be legally binding, and that principle remained in the Family Code of 1968. In cities and larger towns, a couple could avoid the coldness of an office registration by celebrating their marriage in a more attractive government-run "wedding palace." In an effort to combat divorces caused by too-hasty marriages, the Family Code of 1968 required that the couple give at least one month's notice before a wedding could be celebrated. This waiting period could be extended at the discretion of the local Registry official. For example, the official might have suspected the marriage was just a strategy for getting a residency permit or that one of the couple was marrying "on the rebound" from a failed marriage rather than out of love. For these and many other reasons, a local Registry authority could make a couple wait an extra month or two beyond the 30-day requirement. On the other hand, extenuating circumstances such as a family emergency or the bride's pregnancy might move a sympathetic Registry official to shorten the waiting period. Both newlyweds had to be at least 18 years old, although in special cases local authorities, rather than parents, could consent to the marriage of a 17-year-old girl. As with marriage laws in many countries, close biological relations could not marry each other, and bigamy was prohibited.[37]

The 1968 Family Code provided for the annulment of marriages that violated the law. The annulment process could be started by anyone who thought it necessary and right to do so, even after one of the couple had died. However, if one or both of the couple were under 18 when married, the marriage could not be annulled if the underage person(s) reached that age by the time the annulment issue was brought to court. If the woman had given birth or was pregnant, the marriage could not be voided. Weddings of sheer convenience (for example, in order to get an apartment, a permit to live in a city, or an internal passport) could be canceled, but only if both parties regarded the marriage as false and never lived together as husband and wife.[38]

As in many European countries and parts of the United States, the Soviet Union recognized the principle of community property in marriage. Property acquired before marriage remained with its original owner, but goods acquired during marriage, including salaries, were jointly owned by both spouses. Gifts given to one of the spouses, clothing, and other possessions bought to be used only by one of the couple were not common property. A couple's joint property could be sold only if both agreed to the sale and could be divided up only if there were a death, divorce, or debts. The Family Code of 1968 provided that under certain conditions—if one spouse had custody of children, for example, or if one spouse had been extremely irresponsible—the community property could be divided unequally upon divorce.[39]

In the earliest days of the new Bolshevik government, the process of divorce, as well as marriage, was uncomplicated and informal. "Breakup of the family" was sufficient grounds for divorce in all Soviet courts. Under the Family Law Code of 1926, just as a couple who wanted to marry simply had to go to the Registry and record their marriage, one of the spouses who later wanted to divorce had only to return to the Registry and declare a desire to end the union. Afterward, the other spouse would get a postcard informing him or her that the marriage was over. The postcard also instructed the newly divorced to go to the People's Court (the lowest court) to have problems concerning child custody, child support, and other postmarital legal issues dealt with. The cost of this entire transaction was very affordable: three rubles. The penalty for failure to pay child support was six months of unpaid labor at one's job. After June 1936, both spouses had to present themselves at the Registry and the fee for divorce jumped: 50 rubles for the first, 150 for the second, and 300 for the third or more. In 1944 the procedures for divorce became even more complicated. The couple had to go first to a People's Court to try for a reconciliation. If the People's Court decided reconciliation was impossible, the couple next went to the District Court, which had the power to grant divorces. Fees for divorce continued to escalate, and there were other difficulties. District Courts could be far from the couple's residence, and since most people did not own cars and public transportation tended to be overcrowded and unreliable, it could be expensive and complicated to transport the necessary witnesses, such as colleagues and neighbors. In 1965 the two-step process was abolished, and divorces were again handled through the nearest People's Court, which may have caused the divorce rate in Leningrad to triple in one year. Starting in 1968, a married couple with no minor children who both agreed they wanted to end the marriage could petition for divorce at the Registry, wait three months, and be officially divorced. A man could not get a divorce without his wife's consent while she was pregnant or within a year after their child was born. Divorced parents who did not have custody of their children were legally obligated to pay child support to the custodial parent, the amount depending on the spouse's income and number of children. Such sliding-scale child support payments had been established under a 1936 decree that at that time mandated that the noncustodial parent (usually the father) pay one-fourth of his salary for one child, one-third for two children, and one-half for three or more offspring. The 1936 law also stiffened the punishment for "deadbeat dads" by imposing a two-year prison sentence for nonpayment. But problems of finding the nonpaying father (not a high priority for most local authorities), bringing him to court, and getting cooperation from employers and court officials were obstacles that very often made the child support law an empty promise for Soviet women, even when they were ex-wives of important Party officials.[40]

Able adults were expected to work and support themselves, so a married person was legally entitled to spousal support only if unable to work, above retirement age (60 for men, 55 for women), pregnant, or caring for a baby during its first year. The Family Code of 1968 emphasized the importance of family responsibility: the law required parents to maintain their handicapped children, children to support needy parents, orphans to be supported by close relatives, and in general for relatives to be responsible for one another. Even after divorce, the law recognized a variety of circumstances, such as disability, which might require continued ex-spousal support.[41]

Support of Dependent Relatives

Because revolution, civil war, and famine had created millions of homeless, roving, starving, and often lawless children (called *besprizorniki*), the Family Code of 1926 encouraged adoption. As in the United States, Soviet adoptees had full legal rights and responsibilities within their adoptive families, including rights of inheritance, and no legal connection to their biological parents. People who wished to nurture and be responsible for a child, short of adoption, could choose an option called "dependency." A child taken in as a dependent remained legally part of his biological family, but the sheltering family assumed caregiving responsibility until he or she reached 16. In 1936 a third option was   **Children** introduced, called *patronat*, a kind of state-supported and supervised foster care. Under *patronat*, the Ministries of Health and Education were to pay the child's caregiver a monthly stipend to help cover expenses of child rearing and education, until age 16. Unfortunately, Soviet parents were hard-pressed to keep their own children fed and sheltered, much less take in others. The laws designed to promote adoption and nurturing were powerless to save or soften the lives of thousands of children for whom there were no welcoming families.[42]

Under a law of 1944, an unmarried mother could give her child to the state to be raised in an orphanage, or she could keep her child and get some support from the state; she could not try to force the father to support his child or bring a paternity suit against him. A line was drawn through the space for the father's name on the birth certificate of the child of unwed parents. The Family Law of 1968, however, enabled a woman to bring a paternity suit against the man she believed to be the father, and if she succeeded in proving her case, he was required to fulfill his legal paternal obligations. If the child did not have a legal or acknowledged father, the mother entered a male first name and patronymic (the father's name, which Russians use for a middle name) plus her last name on the birth certificate in the space allotted for the father's last name. This was to protect the child from embarrassment later in life.[43]

From the early days of Bolshevik power until April 7, 1935, laws regarding juvenile crime harmonized with progressive European lawmaking. A child could not be tried as an adult until age 14 or 16 (depending on the crime), and even delinquents   **Juvenile Crime** between 16 and 18 were dealt with less harshly than older criminals, with an eye to reform through education. During the 1920s and early 1930s, most juvenile offenders in the USSR had their cases heard in special Juvenile Affairs Commissions run by the Ministry of Education (Narkompros) rather than in court. These commissions consisted of three people: a chairman from the Ministry of Education, a physician, and a judge. Juvenile cases could go to court only if they were referred there by a commission. Theoretically, commissioners could do such things as remove children from bad homes and place them in state juvenile facilities such as children's homes and (for more serious offenders) "labor homes," find jobs for them, place them with relatives, or make supervisory home visits. But in big cities like Moscow, the commissioners' huge caseloads overwhelmed the available manpower and juvenile facilities. Many regions had no children's homes whatsoever. As a result, commissioners were forced to turn children back to the streets or remand them to adult courts and a likely prison term among adult criminals. Thus children who

A group of homeless and abandoned children (*besprizorniki*), victims of wars and famine, in the Volga region around 1921. Reproduced from the Collections of the Library of Congress, LC-USZ62-096830-328551.

stole to survive became prey to, and hardened products of, adult prisoners' brutality. By law, the commissions were supposed to reduce children's sentences for given crimes according to a certain formula: 14- to 15-year-olds got half of what an adult offender would get for the same crime; 16- to 17-year-olds, two-thirds. The decree of April 7, 1935, which was handed down suddenly, directly from Stalin, meant that children as young as 12 would henceforward be punished as adults, with full criminal penalties. This happened at a time when new waves of vagrant children had recently been, and were about to be, created by collectivization, famine, the Great Terror, World War II, and mass deportations of Soviet nationalities from their homelands. Juvenile Affairs Commissions were eliminated and replaced, in a few big cities, by juvenile courts that generally dealt with young offenders quickly and harshly. Although the edict opened the door to the execution of minors, it is not known whether any children were actually sentenced to death as a result. Secret police-operated labor camps were set up for homeless juveniles; children's homes came under police supervision as well. In 1943, an executive order established special NKVD-run "reformatory colonies" for children 11 to 16 years old accused of petty crimes, including vagrancy. According to the order, such children were to be sent away at the discretion of the secret police, without any court proceedings.

A very common criminal charge against juveniles was "hooliganism," which generally meant unruly, often drunken or vandalistic behavior in public places. After Stalin, the age at which one could be punished as an adult was again raised to 14 or 16, depending on the seriousness of the crime. Perpetrators under 18 at the time of a capital offense were exempted from the death penalty.[44]

From 1920 to 1936, abortions on demand were free and legal as long as they were performed by a doctor in a hospital or clinic. In 1936, in response to the declining population and birth rate, Stalin issued a decree banning all abortions except where necessary to pro-   **Abortions** tect the mother's life or prevent inherited diseases. Women were promised financial bonuses for large families, and penalties against employers who discriminated against pregnant women were increased, as were penalties against men who failed to pay alimony. At the same time, a secret decree ordered a ban on contraceptives. These measures did not succeed in raising the birth rate but did create a thriving underground business for elderly peasant women who migrated illegally to cities to work as abortionists. The clients of peasant and other underground abortionists often ended up in hospitals and morgues. Women with money and connections might find a doctor willing to declare the pregnancy a threat to the patient's physical or mental health, or, failing that, one who would terminate the pregnancy safely though unlawfully. Abortion remained the main Soviet form of family planning, becoming legal again in 1955.[45]

Most Soviet families lived in extremely cramped quarters; basic consumer goods, including groceries, were scarce, and women were the workhorses who had to hold down full-time jobs as well as shoulder the responsibilities of child care, shopping, cooking, and cleaning. At least in the non-Muslim republics there was strong incentive to keep families small, whatever the shifting laws, decrees, policies, and promises of Party and state might be.

NOTES

1. Zhores A. Medvedev and Roy A. Medvedev, *A Question of Madness*, trans. Ellen de Kadt (New York: W. W. Norton, 1979), 26–27.

2. Louise I. Shelley, *Policing Soviet Society: The Evolution of State Control* (London: Routledge, 1996), 31; Peter H. Solomon, *Soviet Criminal Justice Under Stalin* (Cambridge, UK: Cambridge University Press, 1996), 28.

3. Dina Kaminskaya, *Final Judgement*, trans. Michael Glenny (New York: Simon and Schuster, 1982), 14; Masha Gessen, "Rotting in a Russian Jail," *New York Times*, June 21, 2000, late edition final, sec. A, p. 23, col. 1.

4. Solomon, *Soviet Criminal*, 41; Soviet Union—A Country Study (http://lcweb2.loc.gov/cgi-bin/query/r?frd/ctudy:@field(DOCID+su0008)) (accessed October 2003).

5. Eugene Huskey, *Russian Lawyers and the Soviet State: The Origins and Development of the Soviet Bar, 1917–1939* (Princeton, NJ: Princeton University Press, 1986), 229.

6. Solomon, *Soviet Criminal*, 112.

7. Kaminskaya, *Final Judgement*, 24, 29–38, 44; Shelley, "The Structure and Function of Soviet Courts," in *The Distinctiveness of Soviet Law*, ed. F.J.M. Feldbrugge (Dordrecht, The Netherlands: Martinus Nijhoff, 1987), 212–13; W.E. Butler, *Soviet Law* (London: Butterworth, 1983), 79.

8. Roy D. Laird and Ronald A. Francisco, "Observations on Rural Life in Soviet Russia," in *Contemporary Soviet Society: Sociological Perspectives*, ed. Jerry G. Pankhurst and Michael Paul Sacks (New York: Praeger, 1980), 144.

9. Leonard Schapiro, *The Government and Politics of the Soviet Union* (London: Hutchinson University Library, 1965), 70, 67; Woodford McClellan, *Russia: The Soviet Period and After*, 3d ed. (Englewood Cliffs, NJ: 1994), 63, 210–11.

10. McClellan, *Russia*, 63–64; John M. Thompson, *A Vision Unfulfilled: Russia and the Soviet Union in the Twentieth Century*, with historiographic essays by William Gleason (Lexington, MA: D.C. Heath, 1996), 182.

11. McClellan, *Russia*, 63–64; Schapiro, *Government and Politics*, 68.

12. Thompson, *Vision*, 231; Sheila Fitzpatrick, *Everyday Stalinism: Ordinary Life in Extraordinary Times: Soviet Russia in the 1930s* (New York: Oxford University Press, 1999), 17, 19, 26–28; Vadim Medish, *The Soviet Union*, 3d ed. (Englewood Cliffs, NJ: Prentice-Hall, 1987), 88; "Politics and Government" in Soviet Union—A Country Study.

13. Schapiro, *Government and Politics*, 49, 51; Merle Fainsod, *How Russia is Ruled*, rev. ed. (Cambridge, Massachusetts: Harvard University Press, 1964) 367–69; McClellan, *Russia*, 61–62; David MacKenzie and Michael W. Curran, *A History of Russia, the Soviet Union, and Beyond*, 5th ed. (Belmont, California: West/Wadsworth, 1999) 431.

14. "The Constitution of the USSR (As Amended by the Sixth Session of the Seventh Supreme Soviet of the USSR)," in David Lane, *Politics and Society in the USSR* (New York: Random House, 1971), 535–55.

15. Schapiro, *Government and Politics*, 87, 96–97, 99–100, 191–92; Edward Braun, "Meyerhold: The Final Act," *New Theatre Quarterly* (9 (1993): 3–15. Reprinted in *Enemies of the People: The Destruction of Soviet Literary, Theater, and Film Arts in the 1930s*, ed. Katherine Bliss Eaton (Evanston, IL: Northwestern University Press, 2002), 145–62; Lane, *Politics and Society*, 535–55.

16. Eugenia Ginzburg, *Journey into the Whirlwind*, trans. Paul Stevens and Max Hayward (New York: Harcourt, Brace and World, 1967), 153–54.

17. McClellan, *Russia*, 270.

18. McClellan, *Russia*, 64.

19. "Politics and Government" in Soviet Union—A Country Study.

20. Schapiro, *Government and Politics*, 111, 115–16; Harvey Fireside, *Soviet Psychoprisons*, with foreword by Zhores A. Medvedev (New York: W.W. Norton, 1979), 135; McClellan, *Russia*, 64; Andrei Amalrik, *Notes of a Revolutionary*, trans. Guy Daniels (New York: Alfred A. Knopf, 1982), 101; Solomon, *Soviet Criminal*, 192.

21. Shelley, *Policing*, 135–39; Robert Conquest, *The Soviet Police System* (New York: Frederick A. Praeger, 1968), 30–33.

22. Christopher Andrew and Oleg Gordievsky, *KGB: The Inside Story* (New York: HarperCollins, 1990), 64; Solomon, *Soviet Criminal*, 19.

23. Conquest, *Soviet Police System*, 17.

24. Shelley, *Policing*, 131; McClellan, *Russia*, 136; Nadezhda Mandelstam, *Hope Against Hope: A Memoir*, trans. M. Hayward (New York: Modern Library, 1999), 284–88.

25. Sheila Fitzpatrick, *Stalin's Peasants* (New York: Oxford University Press, 1994), 92–95; Shelley, *Policing*, 132; Robert Conquest, *Agricultural Workers in the USSR* (London: Bodley Head, 1968), 92.

26. Fitzpatrick, *Stalin's Peasants*, 93; E. L. Johnson, *An Introduction to the Soviet Legal System* (London: Methuen, 1969), 142; Shelley, *Policing*, 131.

27. Shelley, *Policing*, 131–33, Solomon, *Soviet Criminal*, 192.

28. Johnson, *Soviet Legal System*, 49, 58–59; Peter H. Solomon, "Soviet Criminal Justice and the Great Terror," *Slavic Review* 46, nos. 3–4 (Fall/Winter 1987): 396, 409; Solomon, *Soviet Criminal*, 114; Robert Conquest, *The Great Terror: A Reassessment* (New York: Oxford University Press, 1990), 283; McClellan, *Russia*, 188; Vladimir Gsovski and Kazimierz Grzybowski, eds., *Government, Law and Courts in the Soviet Union and Eastern Europe*, vol. 2 (New York: Frederick A. Praeger, 1959), 940.

29. Solomon, *Soviet Criminal*, 46; Johnson, *Soviet Legal System*, 58.

30. Johnson, *Soviet Legal System*, 55.

31. Conquest, *The Great Terror*, 283–84.

32. Conquest, *Great Terror*, 285; Elena Bonner, *Mothers and Daughters* (New York: Alfred A. Knopf, 1992), 323.

33. Conquest, *Great Terror*, 285; Ginzburg, *Journey*, 373; David R. Shearer, "Crime and Social Disorder in Stalin's Russia," *Cahiers du Monde Russe* 39, 1–2 (January–June 1998): 134.

34. Conquest, *Great Terror*, 286–87; Ginzburg, *Journey*, 334; Solomon, *Soviet Criminal*, 231–32; Mandelstam, 212.

35. Conquest, *Great Terror*, 287.

36. Johnson, *Soviet Legal System*, 171–72.

37. Johnson, *Soviet Legal System*, 173–74; Peter H. Juviler, "Whom the State Has Joined: Conjugal Ties in Soviet Law," in *Soviet Law after Stalin*, ed. Donald Barry, George Ginsburgs, and Peter B. Maggs (Leyden, the Netherlands: A. W. Sitjhoff, 1977), 128.

38. Johnson, *Soviet Legal System*, 175.

39. Johnson, *Soviet Legal System*, 176–77; Juviler, "Whom the State," 130.

40. Johnson, *Soviet Legal System*, 177–80; Juviler, "Whom the State," 122, 130; Roberta Manning, "Women in the Soviet Countryside on the Eve of World War II, 1935–1940," in *Russian Peasant Women*, ed. Beatrice Farnsworth and Lynne Viola (New York: Oxford University Press, 1992), 210–11.

41. Johnson, *Soviet Legal System*, 185; Juviler, "Whom the State," 130.

42. Johnson, *Soviet Legal System*, 186–87; Bonner, *Mothers and Daughters*, 304; Nina Kosterina, *The Diary of Nina Kosterina*, trans. Mirra Ginsburg (New York: Crown, 1968), 45; Nina Markovna, *Nina's Journey: A Memoir of Stalin's Russia and the Second World War* (Washington, DC: Regnery Gateway, 1989), 26.

43. Johnson, *Soviet Legal System*, 187–88; Juviler, "Whom the State," 122, 139.

44. Gsovski, 938–39; Solomon, *Soviet Criminal,* xvi, 200, 201–2, 205–8; Markovna, *Nina's Journey,* 26; Shelley, *Policing,* 34–35; Shearer, "Crime and Social Disorder," 120–130; Johnson, *Soviet Legal System,* 159–60; Alan M. Ball, *And Now My Soul Is Hardened: Abandoned Children in Soviet Russia, 1918–1930* (Berkeley: University of California Press, 1994), 1–17, 120–26, 196.

45. Solomon, *Soviet Criminal,* 213–14; 217–19; Juviler, "Whom the State," 123, 138.

4

The Military

The Workers' and Peasants' Red Army, predecessor of the many-branched Soviet Armed Forces, was begun in March 1918 when Lenin assigned Leon Trotsky to form a tough new fighting force. With that army, the Bolsheviks aimed to maintain their one-party dictatorship and regain the territory of the Russian Empire. Opposed to the Reds in the Civil War of 1918–1921 were the Whites, who represented an extraordinary range of political viewpoints, from monarchists to anarchists. Most White officers had served in the former Imperial Army during World War I and now commanded peasant soldiers, many of whom were also veterans of that war.[1]

Bolsheviks wanted their army to be very different from the tsars' and other traditional armies. They envisioned an all-volunteer, democratic organization consisting mainly of loyal urban workers, a band of brothers in which working-class officers did not consider themselves superior to their men or expect special privileges, wore uniforms that looked like the enlisted men's, and had no titles of rank. But Trotsky insisted on a clear chain of command and iron discipline. Early Bolshevik leaders also had in mind an army in which common soldiers, unlike the tsars' troops, were treated respectfully, not abused by their officers, and housed, fed, and clothed decently. For the most part, throughout the Red Army's history, those conditions were met only now and then, if a senior officer happened to care. Nonetheless, a spirit of unity between officers and men was apparently not unusual through the 1920s and early 30s, and perhaps during World War II. One colonel, caught up in the massive military purge of 1937, recalled his prearrest career in the Red Army and what it meant to him:

I liked the absence of routine in my work, the opportunity we had for a wide range of studies, the opportunity for advancement, and the fact that there was no gulf between the officers and the soldiers. I worked hard to prepare myself for leadership and trained my officers in the same way; this gave me great satisfaction.[2]

Even during the Civil War, however, officers were "informally" allowed to abuse their peasant soldiers, even hit them in the teeth with a rifle butt, despite Trotsky's disapproval, so it is not surprising that peasants deserted by the hundreds of thousands. Besides running away to avoid being assaulted, peasant soldiers deserted because they were tired of fighting, or to defend the interests of their villages, to fight against having their produce requisitioned and free market destroyed, and because they did not like being ordered around by aristocratic officers who had once served the tsar. Officially, the number of Red Army deserters during the Civil War was between three and four million, not counting tens of thousands of unrecorded AWOLS. Trotsky decreed that if caught, deserters and anyone who helped them were to be shot and houses that sheltered them burned down. But in practice, runaways were usually just sent back to different units. If they wished, deserters could, and thousands did, wait for the Trotsky-ordered general amnesties, during which they returned to duty unpunished. Presumably no questions were asked concerning the whereabouts of their government-issued equipment.[3]

Since deserters tended to "liberate" uniforms, weapons, and whatever else fell into their hands and was portable, scarce supplies got scarcer. Many soldiers had no uniforms and could not go outdoors in freezing weather for lack of footwear. Frequently they did not have enough food, and malnutrition made them vulnerable to deadly diseases. In order to get food and other necessities, soldiers often preyed violently on local people. Even the gentle Isaac Babel, employed as a government journalist with a cavalry unit, grabbed bread from a child's hands while weeping peasant women watched soldiers loot their food. Sometimes scarcity turned soldiers into mutineers who deposed their commander and chose his replacement themselves. At other times, it led to passive resistance—soldiers refusing to fight until they had received food, warm clothing, and the like. There were also bloody mutinies inspired by peasant soldiers' hatred of Communists and Jews, whom they blamed for their miserable lives. An official investigation into a 1920 mutiny of mainly peasant soldiers revealed that in one village they had murdered 21 Jews, and wounded 12, while in another, "drunken Red Army men raped almost every woman...." In Vakhnov,

eighteen homes were burnt, twenty men killed, women raped in the streets in full view of the townsfolk and the younger women taken away like slaves in transports. Events of this kind took place in Annopol, Berezdovo, Krasnostav, Tarashcha and other places.

Babel recorded in his diary that his division commander routinely ordered the men not to "waste cartridges" on prisoners, but instead to "stick them." Along with privation, the propensity to commit atrocities against enemy soldiers and helpless civilians remained a feature of Red Army life, to the end.[4]

Despite their widespread discontent with army life, millions of peasants continued to be drafted into the Red Army, if only because there were far more peasants than any other group, and the urban workers favored by the Bolsheviks did not volunteer in great numbers. Prosperous peasants (kulaks), however, were excluded from the privilege of serving, as were members of the merchant class (bourgeoisie) and former nobility, except when the army needed their expertise. For example, Trotsky established an officer corps that depended heavily on aristocratic former tsarist commanders, though they were called "military specialists" rather than officers. Like conscripted peasants, former imperial officers were seldom willing to serve, but they feared arrest and what might happen to their families if they refused or deserted. Since the government did not trust these "military specialists," it created a new kind of military official, that of political officer (also called military commissar or simply commissar), to keep an eye on the aristocrats. Commissars also carried out political indoctrination among the troops. In his satirical novel about Soviet life on the eve of World War II, Vladimir Voinovich depicts his peasant hero, Private Ivan Chonkin, at a political education meeting conducted by Yartsev, his unit's Senior Politruk (a *politruk* was a commissar who, among his other jobs, organized and led discussions). The subject is "The Moral Character of the Red Army Soldier."

"Who would like to go first [to summarize the material]? Chonkin?" [Yartsev] asked, amazed that Chonkin had raised his hand.... "I'm not prepared, Comrade Senior Politruk," Chonkin mumbled hesitantly, dropping his eyes. "So why did you raise your hand?" "I didn't raise my hand, Comrade Senior Politruk. I was getting a beetle out. Samushkin put a beetle down my back."[5]

Later in the meeting, Chonkin's naive question, "Is it true that Stalin used to have two wives?" evokes a horrified, furious response from Yartsev, who pronounces the hapless private a "disgrace, not only to [the] unit and company, but to the entire Red Army as well." Voinovich's satire notwithstanding, many soldiers liked and admired their commissars for their ability to boost morale before a battle, or just for their friendship. But for young people about to risk their lives, a charismatic political officer's presence and pep talks must have been a psychological substitute for chaplains and other religious comforts banned in the armed forces.[6]

THE SOVIET ARMED FORCES

In the late Soviet era, the military consisted of five main "forces" under the Ministry of Defense, as well as forces under the Ministry of Interior and secret police (KGB from 1954). The Ministry of Defense services were the Strategic Rocket Forces, Ground Forces (Army), Troops of Air Defense,

Air Forces, and Navy. Other Ministry of Defense groups, such as the Rear
Services of the Armed Forces, Civil Defense Troops, and (the least prestigious) Construction Troops, did not belong to any one service but were
sent where needed, as were the Special Troops of support personnel—
engineering, chemical, signal, road building, railroad building, and automotive.

The KGB and Ministry of Interior (MVD) each had their own elite,
highly trained, and well-equipped uniformed forces known collectively as
Security Troops   Security troops. During each semiannual draft call up,
agents from these government departments reviewed
the new conscripts' files. Those assigned to one or
another of the Security troops were vetted for intelligence, physical fitness, and political dependability, a quality demonstrated in part by membership and activity in the Party, Komsomol (the youth organization for
prospective Party members), or both.[7]

Internal Troops, which were Security Troops subordinate to the Ministry of Interior, maintained political security and calm within the country's borders and guarded prisons and prison camps. Internal Troops were
stationed in every Soviet town over a certain size. Border Troops, a branch
of the KGB Security Troops, included air and naval units as well as ground
forces. They were the first military units encountered by visitors entering
the USSR, and probably the last those leaving would see. A human "iron
curtain," Border Troops did whatever it took to ensure that illegal,
unwanted, or suspect foreigners were turned back or arrested and that no
one left the country without official permission. To keep their land closed
and isolated, Border Troops used

hidden and open physical and electronic barriers…detection and alarm devices,
explosives, trip wires, and observation posts.… aircraft…foot, horse-mounted
and vehicular patrols…Specially trained…dogs…patrol boats…ambushes,
trenches, ditches…searchlights, electronic and infrared devices, telescopes,
mines,…fences, wire, ploughed areas…The entire 60,000 kilometers of border
[was] patrolled on the ground, by water, or through the air around the clock, day
in and day out.[8]

Those entering or leaving the country were thoroughly checked by Border
Troops, who looked for any kind of "subversive" literature, music, art,
and so on. Border Troops also inspected all means of transportation to
make sure nothing was hidden inside. No one was allowed to live near or
to stroll or drive around the immediate border area. Yet another branch of
KGB Security Troops, Signal Troops, were responsible for installing, main-
taining, monitoring, and overseeing security for communications facilities
linking high government, Party, and military and secret service offices and
bases throughout the USSR. There were also special KGB guard units for
protecting the Kremlin and other important government office sites in

Moscow and elsewhere. The KGB, in another aspect of military security work, planted informers disguised as ordinary soldiers and sergeants within military units, the better to report on politically suspect behavior or conversation.[9]

What follows concentrates mainly on the Red Army, since it was the largest, as well as the original, Soviet armed force, the military branch most draftees served in or tried to avoid serving in.

A SOLDIER'S DAILY LIFE, 1922–1939

Like most members of Soviet society, soldiers had to endure substandard housing plus shortages of food, clothing, and other basic necessities. They often had to live in tents for months, since the number of men being drafted always raced ahead of the government's ability or willingness to provide more substantial housing for them. Even brand-new barracks were likely to have been shoddily built, far from weatherproof, with no indoor plumbing or electric lights. Soldiers often also lacked bathhouses. The degree to which conscripts ate well or at least had enough food depended on how concerned their officers were about their diet. As a result of the famine of 1932–1933, the government ordered all units to grow their own food and raise their own livestock. Such military farms raised cows, pigs, bees, rabbits, wheat and other cereals, and fruit. Much time was diverted from military training while soldiers became field hands under officer farm managers, but they had to eat, and such agricultural enterprises were an integral part of major Soviet army units until the fall of the Soviet Union. Military farms usually had the same problems as nonmilitary ones: poor management, roads, housing, and equipment, and unwilling workers. When such farms did not produce enough the soldiers' diet suffered. Besides being assigned to work on military farms, soldiers were often used as a source of free labor to work on civilian collective farms as well as in any other areas of the civilian economy. Even though soldiers got no reward for their extramilitary work, it is likely that people higher up the chain of command profited. It is also likely that the many hours spent in field-hand work, railroad and apartment house building, and other kinds of heavy labor contributed to the army's chronic morale problems. There was generally no effective way to get grievances resolved. Soldiers wrote letters of complaint, sent them to the official channel (the Bureau of Red Army Men's Letters), and in most cases waited in vain for a response.[10]

The USSR was drastically unprepared for the German invasion of Russia in 1941, in great part because Stalin had signed a nonaggression treaty with Hitler and because of the deadly purge of the Soviet military in 1937 and 1938. First came the arrests and executions of Marshal Mikhail Tukhachevsky, a former chief of staff and Civil

A Soldier's Daily Life during World War II (1941–45)

War hero, and other high Red Army officers, on grounds of treason. Suddenly it seemed that antigovernment conspiracies were everywhere in the military. By the time Stalin finished flushing out supposed armed forces traitors, some 40,000 officers had been discharged, many to be shot or sent to the gulag. The victims were mainly senior officers, including most of the marshals, army commanders, corps commanders, divisional commanders, and all but one navy fleet commander. When the purges were over, fewer than half of the senior Soviet officers were still alive. They had been convicted on false evidence, their confessions extracted under torture, but no one knows why Stalin went after them. When the "Winter War" with Finland (1939–1940) showed how much the Red Army needed officers with military expertise and war with Germany loomed or had already begun, more than one-fourth of the surviving arrested officers were freed, reinstated in their former rank, and sent into war.[11]

Naturally the purges degraded morale in the armed forces. Officers had to wonder whether any one of their orders might get them arrested, while soldiers and junior officers questioned how they could trust a senior officer's judgment, since so many had been convicted of treason. And who knew whether an arrested officer's replacement might not also turn out to be an "enemy of the people"? Officers' arrests may have contributed, in the late 1930s, to a decline in military discipline and a significant rise in accidents, suicides, and self-inflicted wounds among servicemen. And when war began, thousands of new, inexperienced officers paid with their lives for lack of training, as did millions of soldiers under their command. Even experienced officers, however, might be summarily executed for losing a battle. To save their own skins, officers sometimes denounced each other as traitors.[12]

Even though millions of Soviet citizens supported the war effort, desertion remained a chronic, widespread problem throughout the conflict, as it had been during the Civil War. Tens of thousands of soldiers assigned to defend border areas (Ukraine, Byelorussia, Lithuania, Latvia, and Estonia) at the beginning of the war ran away or deserted to the German side because they hoped the Germans would bring their countries independence from the Soviet Union, or they sympathized with Nazi anti-Jewish policies, or both. Many deserted because they had been alienated by Soviet terror.[13]

The government tried to fix the problem by threatening soldiers with terrible reprisals if they retreated or fled, or (in the case of officers) did not prevent their men from doing so. A decree of August 1941 ordered officers'—including commissars'—families to be arrested if their men deserted. On September 12, 1941, Stalin decreed that special NKVD (secret police) detachments be sent to the front lines with orders to shoot any soldiers who tried to run away, a tactic that had also been used in the Civil War. In 1942, Stalin ordered "not one step backward" for soldiers in battle, adding special regular army "blocking detachments" to the NKVD troops already assigned to shoot retreating soldiers. In addition, the order created penal battalions for disobedient or "cowardly" soldiers and their officers. These units were sent into battle ahead of regular troops, to attract enemy fire or become human mine sweepers. Jokes about or criticisms of military or government policies could land a soldier in a penal battalion and nearly certain death.[14]

The Germans treated Soviet prisoners of war worse than they did other Allied prisoners because according to Nazi racism, Jews, Slavs, and Asians were the most inferior groups, and the USSR was composed mainly of Jews, Slavs, and Asians. Stalin considered his soldiers traitors for having been captured and readily abandoned them to their fate. The Red Cross was not allowed to deliver them food parcels from home or to try to protect them in any other way. As a result, Soviet POWs died by the hundreds of thousands in German prison camps, from starvation, disease, cold, and executions. When the other Allied POWs shared food packages with their Soviet comrades, starving Red Army prisoners "jumped on these gifts like a pack of dogs on a bone."[15] The cheapness of their lives, to the Germans, is reflected in the fact that 600 were murdered in September 1941 in the first mass killing experimental use of Zyklon B poison gas at the Auschwitz death camp.[16]

Those not captured also had only slim chances for surviving. Untrained or barely trained, ill equipped replacements for wounded and killed soldiers were sent to the front lines and "shov[ed]...in front of the Germans." One such replacement, Gabriel Temkin, lived to write about his experiences as a raw recruit sent to combat with no weapons instruction and no weapons. When asked about preparation, a political officer told the men they would soon have on-the-job training. When he arrived at the front in May 1943, Temkin found weapons aplenty, left behind on the battlefield by hundreds of slain Red Army predecessors. He and his fellows simply picked up the guns and began shooting at the enemy as best they could. The Germans "were not caught by surprise," he recalled. "Their heavy machine guns began to crackle and mowed down our soldiers." In the course of 10 days' savage fighting, Temkin's division lost about 200 men per day, losses regularly replenished by more new untaught recruits, though no territory was gained. In fact, at the beginning of World War II, the chances were that more than 60 of every 100 soldiers would be either dead or captured within six months. Nevertheless, many struggled courageously against the terrible odds.

The resistance by the garrison of the Brest fortress was heroic, despite the fact that the command had abandoned it. The fortress was besieged on all sides by the Germans but continued to resist for twenty-eight days. The few survivors, after unprecedented suffering at the hands of the Germans, ended up in Soviet prison camp in [Siberia] as "traitors to the homeland." They were not rehabilitated [freed and/or their names cleared] until many years after the war.[17]

But the tide was turning. After the Germans were routed from Stalingrad in February 1943, people knew the enemy would be defeated. By 1943 the devastation Germans had wrought on the USSR's heavy industries was being overcome. In 1944, Soviet military production was about four times greater than it had been in 1940, surpassing the Germans' war industry capabilities. By dint of working 55-hour weeks, Soviet engineers and laborers were each month pumping out thousands of airplanes, tanks, guns, mortars, and machine guns as good as, or better than, the Germans', as well as millions of bombs, shells, and mines. That same year saw the beginning of an American-British-Canadian program (Lend-Lease) that gave the Soviet war effort billions of dollars' worth of food, motor vehicles (Studebakers, Dodges, and Jeeps), clothing, gasoline, raw materials, weapons, ammunition, explosives, materials for heavy industry, railroad equipment, medicines, textiles, tanks, and planes. Not only regular armed forces troops benefited. After the Battle of Stalingrad (now Volgograd), the government also allotted partisan bands (guerrilla fighters behind enemy lines) more and better supplies of guns, food, and medicine, so that in 1943 and 1944 many more fighters joined the partisans. These developments may have buoyed troops' morale even though by war's end, Red Army dead and wounded far outnumbered casualties suffered by other Allied forces. Estimates vary, but probably around 26.6 to 42.7 million Soviet soldiers and civilians were killed during World War II. As one historian commented, "Both the scale of the figures and their imprecision is a testament to man's inhumanity to man." The number of German soldiers and civilians killed in the war amounted to about a third of the USSR's losses. In comparison, Great Britain and its Commonwealth countries lost 42 times fewer soldiers and civilians; the United States (whose losses did not ordinarily include civilians) lost 72 times fewer people. Soviet war dead included millions of civilians as well as combatants because much of the war was fought on their land for three and a half years, by an invader who succeeded in carrying out policies of mass murder against millions of Jewish residents and brutalities against millions in other Soviet ethnic groups. In addition, the USSR's war with Germany was a war of attrition: both sides ruthlessly used people as *materiél,* and the USSR had more people to expend.[18]

Besides the millions of soldiers who died in combat, hundreds of thousands of troops succumbed to infectious diseases like typhus and cholera, as well as from a lack of prompt, skilled emergency medical care, whether in the field or behind the lines. Hospitals behind the lines were shabby, unheated, and generally filthy, with few male orderlies who could restrain violent, battle-shocked patients. Inpatients fled if they could, even if it meant foregoing crucial surgery.[19]

In his memoir, Igor Kaberov, a much-decorated World War II combat pilot and officer, survivor of 132 air battles, tells of good times and bad. We learn from Kaberov how physically and mentally exhausting it was to be in the middle of an airborne firefight: once after such a fight, he landed his plane on the runway and immediately fell asleep, to the consternation of his technician, who thought he must have been wounded. The air force suffered from a lack of crucial supplies, as did the other services. For example, many planes in Kaberov's squadron lacked oxygen masks, so pilots were limited in how high they could fly, giving the Germans an advantage. The men lived in flimsy shelters hidden from German pilots' view under forest cover, or in hillside dugouts. Pilots were expected to take time out for rest and recreation—sometimes zealous airmen were even ordered to do so. When not risking their lives, the men in Kaberov's unit celebrated their camaraderie by telling jokes, singing, and dancing. Kaberov himself entertained his fellows by playing his accordion and helping to publish a daily squadron newsletter. Women cooked for them. Presumably because he was an officer, in two years (1941–1943) of frontline duty, Kaberov was allowed furloughs from his assignment in the Baltic. He visited his family in Vologda, traveled to Moscow more than once, and even went to Leningrad to visit friends when that city was under siege, an experience more depressing than restful. Death stalked airmen's lives; when a pilot was killed, his comrades toasted him with a hundred grams of vodka.[20]

At war's end, over two million Soviet citizens—POWs and others—were repatriated, often by force, from Germany and other European countries with the help of British and American authorities. Stalin presumed they were German collaborators, as thousands had been. For thousands of others, however, the only traitorous act was having been captured. The hapless returnees were automatically tarred with the same brush and dispatched to the same fate: execution or long prison camp sentences. Only 15 to 20 percent escaped such punishments after they arrived on Soviet soil.[21]

Thanks to its new military might, the Soviet Union had leaped forward in world power and prestige, but remarkably, the daily life of soldiers after the war was not much different than it had been before the war. When Alexander Lebed arrived in 1985 to command the garrison of the 331st Airborne Regiment, he saw that the whole base was "a trash heap without a single visible trash can or dumpster." Sanitary conditions were ghastly. All the garrison's soldiers were crowded into only two barracks; maybe that was the reason for the "total disregard for cleanliness." In the lavatory, "toilets and sinks were broken and three-fourths of the faucets were twisted off."

The walls were covered with slime and mildew. Everything was overflowing, leaking, and smelled terrible. In the sleeping facilities, the side tables and stools were broken, and the entire hall had only two or three light bulbs, which were coated with dust.[22]

Such day-to-day existence in the midst of poverty and filth, bred in the soldiers, Lebed believed, "Boredom, hopelessness, and the desire to do something nasty, mean, and cruel to your neighbor." Lebed claimed that with difficulty, he was able to set things right on the base.

INDUCTION AND CONSCRIPTION

According to law, all healthy, physically and mentally normal males were obligated to do military service. In the years following the Civil War, there was an annual draft from September 1 to mid-November, which in 1967 changed to twice yearly, May–June and November–December, so that young farmers could help complete spring planting and fall harvesting. Men ages 21 through 30 were draft age until 1936, when the age was lowered to 19, but in 1942 and 1943, so many Soviet soldiers were killed that teenagers as young as 15 were sent to the front lines. The 1967 Law on Universal Military Service lowered conscription age to 18, and teenage boys had to register with their local draft board induction center (military commissariat) between January and March of the year they turned 17. In accordance with that law, women with special technical skills, including medicine, also had to register for the draft. As it happened, the government, post-1967, chose not to draft them, but women between 19 and 40 could voluntarily enlist. Soldiers were in the reserves until age 50, officers until 65.[23]

As with all other aspects of Soviet life, the Party was intensely involved in the conscription process. Originally, kulaks, former members of the nobility, bourgeoisie, religious believers, and conscientious objectors were banned from service. In 1936 the "Stalin Constitution" outlawed such restrictions, and in 1939 religious believers and other conscientious objectors lost their exemptions. In 1967, length of compulsory service was reduced a year, to two years in the Army, Air Force, Border and Security Troops, and three in the Navy, Coast Guard Combat Units, and Navy Border Troops.[24]

All young men were supposed to take two years of preinduction basic military training, but in reality such training, when it was provided, was often insufficient. Military commissariats kept files on all draft-eligible men, and when a man was called up decided, based on the information on file, which branch of service he would go into. In the regular armed forces, the Air Force and Strategic Rocket Forces took those with high intelligence, a good education, physical fitness, and clean political record. The Navy set the bar lower, looking for physical fitness more than intelligence. (Igor Kaberov, who passionately wanted to be a Navy fighter pilot and eventually achieved that goal, was twice rejected from pilot training, first for being "badly proportioned," and later for having flat feet.) The KGB and Ministry of the Interior also competed for the cream of young recruits, to the displeasure of Army officials, who did not want only leftovers. The least desirable—criminals, the chronically ill, the politically suspect— were generally assigned to construction battalions. The government was not eager to see ethnic minorities supplied with weapons, except to keep other minorities under control, so they were also usually sent to construction or other noncombat battalions and were unlikely to be given much if any weapons training.[25]

DEFERMENTS

There were three main types of draft deferments: education, family hardship, and health.

High school students were deferred until graduation if they were under age 20. Those enrolled as full-time students at the college level were entitled to deferments until age 27. A man who reached 27 and still had a student deferment joined the reserves, which meant the chances were good he would never have to serve in active duty. In the late 1970s, a bright Moscow 17-year-old who attended an elite special high school for biology told an American journalist that her male classmates were eager to avoid being drafted into the "ghastly" army and that parents tried to help by searching for physical defects in their sons. After Soviet forces invaded Afghanistan in 1979, however, the government needed to beef up its military manpower and so became much less generous with student deferments. Most were discontinued in 1980 but reinstated in 1989, thanks perhaps to the end of the war in Afghanistan and pressure from grassroots groups dominated by students' mothers.[26]

Because soldiers were paid no more than pocket money, men who were the sole support of invalid parents, two or more minor children, or dependent siblings got a deferment until age 27 and then entered the reserves. Although not a cause for deferment, Party officials knew that soldiers' morale plummeted when they had unhappy news from home, and local agencies were supposed to act quickly to resolve a soldier's family problems. Unfortunately, local authorities often ignored such complaints. In 1936, a special investigation revealed severe cases that had not been remedied. In one that a city soviet failed to address, a soldier's wife and 10-year-old child lived in abysmal circumstances despite the wife's many requests for help. Another soldier's wife, who lived with their 10-month-old baby in an unheated apartment, supported herself and the infant by hawking vodka and denatured alcohol on the street. The official investigation revealed that her village council decided to help, not by getting her a heated apartment and decent job, but by ignoring her illegal street vending. In another case,

The secretary of the Khokhlovsk village [council], Comrade Sazonov, to the question whether he visited the families of soldiers or interested himself in how they lived, answered: "Why visit them? There isn't enough time, and if necessary they will come themselves."[27]

The 1936 investigation resulted in stern orders from above to reform the handling of soldiers' and their family's complaints; as a result there may have been some improvements, at least for a time.[28]

A physician sat on each local draft board. These doctors had lengthy, complicated, and secret, official guidelines for determining who would be assigned to what kind of military duty and who might be exempted or deferred. For example, a youth with diabetes or asthma or other illness might well be found unfit for combat duty, but not unfit to serve in a construction battalion. Cases of self-mutilation as a way to avoid army service (or to be discharged from active duty) occurred, but it was more common to use *blat*—the tried-and-true combination of influence, networking, and bribes—to have a physician declare a young man mentally unfit. Schizophrenia was a favorite diagnosis, which if successful meant several months in a mental hospital rather than two years in the service. New secret medical guidelines issued in 1987 ended many previous health exemptions. Young men with cardiovascular diseases, asthma, tuberculosis, digestive problems, histories of mental illnesses, and many other pathologies lost their exemptions. As a result, many sickly youths were assigned to construction battalions to do heavy labor alongside criminals and ethnic gangs. If they survived long enough, the luckier ones might eventually be deemed unfit for army life and given early discharges.[29]

The use of *blat* to avoid the draft could be tailored to local conditions. One young Azerbaijani man gave 10 sheep to the local draft board chief so that he would be assigned to a construction battalion within walking distance of his house. Another strategy obtainable through bribes involved having one's name removed from the draft list. Many Russian soldiers believed ethnic minorities were wealthier than they, and so could more easily buy their way out of military service.[30]

During the war in Afghanistan, corruption at local draft boards became especially intense. People noticed, often bitterly, that boys who lived in major cities with large, well-educated, white-collar populations were much less likely to be drafted than boys from the country or smoky industrial towns, who did not have access to important power networks. The Red Army, as one officer remarked ironically, was becoming once again an army of workers and peasants.[31]

INDUCTEES

A young man who could not get or did not want a deferment faced certain rituals at induction time. He might be both the guest of honor at, and the excuse for, a number of farewell parties characterized by tables groaning with food and freely flowing vodka. It was traditional for parents to propose toasts until their son was falling-down drunk. Fathers and guests who had served reminisced about their army days, prophesying that the experience would "make a man" of the new recruit. Then it was off to the induction center, where drinking might continue amid patriotic speeches, emotional embraces, and tears. Since Russian families were small and children customarily lived in their parents' cramped apartment or room at least until marriage, parents were likely to be sending off an only child from whom they had never been parted for more than a few hours or days. Because furloughs were rare and postings were distant, parents knew they would probably not be seeing their offspring for two or three years. Once parted from their families, new recruits were inspected for various vermin, tested for contagious diseases, given a steam bath and a skull-revealing haircut, and had their clothes disinfected. Then they waited a few hours, or for a week or longer, for a "buyer" to choose them.[32]

Military agents called buyers were sent from armed forces units around the country to ensure the ethnic mix within a unit was exactly what the government wanted. For example, if orders came down from the general staff that a certain Air Force unit needed a hundred Slavic (Russian, Ukrainian, Byelorussian) men and three Uzbeks, a buyer would be dispatched at induction time to Leningrad or Kiev or some other area with a Slavic majority. Another buyer would be sent to an Uzbek military commissariat to acquire three promising young men from that region. (Elite troops had strict, unpublished quotas as to how many minority youth would be admitted.) After they arrived, buyers scanned the draft board's files and then chose whom they wanted.[33]

A new inductee's former lifetime in a cramped one- or two-room apartment may have been good preparation for crowded barracks. But it must have been unnerving to be suddenly torn from the devotion and home cooking of mothers and grandmothers to 6:00 A.M. reveilles and scanty, unappetizing meals. Perhaps mother and grandmother would soon receive a photo of their darling in uniform—heavy khaki shirt, jodhpur-style pants, high boots, and the Russian army version of socks,

two elaborately folded rags that can be washed out and hung over the bed each night. The whole ensemble is topped by a tiny folded peak of material that perches precariously upon the smooth bald head.

Now their sons resembled "confused, convicted, horseless cavalrymen" about to be transported to parts unknown.[34]

STATIONING PRACTICES

Where the recruits were off to and which service they were assigned to was a secret carefully kept from conscripts and their families. Even the *blat* of worried parents could not ordinarily drag that information from a buyer or his assistants. "I figured out that I would be in the Air Force because of the tags the buyer was wearing," a former enlisted man recalled. "But no one would tell us until we actually arrived there." Another man was told he was going into a "high frequency communications unit," but at journey's end found himself part of the Border Troops. New recruits en route to their assignments were closely guarded, to prevent them from running away and also to foil relatives' attempts to snatch them back. When Azerbaijani parents were successful in retrieving a son, they ran for the mountains. Citizens of the Komi Republic who grabbed their sons from conscription trains, headed for the forest.[35]

Especially during the Soviet war in Afghanistan (1979–1989) new conscripts were lied to about where they were going, often being told they were en route to Poland or some other safe place.

They were generally sent under guard: frightened, half-trained boys, kept behind barbed wire, pacified with vodka until the armed military policemen came to herd them to their plane like convicts.[36]

Before the 1930s, Soviet soldiers were stationed in their home regions, but in the mid-1930s, the government adopted the practice of sending them very far from their homes, for as long as their tour of duty lasted. There were various reasons for that policy. Stalin did not want to risk having a group of young Uzbeks, for example, armed and ready to rebel, stationed in their homeland, surrounded by sympathetic countrymen. Being assigned hundreds of miles from home also made desertion or retrieval by one's family difficult. Finally, if soldiers were ordered to put down a rebellion, the government figured they would be more willing, perhaps even eager, to shoot down ethnic "others." "A Russian soldier probably would not shoot at Russian women," a former Soviet serviceman explained, "but a Kazakh would. He would say, 'They are Russians. Let's go get them.'" So Russian recruits went to Kazakhstan, Kazakhs went to Ukraine, Ukrainians went to Georgia, Uzbeks to Russia, and so on. Construction battalions, railroad support units, and other troops who were unarmed and generally had little or no weapons training were exceptions to this rule; it was not unusual for such battalions to be composed of men who lived in the republic where they were stationed.

Soviet military bases tended to be at a distance from cities and towns in order to isolate soldiers from local civilians. Especially in Central Asia and the Caucasus, soldiers often did not get to visit the nearest town until after their discharge, partly for their own protection from hostile civilians. Often servicemen were confined to base during their whole tour of duty, not only for protection but also to prevent friendships between soldiers and civilians, especially in border areas where guards were expected to shoot down border crossers. Those stationed in Russian areas, however, could usually go into town regularly. Officers, who lived in special housing next to the base, were free to travel into nearby towns and other places.

Since it was the armed forces' official language, fluency in Russian played a major role in determining who got assigned to which unit and was likely to be promoted. Very many non-Russian recruits, especially those from rural areas, did not know the language and so were assigned to construction and other support units, or to Interior Troops meant to put down civil disturbances. Minorities fluent in Russian, on the other hand, had a good chance of being assigned to more important, more highly technical jobs, with weapons training. Minorities in combat units were supposed to use Russian at all times, under threat of punishment if they reverted to their native tongue. In reality they usually spoke Russian only in front of their officers and NCOs, not when they were together with countrymen. In construction units, soldiers spoke their native languages without hindrance even in front of officers, unless they wanted to be promoted to sergeant. Sometimes officers and sergeants in construction battalions spoke to their men in non-Russian languages if they could, but most often communication between Russian-speaking officers and national minorities was a problem. The military provided no special language training programs; rather, minorities were expected to learn Russian however they could, and often they did, if only primitively. But inability or seeming inability to speak Russian could be a strategy for evading work, or so Russian soldiers and officers often suspected. Those suspicions caused nasty racial slurs, fights, and even jail time for suspected shirkers, but linguistic problems were not the only cause of racial tensions in the military. Racism was a fact of daily life soldiers brought with them from their ethnic and civilian world.

Racial discrimination and racially motivated violence on the part of soldiers and sergeants was often brutal. Central Asians were made to do the worst jobs, like cleaning toilets. In the mess hall, Asians often ate last, Russians and Ukrainians first. "If I worked with a screwdriver," an ex-soldier said, "the Central Asian work[ed] with a shovel." Although there were few or no checks on common soldiers and NCOs expressing their racism in words and actions, senior officers were less likely to show racism in public. They also tended to ignore or actively cover up incidents of ethnic and other violence in order to keep their own record free of any hint they could not control their men's behavior. It is not unlikely that some officers and NCOs were amused by fighting among ethnic and national groups in their units and saw these conflicts as diverting blows away from themselves. Because of linguistic problems, less education, and racial prejudice, non-Slavs were scarcest in services that depended on sophisticated technology, such as the Strategic Rocket Forces, the Air Force, and the Navy. Hatred, of course, cut both ways; ethnic minorities took their revenge on Russian soldiers when they could.

HAZING OF NEW RECRUITS: DEDOVSHCHINA AND GRUPPOVSHCHINA

The brutal hazing of new recruits was a widespread, often lethal practice similar to abuses in prisons and in some vocational-technical schools, places where many youths had spent time before entering the military. The oldest variety of hazing, called *dedovshchina* (rule of the grandfathers), began to be publicly acknowledged and discussed only during glasnost; possibly its roots go back to tsarist times. During their first six months in the military, new recruits were exploited by the "old men" (*stariki*) doing their final six months of service. The abuse took many forms. New recruits were forced to be servants to outgoing short-timers, taking on their menial duties, handing over money, allowing possessions to be stolen. It was wise to leave pens, razors, watches, and other amenities of daily life at home. Once their first six months were up, recruits waited a year for their turn to haze newcomers. Sergeants lacked authority because most were also short-term conscripts and were often themselves victims of *dedovshchina*. The chronic shortages of basic military materials, such as uniforms and gear, motivated theft, but hazing also often meant savage physical abuse. Military prosecutors were ready and willing to go after offenders, but most officers simply turned the barracks over to the inmates and covered up abuses in order to safeguard their own careers. With no one to turn to for protection, it was not unusual for helpless recruits to commit suicide or desert. In one horrible example of *dedovshchina*, a young Lithuanian recruit, Arturas Salauskas, requested a transfer after having undergone an "initiation" beating.

Trapped late at night on a transport train three days before his transfer, the young recruit was beaten, burned, and raped by seven of his fellow soldiers. He responded by shooting them all, as well as a civilian conductor.[37]

Some 4,000 soldiers were tried for hazing in 1985, but that number was probably only a fraction of the attacks carried out, since most victims were afraid to report their tormentors, and officers usually refused to acknowledge complaints.[38]

Gruppovshchina, "rule of the group," arose in the later Soviet period as more and more national minorities were drafted. In units dominated by non-Slavic groups, ethnicity substituted for seniority in the pecking order, and woe to Russian recruits caught in a unit dominated by a non-Slavic gang. Many young men who entered the army fit, healthy, and with plans for the future were returned to their parents as corpses, murdered or hounded to suicide by the predators within their own ranks.[39]

After glasnost made it possible, thousands of people wrote letters to editors, protesting brutal hazing. A woman wrote to the popular magazine *Ogonyok* (*A Small Fire*) about her two sons' experiences and about the even worse hazing of a colleague's son, who

had been beaten up so badly that there wasn't an untouched spot left on him: he had refused to wash the grandfathers' socks. Newcomers were beaten with belt buckles so hard that the [star insignias] were imprinted on their behinds.

The letter writer asked, "Where are the commanders? Where are the political officers? It seems impossible that they don't know anything." In another letter, a man recounted the death of his sailor son, after having been beaten by an "elder" who ruptured his spleen. "What for? For not bringing his cigarettes in time or for not making tea." According to the grieving father, the ship's captain admitted, at the murderer's trial, that he [the captain] "had no authority; he had reported [the hazing] to all the higher-ups but had received no help." In this case, the murderer was sentenced to nine years in a maximum security labor camp.[40]

Glasnost brought with it increasing freedom for news media to report on bad things happening in the military as well as in civilian daily life. As horror stories about military life became ever more widespread, thousands of youths who had no legal ways to get out of serving looked to their parents to help them avoid the draft or desert. Parents' groups learned to use the media to publicize their concerns, effectively lobbied local and national governments, counseled draft evaders and their parents, and sheltered inductees fleeing the military.[41]

Some soldiers, however, especially Ukrainian peasants, willingly enlisted because for them the military offered a step up the social ladder. Village boys who reenlisted as NCOs were rewarded with internal passports entitling them to travel freely within the Soviet Union—a privilege most other peasants did not have—and to settle in any city, a rare perk for anyone. Otherwise, after serving their compulsory two or three years, rural conscripts had to go back to their villages passportless, with no sure exit to a better life and decent wage. Moreover, former NCOs could choose well-paying jobs either in the militia or in the KGB.[42]

MEDICAL CARE AND HEALTH

During World War II, medical care for those at the front was very undependable. Although there were many heroic medics, too often, advance planning for transporting soldiers from the battlefield was poor, or medics were most interested in saving their own necks. Thus, wounded fighters might lie where they had fallen for hours or days before getting any treatment, or they might be abandoned altogether. By the time of the Afghan war, however, the military had a modern helicopter airlift system for evacuating casualties to networks of hospitals and emergency care centers. But once the wounded were brought to a care center, doctors, nurses, and medics had to contend with the same shortages and second-rate equipment that plagued civilian medical care. Many of the medical personnel and officers did what they could to supply what was lacking. Officers on leave brought black market medical supplies back with them to Afghanistan, or spent their hard currency vouchers on Western medical equipment, or even joined commando raids on enemy supply convoys in order to collect Western medical supplies.[43]

OFFICERS

Party membership was part of an officer's career path, just as it was for those in civilian life. From 1928 to 1941, turnover in the officer corps was very heavy, in great part because living conditions, salary, and social prestige for junior officers were low compared with that of civilian managers. Between 1925 and 1936, 47,000 officers left the military, but not always voluntarily and not always into better jobs. Military tribunals sentenced many thieving officers to prison or firing squads. Public drunkenness was common among officers, as was their alcohol-fueled violence.

Junior officers, unlike enlisted men, had to pay for their own uniforms, including boots, which could be quite expensive, food, and furniture for their quarters. In the 1930s junior officers had the same housing problems as most others in civilian life: separate families were crowded together in tiny spaces in dilapidated substandard buildings, with no plumbing or heat during the hard Russian winters, conditions even senior officers (colonels and generals) sometimes had to endure. In 1935, as part of an effort to recruit more men into the officer corps, the government gave officers a pay raise, introduced dress uniforms, and reintroduced titles of rank, which had been taboo since the Revolution. The word "officer," however, was not brought back into use until 1943. With their higher pay, nattier uniforms, and traditional military ranks, some senior officers, like those in tsarist times, started thinking of themselves as better than other men. However, the great purges of officers in 1937–1938 must have shaken such arrogance and whatever sense of security or confidence officers had in their high station. On the other hand, privations they suffered must have seemed trivial in comparison with the terrifying roundups and executions.[44]

During the cold war years (1946–1991) junior officers shared with civilians the same deprivations of the civilian population. In the 1980s, 165,000 officers had to find their own often substandard housing and pay for it out of their own pockets. One described his home as a "plywood hut without any so-called amenities . . . only cold [water], and it is out in the courtyard." Furthermore, the officer complained, there was not enough heat, medical care was dangerously inadequate, there was no nursery or kindergarten, and food was hard to find. Soviet junior officers stationed in East Germany had to endure living standards below that of most East German citizens. By the end of the Soviet period, however, senior officers were living very well and enjoyed social prestige. Generals earned much more than most civilian managers and enjoyed perks such as having summer homes built with government supplies and free military labor.[45]

The officer corps was almost entirely Slavic, a bias that only increased with time. Jewish, central Asian, Caucasian, or Baltic officers were rarities. Eventually about 80 percent of officers were Russians and most of the rest Ukrainians and Byelorussians. Unofficial policy, especially after World

War II, discouraged non-Slavs from applying to officer schools and rejected most minorities who did apply. The few minorities who graduated from military academies and became career officers quickly hit a "glass ceiling" that barred their way to promotion. So in order to get enough qualified Russian officers, the government fell back on "involuntary recruitment": a Russian university graduate, usually under 30, with a needed specialty (including medicine) was approached and offered a deal he could not refuse—join the military as an officer for a limited term (two to five years). Refusal could result in loss of one's diploma and ruination of a career. Once the recruit was in its clutches, the military could extend his contract without his consent and sometimes did. Although in the early 1980s the government began an effort to get more minorities into officer schools, it was also the case that most non-Russians did not want to be Soviet commanders. They felt no particular loyalty to the government and no desire to renounce their culture, which they would have had to do in order to build a military career.[46]

Ethnic Makeup of Officers

Soviet officers distanced themselves from their troops, just as officers had done before the Revolution. Also as in the tsar's army, they felt free to beat soldiers and did, without fear of punishment. One Afghanistan-era commander admitted that officers sometimes beat soldiers unmercifully: "I saw it myself, though I didn't do it personally. I often tried to stop other officers, literally holding their hands. But I have never done it myself. Well, in rare cases, I did slap a soldier." A newly discharged young man wrote a letter to *Ogonyok*, complaining that his commanders used soldiers as personal servants and even, in one case, kept soldiers beyond their discharge date in order to build him a wine cellar.[47]

Officers' Mistreatment of Soldiers

WOMEN IN THE MILITARY

According to the Soviet constitution, men and women were equally required to defend their country. During World War I, the Provisional Government formed women's battalions to shame the many male deserters into returning to the fight. During the Civil War, tens of thousands of women volunteers (2 percent of the force), many of them soldiers' wives or sweethearts, joined the Red Army. Most were nurses or administrators, but some fought alongside male soldiers. For many, these women warriors signaled the beginning of a new era of gender equality. In his Civil War diary, Isaac Babel described the female cavalry he saw in 1920.

The squadrons go into battle, dust, din, bared sabers, furious cursing, and they gallop forward with their skirts tucked up, covered in dust, with their big breasts, all whores, but comrades, whores because they're comrades, that's what matters, they're there to serve everybody, in any way they can, heroines, at the same time, despised, they water the horses, tote hay, mend harness, steal from the churches and from the civilian population.[48]

An article Babel wrote for the Red Army newspaper, *The Red Cavalryman*, presents a harsh picture of the indignities army nurses had to endure in order to treat the wounded. The nurse Babel visited when he had a sore throat worked out of a corner of a crowded "smoky hut, filled with fumes and rankness." As she bandages the wounded, some "troublemakers" try to distract her with "the most blasphemous, unnatural curses." When the squadron has to ride off, the nurse, who owns "neither cloak nor coat," joins them, ill-dressed as she is against the bitter cold and rain. "Her pitiful thin dress flutters in the wind, and her frozen red toes show through the holes of her shoes." The nurse tends to the wounded on the battlefield, under the crossfire of machine guns and explosion of shells. She drags bloodied soldiers off the field on her shoulders "with disdainful calm." When the fighting is temporarily over, and she is once again settled, with the rest of the platoon, in a corner of a dirty hut, she resumes her "bandaging, bandaging, bandaging...." while the men taunt her. At day's end, "Nobody helps her, nobody puts down straw for her to sleep on, nobody fluffs up her pillow."[49]

During World War II, huge casualties caused a drastic shortage of able-bodied men, so the military recruited women as volunteers and also drafted them, although policies for drafting and promoting women were not consistent. Approximately 800,000 women served in combat and noncombat roles of every kind—besides being fighters and snipers, they were clerks; doctors; nurses; paramedics; cooks; postal workers; radio, telegraph, and telephone operators; construction workers; train engineers and crew on dangerous frontline routes; and military truck drivers. Many women who worked behind the lines were called on to fight at critical moments.[50]

The government apparently never kept hard statistics on the age, nationality, or rank of women in the military in World War II, but in general, most were probably teenagers and low in rank. Few were trained as NCOs or admitted to officer training. Of those who did become officers, most were political workers, attached to brigades and divisions, who served as Party organizers, Komsomol leaders, newsletter and newspaper editors, political indoctrinators, and so forth. Like male political officers, women commissars were expected to, and did, fight in frontline combat and often lost their lives. As the war ground on, the line between combat and noncombat duties faded—nurses often carried guns and used them while rescuing soldiers on the battlefield. Beginning in mid-1942, women began showing up on the front lines as regular army soldiers, sometimes fighting in all-female, sometimes in mixed, combat units. Altogether over a million women served in army units and partisan bands.[51]

Partisans were guerrilla fighters who carried out sabotage operations in enemy-held territory by shooting, sniping; burning buildings; and blow-ing up bridges, trains, and railroad tracks. If caught, they were tortured and executed. Like their regular army sisters, Soviet women partisans in World War II fulfilled a range of overlapping roles, from medics to machine gunners to cooks, washerwomen, and lovers. The extent to which women were treated as equals by male partisans varied widely, depending on the group. Some bands preferred to keep females "in the kitchen," as one would-be woman fighter complained. Nina Kosterina was allowed to be a partisan even though her father and other close relatives had been arrested as "enemies of the people." In 1941, before departing her Moscow home to parachute behind enemy lines, Nina wrote in her diary, "I have a single thought: perhaps my action will save father?"[52] Many male soldiers resented women fighters, and sexual rivalries and jealousies were common in mixed partisan bands and army units.[53]

Few women served in the Soviet Navy in World War II, but they made a significant contribution to the Air Force. During the 1930s, Soviet women pilots achieved more world flight records than women pilots in any other country and were almost a **Women in the** third of all pilots trained in the Soviet Union. When war **Air Force** came, women made up 24 percent of Air Force personnel. There were three all-female Air Force regiments; their assignments, whether as flight crews or ground crews, were no less dangerous or difficult than those given to male colleagues. Yet as in civilian life, women military personnel were not allowed to escape working double shifts. They might risk their lives on the battlefield and still be expected to cook and launder for the men, and be the first on hand with medical care for wounded comrades.[54] Female or male, those serving in the Air Force during World War II probably had a more fulfilling experience than infantry soldiers.

As soon as Germany was defeated, most women were immediately discharged from service, and their contributions were largely ignored. Although they received many thousands of military decorations and suffered proportionately higher losses **Women World** than their male colleagues, Soviet women veterans **War II Veterans** were not allowed to participate in the massive postwar Moscow Victory Parade (June 24, 1945). Instead, they came home to official policies demanding their fast return to a steady, full-time civilian job, childbearing and nurturing, shopping, cooking, laundering, and cleaning. In a speech to a group of recently discharged female veterans, President Kalinin praised them for having "won equality for women…in the defense of your country, weapons in hand." Then he counseled them: "Do not give yourself airs in your future practical work. Do not speak of the services you rendered, let others do it for you. That will be better." Except for celebrations of Victory Day on May 9, when women veterans traditionally emerged, medal-bedecked, most official histories and commemorations bypassed them. Not until the 1960s did the military once again recruit large numbers of women specialists. In the late 1980s there were several thousand women in the armed forces, in medical, communications, and administrative jobs; most held the low rank of warrant officer. Women served in the Afghan war, in a much more limited role than they had in World War II; they were not sent in to fight but served in medical and other support roles. Nevertheless, female medics were frequently in danger, especially when they worked under fire to remove the wounded. At least 12 servicewomen died in Afghanistan. Females were never admitted to military academies, the main route to promotion in the officer corps.[55]

CHILDREN IN THE MILITARY

It had been traditional since tsarist times to boost the number of fighters and support troops by adopting male orphans (called "sons of the regiment") into a unit. The Soviet Army continued the practice during World War II, but because these adoptions were unofficial, it is not possible to know exactly how many thousands of children, ages around 6 to 16, were involved. Many of them fought on the front lines. While the Imperial Army adopted only male orphans, during World War II the Red Army began adopting young parentless girls. Besides being fighters, orphans also served as medical corpsmen and radio operators. Sometimes they were outfitted in miniature uniforms and awarded medals "for valor and service."

Prisoners were another source of manpower, in military and civilian life, in war and peace. After the German invasion, hundreds of thousands of men, including recently "purged" officers, were released from prison camps and exile in order to fight or work in industries. Sometimes their wartime assignments matched their preprison lives in weird ways, as when the playwright Nikolay Erdman, arrested and sentenced to exile for writing satirical fables, was freed into a secret police song-and-dance ensemble as a "literary consultant." His job was to write sketches intended to pump up soldiers' morale. Alexander Gorbatov was released just before the German invasion in 1941. After he was freed, Gorbatov met with the Commissar of Defense, who expressed his pleasure that the former officer was still alive, encouraged him to "have a rest, get better," and informed him that his former army rank and 30 months' back pay were waiting for him. When the war ended, Gorbatov, a general who tried to fight well *and* keep his troops' casualties low, was promoted to Commandant of Berlin.[56]

A kind of impromptu mobilization was common during the Civil War and World War II, when battlefront units increased their numbers by forcing able-bodied men who happened to live in the area into combat, without military training, uniforms, or weapons. Sometimes authorities went searching for recruits by landing a helicopter in remote terrain. "[They] look around, see a guy of approximately military age, and just take him."

Because of this, one guy was brought to our construction battalion who actually was an Iranian citizen. He had crossed the border in the mountains—some of them don't even know a border exists there—and they caught him and put him in service. ... He served with us for a year and a half before they got it straightened out.[57]

AFGHANISTAN

In December 1979, the government sent troops into Afghanistan to defend the Soviet-backed government of the Democratic Republic of Afghanistan (DRA) against rebellious Islamic "holy warriors" *(mujahideen)*. Altogether, some 642,000 Soviet soldiers served in Afghanistan from 1979 to 1989.

As in the past, soldiers usually had no leave during their stint. Mixing with the local population was forbidden and dangerous (though it did occur), and there were few or no opportunities for recreation. Soldiers were sent into the Afghan mountain and desert wildernesses, with their constant strong winds, extremes of hot and cold weather, and gun-clogging dust and sand, without sufficient water. Close to 15,000 *afgantsy* (soldiers of the war in Afghanistan) were killed by Afghan guerrillas during the 10-year war. Thousands of survivors, men and women, came home wounded in body and mind. All the harshest aspects of Soviet military life: bullying, drug and alcohol abuse, mistreatment by officers, crime and corruption continued and intensified in Afghanistan.[58]

Afghanistan was a rich breeding ground for diseases such as jaundice, malaria, meningitis, dysentery, hepatitis, typhus, and skin diseases, which often were more life-threatening than the mujahideen. Besides having to shelter in ramshackle barracks with no heat, toilet, or washing facilities, *afgantsy* had to endure hunger—a regular feature of army life from the Civil War on. The stingy rations were often so distasteful that soldiers spent their 10 rubles per month (the equivalent of just a few dollars) on food, or bought liquor and drugs when they could. Some committed suicide. Others stole government property and resold or bartered it to Afghans. Marketable items included gasoline, boots, uniforms, construction materials, automotive spare parts, rifles, and other weaponry, large and small. Kabul even had a special bazaar for the loot.

Dedovshchina in Afghanistan added a new twist: recent arrivals were hazed even if they had already served their first six months and been the victims of *dedovshchina*. Only this time, the tormented sometimes found an opportunity to strike back. In the midst of a firefight with the enemy, "grandfathers" might get picked off, dispatched by their erstwhile victims and not the Afghan enemy. Brutal officers had reason to be wary of their men since there were cases of soldiers murdering officers while other soldiers simply stood by and watched.

Soviet soldiers committed atrocities on the mujahideen as well as on unarmed noncombatants, and the mujahideen in turn committed atrocities against Soviet soldiers and their Afghan allies, including women and children. One Red Army veteran described a horror he witnessed when four Afghans were "tied, laid on the road, and run over" with an armored personnel carrier. One Afghan "was a [cleric] with a beard and they spared him." The next morning, however, when a soldier refused an officer's order to pour gasoline over the cleric and burn him, the officer angrily slit the cleric's throat. Elsewhere, a Soviet Army search party looking for their missing men found three of their comrades' burned bodies lying near a campfire.

The fourth was put up above the fire like in a grill. Cut off tongues, ears, picked out eyes were spread around. I thought that my heart would never bear such a terror, that it would explode like a grenade.

Both sides generally killed prisoners.[59]

As in previous wars, most who returned physically or emotionally disabled did not get adequate help from either the military or civilian communities. What help they did get often came only after a determined struggle against bureaucratic indifference. Sometimes the paperwork needed to get veterans' benefits started was lost or filled out incorrectly. Although 3,000 veterans needing artificial legs had not received them by mid-1990, most would not have benefited anyway—more than half the veterans allotted Soviet-made artificial legs found them unusable. Disabled veterans of the Afghan war, like all other handicapped Soviet citizens, had to deal with social attitudes and official policies that stigmatized them as invalids and pariahs, assigned them low-level jobs and paltry pensions, and did nothing to make the outside world, including public transportation, accessible.[60]

Increasingly as the country lurched toward the collapse of its government, resistance to military service grew stiffer, especially in the minority republics, where not serving became a matter of honor, abetted by sympathetic local officials. In 1990 and 1991, only 79 percent of those called up, countrywide, responded, and most of them were ethnic Russians. Of those who did answer the draft call, many subsequently deserted. Many officers became less enthusiastic about their career choice when, thanks to glasnost, they could compare their standard of living with that of officers in NATO armies.

Led by a cluster of ultraconservative generals, the Red Army's inglorious "last hurrah" was its failed attempt in August 1991 to unseat General Secretary Mikhail Gorbachev by force, undo the trend toward an open society that Gorbachev had set in motion, and keep the unraveling Soviet empire intact. Soldiers sent to the Kremlin in tanks were unwilling to attack their fellow citizens, as were many commanders. Prodemocracy civilians even clambered aboard tanks and posed for jubilant photos with the crews. Finally the Minister of Defense ordered the troops to leave; the attempted coup was history, as the Soviet Union would soon be.[61]

In December 1991 the Red Army became the Russian Army, a military that no longer has political workers as officers, but whose living conditions for common soldiers are still so hazardous that Russian mothers struggle to prevent their sons from serving, or travel to Chechen battlegrounds to search for them and bring them home.

NOTES

1. Roger R. Reese, *The Soviet Military Experience: A History of the Soviet Army, 1917–1991* (London: Routledge, 2000), 9, 11, 36–37.

2. Eugenia Hanfmann and Helen Beier, *Six Russian Men—Lives in Turmoil* (North Quincy, MA: Christopher Publishing House, 1976), 40.

3. Reese, *Soviet Military*, 1–4, 7–8, 12–15; 31; Milan Vego, "The Soviet Naval Officer Corps," *Soviet Armed Forces Review Annual* (*SAFRA*) 9 (1984–85): 271.

4. Reese, *Soviet Military*, 12–15, 31–33, 36.

5. Vladimir Voinovich, *The Life and Extraordinary Adventures of Private Ivan Chonkin*, trans. Richard Lourie (New York: Farrar, Straus, and Giroux, 1977), 25.

6. Vego, "Soviet Naval," 271–72; Reese, *Soviet Military*, 1–4, 7–8, 22, 71, 128–29; Voinovich, *Ivan Chonkin*, 29–30.

7. James T. Reitz, "The Soviet Security Troops—The Kremlin's Other Armies," *Soviet Armed Forces Review Annual* 6 (1982): 291–92; Harriet Fast Scott and William F. Scott, *The Armed Forces of the USSR*, 3rd ed., revised and updated (Boulder, CO: Westview Press, 1984), 142–43.

8. Reitz, "Soviet Security," 286.

9. See ibid.

10. Reese, *Soviet Military*, 65–69, 157–59; Alan Bookbinder, Olivia Lichtenstein, and Robert Denton, *Comrades: Portraits of Soviet Life* (New York: Plume, 1985), 48; *The Soviet Union: A Country Study*, "Security Troops of the Committee for State Security," http://lcweb2.loc.gov/frd/cs/sutoc.html. Scroll down to "The Armed Services." Accessed December 2002.

11. Scott and Scott, *Armed Forces*, 19; Alexander V. Gorbatov, *Years Off My Life: The Memoirs of a General of the Soviet Army*, trans. Gordon Clough and Anthony Cash (New York: W.W. Norton, 1964), 108; Hanfmann and Beier, *Six Russian Men*, 41.

12. Mark Von Hagen, "Soviet Soldiers and Officers on the Eve of the German Invasion: Toward a Description of Social Psychology and Political Attitudes," in *The People's War: Responses to World War II in the Soviet Union*, ed. Robert W. Thurston and Bernd Bonwetsch (Urbana: University of Illinois Press, 2000), 195–96.

13. Reese, *Soviet Military*, 112–13; William C. Fuller Jr., "The Great Fatherland War and Late Stalinism: 1941–53," in *Russia: A History*, ed. Gregory L. Freeze (Oxford, England: Oxford University Press, 1997), 333.

14. Reese, *Soviet Military*, 114–18; Von Hagen, "Soviet Soldiers and Officers," 189; Christopher Donnelly, *Red Banner: The Soviet Military System in Peace and War* (Coulsdon, England / Alexandria, VA: Jane's Information Group, 1988), 82–83; Mikhail Heller and Aleksandr Nekrich, *Utopia in Power: The History of the Soviet Union from 1914 to the Present,* trans. Phyllis B. Carlos (New York: Summit Books, 1986), 444.

15. Aleksandr Solzhenitsyn, *The Gulag Archipelago 1918–1956: An Experiment in Literary Investigation,* trans. Thomas P. Whitney, vols. 1–2 (New York: Harper & Row, [1973] 1974), 219.

16. Heller and Nekrich, *Utopia in Power,* 389–90.

17. Heller and Nekrich, *Utopia in Power,* 445.

18. Alexander Werth, *Russia at War 1941–45* (New York: E.P. Dutton, 1964), 619–28, 415–16; Donnelly, *Red Banner,* 81–82; Walter G. Moss, *A History of Russia,* vol. 2, *Since 1855* (New York: McGraw Hill, 1997), 277; *The Road to Berlin* and *The Road to Stalingrad,* PBS documentary, DVD; Heller and Nekrich, *Utopia in Power,* 443–44; Reese, *Soviet Military,* 1243–24; Michael Haynes, "Counting Soviet Deaths in the Great Patriotic War: A Note," *Europe-Asia Studies* 55, no. 2 (2003): 303–9.

19. Catherine Merridale, *Night of Stone: Death and Memory in Twentieth Century Russia* (London: Penguin Books, 2001), 239–40.

20. Aaron Kruger, "Battles over the Baltic," August 23, 2000, review of Igor Kaberov, *Swastika in the Gunsight: Memoirs of a Russian Fighter Pilot, 1941–45,* trans. and abridged by Peter Rule (Phoenix Mill: Sutton Publishing, 1999).

21. Reese, *Soviet Military,* 102; Fuller, "Great Fatherland War," 338; Heller and Nekrich, *Utopia in Power,* 450–52.

22. Reese, *Soviet Military,* 154–55.

23. Herbert Goldhamer, *The Soviet Soldier: Soviet Military Management at the Troop Level* (New York: Crane, Russak and Company, 1975), 4; Steven L. Solnick, *Stealing the State: Control and Collapse in Soviet Institutions* (Cambridge, MA/ London: Harvard University Press, 1999), 176–77; *The Soviet Union: A Country Study,* "Women in the Armed Forces" and "Reserves and Wartime Mobilization."

24. Reese, *Soviet Military,* 56–57.

25. Reese, *Soviet Military,* 57–58, 149; Alexander R. Alexiev and S. Enders Wimbush, "The Ethnic Factor in the Soviet Armed Forces," in *Ethnic Minorities in the Red Army: Asset or Liability?* ed. Alexander Alexiev and S. Enders Wimbush (Boulder, CO: Westview Press, 1988), 130; Kruger, "Battles over the Baltic."

26. Goldhamer, *Soviet Soldier,* 7; Reese, *Soviet Military,* 156; Robert G. Kaiser, *Russia: The People and the Power* (New York: Pocket Books, 1977), 35; Solnick, *Stealing the State,* 177, 187, 196–97.

27. Merle Fainsod, *Smolensk under Soviet Rule* (New York: Vintage Books, 1958), 331–33.

28. Ellen Jones, *Red Army and Society: A Sociology of the Soviet Military* (Boston: Allen & Unwin, 1985), 53–54; Solnick, *Stealing the State,* 177; Reese, *Soviet Military,* 156; Goldhamer, *Soviet Soldier,* 7.

29. Solnick, *Stealing the State,* 177–78, 180, 192–93.

30. Mark Galeotti, *Afghanistan: The Soviet Union's Last War* (London: Frank Cass, 1995), 29–30; Alexiev and Wimbush, "The Ethnic Factor," 130.

31. Reese, *Soviet Military,* 175; Jones, 53; Alexiev and Wimbush, "The Ethnic Factor," 127–30; Galeotti, *Afghanistan,* 30.

32. Bookbinder et al., *Comrades*, 43–49; Reese, *Soviet Military*, 57, 157; Solnick, *Stealing the State*, 183–84.

33. Alexiev and Wimbush, "The Ethnic Factor," 133.

34. Bookbinder et al., *Comrades*, 45–46.

35. For the "Stationing Practices" section, see Alexiev and Wimbush, "The Ethnic Factor," unless otherwise noted.

36. Galeotti, *Afghanistan*, 34.

37. Solnick, *Stealing the State*, 185.

38. Reese, *Soviet Military*, 150–51; Christopher Cerf and Marina Albee, eds., *Small Fires: Letters from the Soviet People to Ogonyok Magazine 1987–1990*, trans. Hans Fenstermacher (New York: Summit Books, 1990), 173; David R. Stone, "Review of *The Soviet Military Experience*," *Slavic Review* 60, no. 3 (Fall 2001): 654; Solnick, *Stealing the State*, 184–85.

39. Solnick, *Stealing the State*, 184; Galeotti, *Afghanistan*, 37.

40. Reese, *Soviet Military*, 150; Cerf and Albee, *Small Fires*, 174, 176–77.

41. Reese, *Soviet Military*, 156–57; Solnick, *Stealing the State*, 196–210.

42. Alexiev and Wimbush, "The Ethnic Factor," 150–53; *The Soviet Union: A Country Study*, "Noncommissioned Officers," http://lcweb2.loc.gov/cgi-bin/query/D?cstudy:1:./temp/~frd_GcYE::

43. Reese, *Soviet Military*, 118–19; Galeotti, *Afghanistan*, 68.

44. Reese, *Soviet Military*, 81–85; Vego, "Soviet Naval," 274.

45. Reese, *Soviet Military*, 147–48; *The Soviet Union—A Country Study*, "Officers," http://lcweb2.loc.gov/cgi-bin/query/r?frd/cstudy:@field[DOCID+su0505]

46. Alexiev and Wimbush, "The Ethnic Factor," 153–55; 156, note 7; 164–65.

47. Reese, *Soviet Military*, 146; Cerf and Albee, *Small Fires*, 174–75.

48. Reese, *Soviet Military*, 17; *The Soviet Union—A Country Study*, "Women in the Armed Forces."

49. Isaac Babel, *The Complete Works of Isaac Babel*, ed. Nathalie Babel, trans. with notes by Peter Constantine (New York: W. W. Norton, 2002), 374–75.

50. Susanne Conze and Beate Fieseler, "Soviet Women as Comrades-in-Arms: A Blind Spot in the History of the War," in *The People's War: Responses to World War II in the Soviet Union*, ed. Robert W. Thurston and Bernd Bonwetsch (Urbana: University of Illinois Press, 2000), 212–15; Reese, *Soviet Military*, 108; Kazimiera J. Cottam, "Soviet Women in Combat during World War II: The Rear Services, Partisans and Political Workers," in *Soviet Armed Forces Review Annual* 5 (1981): 277; *The Soviet Union— A Country Study*, "Women in the Armed Forces."

51. Conze and Fieseler, "Soviet Women as Comrades," 212–13; Cottam, "Soviet Women in Combat," 275, 290; Reese, *Soviet Military*, 109.

52. Cottam, "Soviet Women in Combat," 280–81; Nina Kosterina, *The Diary of Nina Kosterina*, trans. Mirra Ginsburg (New York: Crown Publishers, 1968), 190.

53. Cottam, "Soviet Women in Combat," 275; Conze and Fieseler, "Soviet Women as Comrades," 213, 226; Reese, *Soviet Military*, 108–9.

54. Conze and Fieseler, "Soviet Women as Comrades," 213; John M. Thompson, *A Vision Unfulfilled: Russia and the Soviet Union in the Twentieth Century* (Lexington, MA: D.C. Heath, 1996), 348–49; Cottam, "Soviet Women in Combat," 281, 290; Christine A. White, introduction to *A Dance with Death: Soviet Airwomen in World War II*, edited by Anne Noggle (College Station: Texas A&M University Press, 1994), 3, 12.

55. Conze and Fieseler, "Soviet Women as Comrades," 214, 226–27; Cottam, "Soviet Women in Combat," 291; *The Soviet Union: A Country Study.* "Women in the Armed Forces"; Galeotti, *Afghanistan,* 40–43; Reese, *Soviet Military,* 153–54.

56. Reese, *Soviet Military,* 110–11; Joseph E. Brandesky Jr., *Nikolai Erdman's* The Mandate *and* The Suicide*: Critical Analyses* (Ph.D. dissertation, University of Kansas, 1991), 53; Gorbatov, *Years,* 152; David M. Glantz, *Stumbling Colossus: The Red Army on the Eve of World War* (Lawrence: University Press of Kansas, 1998), 58–59.

57. Alexiev and Wimbush, "The Ethnic Factor," 135; Reese, *Soviet Military,* 110–11.

58. Galeotti, *Afghanistan,* 34–36; Michael Wines, "The Veterans: Russians Recall the 'Giant Mincer' That Was Afghanistan," *New York Times,* September 29, 2001, B7.

59. Galeotti, 35, 37; Reese, *Soviet Military,* 166–72.

60. Galeotti, *Afghanistan,* 67–83; Reese, *Soviet Military,* 166–67; Sarah D. Phillips, "Living in a 'Parallel World': Disability in Post-Soviet Ukraine," University of Illinois at Urbana-Champaign Russian and East European Center, *Center News* 100 (Fall 2002), 1–2.

61. Reese, *Soviet Military,* 175–78, 182.

5

Economy, class structure, food, clothing, and shopping

In the decade before World War I the Russian Empire's economy grew substantially, but then came years of war, revolution, and famine, costing the lives of millions and wiping out that material progress. Factories and transportation systems were heavily damaged or destroyed, and agriculture was in a shambles. Armies clashed across the landscape, confiscating produce and animals, making the routines of sowing and harvesting difficult or impossible. Hordes of civilians deserted cities for the countryside, searching for food. War's upheavals and brutalities combined with the anti–private business attitude of the Bolsheviks forced many private businesses, big and small, to close up, and many businesspeople fled the country. When the Civil War ended in 1921, Lenin introduced the New Economic Policy (NEP) in order to save his Party and rescue the economy by permitting the existence of small private businesses and farming. According to the plan, small private enterprises were to coexist inside the main socialist economy of government-owned businesses, industries, and public services, such as banks, utilities, schools, transportation, communications, and heavy industry. During NEP, which lasted until 1928–1929, the Soviet economy improved and Soviet arts flowered as they never would again.[1]

The 1930s were marked by an extraordinary turn of events in the lives of Soviet citizens. Society was shaken from top to bottom. The Bolsheviks had overthrown the liberal democratic Provisional Government in October 1917 and then crushed a number of political opponents in the Civil War of 1918–1921. Now the question was, what paths should the new state follow? What must it become, what means must be employed, to attain the goal of communism, that utopia of no state at all? Party leaders could not agree on a single path. Lenin might have pointed the way, but he died. NEP was hardly the answer; Lenin himself had characterized it as a temporary retreat, a step backward. It was Stalin and the so-called Stalin Revolution of the 1930s that decided the issue and stamped Soviet society with its fundamental identity. Stalin ended NEP, killed most Bolshevik leaders of 1917 (the "Old Bolsheviks"), replaced Party leaders with his own cult-dictatorship, and greatly expanded police terror and the prison system.

What happened to the economy in the 1930s was no less revolutionary than what happened politically. On the one hand, Stalin's regime swept aside NEP enterprises and private farming quickly and ruthlessly. On the other, it forced peasants into state-owned or supervised collective farms, smashing the considerable opposition without mercy. At the same time, the regime marshaled the vast labor and natural resources of the land into a great industrial complex. There are many ways to gauge the traumatic consequences of these changes on the lives of common people. Millions of persons were swept into the vast Security Police (secret police) prison system (gulag), where they became slaves, the largest single group in the industrial labor force. Millions of peasants died as a result of the government's program of forced collectivization or its deliberate disregard for victims of the great famine of 1932–1933. The number of livestock was also greatly reduced as peasants slaughtered their animals (to eat or sell the meat) rather than turn them over to the collective farm (*kolkhoz*). Such behavior was brutally punished. Still, in the end the state was forced into a compromise, allotting farmers small plots of land for raising food and livestock to consume and sell, in return for working the *kolkhoz*. Sales of produce and animal products from these little allotments remained an important part of the economy throughout the Soviet period, both for peasants and for townspeople who shopped at farmers' markets for high-priced food and homemade goods not available (or of poorer quality) in government stores. Cultivation of small personal land plots became the largest private business in the USSR and the third-largest source of jobs.

By 1940 the country had settled into the official and unofficial economic systems that characterized it to the end. The State Planning Committee (*Gosplan*) designed the nation's economy. Gosplan set short-term (annual) and long-term (five-year) production targets. Except for collective farms, managers and workers were given special awards if they fulfilled or overfulfilled their targets. In I. Grekova's short story "Ladies' Hairdresser," a much-sought-after young hairstylist finds himself under attack by jealous colleagues who say he spends so much time on each of his customers that "the [production] plan suffers." In order to squeeze him out of the salon, someone steals his address book to use as evidence that he has illegal private clients. The hairdresser laments that to fulfill the plan he would have to turn his art "into hack work."

These days, for example, a fashionable hair-do requires bangs. I have to think about those bangs, which takes up more time than a whole permanent. It doesn't fit into the existing system.[2]

The government controlled and subsidized prices for groceries, mass transportation, education, child care, apartment rents, hotel rooms, restaurant meals, and health care and kept these goods and services cheap. However, the problem was always availability and quality. There was little that people wanted and needed that was not chronically in short supply, of poor quality, or both.

Most able-bodied adults worked for the government. By the late 1960s they put in around a 40-hour, five-day workweek and by the mid-1980s had a higher standard of living—in terms of housing, medical care, income, social services, education, and city residency—than in the Stalinist era but still lacked many of the consumer goods and modern conveniences Americans took for granted.[3]

Although all workplaces had a branch of the state trade union system, *profsoiuz*, unions were government-operated paper tigers without the right to call strikes, protest wages or working conditions, demand changes in management, and so forth. Nevertheless, after Stalin, laborers did go on strike when they were enraged about the poor circumstances of their work

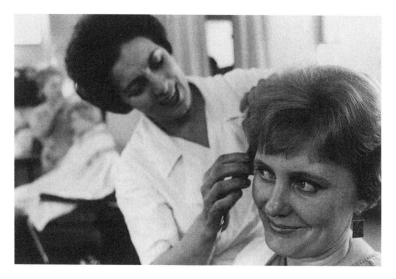

A Soviet woman and her hairdresser, 1967. Reproduced from the Collections of the Library of Congress, Prints & Photographs Division, Look Magazine Photograph Collection, LC-L9-67-3337.

Men working, probably 1959. Reproduced from the Collections of the Library of Congress, LC-U9-2830-328550 #15.

and lives. In 1962, when the government announced a reduction in take-home pay and an increase in the price of meat and butter, workers first in Novocherkassk and then across the country went on strike, demonstrating and rioting, a show of anger not seen since the early days of the revolution. In summer 1989, shortly before they were given the legal right to strike, miners walked out demanding more and better consumer goods, especially food staples. In spring 1991, just before the government collapsed, 300,000 of 1.2 million miners and other workers participated in strikes and slowdowns for two months, demanding not only higher wages and improvement of their miserable, dangerous working conditions, but an end to the Soviet economic system.[4]

Not only free workers contributed to the economy. Prisoner labor was a significant part of the economy until Khrushchev began systematically reducing prison camp populations after his 1956 anti-Stalin speech. Prison slave labor was used for a wide variety of occupations, including highly specialized technical and scientific jobs, but prisoners mainly did work that was particularly dangerous and exhausting, such as mining (the export of prisoner-mined gold was an important source of money for the Stalin government), logging, and construction (of roads, railways, factories, and huge canal projects). Much of this backbreaking slave labor was done in the Arctic Circle, a place to which few people would willingly go. Prisoners contributed heavily to the Soviet war effort during World War II, producing much-needed goods for the military, such as food, cloth for uniforms, and hand grenades.[5]

Although all able-bodied people were promised work, there was unemployment. Farmworkers were often seasonally jobless; new graduates might be unemployed for shorter or longer periods; sometimes people quit to search for something better, perhaps in a place they would rather live. Those who were in political trouble—but not in prison—were very likely to remain jobless, which put them in danger of being arrested as "parasites" or forced to work in very low level jobs.[6]

Small pensions (or no pensions) encouraged many who had reached retirement age to keep working full- or part-time. In the early 1980s, the average pension of 40 rubles, or $53, a month was below the poverty line. To make up the shortfall, retirees often took menial jobs as doormen, watchmen, street vendors, theater cloakroom attendants, street sweepers, elevator operators, and cleaning ladies. Pensioners had a cap on how much they could earn before their pension was docked, but their earnings were low enough and the cap high enough to encourage them to keep working.[7]

Women made up a large portion of the labor force for a variety of reasons. Official Soviet philosophy proclaimed women's right to work outside the home; even without that encouragement, low salaries made it imperative

Street sweepers in Arkhangelsk. They are clearing snow off trolley tracks, around 1920. Reproduced from the Collections of the Library of Congress, LC-USZ62-12262.

for most wives to contribute income, though for many the "double shift" was exhausting. In I. Grekova's novella *The Hotel Manager* the heroine Vera is a colonel's full-time housewife. When she enters the hospital to get an abortion, she has to endure the contempt-plus-envy of her fellow patients in the abortion ward, all of whom are "working women: drivers, stockroom attendants, librarians, guards, even a woman judge."[8]

In Natalya Baranskaya's short story "A Week Like Any Other," the heroine's husband tries to persuade his wife to quit her job so she can be a full-time caretaker of their children and himself, but what Olga wants is to keep her outside job and have her husband take some of the burden of homemaking on himself. "What you're suggesting would kill me," she says;

What about my five years at the university, my degree, my seniority, my research? It's easy enough for you to dismiss it all, but if I didn't work I'd go mad, I'd become impossible to live with.[9]

Unlike collective farmers in the earlier years, who were paid with produce, urban workers were paid mostly in cash; the amount depended on how much social prestige the job had as well as its perceived importance to the economy. Tractor drivers earned more than cowherders, university professors more than street sweepers, star singers more than members of the chorus. However, since resources went mainly into heavy industries and the military, rather than manufacturing consumer goods, such goods were chronically in short supply, and even good wages did not guarantee getting them. People often needed more than cash; they needed time to stand in line, networking connections for help in locating and acquiring products, and goods or skills to barter for what they wanted. Consumer goods were not only scarce, they were also unevenly distributed. Moscow had more than other cities, major cities more than smaller ones, while villages ended up with little or nothing. Besides location, when it came to acquiring scarce commodities social class weighed heavily.[10]

CLASS STRUCTURE

Anyone who was ambitious knew that the main prerequisites for social climbing were Party membership; education; Russian nationality or language ability; and residence in an important Soviet city, preferably Moscow or Leningrad. Full-time Party workers were guaranteed special benefits and social status. The tip of the social pyramid consisted of the highest Party bosses (the secretary-general and other members of the Politburo), then government ministers, the most senior military commanders, top officers in the secret police and militia, diplomats, directors of large enterprises, and top-ranking academics, artists, performers, and scientists.

Perks available to the internationally known painter Ilya Glazunov, a "People's Artist of the USSR," show the kind of luxuries available at the

A worker in a textile factory, Moscow 1955. Reproduced from the Collections of the Library of Congress, Lot 7401 #13.

top: spacious penthouse apartment, expensive Western furniture, valuable paintings and carpets, fine food and drink, and a white Mercedes sedan (few ordinary citizens owned cars, let alone pricey foreign models). Top Party officers had the use of state-owned cars with drivers, private apartments, summer homes, servants, and foreign travel, the most luxury at the least cost to themselves. Retired officers jumped the line for private apartments wherever they wanted to live within the USSR and could select a well-paid second career, especially in security-related fields.

Beneath the military elite were the ambitious middle classes—middle- and lower-level Party officials, white-collar workers, managers, professors and other academics, teachers, doctors, hardworking black marketeers, and so forth. These people lived very well in comparison to the classes below them and their parents' and grandparents' generations, and they knew it. They were also conscious of the special privileges accorded to the classes above them and aimed for a piece of that pie, if not for themselves, then for their children. However, a "middle class" standard of living in the Soviet Union was much lower than that in other developed countries. Lower-level urban workers were the class below the middle class. Except for prisoners, peasants—agricultural workers on collective farms—were the lowest social class. Farmworkers on state farms were regarded as "workers" rather than "peasants," which placed them a cut above peasants on the social ladder.[11]

A shoeshine woman in a Caucasus railway station cleaning and polishing the
boots of a Soviet officer in the 1950s. Reproduced from the Collections of the
Library of Congress, LC-USZ62-100130, Lot 6488.

Although the Bolsheviks had declared the Soviet Union a state by and
for workers and peasants, in reality, "If you had a grandmother or a
grandfather who came from a village…you didn't talk about it. You hid
them, so to speak." The situation had been quite different in the 1920s and
30s, when (the world having been turned upside down), being a member
of the nobility, a businessperson, an officer of the tsar's armed forces, a
wealthy peasant, or a priest could cost a person liberty or even life itself.
Such people often fled into the lower classes. Their children took factory
jobs to qualify for higher education, to rebel against their parents, or simply because they were proud to be known as "proletarians."[12]

Since the government's system of distributing food, clothing, and other
goods and services, from education to transportation to health care and
anything else, largely ignored the countryside and small towns, big-city
residency was an important status symbol for people of all classes.
Moscow conferred the biggest bragging rights because it was the seat of
government and center of power. Muscovites as a group were wealthier;
more sophisticated; and better clothed, fed, and educated than residents
of any other Soviet city, including Leningrad. In the early 1980s about a
million visitors came to Moscow every day for shopping.[13]

The upper classes lived in clean, well-maintained apartment buildings, in contrast to littered working-class buildings with their smelly stairwells. It was usual for a building in an upper-class area to have a vigilant retiree sitting in a glassed-in booth just inside the entrance. These elderly gate-keepers recognized all the residents and kept track of everyone's comings and goings. Kiril, whose mother was a cleaning lady and father a night watchman, and who passed the entrance exam to an elite Moscow "special" high school, quickly discovered the social gulf separating him from his wealthy classmates. Unlike his family, his friends had VCRs, color TVs, imported furniture, and fashionably faded jeans and other imported clothing, and they ate foods not available to the general public, much less cleaning ladies. "I looked like a village bumpkin in my Russian-made clothes," Kiril complained. "I felt ashamed and uncomfortable when [my friends and I] were together."[14]

At home and at work men were the privileged class. A working woman might spend as much as two hours a day, every day, searching for goods and standing in lines, and return home to do the household chores. Olga, the young working mother in Baranskaya's story, copes with her professional and household responsibilities. On a typical weekday evening, laden with heavy shopping bags, she rushes home (by overcrowded subway and bus) to her Moscow apartment, anxious about whether her husband has remembered to feed the children—he hasn't! The kids have been munching bread while her husband, Dima, reads a technical journal. In a whirl of activity, Olga (who has been going nonstop since 6 A.M.) lights the stove and puts on potatoes, water, milk, and cutlets. This will be her first meal because she did not have time to eat breakfast or lunch. After supper Olga bathes the children and puts them to bed. It is 9 P.M. While Dima continues to read and sip tea, Olga washes dishes, then her children's clothing and handkerchiefs. Then she mends her son's tights and gets the children's clothing and supplies ready for the next morning. Her husband brings her his coat so she can sew on a button. After that "the sweeping still has to be done, and the rubbish taken out. The last is Dima's job." A popular joke illustrated Soviet women's second-class citizenship. A shipwrecked Russian couple are cast away on a deserted island. When after many months rescuers finally arrive, only the man is found, snoozing in the sun. "Where is your wife?" the rescuers ask him. "The masses are working in the fields," he replies. To their credit, Russian husbands were often the family fixers, repairing household items that went on the blink, including the car and plumbing, for families that had those items.[15]

SHOPPING

Shopping was an unrelenting concern of most people's daily lives. Because there were constant shortages of everything except bread and vodka, people did not so much shop as forage for food and other common household purchases. As a Soviet woman pointed out to Hedrick Smith, long lines were the norm for just about anything, including "a decent purse, a nice writing table, a typewriter, a good woman's bra,"

—not a floppy, ugly Soviet one with no support and no adjustments, made for big-bosomed country girls. But a Czech bra or a Polish one, white and pretty instead of blue and baggy with rose buds.[16]

Ordinarily people had to stand in line three times for each purchase in a small store or department of a larger store: the first time, to view the product and find out the cost, then to pay and get a receipt, and finally to be handed the item. However, seasoned shoppers knew ways to shortcut the process. In a slow-moving line one asked the person behind to hold his or her place, then queued up in a faster-moving line. The placeholder had an obligation to help defend your right of return against the onslaughts of anxious and irritated shoppers farther back in line. It was not uncommon for people to wait in line for hours, during which time the items they had been waiting for were sold out. By the 1980s, self-service food stores with express checkouts were slowly appearing in city centers and suburbs, but the three-line system still predominated for groceries and many other goods.[17]

It was difficult or impossible to predict when particular items would suddenly appear in the markets or just as suddenly disappear for a long time, so people left home in the morning with a good supply of cash, and containers tucked inside a briefcase (the shopping luggage of choice for men) or net bags (the latter were called *avoski*, from *avos*, "perhaps," and were carried by women), or plastic bags, just in case something good (beef, say, or Yugoslav toothpaste) suddenly appeared for sale. When that happened people tried to gather as much of the product as they could, for their immediate family, for friends and relatives, for stockpiling, and for barter. Villagers periodically traveled to cities on the chance of a shopping opportunity.[18]

Goods not available in shops might suddenly pop up in small kiosks scattered around cities. City shoppers, always alert, checked regularly, knew which outlets were most likely to offer the best goods or hard-to-find fresh fruit and vegetables, picked up tips from friends and coworkers, and reacted quickly to the sight of a line forming, a signal that something scarce might be for sale. The queue could also mean only one clerk was working and the wait would be long. The usual practice was to quickly grab a place in line and only then inquire what was for sale. For big-ticket items like rugs or cars, people might queue for some 18 hours, outdoors in freezing weather, merely to get their names on a list, for delivery a year or more later.[19]

Patience to queue up for long periods was not the only prerequisite to successful shopping. As often as not, people got everything from food to theater tickets "under the counter." Those whose jobs gave them access to consumer and other products regularly and illegally skimmed off a certain amount for personal use. For example, a good piece of pork was likely to find its way onto the butcher's family table, and another piece might quietly change hands at the back door of the butcher shop in payment for skilled carpentry. Factory workers routinely helped themselves to plant equipment—whatever they could carry out in their pockets or under their arms. Agricultural workers stole food and materials from state and collective farms. Milkmaids concealed the theft of milk by watering down what remained, a prelude to further dilutions when the milk reached stores.[20]

Material goods were not the only things in short supply. It was extremely difficult for ordinary people to get tickets to the best cultural events, particularly in Moscow, the cultural center. The hottest tickets were reserved for foreign tourists, high Party officials, and VIPs from abroad. Others needed, besides the price of the ticket, special connections, such as a carefully cultivated relationship with the box office ticket seller, and the means to return the favor in some way.[21]

The *rynok,* or peasant market, was one alternative to state outlets. A *rynok* might be outdoors or inside long, low buildings that could be closed up in winter. Peasants, sometimes entire collective farms, rented stalls for selling their produce. Unlike the fixed low prices at state stores, peasants could set their own prices. Produce from the *rynok* tended to be smaller, less uniform, less glossy, but more flavorful than American produce. Besides food, sellers offered a host of items, from flowers to handcrafted beeswax candles and wooden spoons. Everyone, including grandmothers and teenagers, lined up at a "yellow cylinder that resembled…a child's toy locomotive enlarged" that dispensed *kvas,* a sour beer made by pouring water over rye bread and waiting for the bread to ferment.[22]

Some cities had special stores called *beryozki* (singular, *beryozka*) where foreign tourists, diplomats, foreign correspondents, and a few privileged Soviets with Western money could shop. Here, people did not have to wait in line to buy scarce goods. Unlike ordinary state shops, *beryozki* were pleasant: decorated, carpeted, clean, well-lighted, heated in winter, with a variety of attractive goods artfully arranged, and staffed by people who appeared to be friendly. One such Moscow store had two rooms, a larger one for European and American beer, wine, liquor, cigarettes, and candy and a smaller one for imported canned goods and first-quality meat, dairy products, and produce. *Beryozka* wares were better and cheaper than those in peasant markets or state shops—if those outlets carried such things at all. One Moscow *beryozka* was located in a grimy, lower-class industrial section of the city. The shabbily dressed working people who passed the shop carrying their homely, hard-won purchases paused in front of its alluringly curtained-off window before trudging on their way. Sometimes such special stores had purposely misleading signs at their entrances, such as "Bureau of Passes." If the unprivileged tried to enter, a guard stopped them.[23]

A day at the collective farm market, summer 1959, Sverdlovsk. Unloading bags of produce. Reproduced from the Collections of the Library of Congress, LC-U9-2837-328550 #4.

A day at the collective farm market, summer 1959, Sverdlovsk. Outside the central collective farm market. Reproduced from the Collections of the Library of Congress, LC-U9-2837-328550 #11.

A day at the collective farm market, summer 1959, Sverdlovsk. Shopping. Note how the grapes are placed in paper cones. Reproduced from the Collections of the Library of Congress, LC-U9-2837-328550 #28.

A day at the collective farm market, summer 1959, Sverdlovsk. Buying tomatoes. Reproduced from the Collections of the Library of Congress, LC-U9-2837-328550 #21.

In contrast, public access shops were grimy, unheated, dimly lit, undecorated, with sales clerks who were rude if not downright hostile. In a butcher shop in Tashkent, an elderly woman who had waited in a long, slow-moving line finally reached the counter. Then she had to cool her heels while the butcher conversed with his friend. When she asked to be waited on, the butcher replied, "Next, I suppose you'll want me to cram it in your mouth for you." Goods in high demand were first skimmed by employees and what was left sold out quickly. Less attractive wares decayed or gathered dust on shelves until they were thrown out. The story circulated of a would-be customer who entered what he thought was a cheese store, but was told, "This is the store that doesn't have meat. The store that doesn't have cheese is next door."[24]

Since convenience foods common in the West, such as mixes and prepared frozen and canned food, were scarce or unavailable, home cooks made meal ingredients from scratch, including mayonnaise and fruit and vegetable preserves. The quality and quantity of home cooking depended on availability of ingredients, personal connections, and amount of time the housewife could spare for cooking. For special occasions Russians were fond of long-drawn-out feasting and drinking at home or in one of the few decent public restaurants. At a home party, guests arrived in the early evening or late afternoon, sat around the table dipping into the many courses, celebrating late into the night and often into the next day or days. A typical multicourse feast would usually start with appetizers (*zakuski*), which might include red and black caviar on dense brown bread, smoked salmon, pickled or marinated mushrooms, salted herring, herring salad with pickled beets, salami, pickled cucumbers, beet salad, and soups (perhaps clear red beet *borsch* or cabbage *shchi*), another course, then the main meal and dessert. For drinks there would be freely flowing vodka along with other alcoholic drinks such as cognac, wine, and Soviet champagne (which was sweet rather than dry), with sweetened hot tea accompanying the dessert course. Much time and money were spent hunting and gathering ingredients and then preparing such feasts. People with little money or few or no shopping connections hosted suppers as lavish as they could manage—saving up rubles and food and depending on friends and relatives to contribute to the meal.[25]

FOOD AND SOCIAL CLASS

The top elite, including leaders in the arts, had special restaurants open only to members, their families, and guests. These restaurants, unlike public ones, provided well-prepared luxury food (e.g., steak, caviar, and shellfish); attentive, friendly service complete with clean tablecloths; and also carry-out privileges: members could walk into the kitchen and buy nicely prewrapped raw meat or telephone ahead to have such items ready for pickup. The top elite, such as KGB officers with the rank of captain and above, had their phone orders boxed and delivered weekly to their homes or desks by an unmarked van. The higher the social class, the easier it was to get good food at bargain prices. In his satirical novel *The Master and Margarita,* Mikhail Bulgakov provided a glimpse of the closed world of Soviet privilege in the form of the Moscow Union of Soviet Writers, housed in a beautiful mansion. Outsiders could only turn green with envy at its restaurant, not only because it occupied two fantastically decorated rooms, had tables adorned with silk-shawl-draped lamps, and was closed to ordinary folks, but above all because its delicious food "was served at the most moderate, most reasonable prices."[26]

The lower urban social classes—office and factory workers—often had access to workplace canteens, from which they could order groceries weekly. The quality of canteen food depended on how valued the particular workplace was. Employees who manufactured computers or military weapons had better-stocked canteens than workers in the legal system or agriculture bureaucracy, for example. A common way for workers at a large enterprise to order food through their workplace was for small groups of employees each to appoint a woman member to take their orders, which she then transmitted to the enterprise's purchasing officer, who in turn had access to food stocks not available in public grocery stores. Weekly notices were posted listing what foods were available that week, but employees could not simply pick and choose what they wanted. Instead, they had to buy according to prearranged lists. Generally each list contained at least one scarce item plus several less enticing ones. People chose lists that contained something they desired, resigning themselves to buying the unwanted add-ons. In this way some workers enjoyed a slight privilege over those who depended entirely on street shopping, and the government got rid of its surplus merchandise. A former employee in a Moscow architecture institute told how one time she bought a list with scarce canned coffee, two pounds of sugar, a box of stale cookies, and a box of chocolates. "Well, I didn't want the cookies or the chocolates, but I ordered the list anyway to get the coffee." As it turned out, by the time lower-level workers got their orders, there was no more coffee, so she had to wait until the following week and order the list again. Another time she ordered a list heavy on meat and vegetables, most of which was nearly inedible, but there was some good sausage and beef, so she was happy with her purchases. Money wasted on unwanted or moldy list items was the price people paid for not having to stand in line for the much-desired coffee and fresh beef. Within each workplace, the higher the official, the better the food available to that person and the easier it was to obtain.[27]

For unprivileged Muscovites, Moscow state shops in the summer of 1978 had a sufficient supply of bread, cheese, butter, eggs, sugar, cookies, jars of small pickled cucumbers (gherkins), canned fish, and canned vegetables. Cabbages were just about the only fresh vegetable regularly available; potatoes and carrots occasionally showed up but were often decomposing by the time they reached store shelves. Tiny onions appeared once in a while. Small green apples were the only fresh fruit available. People could buy tomatoes in the *rynok,* along with a limited selection of other fruits and vegetables, at high prices. It was difficult to find other groceries. "Fresh" milk was often sour, watered down, or both; cheap sausage and chicken were scarce; and whatever was to be had in butcher shops was doled out in small chunks. In the farmers' market lumps of pork fat sold for twice the state price.[28]

In "A Week Like Any Other" Olga's women colleagues in a research institute take turns shopping for themselves and each other. The day's designated shopper takes her lunch break from two o'clock to three o'clock when stores are less crowded. Olga dreads it when the chore falls on her, not only because she has to lug heavy bags, but other shoppers resent that she is buying in bulk. "Opening a café, are you?" one of the women in line yells at her. Nevertheless it was common for people to buy for others whenever something good suddenly appeared. Good shoppers carried in their heads an impressive data bank of friends' and relatives' color preferences and shoe, clothing, and underwear sizes.[29]

FOOD SUPPLIES DURING WORLD WAR II

Goods and services were rationed whether or not ration tokens were handed out. Nevertheless, there were periods when rationing was formalized by allotting coupons that theoretically entitled—and limited—people to a certain amount of food and other consumer goods. Food had been rationed from 1918 to 1923 as well as during forced collectivization of farmland in the 1930s. When food shortages became severe during World War II the government rationed basic foods such as milk, butter, and meat (including fish and fish products, eggs, flour, sugar, tea, and bread), but supplies fell short of even the small amounts allotted. Most peasants were expected to live on their own produce, so they did not get ration coupons. Rural non-farmworkers and peasants whose farms grew nonfood crops had a separate rationing system. Even though the military was generally allotted more and better food than civilians, common soldiers often went hungry.[30]

The amount, variety, and quality of rationed groceries people were entitled to depended on the kind of work they did. Although rationing was supposed to insure that everyone got the necessary amount of the five food groups, bread was often the only fare actually available; obtaining other rationed provisions "became a perpetual crap shoot." Workers and their families had the right to a given amount of meat per month—if they could locate it. In apportioning rationed food, authorities divided the population into four categories, with quantities apportioned in descending order from one to four: (1) blue-collar workers, workers in war-related industries, scientists, and technicians; (2) white-collar workers; (3) dependents of the preceding categories; and (4) children.

It was common for the state to make sudden unannounced changes in the rations, depending on what and how much was available at the time.

Nor were food allotments the same around the country, although officially they were supposed to be. For example, workers in Murmansk were allocated more, probably because of the severely cold Siberian climate and lack of access to farmers' markets, while in other cities rations fell below official norms, as scarcity increased. When food allotments fell, foreign and Soviet journalists were not allowed to write about it. In Novosibirsk in 1942, the monthly bread ration for blue- and white-collar workers fell from 800 grams to 400, and from 400 to 300 for dependents, while the meat ration fell from 1,800 to 1,200 grams for white-collar workers. A former resident of Kuibyshev recalled that during the winter of 1941–1942, people who gave blood for wounded soldiers were rewarded with ration cards, money, and a three-course meal right after the donation. Because rationed nourishment was insufficient and undependable, people made up the shortfall by buying from the private peasants' markets, bartering possessions and services for food, and using whatever other legal and illegal strategies got them the sustenance they and their families needed. Because the German army besieged Leningrad for 28 months during 1941 and 1942, and the government had not made adequate preparations for that possibility, all supplies were cut off for a time, and Leningraders froze and starved. The rationing system meant little when there was hardly any food to distribute. People ate wild grasses and herbs, cats, dogs, rats, mice, pigeons, bulbs from the botanical gardens, and even each other.

I saw dead people on the street, frozen, without parts of their bodies. I once saw a man walking on the street with a part of a body sticking out of his pocket. People went crazy. The hunger made people crazy.[31]

When Elena Kochina took her starving daughter to a Leningrad clinic in January 1942 a nurse warned her not to "leave the child unattended" because "We've had cases of children being kidnapped." All open spaces in and near the city were used for planting vegetables, but such efforts hardly dented people's need for food. Perhaps as many as 40 percent of the city's population died of disease, starvation, and cold during the German blockade.[32]

In her diary entry for January 2, 1942, Kochina described her yearning for bread. "Bread! Soft, fragrant, with a crunchy crust. The thought of it drives us crazy."

It tastes better than chocolate, it tastes better than cakes, it tastes better than sweet rolls. We don't want anything the way we want bread.[33]

CLOTHING

Foreigners were easily spotted by the superior quality and style of their clothing. Shoes were a dead giveaway, as illustrated in an episode of the movie *East-West* when the stylishly dressed heroine, trying to escape the USSR, is almost nabbed by Russian guards who notice her homely shoes. Because Soviet-made clothing lagged behind Western fashions; lacked variety in colors, styles, and sizes; and was often of poor quality, anyone with a sewing machine and the skill to use it was kept busy. Of course people also needed connections for acquiring good, attractive fabric. Women prized Western fashion magazines like *Vogue* for the sheer pleasure of browsing through their pages, but also because skilled home seamstresses could study the photos and replicate the styles on their machines. Another strategy for acquiring clothes was to approach a foreigner in the street and offer to buy them off her back. "One woman...drew me aside in a bus line," Andrea Lee recalled, "and asked me in a low voice what I would take for my sweater."

"Why do you want it?" I asked. "It's not pretty." "It's wool," she said, "We used to have wool, but it's [scarce] now."[34]

CARS AND OTHER DURABLE GOODS

From about the 1960s, city folk began acquiring such luxuries as small refrigerators, sewing machines, radios, TVs, stereo systems, tape recorders, vacuum cleaners, washing machines, and cars. In 1965, about one-fourth of all families had a television set, one-fifth a washing machine, and one-tenth a refrigerator. By 1989 a large majority of urban and rural families had TV, about three-fourths had washing machines and refrigerators or freezers, according to a Soviet survey. By then it was also common among most (non–collective farm) families to own vacuum cleaners, sewing machines, and tape recorders; one-fifth of non–collective farm families had their own car. But clothes dryers, dishwashers, and microwaves were rare, and even appliances that could be acquired new were antiquated from the start. A standard 1970s model Soviet-made washing machine held only three or four pounds of laundry and had no spin-dry, and all cycles had to be started manually; refrigerators were tiny compared to foreign ones, and few had freezer compartments. At the end of the Soviet era, many people were still using their apartment balconies as places to dry laundry and cool perishable food. Those without balconies dried laundry on inside lines and hung their groceries outside a window in a net bag. Even when they had appliances and TVs most country people in 1980 still lived without paved roads, indoor plumbing, central heat, or telephones.[35]

FINANCIAL TRANSACTIONS: GETTING AND SPENDING

In an economy of empty stores and years-long waiting lists for cars, apartments, and major appliances, people needed more than just rubles to buy things. They needed social status and *blat* as well as money. Soviets without Western liquor, wine, chocolate, cigarettes, and the like for bribing hotel managers would have to sleep elsewhere. Those at the pinnacle of society had the least need for money because the state handed them the necessities of life and so much more. People at the very top had government cars and drivers; spacious centrally located subsidized private apartments; access to the best free health care; summer homes; and state-subsidized food, clothing, and travel.

Particularly in rural areas, people needed more than money to get material goods. A *kolkhoznik* loaded with rubles from successful sales of vegetables from his plot would need special influence beyond rubles to move to the head of the waiting list for a telephone or car, ahead of the farm manager's father-in-law and daughter, for example. People who volunteered to work in Siberia for a few years automatically moved to the head of such lists when they returned from their stints. Most people knew nothing of credit cards, and checking accounts were slowly coming into use only toward the end of the Soviet era, for a few of the privileged. Such checks, however, were not widely used, were good only in shops for purchases of 200 or more rubles, and could not be used for paying bills, and most salesclerks, not knowing what they were, would not accept them. Nevertheless, as an upper-middle-class Moscow woman proclaimed, showing off her checkbook, "We do have them, and so we do have what you have in the West." A much more powerful substitute currency was the "certificate ruble"—government-issued documents the state gave to Soviet citizens in return for their Western money, which it was illegal to own. One could use certificate rubles to shop in a *beryozka*. Sometimes people received hard currency from friends or relatives abroad, but usually those who owned that kind of valuable cash were privileged elites such as scientists and other scholars granted the opportunity to travel to the West to earn salaries there. In the late 70s, those who obediently and legally exchanged their dollars for certificate rubles at a Soviet bank received an exchange rate of one to one, minus tax. Those who exchanged their dollars on the black market got about 20 rubles for each dollar. Soviet citizens were legally barred from trading rubles for foreign currency, though many did.[36]

PRIVATE ENTERPRISE AND PRIVATE PROPERTY

Various kinds of private enterprise and private property were legal, but the state owned all land, mineral rights, mass transportation systems, and factories. People were not supposed to be middlemen, but *kolkhozniki* would sometimes go to the city, load up on goods not available on the *kolkhoz,* and then return and illegally resell at a higher price to the folks back home. By the same token it was illegal to buy an apartment in order to rent it for extra income. But as with other forbidden activities, people went ahead with their profit-making enterprises while officials looked the other way, often extending a hand for a bribe. There were fine lines between legal and illegal transactions. While it was against the law to be a middleman, people were allowed to own and sell their personal property, things like clothing and household goods, including radios, TVs, and sound systems as well as hand tools, cars, apartments, and houses. Many who could afford them bought jewelry, paintings, and rare books as investments. Other private financial assets ranged from lottery tickets to savings accounts (with a state-owned bank). Although people legally received interest on savings accounts, it was generally illegal to receive income from one's property, although "under certain circumstances," people could take money for subletting an apartment or renting a room to a student. It was legal to lend a friend money but illegal to charge interest, which is not to say that it was not done.

Just as Eskimos have many words to describe snow, Soviets had a rich vocabulary for illegal and semilegal transactions. Things could be gotten, for example, *nalevo* (on the left). *Nalevo* was the most general phrase and applied to a wide range of strategies for avoiding waiting in line or doing without. Within that range, people might buy a rug, say, *po znakomstvu* (through a contact, say, from a friend who worked in a rug factory, a transaction "more improper than illegal"). *Po znakomstvu* often did not involve any money changing hands; rather, recipients knew their contact expected a return favor sometime in the future. *Po blaty* (through pull) had overtones of bribery or knowing someone important, or both; *Na chernom rynke* (on the black market) implied an illegal transaction and usually involved goods gotten from an entrepreneur looking to make a profit. The American writer Andrea Lee met a Moscow black marketeer, Olga, who specialized in buying and selling foreigners' clothing and doodads. Olga wheeled and dealed mainly in jeans—the "money crop" of the Soviet black market—and currency, with probably a bit of drug dealing on the side. Having changed foreigners' dollars to rubles on the black market she then took the dollars to *beryozki* and bought all manner of goods not available in Soviet stores (such as furs, fashionable shoes, jewelry, and radios), which she sold at a big markup to Russians. She also sold antiques such as icons and samovars (large urns for brewing and serving tea) to foreigners. Although her business was risky, Olga seemed impervious to prosecution, perhaps because she was the daughter of a high official; some suspected a secret police connection. If Olga stayed in the black market business into the mid-1980s, she probably would have had a new business expense—a hefty monthly payment to a "protection" racketeer. In the liberalized business atmosphere of the later 1980s, gangsters popped up to prey on legal and illegal business, large and small. Those who did not pay up were in danger of being murdered.

People legally sold furniture and various personal property on commission in state-owned secondhand stores, swapped apartments, advertised property and apartments for sale or swap on street bulletin boards (some set up by the state, others informally tacked onto posts or buildings), or advertised in newspapers. Many people privately sold their skills and labor, such as hairstyling, handcrafting, or various kinds of repair work or worked privately in semiskilled and unskilled jobs: as nannies, laundresses, or housemaid-cooks. For women, such unskilled household jobs were a way to escape the village and enter city life. People who worked for the state and moonlighted were within the law as long as they did private work on their own time.[37]

GRANDPARENTS' CONTRIBUTION TO THE ECONOMY

Because of extreme housing scarcity in cities and household traditions in the country, one or two grandparents often lived with their children and grandchildren. Whether or not they all lived under the same roof, grandparents were important contributors to the economic well-being of their country and family. If they worked after retirement, they were likely to contribute their pension money and wages to help pay household expenses. Even if they went into full-time "retirement," however, they often were indispensable helpers to their children's households. Retired grandparents traditionally helped working daughters and daughters-in-law survive by tending grandchildren, cooking, cleaning house, gardening, or simply searching and waiting in line for groceries and other consumer goods. The latter could easily be a full-time job in itself. During the Stalin terrors grandparents were often the only ones left to raise their grandchildren. In the later Soviet period, however, many middle-aged women were refusing the traditional *babushka* role of nurturing a second family—they wanted a fulfilling life of their own.

NOTES

1. James R. Millar, *The ABCs of Soviet Socialism* (Urbana: University of Illinois Press, 1981), 3, 5, 7–8, 21–24, 35, 108–10; William Moskoff, *The Bread of Affliction: The Food Supply in the USSR during World War II* (Cambridge, England: Cambridge University Press, 1990), 135–51.

2. I. Grekova, "Ladies' Hairdresser," in *Russian Women: Two Stories*, trans. Michel Petrov (San Diego: Harcourt, Brace, Jovanovich, 1983), 55.

3. Walter G. Moss, *A History of Russia*, vol. 2, *Since 1855* (New York: McGraw-Hill, 1997), 433, 444; Wolfgang Teckenberg, "Consumer Goods and Services: Contemporary Problems and Their Impact on the Quality of Life in the Soviet Union," in *Quality of Life in the Soviet Union*, ed. Horst Herlemann (Boulder, CO: Westview Press, 1987), 34.

4. David Remnick, *Lenin's Tomb: The Last Days of the Soviet Empire* (New York: Vintage Books, 1994), 414–17; M.K. Dziewanowski, *A History of the Soviet Union and Its Aftermath*, 5th ed. (Upper Saddle River, NJ: Prentice Hall, 1997), 327; Lois Fisher, *Survival in Russia: Chaos and Hope in Everyday Life* (Boulder, CO: Westview Press, 1993), 165–75; Moss, *History of Russia*, 444.

5. Aleksandr Solzhenitsyn, *The First Circle,* trans. Thomas P. Whitney (New York: Harper & Row, 1968); J. Otto Pohl, *The Stalinist Penal System* (Jefferson, NC: McFarland, 1997), 39–46; Millar, *ABCs,* 117.

6. Millar, *ABCs,* 107.

7. Hedrick Smith, *The Russians,* rev. ed. (New York: Ballantine Books, 1984), 91.

8. Millar, *ABCs,* 104–05, Grekova, *Russian Women,* 110–11.

9. Natalya Baranskaya, *A Week Like Any Other: Novellas and Stories,* trans. Pieta Monks (Seattle, WA: Seal Press, 1990), 60.

10. Millar, *ABCs,* 93.

11. David Willis, *Klass: How Russians Really Live* (New York: Avon Books, 1987), 11–16; Raymond E. Zickel, ed., *Soviet Union: A Country Study,* 2nd ed. (Washington, DC: Library of Congress, Federal Research Division, 1991), 211–12, 214–16.

12. Willis, *Klass,* 67; Sheila Fitzpatrick, "The Problem of Class Identity in NEP Society," in *Russia in the Era of NEP: Explorations in Soviet Society and Culture,* ed. Sheila Fitzpatrick, Alexander Rabinowitch, and Richard Stites (Bloomington: Indiana University Press, 1991), 12–33.

13. Millar, *ABCs,* 99; Moss, *History of Russia,* 441.

14. Fisher, *Survival in Russia,* 10–11.

15. Moss, *History of Russia,* 441; Baranskaya, 23–24.

16. Smith, The *Russians,* 84–85.

17. Smith, *The Russians,* 85–86.

18. Millar, *ABCs,* 100–01; Smith, *The Russians,* 79–80.

19. Mervyn Matthews, *Poverty in the Soviet Union: The Lifestyles of the Underprivileged in Recent Years* (Cambridge, England: Cambridge University Press, 1986), 60; Smith, *The Russians,* 83.

20. David Satter, *Age of Delirium: The Decline and Fall of the Soviet Union* (New York: Alfred A. Knopf, 1996), 176–77, 188.

21. Millar, *ABCs,* 94.

22. Andrea Lee, *Russian Journal* (New York: Vintage Books, 1984), 17–19; Millar, *ABCs,* 94.

23. Willis, *Klass,* 27; Lee, *Russian Journal,* 163–64.

24. Smith, *The Russians,* 87.

25. Moss, *History of Russia,* 447; Dora O'Brien, *From Moscow: Living and Teaching among the Russians in the 1990s* (Nottingham, England: Bramcote Press, 2000), 45; Smith, *The Russians,* 160; Sydney Schultze, *Culture and Customs of Russia* (Westport, CT: Greenwood Press, 2000), 68–73.

26. Willis, *Klass,* 2–3, 6–7, 19–35; Mikhail Bulgakov, *The Master and Margarita,* trans. Mirra Ginsburg (New York: Grove Weidenfeld, 1967), 61.

27. Willis, *Klass,* 21–23.

28. Matthews, *Poverty,* 60.

29. Baranskaya, 14; Smith, *The Russians,* 80–81.

30. Alena V. Ledeneva, *Russia's Economy of Favours: Blat, Networking, and Informal Exchange* (Cambridge, England: Cambridge University Press, 1998), 90–94; Moskoff, *Bread,* 136–37.

31. Moskoff, *Bread,* 197.

32. Moskoff, *Bread,* 136–42, 148–50, 185–97; Elena I. Kochina, *Blockade Diary,* trans. Samuel C. Ramer (Ann Arbor, Michigan: Ardis, 1990), 72.

    33. Kochina, 67–68.
    34. Lee, *Russian Journal*, 22.
    35. Moss, *History of Russia*, 434–35, 445; Smith, *The Russians*, 79.
    36. Willis, *Klass*, 90–95, 97–100.
    37. Millar, *ABCs*, 88–90, 96, 99; Lee, *Russian Journal*, 23, Fisher, *Survival in Russia*, 7–26.

6

Rural Life

HISTORICAL CONTEXT

Rural life in the Soviet Union was extremely difficult. The seasonal rhythm of farmwork was, of course, interrupted by good times and joyous occasions, but the peasant (*krest'ianin* or *muzhik*) was among the hardest working and least rewarded of citizens and was especially vulnerable to natural and human-made disasters. In the perilous so-called Thirty Years War of the twentieth century (1914–1945) peasants of the Russian Empire and Soviet Union suffered great calamities. After World War II peasants were no longer victimized by such great misfortunes but continued to be treated as second-class citizens. Soviet leaders talked about the immense importance of agriculture and the need to increase food production, but industry and defense were always first in line for state support. Large investments, when they came, were sometimes poured into ill-conceived giant projects, like plowing up vast tracts of arid grassland. Meanwhile, the life and work of peasants continued to be characterized, as it had been in the past, by low productivity and a poor standard of living.

The late tsarist and early Soviet years brought extraordinary changes to village life. But much remained the same. Emancipation of the serfs (1861 and 1864) did not entirely lift peasants from servile status, nor did economic growth prevent famines. Though emancipation freed former serfs from the reign of their landlords, they were still tied to the village commune (*mir*) and collectively responsible for its debts and taxes and subject to its often outmoded methods, especially the farming of multiple strips of

Sowing spring barley at the Lenin Collective Farm, Krasnodar Region, 1955.
Reproduced from the Collections of the Library of Congress, LC-USZ62 / 328551 /
098691.

land. Because emancipation allotments were inadequate for, or barely met,
their needs, freedmen sometimes had to work the fields of their former
masters, as well as their own. Peasants did manage to purchase additional
land, but this was largely offset by two circumstances: rapid growth in the
number of peasants and their continued use of inefficient ways of farming.

During the relatively prosperous years between the revolution of 1905
and World War I, Peter Stolypin (prime minister, 1906–1911) began a program to change rural life fundamentally, vigorously promoting private
individual ownership of farmland at the expense of the commune. As a
result, nearly half the heads of peasant households owned their land by
1916. However, the Stolypin reforms were interrupted and largely undone
by war and revolution. In 1917–1918 what remained of the old estates,
much public land, and many of the recently enlarged private holdings of
better-off peasants was taken over, often violently, by the mass of mainly
poor peasants. The result was a substantial increase in peasant land and a
leveling of peasant wealth in terms of livestock and acreage per household. There were substantially fewer peasants who had no land or animals
and fewer peasants with large farms. Various types of farms took shape,
ranging from the private family farm (*khutor*) to the completely socialized
collective (*kommuna*) in which peasants were housed and ate together and

land, animals, tools, crops, and buildings were held in common. Most numerous, by far, were farms joined together in the old traditional *mir* where the village community periodically reallocated land so as to maintain an even distribution based on the number and size of households.[1]

The gains made by peasants in the tumultuous months following the overthrow of monarchy (March 1917) represent a short-lived acquaintance with good fortune, followed as these gains were by the grinding civil war of 1918–1921 and great famine of 1921–1922. In the civil war both Reds (Bolsheviks) and Whites (anti-Bolsheviks) expropriated grain from peasants, but the Reds devised an especially systematic and brutal method that set poor and better-off peasants, called kulaks *(kulaki,* singular: *kulak)* against each other and included armed expropriation teams of Party-led workers. In the Red- and White-controlled zones peasants sharply reduced their production of grain since it was likely to be taken with little or no payment. Sometimes all the peasant's grain was taken, even seed for

Dinner in a Ukrainian peasant house, 1950s. The family is sitting down to an evening meal of soup and bread. The photographer gave this family strips of film to tie back their window curtains. Reproduced from the Collections of the Library of Congress, LC-USZ62-100129.

the next year's planting. Forced requisitions, reduced planting, and drought resulted in poor harvests for 1920 and widespread starvation during the next two years. "War Communism," a Red slogan for the ruthless, all-out effort to defeat the Whites, succeeded. But just as victory appeared secure, peasant resentment toward War Communism exploded into violent opposition against the Bolshevik expropriators. The revolt of Kronstadt sailors in March 1921 (see chapter 1), in part a sympathetic response to the peasant movement, was a clear indication that anti-Bolshevik resentment ran deep and went beyond the village. So serious was this threat to the Communists that Lenin decided to make a dramatic tactical and ideological retreat by introducing the New Economic Policy (NEP). At its heart NEP restored to peasants their incentive to produce: to cultivate the land as their own and sell or otherwise dispose of their produce as they determined, paying a reasonable tax in kind or money. Forced requisitions were abolished. Details remained to be worked out, but the plan called for a significant shift in the direction of a market economy. In the history of Soviet peasants NEP (1921–1928) was a rare episode of relative peace and prosperity.

For Bolsheviks, however, an economy dominated by industrial workers was politically imperative and so it is not surprising that many in the Party had misgivings about NEP favoritism toward peasants and private enterprise and were eager to harness agriculture to the building of industry. Stalin answered their concerns, beginning in the late 1920s, by pushing industrialization at a blistering pace and at the same time ruthlessly collectivizing Soviet agriculture, turning it into the servant of industry and cities.

KOLKHOZNIKS AND SOVKHOZNIKS

Collectivization of agriculture in the 1930s meant that private farming was replaced by large state-controlled agrarian enterprises. Most farms were joined together into large collectives (*kolkhozy*; singular, *kolkhoz*) and the former peasant proprietors into the collective worker-members (kolkhozniks, Russian, *kolkhozniki*). A smaller area of farmland was turned into agricultural factories or state farms (*sovkhozy*; singular, *sovkhoz*) where former proprietors were employed as wage earners. Stalin and his government met the peasants' considerable resistance to these changes with ruthless and uncompromising force. Kulaks were the most unfortunate, more so even than the kolkhozniks and their counterparts, the state farm workers (sovkhozniks, Russian, *sovkhozniki*). Kulaks stood to be the greatest losers and, as a group, most strongly opposed collectivization. Millions of them, including women and children, were executed outright or died as a result of imprisonment in camps or other brutal treatment. "They mostly kicked out those [kulaks] who had lots of kids," one witness recalled.

Then they'd bundle them into a cart, and there'd be no room for any belongings. All the poor wretches could carry were little cases for a change of clothes.... Off the family went, and where to?...They spent the winter living in tents, the whole winter. They all caught colds, some died.[2]

Collectivization of agriculture in the USSR was one of the great disasters of the twentieth century. Besides the massive destruction of humans, tens of millions of farm animals were destroyed by peasants who did not want to see them taken away and collectivized with the livestock of others. The result of this slaughter was to make even more serious the scarcity of meat and other animal products and also to drastically reduce animal draft power and natural fertilizer. Composition of the peasant farming community was also radically altered. Of the more enterprising and hard-working peasants, those not killed or sent to labor camps, many left the countryside, if they could, to seek work in industry. The largest group among these migrants to cities and factories were younger males. Thus, in the beginning the new Soviet agriculture was born in crisis and, in part because industry always took first place in the Party's economic plans, was never wholly raised from its depressed circumstances.

In exchange for their labor *kolkhozniki* were promised a lifetime stake in a member owned and governed large farm and cradle-to-grave benefits. Except for the lifetime commitment, the reality turned out to be much different from the promises: central planning rather than local self-government, marked inequalities in wages, little if any time off or time for hobbies or cultural pursuits, and few or no amenities of city life. Before 1976 kolkhozniks did not receive internal passports, so they had difficulty traveling away from their farms. Most collective farmers' pay and benefits were quite meager. Andrei Amalrik, a Russian dissident writer sentenced in 1965 to exile and labor on the "Kalinin" *kolkhoz* in western Siberia, compared collective farming to a sentence of lifelong slave labor.[3]

Forced to choose, peasants usually opted for the collective. Party leaders, on the other hand, saw state farms as the ideal way to organize socialist agriculture and, at first, gave them preferential treatment. In fact, the two types of farms were quite similar and in the post-Stalin decades what differences existed were further minimized. In a major readjustment of Soviet agriculture, beginning in the 1950s and 60s Party central planners began to narrow the most obvious inequalities, wage differentials for example, between collective and state farms, among various classes of farmworkers, and between them and industrial workers. Heavy state investments in agriculture were made to increase production and raise the quality of life on collective farms closer to that on state farms.

Another event that narrowed the differences between the two types of farms was the decommissioning in 1958 of Machine Tractor Stations. These had served groups of neighboring kolkhozes for 30 years, spreading around the resources of mechanized power but also serving central planners as a means of controlling farm operations. Beginning in 1949, however, the state set out to combine kolkhozes into fewer but much larger units, and as a result it became convenient to require them to have and operate their own machines. At the same time collective farms were being merged, the government was substantially increasing the number of state farms, so that by the 1980s state and collective farms came to resemble each other in size and number.[4]

THE *KOLKHOZ*

The average Soviet village in the early 1980s had 225 residents; a typical *kolkhoz* in the 1960s would include one or more villages (Andrei Amalrik's included five). Kolkhozes held a (theoretically) permanent lease on their state-owned land. Heavy machinery and profits belonged to the *kolkhoz*, as did most of the livestock and crops. According to their government charter (formulated in 1935; slightly revised in 1969 and amended again in 1988), a *kolkhoz* was supposed to be run by general meetings of all its members, meetings at which members would decide production goals, budget, health and safety regulations, and members' wages.[5]

Such a democracy never materialized, for reasons both practical (some collectives had several thousand members) and political (Moscow was not about to surrender its collective farm system to local control). Various alternatives, featuring farmer-elected delegates, were tried or promoted on paper, but most members did not have a voice in running their *kolkhoz*. In practice, it was run by the farm's chairman or a combination of chairman and *kolkhoz* board, all of whom were appointed by and served at the pleasure of local Party authorities. The chairman, board, and other farm officials had it in their power to decide, among other things, whether kolkhozniks worked overtime, on holidays, or at night or had paid holidays. Much depended on a *kolkhoz*'s location and management, but all too often, kolkhozniks ended the fiscal year with little or nothing to show for their work on the farm. Until 1964, *kolkhoz* members did not get the standard pension and disability benefits to which all other Soviet workers were entitled. Each communal farm was expected to use its profits to take adequate care of its members in illness, maternity, and old age, as well as to provide other benefits such as centers for culture and entertainment and the building and equipping of schoolhouses and day-care facilities. The problem was that many such farms were unprofitable and could not help their members either individually or as a community. And even if a collective farm finished a year in the black, the farm chairman or Moscow might have their own plans for the surplus—plans that did not include enhancing the kolkhozniks' quality of life, or security in old age. In his story *Matryona's Home*, Aleksandr Solzhenitsyn paints a vivid picture of the harsh life of an elderly, sickly woman who because of illness has been dumped from her *kolkhoz* and must survive as best she can on her own small crop of potatoes and onions, milk from her goat, stolen heating fuel, and a tiny war widow's pension. When aged kolkhozniks did get a pension, it was generally much lower than that of other retired Soviet workers. For most kolkhozniks, old age and poverty walked hand-in-hand.[6]

Alone among Soviet workers, collective farmers were paid not according to the number of hours per day or month they devoted to their jobs, but according to a complicated credit system, introduced in 1930–1931 (phased out beginning in 1966), called the *trudoden'* (labor-day). The number of labor-days a *kolkhoznik* might earn in a year was calculated according to **Payment of Kolkhozniks** amount plus skill level of work done for the *kolkhoz*. The assignment of labor-day credits for given kinds of work varied from one *kolkhoz* to another and changed over time, but a typical unskilled field laborer, whose work was sweaty and seasonal, might have earned only .5 labor-day credits by the end of a summer's day, whereas a tractor driver in the same period could tuck 4 to 7 labor-day credits into his account. Dairymaids and white-collar farm personnel also received more credits for work done than did fieldworkers, who in any case could earn little or nothing in the off-season. The *kolkhoz* chairman was at the top of this earnings pyramid. Each labor-day unit was worth a certain amount of farm produce or combination of money and produce. Once a year, when labor-day credits were totted up, kolkhozniks hoped to receive their earned allotments. Collective farmers called this system "working for checkmarks" because in earlier days, illiterate farm accountants put check marks rather than numbers next to a worker's name, to show the number of labor-days earned. By the 1960s kolkhozes had gone to a system of payment whereby members were paid monthly or quarterly cash advances on their earnings. Whether in cash or kind, wages were dependent on a *kolkhoz*'s ability or willingness to pay, so that in hard times or less productive regions, farmworkers and their families often got little or nothing from their collectives.

In the summer of 1952, a group of Moscow University students spent their holiday touring Moscow province, overnighting in peasant huts. The poverty they saw prompted one of the students, V. M. Bykov, to write a letter to Stalin himself.

On many kolkhozes along our route [the kolkhozniks receive] 160–200 grams [somewhat less than 1/2 pound] of grain per labor-day. If you consider that they get only a small amount of other produce... then it's clear that life in many villages is very hard. Basically, they live by means of their personal garden plots, a fact which is not comforting.[7]

Bykov goes on to describe the primitive conditions of one of the farmer's homes where he and his friends had spent a night, a home in which "there were not even kerosene lamps."

Andrey Amalrik discovered that even by working ceaselessly he could not earn enough labor-days to pay for a subsistence diet. His daily quart of milk cost him six rubles a month, between a third and a half of his monthly salary. Even at the end of the year when he received the cash balance owed on his salary, plus grain, which he sold, he could not pay what he owed the *kolkhoz* commissary. Unlike non–prisoner labor he did not have a personal garden plot or livestock to help fill his belly. In 1966 First Secretary Leonid Brezhnev introduced a plan to pay kolkhozniks like other Soviet workers: a guaranteed monthly cash salary would henceforth replace the labor-day system and raise farmers' salaries closer to what other blue-collar workers earned. Unfortunately Brezhnev's plan often turned out to be a blessing on paper only because each *kolkhoz* manager could set his own pay scales for his farmers. And even the 1988 *kolkhoz* charter did not mention a minimum wage for kolkhozniks, a benefit long enjoyed by state farmers and other workers.[8]

The original 1935 statute (charter) governing kolkhozes said nothing about how people might apply for admission. Apparently those who

Collective Farm Membership

crafted the charter presumed *kolkhoz* children were born to the hoe, milkmaid's pail, or tractor. The slightly revised 1969 charter created a formal procedure for children of collective farmers to apply for membership at age 16, and these teenagers constituted most of the new recruits to farm life. Less often *otkhodniki* (people who left the collective farm) returned. Sometimes people transferred from one commune to another. The *kolkhoz* assembly could vote in or reject an outsider who wanted to join their farm.[9]

Stalin's 1935 charter did not spell out a way to leave the collective, although many did, usually to get nonfarming jobs. The 1969 charter and its later revisions were vague about whether a member had a right to

Leaving the Collective Farm

withdraw without the agreement or permission of collective farm management, other members, or both. However, in 1988 peasants were granted the right to apply in writing to leave, an application that had to be presented three months ahead of time. This was in contrast to all other workers, who were required to give only two weeks' notice—another example of the lowly status of kolkhozniks.

Kolkhozniks who wanted to leave their farm and find work elsewhere needed two documents: an internal passport, issued to all other workers at age 16 (see chapter 3) and a "labor book," an employment record urban workers automatically received when they got their first job. Most kolkhozniks had neither, until a law adopted in 1974 mandated that all collective farmers be issued passports, to be distributed over a five-year period beginning in 1976. But even before that time young people had been leaving farms in droves, obtaining passports by various strategies, or they just left—without a passport or labor book. One popular technique for getting a passport was to establish urban residence before age 16 by

living with a town relative and then, at 16, applying to the town's authorities for a passport, using the relative's address.

Even collective farmers with passports were not free to settle down
wherever they wished. Like all Soviet citizens they needed residency permits to live in a city. The ease or difficulty of getting such a permit
depended on the city's attractiveness. If it was a major cultural center
(such as Moscow, Leningrad, or Kiev) with a relatively high standard of
living, or a town located in a pleasant, popular resort area, a residency
permit would be hard to come by. On the other hand, many cities in
unpopular locations were crying for workers. Peasants willing to move to
an ordinary smaller town or to Siberia, for example, usually did not have
problems getting residency permits, but most who left their farms did not
go far. Most young ex-kolkhozniks worked in small towns near the farm
where they were raised. In big and small ways the government's refusal,
until late in the Soviet era, to issue internal passports and labor books to
collective farmers, and its continuing residency permit requirement, crippled the kolkhoznik's constitutional right to freely choose a line of work.[10]

Collective farmers had few incentives to work efficiently and conscien-
tiously for their *kolkhoz*. Low wages encouraged them to devote themselves to nurturing the small gardens and few animals the state allowed
them to keep on their own. Peasants who tried to raise the overall work
standard were not appreciated by their fellow farmers and risked getting
beaten up.[11]

THE *SOVKHOZ*

During his term as First Secretary (1953–1964), Nikita Khrushchev
sought to promote and develop state over collective farms. State farms
were government owned and controlled and managed like factories. Each
was headed by a director and his assistants. Unlike the *kolkhoznik*, whose
income and working conditions heavily depended on the quality of his
farm and whims of his bosses, a *sovkhoznik* was a regular government
employee, like employees of other Soviet enterprises, with state-prescribed
pay scales, including minimum wage; a 41-hour, five-day week; social
security; vacations; holidays; internal passport; disability insurance; and
maternity leave. A comparison of state and collective farm households in
Moscow province in the late 1960s showed that proportionately more
sovkhoz than *kolkhoz* families owned TV sets and books, subscribed to newspapers and magazines, and took adult education courses, probably
because sovkhozniks had a somewhat shorter workday than kolkhozniks
and made more money, on average 30 to 40 percent more. Because state
farmers had a slightly better quality of life than collective farmers,
kolkhozniks sometimes switched to state farms when and where they
could. As like as not, however, the peasant's real goal was to migrate to a
city—it was easier to make that move from a *sovkhoz* than from a *kolkhoz*.[12]

OTHER FARMWORKERS

Often collective farm managers needed to temporarily enlarge their workforce in order to increase harvests or get construction work done, so they contracted with privately organized, semilegal groups of migrant "wildcatters" (*shabashniki*). Because their income depended on the size of the harvest, shabashniks often worked longer and harder days than most kolkhozniks. These migrant workers often lived in abominable conditions, and even though many collective farms could not meet production quotas without the extra farmhands, authorities sometimes arbitrarily forced them to move on before the harvest season was over.

In the 1930s Soviet officials hounded traditional rural craftsmen as capitalists. Those who continued to practice their craft left the villages for towns and cities where they joined state-run artisan cooperatives or found some other way of making a living. Farmers who in pre-Soviet times made household necessities for themselves or to sell needed to devote most or all of their spare, non-*kolkhoz* labor time to tending their own gardens and livestock, working in town factories, or both in order to make ends meet. Authorities frowned on selling handmade artifacts in the marketplace, and *kolkhoz* craftsmen, no matter how skilled, were not credited with labor-days for such work. Given the extreme scarcity of factory-made consumer goods, country and city folk alike badly needed the artisans' expertise in making all kinds of everyday products from rope to lace to shovels. In the 1930s, millers, who were particularly persecuted as kulaks, were arrested or run out of villages, even though the newly founded kolkhozes could hardly do without their special knowledge. In the unofficial (illegal and semilegal) economy, however, artisans were well paid. A village stove maker, for example, could make about 10 times as much a month as a *kolkhoznik*, though he risked being arrested as a self-employed "parasite."

There were, besides the kolkhozes and sovkhozes, a variety of public and private (or personal) farming operations. A few private farms were even left to exist here and there in isolated parts of Soviet Asia, though they were not allowed to employ hired workers and had little consequence for the whole economy. More important for food production was the massive but rather wasteful program of sending millions of city "volunteers" (e.g., industrial workers, komsomol youth, pensioners) out to the farms to help at harvest time. Other programs provided factory workers and others with land for their own personal gardens. Most striking was the remarkable productivity of the small private plots of kolkhozniks and sovkhozniks. During the last decades of the Soviet Union, when, despite large investments in agriculture, the country had to import huge amounts of grain, these personal plots were producing most of the potatoes and a sizable portion of other vegetables as well as meat, milk, and eggs.[13]

THE HOUSEHOLD GARDEN PLOT AND LIVESTOCK

Fresh fruit and vegetables, meat and dairy products, and other farm-produced items were chronically unavailable or of low quality in government shops. But high-priced, quality produce could be legally bought at peasants' market stalls. These goods were the products of the small plots of land and few animals allotted to kolkhozniks and other rural people.

Here, an unshaven peasant missing some front teeth offers skinned rabbit. There, a rolypoly Russian shows off farm-fresh eggs.... An old woman...offers a hunk of *tvorog* (sweetened homemade cottage cheese) on waxed paper, or a sample of *smetana* (sour cream) from a white enamel bucket.[14]

Other good things peasants were selling on the day of that particular Moscow farmers' market included honey, pears, dried mushrooms, cucumbers, beets, radishes, carrots, dill pickles, sauerkraut, and purple grapes, all fresh and homegrown and mostly unavailable in state shops.

Personal garden plots and animal husbandry—for profit—was clearly a violation of socialist principles. That such private enterprise was more or less tolerated by Communist authorities is a clear sign of its importance to the country's food supply. The remarkable success of these small enterprises reminded people of the defects in state-run agriculture and showed that the lowly *kolkhoznik* could be an efficient producer even in very narrow circumstances. Rules governing private farming varied from place to place and over time, but a typical peasant household had the right to keep a cow with a calf up to one year, a heifer or bull up to two years, one sow with pigs up to three months or two hogs being fattened, up to 10 sheep and goats (combined), beehives, poultry, and rabbits. Kolkhozniks were not supposed to have their own horses, which had to be rented or borrowed from the *kolkhoz*. Not surprisingly, people often overstepped these limits, if they could. The private garden plot was the surest way, often the only way, of providing one's family with sufficient food and some cash. Even into the 1980s, about half of a rural family's food supply was still being produced on their land allotment, worked mainly by the woman of the house. In western Siberia, for example, in the late Soviet period, women devoted nearly 23 hours a week to the family garden, almost twice as much time as men, who by tradition avoided gardening except for occasional tasks such as building or repairing sheds and preparing ground in the spring. Others, besides kolkhozniks, who could have private gardens were state farm workers; loggers and foresters; rural teachers and health care workers; communications and transport workers; agricultural specialists; and, often, factory employees as well as city residents who owned a *dacha* (summer house). Plots legally ranged in size from about half an acre to a little under two acres, although people stretched those limits if they could. The right to cultivate a small private plot and keep a few ani-

Soviet farm women shopping for shoes in a rural store in the
Ukraine, 1954. Reproduced from the Collections of the Library of
Congress, Lot #6488.

mals was a job benefit, like health insurance, paid leaves, and social security.

Private plots could be the source of holiday diversions, especially for
many southern peasants (Georgians, Uzbeks, and Azerbaijanis). At harvest time they piled their fruits and vegetables into baskets, bought cheap
plane tickets, and flew to northern cities to sell to city dwellers who might
not have laid eyes on a fresh fruit for months. On such trips peasants
could combine business with pleasure. First, they would set up shop in the
designated marketplace and sell their produce. That done, there might be
time for a day or two of leisure to enjoy city life, shop for goods unavailable in the country, and visit city relatives and friends before returning to
the farm with some rubles and store-bought items ranging from children's
toys to warm clothes. For the mass of peasants, who traveled to the nearest town or city only to market their goods, it was still an excursion—a
chance to get away from the farm, see a piece of the outside world, meet
people, and exchange news and gossip.[15]

PEASANT WOMEN

Most Russian farmworkers were women. Throughout the Soviet era (as well as before) they did the heaviest, most monotonous and poorly paid work, with the least chance for advancement, under the worst physical conditions. Soviet peasant women endured the rude behavior and disdain of their male bosses, with little or no child care or housekeeping help from their husbands. Into the late Soviet era and beyond, most rural women were still doing the family laundry by hand, in water they had carried in buckets from the local well or pump, or in a river, in all weathers. Most also baked their own bread. The closest most women got to any kind of managerial work on the farm was as "field-team" leader, a foreman-type job in which women supervised mostly female work brigades.

Although Andrey Amalrik saw mainly anger and mean behavior among women of the "Kalinin" *kolkhoz*, peasant women sometimes showed solidarity in hard times. In Solzhenitsyn's *Matryona's Home*, Matryona and her female neighbors band together in small groups so "they would be less frightened" when they sneak out to steal heating fuel from the state. During the years 1928–1932, Russian and Ukrainian peasant women staged protest riots against being forced into collective farms and government seizure of their land, produce, and livestock. Their well-

Woman doing laundry through the ice, Arkhangelsk, around 1919–1920. Reproduced from the Collections of the Library of Congress; Courtesy of Prof. Gerry Veeder.

founded fears mingled with rumored fantasies that the government would force them to surrender their children to state-run day care centers (in fact, there was never adequate child care for rural families), men would have to share their wives, women's hair would be requisitioned, and the whole village would be forced to sleep under one blanket.

A crowd of women stormed the kolkhoz stables and barns. They cried, screamed, wailed, demanding their cows and seed back. The men stood a way off, in clusters, sullenly silent. Some of the lads had pitchforks, stakes, axes tucked in their sashes. The terrified granary man ran away; the women tore off the bolts and together with the men began dragging out the bags of seed.[16]

Eugenia (Yevgenia) Ginzburg, a teacher at Kazan University, became a political prisoner in a slave labor camp in northeastern Siberia. In 1940 she and other female prisoners were sent into the frozen forest to cut down trees with handsaws and ordered to fulfill a quota of cut trees or be severely punished. Everyone floundered miserably except the peasant women, working quietly and efficiently together in teams:

How quickly and neatly they made the first cuts with the ax! How smoothly and rhythmically they worked the saw! And how obediently the tree fell in the required direction at the feet of these women, used to manual labor from their childhood![17]

MILKMAIDS AND OTHER FEMALE FARMWORKERS

A very traditional job for rural women before and after the revolution was that of milkmaid. Hand milking and other dairy chores were perhaps the most exhausting of all the traditional women's work on state and collective farms. Many farms had neither piped water nor electricity, and where those amenities existed power frequently failed or machinery broke down and went unrepaired. The average milkmaid was assigned 10 to 12 cows, some as many as 18, although on the Kalinin *kolkhoz,* where the cowshed was completely unmechanized, six milkmaids had charge of 25 cows each, a tremendous workload. The Kalinin dairymaids' daily winter routine, which began at six in the morning and often did not end until late at night, included four milkings, plus cleaning out stalls, feeding, hand loading fodder into feeding racks, and hand carrying water for calves. In addition to these daily chores, the women had to take the cows outside for exercise several times a month. As on other kolkhozes, the Kalinin milkmaids were relatively well paid, especially in winter when they earned three times as much as most other kolkhozniks, who might earn little or nothing in the off-season. But the trade-off was grueling relentless labor that few women cared to endure, despite the higher pay. The harsh drudgery of the Kalinin milkmaids' days did not ennoble them. Nasty scenes were frequent; they often accused each other of theft and diluting the milk, screamed obscenities at one another, and when those insults were not effective, hoisted their skirts and mooned their antagonists. Chronically shorthanded, they cursed the women who refused to be drafted into cowshed work:

"Bitches! We've got children too, but we have to work [as dairymaids]—we've got even more kids than you!"

"Shouldn't get laid so often, then you'd have fewer!"[18]

Despite the relatively higher, year-round pay (or labor-day credits), few young women stuck with milkmaiding for long, especially if they had young children at home. Most milkmaids were under 25, not yet married or childless. *Kolkhoz* milkmaids received an average of no more than one day off per week year-round, which gave them fewer days off than any other industrial or agricultural workers. Even into the mid-1960s, a 12- to 14-hour day was considered a normal workload for milkmaids, who did, however, have several breaks during the day. Those who lived close to home could use their break time to get some household chores done.

Year-in, year-out hand milking of large numbers of cows could cause severe, crippling cramps and joint pain in a milkmaid's hands and sometimes in her whole body. She was vulnerable to other ills as well: open sores on fingers, and brucellosis, a highly infectious disease that spreads from farm animals to humans through contact and drinking unpasteurized milk. (As late as the mid-1950s, the Soviet Union had two to three million human cases of brucellosis.) As a political prisoner/slave laborer/medical assistant assigned to a dairy farm in the Arctic circle, Eugenia Ginzburg saw firsthand the effects of year-round, almost round-the-clock hand milking. The dairymaids would come to her during their evening break so that she could "massage [their] hands and put dressings on their swollen fingers, which were chapped so badly they bled." Toward the very end of the Soviet era, when around 200,000 Soviet milkmaids were still milking entirely by hand, a young woman told a newspaper reporter how she and the other dairy women dragged hay and washed everything in cold water in winter, how their hands with open cracks in the skin from the cold and damp got manure inside the cuts: "In the mornings your fingers won't move—my husband has to dress me while I just cry." As dairy units became mechanized, making the work less exhausting, men began to take over, viewing themselves as machine operators rather than milkers.

Most farm women who were not milkmaids did seasonal farmwork connected with hand cultivation and harvesting of crops such as sugar beets, potatoes, cotton, flax, rice, or fruit. This kind of farmwork was labor-intensive and backbreaking. Whatever harvesting machines were available were often out of commission, or worked so poorly that they may as well have stayed in the shed. When harvesting machines were in

A milkmaid, around 1967. Reproduced from the Collections of the
Library of Congress, LC-L9-67-3337 #36A.

use, men operated them while women were assigned manual labor.
Although there was increasing mechanization of farmwork, by the late
1970s and early 80s most field hands were still middle-aged and elderly
women whose lack of education and technical training gave them few
options, and women with young children. One such woman described her
work as a cultivator of sugar beets: "Your back aches and your feet get
heavy. That's what it's like, farming the crop." As time went by ever fewer
women were willing to devote their lives to these poorly paid, unhonored
tasks, and they began to flee the farms.[19]

THE PEASANT HOUSEHOLD

The word *dvor,* which does not have a direct English translation, means
roughly "rural household" or "the family and its farm" or "farmstead."
Unless a widow lived with no adult male relatives, the head of the household (*khozyain*) was a man who expected to receive the obedience due him
as the supreme authority within his *dvor.* After the Revolution, the *dvor*
continued to be the basic social and economic unit among families who
lived on collective farms, but according to Soviet law, people joined collectives as individuals rather than as families. Allowing women to enroll
as individuals did not break the ancient grip of rural patriarchal traditions, but it did sometimes allow families to improve their standard of living, by establishing mixed households in which perhaps only one member
(generally a woman) would labor for the collective *and* care for the house-

hold garden and livestock. Other adult family members could be "independents" who had dependable higher-salaried jobs outside the *kolkhoz*.[20]

GETTING OUT

Before World War II, Stalin drafted thousands of young kolkhozniks to work in heavy industry. The war ended, but migration from the countryside did not. The flow of the best, brightest, best-educated, most energetic young people from country to city was a chronic source of alarm to Soviet authorities. If all capable young adults managed (despite severe legal restrictions) to wriggle out of farm life, who would be left to produce food?

Young people had many good reasons to flee their villages, which had little to offer except lives of grinding boredom and poverty. Whether it was education, health care, indoor plumbing, central heat, music, movies, theater, better pay, child care facilities, groceries and other consumer goods, public services, and sheer social prestige, access was more likely to happen in the city than in the country. When *kolkhoz* youth finished their army service, they often found city work and married city girls. "And once the young men have gone, the girls will also leave—they do not want simply to wither on the vine," as one Soviet citizen observed. Like an immigrant who comes to the United States and then brings the rest of the family over, a *kolkhoznik* who moved to the city became a magnet for relatives, and the family hut on the commune would be left to the care of a grandmother who might see her children and grandchildren only when they visited for a country holiday.

This pattern of migration from farm to cities changed during the course of Soviet power. Originally, most of those fleeing village life were young men, but in the later Soviet period young women—whose prospects in the village were even bleaker and narrower than men's—began to predominate among those who packed their bags and left. Toward the end of the Soviet era peasant girls were often better educated than the boys, but job opportunities for women did not keep up with the rise in educational levels and expectations of country women. Mothers whose lives had been spent "in muck and filth" wanted something better for their daughters and often encouraged their dream of leaving the village, or at the very least, the farm. In Soviet Central Asia, however, the opposite occurred: the rural population kept growing because of a high birthrate, reluctance to leave ancestral homes, and stiffer family-community resistance to female education and independence.[21]

VISITORS TO THE COUNTRYSIDE

Some rural folk regularly had the opportunity to mix and mingle with city people: relatives and former neighbors who had moved to cities returned to visit; many city dwellers had access to a summer house (*dacha*); seasonal workers came and went; and hundreds of thousands of city dwellers, including students, were drafted to work temporarily on farms for little or no pay. Although students and other draftees from urban life regularly appeared at Andrey Amalrik's Siberian *kolkhoz*, the city visitors did not particularly impress their hosts, and vice versa. These "volunteer" workers were usually university students who did their work poorly, and the results were more likely to be wasteful or even disastrous than mutually enriching. In the village of Malinovka a student-built cattle-shed collapsed, fatally crushing a milkmaid and wounding others. Other "volunteers" were drafted out of factories, and they, too, were as often as not a disaster for agricultural production. "The potatoes have been more or less harvested," an exasperated rural Party official wrote to Stalin, "But what kind of harvest is this?"

They [the drafted factory workers] didn't try to pick all the potatoes, because they weren't interested, they wanted to get away as soon as possible, so they only picked the ones lying above ground; over half the potatoes were never harvested.[22]

Model farms equipped with sleek, humming machinery and cheery, well-scrubbed farm families were maintained for foreign visitors to admire, but the Soviet government blocked foreigners from visiting an ordinary collective or state farm "far from the railroad tracks" even for a day or two. This policy cut off Soviet farmworkers from the outside world, as did the infamously poor roads.[23]

TRANSPORTATION

Country roads in the Russian Empire and the Soviet Union were notorious for their thick, impassable, ankle-deep mud. Abominable travel conditions have been so universal and chronic that Russians even have a word for it: *bezdorozhnost'*, or "roadlessness." Just short distances outside of big cities highly traveled roads in certain seasons quickly became mud traps deep enough to "sink a big truck to its axles." Even when road conditions were ideal, few Soviet villagers had their own cars, and local public transportation was often scarce and undependable. Roads branching off main arteries were nearly always unpaved—and often not even roads, but mere narrow paths or wagon-rutted trails. The poorer the republics, the poorer and fewer the roads connecting villages and farms to outlying areas. These abysmal travel conditions affected people's lives physically, psychologically, and culturally. Country folk found it difficult or often impossible to get themselves and their dependents to health care, child care, or educational facilities; to the closest town for shopping; or to see a play or a movie or visit a relative or friend. Nor were mud and the lack of roadside services the only hazards:

Horse and cart remained the most common means of transportation in the countryside. This photo was probably taken around 1967. Reproduced from the Collections of the Library of Congress, LC-L9-67-3337 #23A.

Late in the evening I'm driving to Kraskovo. There's not a single sign on the road indicating where it's leading. Cars are riding without brake lights. Some of them have their headlights dimmed. A truck is stuck in the middle of the road with no flares to mark it. Bicyclists as a rule ride without lights. Pedestrians stroll nonchalantly in the road. A harmonica is playing. In general, as the French say, you're riding right into an open grave.[24]

NOTES

1. Lazar Volin, *A Century of Russian Agriculture: From Alexander II to Khrushchev* (Cambridge, MA: Harvard University Press, 1970), 103–7, 130–60; M. Lewin, *Russian Peasants and Soviet Power, a Study of Collectivization* (New York: W. W. Norton, 1975), 81–106.

2. Olga Litvinenko and James Riordan, eds., *Memories of the Dispossessed: Descendants of Kulak Families Tell Their Stories* (Nottingham, England: Bramcote Press, 1998), 68.

3. Andrei A. Amalrik, *Involuntary Journey to Siberia* (New York: Harcourt Brace Jovanovich, 1970), 174–75.

4. S. Hedlund, *Crisis in Soviet Agriculture* (New York: St. Martin's Press, 1984), 68.

5. Robert Conquest, *Agricultural Workers in the USSR* (London: Bodley Head, 1968), 92, 94, 98, 121–22; Basile Kerblay, *Modern Soviet Society*, trans. Rupert Swyer (New York: Pantheon Books, 1983), 74; Mervyn Matthews, *Patterns of Deprivation in the Soviet Union under Brezhnev and Gorbachev* (Stanford, CA: Hoover Institution Press, 1989), 34–35.

6. Conquest, *Agricultural Workers*, 93–94, 98, 121–22; Peter Maggs, "The Legal Status of Collective Farm Members," in *Soviet Law after Stalin*, ed. Donald D. Berry, George Ginsburgs, and Peter Maggs (Leyden, The Netherlands: A. W. Sijthoff, 1977), 166; Edward Lea Johnson, *An Introduction to the Soviet Legal System* (London: Methuen, 1969), 212–13; Alexander Vucinich, "The Peasants as a Social Class," in *The Soviet Rural Community: A Symposium*, ed. James R. Millar (Urbana: University of Illinois Press, 1971), 321; Demitri Shimkin, "Current Characteristics and Problems of the Soviet Rural Population," in *Soviet Agricultural and Peasant Affairs*, ed. Roy D. Laird (Lawrence: University of Kansas Press, 1963), 82.

7. "Pis'ma vozhdiam," letters to the Leader, *Istochnik* 4 (2000): 98–107.

8. Amalrik, *Involuntary Journey*, 145, 158–60; Sheila Fitzpatrick, *Stalin's Peasants: Resistance and Survival in the Russian Village after Collectivization* (Oxford, England: Oxford University Press, 1996), 145; "*Trudoden'*," in *Bol'shaia sovetskaia entsiklopediia* (Moscow: Izd-vo "Sovetskaia entsiklopediia," 1977); Conquest, *Agricultural Workers*, 102; Matthews, *Patterns of Deprivation*, 35–36.

9. Shimkin, "Current Characteristics," 82.

10. Maggs, "Legal Status," 163–65; Matthews, *Patterns of Deprivation*, 34–35.

11. Fitzpatrick, *Stalin's Peasants*, 142–45.

12. Conquest, *Agricultural Workers*, 106; Jiri Zuzanek, *Work and Leisure in the Soviet Union: A Time-Budget Analysis* (New York: Praeger, 1980), 120.

13. Louise I. Shelley, *Policing Soviet Society: The Evolution of State Control* (London: Routledge, 1996), 135; Fitzpatrick, *Stalin's Peasants*, 159, 161–62; Stephen P. Dunn, "The Soviet Rural Family," in *The Soviet Rural Community: A Symposium*, ed. James R. Millar (Urbana: University of Illinois Press, 1971), 331; Amalrik, *Involuntary Journey*, 152; Johnson, *Soviet Legal System*, 207; Stefan Hedlund, *Crisis in Soviet Agriculture* (New York: St. Martin's Press, 1984), 165–69; Karl-Eugen Wädekin, *Ethnic German Emigres from Rural Areas of the USSR* (Munich: Ost-Europa Institut, 1986), 10–11.

14. Hedrick Smith, *The Russians*, rev. ed. (New York: Ballantine Books, 1976), 265.

15. Smith, *The Russians*, 265–66, 268, 279; Shimkin, "Current Characteristics," 83; Susan Bridger, "Soviet Rural Women: Employment and Family Life," in *Russian Peasant Women*, ed. Beatrice Farnsworth and Lynne Viola (New York: Oxford University Press, 1992), 283.

16. Lev Kopelev, *The Education of a True Believer*, trans. Gary Kern (New York: Harper and Row, 1978), 188.

17. Eugenia Ginzburg, *Journey into the Whirlwind*, trans. Paul Stevenson and Max Hayward (New York: Harcourt, Brace, and World, 1967), 405; Bridger, "Soviet Rural Women," 280, 286, 271; Vucinich, "Peasants as Social Class," 323; Smith, *The Russians*, 269; Norton D. Dodge and Murray Feshbach, "The Role of Women in Soviet Agriculture," in Jerzy F. Karcz, ed., *Soviet and East European Agriculture* (Berkeley: University of California Press, 1967), 249; Aleksandr Solzhenitsyn, *Matryona's Home*, in *The Norton Anthology of World Literature*, vol. 2, expanded edition (New York: St. Martin's Press, 1995), 2311; Lynn Viola, "*Bab'y Bunty* and Peas-

ant Women's Protest During Collectivization," in *Russian Peasant Women,* ed. Beatrice Farnsworth and Lynne Viola (New York: Oxford University Press, 1992), 198–99; Roberta T. Manning, "Women in the Soviet Countryside on the Eve of World
War II, 1935–1940," in Farnsworth and Viola, 1992, 193–96.

18. Amalrik, *Involuntary Journey,* 256.

19. Amalrik, *Involuntary Journey,* 239, 255; Manning, "Women in Soviet Countryside," 216–18; Bridger, "Soviet Rural Women," 274–78, and "Rural Women and Glasnost," in Farnsworth and Viola, 1992, 294–304; Conquest, *Agricultural Workers,* 98; Shimkin, "Current Characteristics," 88; Ginzburg, *Whirlwind,* 51; "Agricultural Workers," in *The Soviet Union: A Country Study* (Washington, DC: Library of Congress Federal Research Division, Country Studies, Area Handbook Series, Soviet Union 1989), http://memory.loc.gov/frd/cs/sutoc.html/ (accessed October 20, 2003).

20. Lewin, *Russian Peasants,* 25; Helmut Altrichter, "Insoluble Conflicts: Village Life Between Revolution and Collectivization," in *Russia in the Era of NEP: Explorations in Soviet Society and Culture,* ed. Sheila Fitzpatrick, Alexander Rabinowitch and Richard Stites (Bloomington: Indiana University Press, 1991), 192, 215; Fitzpatrick, *Stalin's Peasants,* 112–13; Johnson, *Soviet Legal System,* 214 ff.

21. Conquest, *Agricultural Workers,* 116–18; Bridger, "Soviet Rural Women," 290–91; "Rural Women and *Glasnost,*" 295; "Decreasing Social Differences" in *The Soviet Union: A Country Study,* 1989, http://lcweb2.loc.gov/cgi-bin/query/D?cstdy:1:./temp/~frd_ktGi::

22. "Pis'ma vozhdiam," 99.

23. "Decreasing Social Differences"; Amalrik, *Involuntary Journey,* 178; Smith, *The Russians,* 272–74.

24. Unpublished journal of Il'ia Il'f, quoted in Alice Nakhimovsky, "Death and Disillusion: Il'f in the Thirties," in *Enemies of the People: The Destruction of Soviet Literary, Theater, and Film Arts in the 1930s,* ed. Katherine B. Eaton (Evanston, IL: Northwestern University Press, 2001), 219; Horst Herlemann, "Aspects of the Quality of Rural Life in the Soviet Union," in *Quality of Life in the Soviet Union,* ed. Horst Herlemann (Boulder, CO: Westview Press, 1987), 163–66; Smith, *The Russians,* 73, 270–78; Gertrude E. Schroeder, "Rural Living Standards in the Soviet Union," in *The Soviet Rural Economy,* ed. Robert C. Stuart (Towata, NJ: Rowman and Allenheld, 1984), 254.

7

Housing

In cities and countryside, housing was extremely scarce in the Soviet Union, partly for historical reasons. The Soviet government inherited a housing situation that may have been one of the worst in Europe. After the 1917 Bolshevik Revolution the government confiscated private homes and apartments belonging to the nobility and middle classes and redistributed them—often partitioned into single rooms—among workers and peasants and some favored artists. Although the promise (and principle) was to allocate housing strictly according to need, that never happened. As with other consumer goods, the quality of housing one got varied according to Party rank, job importance, perceived political reliability, money (needed in large amounts for down payments and bribery), and influential connections (the latter, called *blat*, tended to be even more important than money alone). Housing conditions worsened under Stalin, who devoted huge financial resources to building factories but neglected to provide decent living spaces for the millions of people pouring into cities from the countryside in order to work in those factories. Housing became even tighter when much of the available shelter in the European USSR was destroyed in World War II. Stalingrad, for example, was 90 percent destroyed, and almost one-third of Leningrad's housing was demolished during the 900-day German siege of that city.[1]

From 1956 into the 1960s the state undertook a massive drive to construct enough apartment buildings to provide reasonably modern, comfortable housing for its urban population. Consequently, by the end of the Soviet era millions of citizens were enjoying private residences for the first time in their lives. Vast faceless 9-, 11-, or 14-story apartment complexes made of cheap prefabricated concrete parts (often as much as 85 to 90 percent concrete) and looking like "huge packing case[s]" were built on the outskirts of Soviet cities. These buildings, which resemble the large low-income housing projects built in some American cities in the 1950s, became dilapidated soon after they were finished and never reached the standards in modernity, comfort, or eye appeal of middle-class housing in Western Europe, the United States, or even some Eastern European countries. One Leningrad resident grumbled that rough cement building blocks jutted out of corners "right into living rooms." From other parts of the Soviet Union came complaints about shoddy construction by workers who were so eager to fulfill quotas based on floor space that new tenants had to spend their own money and time on basic repair and finishing jobs like rehanging doors, plastering, fixing light switches, and the like. Nor did the housing shortage disappear. The government's concerted building program tapered off after the 1960s even though huge housing needs remained. Consequently a chronic (and for many, desperate) housing crisis remained a reality of Soviet life. On the rare occasion when people had a room to rent or an apartment to lease they could legally do so, and it was a seller's market. Especially if the room or apartment was close to a city's center, owners could be picky about tenants and get rents far beyond the (generally unenforced) legal limit.[2]

The advantages of big-city life were supremely important to very many Soviet citizens because the suburban good life Americans envision and strive toward hardly existed in the Soviet Union. For most Soviets, dreams led from villages, small towns, and smaller and medium-sized cities straight to the heart of Moscow or, failing that, to Leningrad, Kiev, and a few other capitals of republics. Although some preferred to live in the country where they could raise their own food, the ideal habitat for most would have been a private, high-ceilinged Moscow apartment, not more than two or three subway stops from the center in a brick or stone building equipped with gas, hot water, central heat, indoor toilet and bathrooms, balcony, elevator, incinerator, and telephone. Ideal apartments were on an upper but not a top floor, because ground floor windows had to be barred against thieves, and top stories, though further from street noise, were vulnerable to leaky roofs. The best education, jobs, entertainment, shopping, municipal services, and transportation (ordinary folk rarely owned a car) were concentrated in a few big cities, so city life meant greater social prestige, better medical care, and career advancement. Amenities of city life ended abruptly at the city limits. Beyond that point, one could no longer expect to find shops, schools, movie theaters, or satisfactory jobs. A typical worker living on Moscow's outskirts dwelled in an apartment building that

stood not on a street but in the midst of a field. No path led to it. You plunged into the deep snow and made your own path. Other apartment houses, each facing in a different direction, were scattered across the snowy fields. There was no street lighting.[3]

Although privately owned housing existed, the state owned over 70 percent of housing in the 1980s, and also carefully regulated privately owned dwellings and private housing transactions, such as when people rented a room within their apartment; or subleased their state-owned apartment; or bought, rented, or sold co-op apartments. Who got what kind of living space depended mainly on money, social class, and how authorities decided to allocate precious housing.[4]

PROCEDURE FOR UPGRADING ONE'S LIVING SPACE

Since housing was always in extremely short supply, people wanting to upgrade often had to wait many years, even decades. If they hoped for a state-owned apartment they had to apply to have their names put on at least one of two kinds of registers. There was a waiting list belonging to enterprises and organizations such as factories, stores, and other institutions with their own housing stock for workers or members, and a waiting list belonging to cities. In the later Soviet period, people were allowed to enter their names on both rolls, but when they had to choose one or the other, they preferred to be on an organization register where people usually moved ahead faster than on city lists. However, rent for organization apartments was considerably higher than for city-owned dwellings—the equivalent of $40 or $50 per month for the former as opposed to $3 or $4 a month for the latter, including some utilities (in Moscow in the 1960s). Factories making products for heavy industry were more likely to provide shelter for their workers than were factories making consumer goods. People living in Moscow and other Soviet European cities tended to get newer and bigger apartments than did those who lived in non-European towns because the government favored its European cities—above all, Moscow—in its allocation of housing money.[5]

Not everyone could get on a housing register. People who already had their "sanitary norm" (a minimum standard for health and decency, set in the 1920s for the Russian Republic) of 9 square meters—about 100 square feet or 10 by 10 feet—of living space per person were very unlikely to get on a waiting list without *blat*. Officially, it was necessary to have less than 7 square meters per capita to get on a list. This was not a difficult requirement to meet since most Soviets never did attain the 9-square-meter "norm" (a measurement that included bedrooms and living rooms but not kitchens, bathrooms, hallways, or storage areas). Because those who lived in dank basements were supposed to have priority for new apartments, some citizens moved up by first moving down, even paying bribes for cellar rooms.[6]

Every year, names were taken from the register and placed on an annual list of those who would get upgraded housing in the coming year. Criteria for being chosen for the annual list were length of time one's name had been on the list, neediness, and "socially useful activity." The latter was a loophole that allowed influential people to jump ahead in the line and get on the annual list quickly. There were many other categories of citizens who were supposed to be given preference, such as people living in extremely dilapidated, unhealthy housing; housing about to be torn down or put to other uses; families with three or more children; high military officers and high secret police officers who had served over 20 years; wounded war veterans; and people sharing a room with strangers. Others who could push ahead onto the annual list were those with connections, or those able to offer hefty bribes to housing officials. Though such bribery was commonplace, it could occasionally backfire. In 1964 the mayor of a district in the Azerbaijan city of Baku and 28 others were jailed for taking bribes for housing. The previous year, in the Tajik Republic capital city of Dushanbe, 24 construction workers' families who had illegally moved into an unfinished apartment building were evicted, and the building contractor who had permitted them to move in lost his Party membership. From time to time, there would be other stories in the Soviet press about public officials who had illegally garnered thousands of rubles by speeding up people's transfers to better housing. In order to limit the number of people on annual lists, the government often banned singles (such as adult children, a grandparent, an aunt or uncle) who wanted to live apart from their relatives from adding their names to the housing register. Except in special cases, those without a residence permit (*propiska*) for a given area did not have the right to apply for housing space there. This created a "Catch-22" situation in which people who worked in the city but lived beyond city limits and faced long, tiresome commutes into town were generally not allowed to register for city living space because they did not live in the city. In 1964 the police chief of the Russian republic, the Soviet Union's largest state, suggested alcoholics be bounced off housing waiting lists, as a way of combating alcoholism. Landing on the annual list did not necessarily mean getting an apartment of one's own, however. For many the new home would be a room or rooms in a communal apartment.[7]

LIVING SPACE

In 1948, a Russian exile living in France reported,

Any time of the day or night officials may enter your dwelling to measure the space you occupy. If it is more than three square meters, someone will probably be billeted with you.[8]

In the 1950s the average living space per person was 5 square meters, about 54 square feet. By 1972 city folk had only 7.6 square meters, or about one-third the living space of American city dwellers and half the average in Western Europe. By 1982 the average living space per person in cities across the USSR was 9 square meters, ranging from 11.3 square meters in Moscow to 6.6 square meters in Dushanbe, the capital of Tajikistan.[9]

According to law some categories of people were entitled to more room, including members of artists' unions, people with certain illnesses, high Party officials, people who received certain government awards, professors and other high-ranking scholars, and high military officers. Those at the top of the privileged groups lived in specially built dwellings with four- or five-room apartments and modern conveniences. For example, in 1961 the Soviet government honored their first-man-in-space hero Yury Gagarin by moving him and his family (wife, two daughters, and parents) from their two-room apartment outside Moscow to a new four-room apartment in the city, a residence replete with its own kitchen, toilet, and bath. Decades earlier Nadezhda Mandelstam was shown around the new elegant Moscow apartment building reserved for members of the Union of Soviet Writers. Writers were assigned to this or that floor, depending on their prestige. In the mid-1930s, however, such privilege could be deadly. When arrests of high Party officials and artists began, it was easy for the secret police to round them up because so many lived in the same buildings. After the writer and stage director Anna Latsis was sentenced (in 1939) to 10 years in a prison camp for "counter-revolutionary activity," her husband, Bernhard Reich, wrote to authorities protesting that the larger, 16-square-meter room of their two-room apartment had been confiscated, forcing him to share the remaining 12-square-meter room with his 20-year-old stepdaughter. Reich pointed out the impropriety of this arrangement and reminded his wife's persecutors that as a member of the Union of Soviet Writers he was legally entitled to living space up to 20 square meters beyond the "norm."[10]

Reich's experience was not unusual. It was customary for authorities to confiscate all or part of a family's living space when a member of that family was arrested. Especially under Stalin, people could acquire better living quarters by denouncing someone whose room or apartment they coveted. Then families of the arrested were evicted, their dwelling sealed at first "with a big reddish-brown seal...a weight hung from a tiny string embedded in the wax." Soon the place would be turned over to others. Shortly after the funeral of the murdered actress Zinaida Raikh her children, ages 19 and 21, were given two days to vacate the family apartment though legally it belonged to them. To ensure quick departure, Raikh's children were harassed by the new occupants, members of secret police chief Lavrenty Beria's staff. After the writer Isaac Babel's arrest one of the police agents made a telephone call to get instructions about whether Babel's companion, Antonina Pirozhkova, would be allowed to keep two rooms of their three-room apartment. Pirozhkova considered it remarkable good fortune that she, the companion of an "enemy of the people," was permitted to retain two rooms for herself and their daughter. Similarly, the narrowing of Ruth Bonner's life and hopes was paralleled by the progressive narrowing and tightening of her family's housing. Before her husband's arrest in 1937, the household (Ruth and her husband, two children, grandmother, maids and nannies) lived in a four-room Moscow apartment that reflected the couple's status as important Party workers. Postarrest, their apartment was sealed and the remaining family members were shifted to a one-room apartment. Finally the family was dispersed: children and grandmother moved to Leningrad, and Ruth Bonner to a room in the courtyard of their former Moscow home. It was a space about the size of a train compartment, which she shared with another woman also awaiting arrest.[11]

AMENITIES

In 1956 less than 3 percent of city people had hot running water; two-thirds had no running water—they had to carry water in buckets from a community faucet, pump, or well. This was an especially burdensome task for women who worked all day and had to squeeze cooking, cleaning, laundry, and shopping into their after-work hours. A farm home with hot water was extremely rare at that time. Public laundry and dry cleaning facilities were available only in cities, and inadequate at that. By the 1970s most new apartment buildings were being built with the basic conveniences of Western modern life: indoor plumbing, hot water, central heat, electric lighting, and electricity for other uses. But millions of people, especially in the countryside, still did not have all or some of those niceties. By the end of 1975, 20 percent of state-owned city housing lacked running water and plumbing, and 50 percent did not have hot water. In the country, as always, those figures were higher. In Novosibirsk Province in 1977, 78 percent of rural houses did not have running water; 95 percent lacked hot water; 89 percent went without indoor plumbing; 90 percent were without central heat. In 1976, the majority of rural houses had gas (59 percent), through use of individual propane tanks, as opposed to 69 percent of urban housing. By the mid-1980s, 9 out of 10 rural homes had electricity, but brownouts and power interruptions happened often, more in the country than in the city. In 1977, in the rural areas of Novosibirsk Province, only 4 percent of households had telephones. What all apartment buildings did have was a general caretaker, the *dvornik*, whose job included reporting to the local militia on the comings and goings of the building's residents and their visitors.[12]

Communal apartments (*kommunal'ki*) were standard housing for city dwellers into the 1960s. For most families this meant being crammed into one room while sharing a common kitchen, bathtub, and toilet with several other families. Households had separate tables in the communal kitchen, and sometimes the toilet room had a detachable seat for each family. "Corridor apartments" were built especially for the communal purpose: a central corridor with rooms opening to it ran the length of the dwelling. One telephone was used in common, but households had separate doorbells and gas and electric meters. In the 1970s around a fourth to a third of Soviets still lived in such conditions; by 1980 20 percent were still living communally. The journalist Hedrick Smith, who lived in the Soviet Union from 1971 to 1974, knew a family of three who shared a nine-room apartment with 54 other people, a population that eventually dwindled to 27. Given the severe housing crunch in major cities, it was not unusual for extended families to inhabit a small room in a communal apartment, and shelter guests besides. One Muscovite grew up in a single room shared with his grandmother, mother, and aunt, but they always gave overnight (or longer) hospitality to a host of out-of-town relatives who visited frequently.[13]

A Moscow communal apartment building was likely to have unlit hallways, nonworking elevators; dirty floors and walls; boards replacing panes of broken window glass; and behind each apartment door, four to eight families. In his realistic novel *Cancer Ward* Aleksandr Solzhenitsyn describes the cheerless home of a fine doctor, Vera Gangart, who has a single room in a communal apartment. Outside the building, the veranda railing is all but invisible under piles of rugs and doormats. Inside, Vera walks along a gloomy interior corridor she can't illuminate because the lights are on different apartment meters. Because she lives on the ground floor, Vera's windows are barred against thieves, which makes her room look like a cell. When she goes to the communal kitchen to fix herself something to eat, she finds that

her neighbor's son, a big strong lad who had dropped out of school, had installed his motorcycle in the kitchen like a kind of barrier. He was in there taking it to bits, whistling as he laid the parts all over the floor and oiled them.[14]

When Eugenia Ginzburg was first released from a Siberian prison camp into exile she made her way to the Siberian city of Magadan, where an old friend and fellow ex-prisoner took her in. Her friend's room of seven square meters was in a building that had once been a hospital hut for the sickest newly arrived prisoners.

We found a badly lighted, dirty corridor with about twenty doors opening onto it. In front of each door there was a mound of rags, boxes, pails and brooms. A pervasive smell of burned grease filled the air.[15]

Her friend had made the space as tidy and welcoming as possible, with a camp bed for Ginzburg and a table covered with a "carefully ironed white rag." In the following year (1948), when Ginzburg was expecting her teenage son to join them, her friend's bosses allocated a larger room, 15 square meters with "a good window," for the three of them. A corner was partitioned off for the teenager; behind the partition was an iron bed, a chair, and a table so that he could do his homework. Two years later, however, Ginzburg was forced to search for living space for herself; her newly adopted daughter; and later, her newly freed husband, Anton Walter (her son had returned to Moscow). The lodging she found was a partitioned area of 8 square meters in a big communal kitchen. The plywood wall allowed for little privacy.

It was not cozy in our new home. There was a constant smell of the remains of cabbage soup, burned milk, and fried fish. The kitchen came to life early in the morning. Fifteen women, several of them former common criminals, were constantly in and out of it, discussing their daily business, quarreling, singing—all at the top of their voices and in the choicest language.[16]

In fact, the use of thin panels that often did not reach the ceiling was a common way of allotting space to individuals and families.[17]

Yet the urge to create coziness remained strong, and Ginzburg's eight square meters of "ex-kitchen space" soon held, besides her husband and tiny daughter, a piano, bookshelves, beds, stools, and tables. Others, also, decorated their single rooms as warmly and lovingly as their means allowed. One couple's room was "full of little rugs, antimacassars, and cushion covers embellished with swans, kittens, water sprites, and deer hunters." On her days off, the wife had created a lace bed skirt for their bed.

When in 1952 Eugenia and her husband were able to get a 15-square-meter room, it was in a barracks surrounded by an unpaved, unlit, dangerous, and usually snowy wasteland; getting mugged on her way home from work after dark was always a strong possibility. Thirty families and 17 children inhabited their corridor; the younger children's favorite entertainment was pedaling up and down the hallway on their tricycles, ringing the handlebar bells and shouting at each other. After Stalin's death Ginzburg once again found employment as a college-level teacher. Pleased with her work, local officials allocated her family of three a room of 20 square meters in a communal apartment shared with only two other households. To Ginzburg and her husband it was like "the Palace of Versailles." The common kitchen was "good," and there was an indoor, heated communal bath and toilet.

Not daring to believe our own eyes, Anton and I tried out the taps in the bathroom. . . . We listened to the flush as though it were a signal from the other world: we had seen all sorts of things in the last two decades, but a lavatory with all modern conveniences was definitely not among them.

The final improbable miracle of miracles was the appearance of a telephone on our table.[18]

After Stalin died, Ginzburg and her husband for the first time in 20 years experienced freedom from fear of being rearrested. They could go to bed at night without dreading a nighttime knock on the door or phone call from the police. They felt that their room was, in Ginzburg's words, their home and their castle.[19]

Soviet authorities as well as outsiders blamed crowded housing conditions for many of society's problems, including tuberculosis, ulcers, worker inefficiency, low birthrates, high worker turnover, rising numbers of abortions, and divorces. It is not surprising that life in close proximity to so many others was frequently a source of friction, inside and outside the family. "My son got married half a year ago," one Leningrad father complained, "and whenever I come home from work they are always kissing and hugging each other. It revolts me, and then they always act offended." Neighbors in a communal apartment were often irritated by another family's failure to do its share of kitchen or bathroom cleaning, by other people's children or pets, arguments over use of kitchen and bathroom, and other territorial disputes. Sometimes people who shared a communal apartment did not speak to each other for years. Ironically, when the Soviet Union fell and inner-city communal apartments were sold to private owners, many elderly people who had known only communal living in old inner-city buildings dreaded the loneliness and difficulty of living alone in a private apartment far from friends, shops, transportation, and central-city conveniences.[20]

STATE-OWNED PRIVATE APARTMENTS

Rents for the heavily subsidized state-owned private apartments were low—no more than 3 to 5 percent of a typical family's monthly income, including some utilities. Most apartments were one or two rooms, a "two-room" apartment meaning a living room and one bedroom, in addition to kitchen, bath, and toilet. A state-owned four to six room dwelling, unusually spacious by Soviet standards, rented for 14 to 16 rubles per month, or $18.20 to $22.30 in 1974. Apartments in more modern state-owned buildings cost somewhat more. Once again, however, some groups got preferential treatment while the law put others at a disadvantage. Those who had received awards for service to the state, such as Hero of the Soviet Union or Hero of Socialist Labor, and military personnel paid only half the usual rent for their living space, while others such as doctors who kept a private practice, private craftsmen, and clergy were assessed rents higher than most people had to pay for comparable housing. Those who had living space beyond the legal limit but did not belong to any of the groups entitled to more space were supposed to pay three times the normal rent for the extra square meters. Because apartments were so small, living rooms generally became bedrooms at night; most apartments did not have a separate dining room.[21]

Cooperative housing, which had existed earlier but got into high gear in 1962 as a way of combating the housing shortage, was a government-approved compromise between owning a house and renting from the state. In the co-operative plan, a group of people who belonged to a common workplace or professional group, or even just shared some common interest, were allowed to finance the construction of an apartment building for themselves to live in. Shareholders had to make a down payment of 40 percent of the apartment's cost (thousands of rubles). The rest had to be paid over 10 to 20 years at an interest rate of around 1 percent. Monthly payments were much higher than heavily subsidized rent payments in a state-owned apartment, but the wait for occupancy was generally much shorter. In 1964 the cost of a one-room co-op was about 2,400 rubles ($2,670); 3,600 rubles ($4,005) for a two-room apartment; and 6,000 to 6,500 rubles for a three-room co-op in Moscow (but not in the center) with kitchen, toilet, bath, and entrance hall. At that time an average industrial worker made around 110 rubles [$122] a month.[22]

Co-op shareholder-tenants (generally a minimum of 60 members) considered themselves owners of their apartments, although Soviet law avoided the word "owner" in its co-op regulations. By the mid-1960s, there were around 4,000 such cooperatives, with 260,000 members, a tiny but affluent fraction of the Soviet population. Once the voluntary cooperative was formed, members negotiated with the city for a plot of land to build on and held meetings to choose an architect and decide on design and landscaping details and which amenities (such as elevators) to include. Sometimes cooperative apartment owners discovered that their rights as "owners" meant nothing. In 1937 the poet Osip Mandelstam and his wife, Nadezhda, found that the co-op they had paid heavily for was, under government connivance, slowly being turned over to a high-ranking secret policeman named Kostyrev, who in return for spying on them would eventually be awarded the whole apartment. At first Kostyrev, who masqueraded as a writer, was installed in one room of their home, even though according to the law, "nobody could be registered for residence in it without our [the Mandelstams'] permission." Eventually the Mandelstams were banished from Moscow and their apartment became Kostyrev's. A law invalidating co-op owners' rights to refuse unwanted tenants in their home was not passed until the end of 1938, but as Nadezhda observed, "In this country they don't wait until laws are passed before putting them into effect!"[23]

DETACHED HOUSES

In the late Soviet period, only a little over 20 percent of urban residents lived in individual, detached houses. Very many such houses had been torn down by the government, and in many larger cities it was illegal to build separate, private homes. The government frowned on such dwellings and made it difficult for people to get credit to build or buy a new detached house. The law limited private houses to no bigger than

60 square meters of floor space, although there were exceptions for important people and big families. Building materials were very expensive and hard to get; a time-honored way to construct a private house in the countryside was to tear down all or part of an existing house in order to recycle the lumber. In Aleksandr Solzhenitsyn's story *Matryona's Home,* the peasant woman Matryona is bullied until she allows her relatives to cart off the top room of her wooden house so that her foster daughter, Kira, and Kira's husband can transfer it to a plot of land in another village.

Many Estonians, however, did manage to privately build new detached homes. In 1959 a *New York Times* reporter marveled at the scale and quality of private home construction in the Estonian Republic, where middle-class families—higher-paid workers, local officials, civil servants, and professionals—were happily building their own sturdy, pretty houses in city suburbs, along paved streets. A three-room pink stucco house being put up by a 40-year-old truck driver even had a garage for the family car. For house-building Estonians of the time, a finished private house was the end result of many years of intergenerational family toil and financial scraping by. The cost of materials was financed with hefty deductions from family salaries.[24]

RURAL HOUSING

In villages, on the other hand, small, very simple one-, one-and-a-half, or two-story detached houses were the traditional homes for country folk since long before the Revolution. Rural homes were very different from the small apartments or communal rooms of urban residents. Most rural families (about 80 percent in the late 1970s) owned their one-, two-, or three-room farmhouse (*izba*), generally made of planks or logs. Country people on average had slightly more inside living space than city people, and each house had its vegetable garden with a privy in one corner of the garden. Especially under Nikita Khrushchev's leadership (1953–1964) the government pushed to replace peasants' private plots and separate houses with city-style apartment complexes, but when apartment buildings were built on farms, the upper stories often remained empty because women refused to bear the added burden of running up and down stairs every time the garden or livestock needed tending.[25]

An above-average peasant house for a family of four in 1970, in the south of Russia near Krasnodar (an agriculturally prosperous area by Soviet standards), was neat looking, brick, about 22 by 25 feet, not including its small enclosed porch. It had two tiny bedrooms, a kitchen, a living room and a *pech'*, a brick or ceramic stove used for both heating and cooking, big enough for a person to sit or lie down on, and in winter the favorite place for sleeping and relaxing. As Solzhenitsyn points out, this traditional Russian stove is inconvenient for cooking because the cook has to shove the pots inside, and so can't watch them. But the *pech'* also has advantages:

You can stoke it up once before daylight, and food and water, mash and swill [for pigs] will keep warm in it all day long.[26]

Many such peasant homes also had small, cheap, more fuel-efficient metal heating stoves, often made from oil barrels. The bedrooms of the Krasnodar home were "bright and pretty with pale blue, lacey bed and pillow covers," but there were no closets. The kitchen had a very small refrigerator, a table with a radio on it—the house had electricity—but no cupboards, sink, or water supply. The family's living room had a couch, dressing table, and TV. On the porch was an electric washing machine, in the muddy yard fruit trees, flowers, and a grapevine growing on a porch trellis. Despite government campaigns and pressures against religion, such a home may also have had the traditional Russian "icon corner," a place set aside for a sacred image, candles, and perhaps various offerings. Similarly, the prosperous village of Saltykovka (population around 7,000 in 1959), 35 miles by train from Moscow, was filled with small wooden cottages, each heated by a *pech'*. Most Saltykova houses had three small rooms downstairs and one upstairs. Telephones were extremely rare in Saltykovka dwellings in the 1950s, and none had indoor plumbing. Instead, water had to be fetched from village wells, which could be as much as 200 or 300 feet distant from the home. Most cottages had electricity, but the low-wattage bulbs cast only a dim light. As always in the Soviet Union, the plots of ground on which these village cabins stood were intensively cultivated to increase the family's food supply and income. Solzhenitsyn's peasant woman Matryona owns a once-sturdy wooden home that over decades has become as poor and shabby as the woman herself. Nevertheless, relatives covet her house not only for its second-story room, but also for its attic, cellar, fenced-in yard complete with latched gates to keep animals from straying, shingled roof, four windows, plus a small attic window "decorated in the old Russian style," spacious ground-floor room, and *pech'*. The timber walls of the main room are covered with five ancient layers of greenish wallpaper, vestiges of more prosperous times. The house has rubber plants by the windows and (since the 1920s) electric lighting, thanks to Lenin's rural electrification campaign. Besides the narrator and Matryona, "a cat, some mice, and some cockroaches [live] in the house." In her yard, Matryona plants potatoes and keeps a goat for its milk.[27]

A Soviet village's upper class (the farm bosses, agricultural experts, engineers, technicians) possessed more comfortable, more attractive living spaces than did unskilled farm laborers, like Matryona, at the bottom of the social ladder. In the Ukrainian village of Terpene, in the 1960s, all the local elite lived in homes with wood floors and tiled roofs, and almost

Thatch-roofed village homes about 20 miles from Kiev, 1918. Reproduced from the Collections of the Library of Congress, LC-USZ62-97673.

half of those houses had stone walls, while most field hands inhabited clay huts, almost a third of which had dirt floors. Some peasant homes in Terpene had thatched roofs (roofs made from straw or other kinds of plant stalks and foliage). In the western Siberian village of Gurevka, in the 1960s, most roofs were thatched and only a few, better houses had slate coverings. Other izbas in European Russia might be thatched, shingled, or planked.

Inside the Gurevka houses, walls and ceilings were whitewashed; some better residences had painted floors. Windows were very small and could not be opened (a protection against the Siberian winter). Most Gurevka houses had two rooms—one for eating, cooking, and preparing fodder for livestock, the other for sleeping. During the day, the bedroom would be neat and cozy, with bedcovers and pillows covering the bed and a romantic, if cheap, print of an idyllic country scene or of a medieval knight and his lady on the wall. Gurevka villagers proudly furnished their homes with modern factory-made items (dressers, round tables, iron bedsteads). Only a few households, whether from poverty or nostalgia, kept the sturdy wooden beds and square handmade tables of times past. The whole village envied one family's leather sofa, which was always covered with a clean white sheet and never sat on. Gurevka houses had outbuildings where livestock were kept, but villagers brought their precious new-born calves and piglets inside their homes. With food always a precious commodity, villagers of Gurevka planted onions, carrots, and cucumbers next to their houses, reserving the one-acre private plots near their homes for potatoes only. They did not grow fruits but gathered wild currants and raspberries from the nearby woods.

After 1962, when Gurevka was electrified, many village houses boasted radios, but since power was generally turned on just for milking times, villagers could listen to the radio only in the early morning, noon, and night until 11 P.M.[28]

Small plank or log cabins were not typical of all parts of the rural USSR, however. In the Kirghiz Republic in 1965, villagers still lived in mud huts and nomadic livestock herders in their traditional yurts (circular domed tents). In the valleys of the Donets and lower Dniepr Rivers, rows of

Russian peasant woman carrying water from a well, around 1920. Such cabins and method of transporting water for household use remained commonplace in village life throughout the Soviet era. Reproduced from the Collections of the Library of Congress, LC-USZ62-96999.

whitewashed mud brick or flimsy wood shacks with backyard outhouses made up the usual mining town. Women and children balancing water buckets on poles across their shoulders paraded to and from the roadside pump. Construction workers sent to the area to build desperately needed apartment complexes only intensified the housing crisis for a time; the cheap materials and shoddy construction of their hastily thrown up apartment buildings were clearly evident.[29]

WORKERS' DORMITORIES

In 1980, 5 percent of city dwellers lived in workers' dormitories. Conditions in such dormitories could be miserable. One factory worker, not a prisoner, who had been transferred to a new industrial area in the east, described his shelter as being a long building, "half dugout, half barn," in which 60 people slept on wooden bunks, with no privacy. They could bathe only every 10 days and were bedeviled by lice. When Vladimir Voinovich was a railway worker in Moscow in 1956, the station workers lived in heated cattle cars, management in antique passenger cars. Four single people were assigned half a cattle car furnished with a "two-tiered rack, and a kitchen that had nothing in it but a wood stove." Families also had half a car, which they tried to make homey with "little curtains and geraniums in the windows" (and the smell of diapers). Toilet facilities were in a wooden outhouse; water was also outside. When Voinovich found a job as a construction worker, he moved into a hostel intended for unmarried workers, where eight people lived in rooms of 96 square feet and enjoyed such amenities as a big kitchen, gas, and "civilized toilets," but no hot water or bathing facilities. When residents married, which was against the rules, "The supervisors...would come bursting into the room, rip down the [partitioning] sheet, make a scene, and chase the husband out." People endured such conditions in order to live in Moscow, and the rent was very cheap.[30]

DACHAS

Dachas are country retreats Russian city people use for summer vacations and weekend getaways. For Russians a *dacha* fulfills a dream of having a place of one's own, getting back to nature, and temporarily escaping the noise, crowds, lack of privacy, cramped living space, and general stresses of city life. In the late 1980s around 60 percent of Muscovites (Moscow residents) and Leningraders had access to a *dacha*. These cottages can range from secluded palatial villas for the very wealthy and influential (in Soviet times the perks of high Party rank included a free or low-rent state-owned country mansion complete with servants) to rough log huts similar to the year-round homes of many villagers, to a rented room in a peasant's house. Specially built settlements in the hills south and southwest of Moscow, at Peredelkino and Krasnaia Prakha, were rural colonies for writers, actors, and directors. Others, including writers, scholars, journalists, and high government officials, had their forest-surrounded summer homes at Nikolina Gora, 25 miles west of Moscow. The outskirts of the pine-forested communities of Zhukovka and Barvikha west of Moscow were *dacha* country for the *crème de la crème* of Soviet society. The Nobel prize–winning physicist and dissenter Andrey Sakharov had his government-issue *dacha* at Zhukovka, although Abramtsevo was the main location for scientists. Summer places reserved for the elite were on side roads forbidden to ordinary people.

Those not entitled to a government-subsidized *dacha* had to compete in a fierce sellers' market. In 1977, a country place with electricity and running water might cost as much as 50,000 rubles ($69,000). But even for people of means it could be difficult to buy a *dacha* because few were for sale. For ordinary city people the *dacha* shortage was almost as serious as the shortage of year-round housing. When Khrushchev in the 1960s made garden plots available to blue-collar workers, the gardeners quickly put up sheds on their little plots and before long the sheds became mini-dachas, even though the authorities forbade them to expand the sheds beyond 270 square feet.

City folk who wanted fresh-air vacations often began their rental hunt in February (hotel stays were usually out of the question because scarce hotel rooms were saved for foreigners and Soviets on official business). Collective farmers, like the one who rented all his rooms and moved into his toolshed for the summer, could turn a nice profit on summer rentals, but a city family without good connections might end up very disappointed in their summer vacation. Vladimir Voinovich rented two rooms in a cottage for himself and his family, only to discover belatedly that the cottage hosted four other families and was near a similar cabin with five households, one of which loudly played a radio all day and well into the night. Sometimes people rented trucks to bring their home furnishings to the *dacha* and back again at the end of the season. A family member (usually the husband) had to make regular runs between country and city because rural grocery stores were scarce and poorly stocked.

A *dacha* for sale, even if it was no more than a shack, always came with a bit of surrounding land, even though all land belonged to the state and theoretically could not be sold. In Estonia, where unimproved land was especially difficult to buy legally, would-be summer-home owners often paid thousands of rubles for nonexistent houses. The land, however, was real enough to build a *dacha* on. Sometimes, if the right price or other inducements were offered, a rural soviet could be persuaded to sell an abandoned farmhouse. For example, a doctor obtained a house on a collective farm in exchange for his occasional services at the local rural clinic.

NEIGHBORHOODS

Although apartment (or room) size and quality depended on social privilege, neighborhoods and apartment buildings did not necessarily reflect the social class of the people who lived there. Especially in older areas, buildings might contain both communal and private apartments. Even within communal apartments, there was a class distinction between those who had smaller and larger amounts of space; some supposedly communal apartments housed one advantaged family. Newer neighborhoods, however, were more likely to have buildings reserved for workers in certain enterprises and agencies, such as the secret police, the Academy of Sciences, certain factories, or artists' unions.

HOUSING EXCHANGES

Exchanging housing with someone else was a common and legal way to cope with the severe need for adequate room. Every big city had its Bureau of Housing Exchanges, which kept files of information about people who wanted to swap housing, but otherwise bureau officials were not helpful. Big-city housing exchanges also published a bulletin for housing exchanges, but this potentially useful publication could be hard to find, especially in Moscow. As a result, across the Soviet Union people regularly and informally gathered outdoors to post advertisements and meet with others who had apartments or rooms to trade. The Moscow housing exchange market, in an old section of the city, was one such lively swap meet. Even in freezing blustery weather one would see

hundreds of people...milling about for hours, like pickets on strike: hands thrust into their pockets, scarves wound tightly against the cold, carrying placards or hand-scrawled signs pinned to their leather jackets and sturdy cloth coats.[31]

People also found out about housing exchanges through notices posted all over cities, wherever others would be likely to see them.

Such exchanges were often extremely complex, involving numerous families and types of shelter. Before the state exiled him to the city of Gorky in 1980 Andrey Sakharov and his wife, Elena Bonner, needed an apartment big enough for themselves, her daughter and son-in-law, two grandchildren, and Elena's mother, Ruth Bonner. They had their eyes on a four-room communal apartment occupied by three separate families, all of whom wanted better living arrangements. Their intricate plan took a year to craft, involved 17 people and five apartments, and finally satisfied everyone except the local soviet executive committee, which vetoed the exchanges on the grounds that one of the women involved would end up with six and three-quarters square meters of living space beyond the legal norm. The real reason for the veto may well have been Sakharov's political nonconformity. Another intricate Moscow "musical chairs" exchange, organized by a young couple with a baby, involved six apartments and eight families, plus 500 rubles to an elderly man who had his doubts about moving. Even when all parties agreed, such complicated swaps had to pass bureaucratic hurdles. The exchange had to be okayed by city authorities to ensure no one violated the complex rules about who was entitled to how much living space, and that everyone involved was permitted to live in the city where the exchange would take place.[32]

IMPACT OF THE HOUSING SITUATION ON FAMILY LIFE

The extreme housing shortage, especially in cities, meant that grandparents, adult children, and grandchildren lived together in cramped conditions. Divorced couples often had to continue living together because there was nowhere else to go. Newlyweds generally started out living with a set of in-laws, an arrangement that could last for decades. If an extended family had their own apartment they might partition it into separate quarters, still sharing kitchen and bathroom. Couples sometimes agreed to marry not for love, but to secure more rooms in a communal apartment or to get a larger private apartment. Divorce could be a strategy for getting a more comfortable place to live. In one case, a married couple with a family of four achieved a roomier apartment by an intricate tactic of getting on the waiting list for a bigger apartment, divorcing so that the ex-husband was allowed to remain in their old one-room apartment while the ex-wife and children got a three-room apartment. Then the couple, divorced in name only, exchanged their one-room and three-room dwellings for a better apartment.[33]

In the twilight of the Soviet Union, emboldened by Gorbachev's policy of glasnost (openness) and perestroika (rebuilding), many Soviets decided to openly do some building of their own. Rather than wait for decades to receive an apartment from the government, thousands of citizens began seizing empty land on the outskirts of cities as sites for hand-built homes. In the fall of 1989 huge squatters' settlements appeared, with shelters ranging from mud huts to small but sturdy brick houses. People who had never in their lives held a hammer quickly learned the basics of home construction. "I just watch the guy next door and do the same thing he does," a young teacher in the Kirghiz capital of Frunze declared. He was rushing to finish the door and install a coal stove so that his family could move out of their single room into a home of their own before winter.[34]

NOTES

1. Henry W. Morton, "Housing Quality in the Soviet Union," in *Quality of Life in the Soviet Union,* ed. Horst Herlemann (Boulder, CO: Westview Press, 1987), 95,

107, 110; Drew Middleton, "Class Distinction in Russia Depicted," *New York Times,* sec. 1, p. 2, col. 2, February 3, 1948; James F. Clarity, "Leningrad Still Finds Housing Is Its Main Problem," *New York Times,* sec. 1, p. 2, col. 3, February 16, 1970.

2. Thomas W. Ennis, "Standardization Is Soviet Approach to an Ambitious Housing Program," *New York Times,* sec. 8, p. 1, col. 2, August 28, 1960; Middleton, "Class Distinction"; Clarity, "Leningrad"; Hedrick Smith, "In Soviet, Ingenuity Is Needed to Find a New Apartment," *New York Times,* sec. 1, p. 1, col. 6, November 11, 1974; Henry W. Morton, "The Contemporary Soviet City," in *The Contemporary Soviet City,* ed. Henry W. Morton and Robert C. Stuart (Armonk, NY: M. E. Sharpe, 1984), 9; Morton, "Housing Quality," 96–97, 104–5; Welles Hangen, "Soviet Expands Donbas Housing," *New York Times,* sec. 1, p. 3, col. 1, October 16, 1956.

3. Middleton, "Class Distinction."

4. Morton, "Housing Quality," 99, 102–3, 110, 112; Ennis, "Standardization"; Morton, "Contemporary Soviet City," 3–5, 9.

5. Donald D. Barry, "Soviet Housing Law: The Norms and Their Application," in *Soviet Law after Stalin, Part I: The Citizen and the State in Contemporary Soviet Law,* ed. Donald D. Barry, George Ginsburgs, and Peter B. Maggs (Leyden, The Netherlands: A. W. Sijthoff, 1977), 4–5; Morton, "Housing Quality," 99; Peter Grose, "Coop Home Fulfills Moscow Housewife's 'Wonderful' Fortune," *New York Times,* sec. 1, p. 19, col. 1, September 5, 1965; Smith, "In Soviet."

6. Smith, "In Soviet"; Morton, "Housing Quality," 99, 107, and "The Contemporary Soviet City," 8; Bernard Gwertzman, "U.S. Survey Shows a Steady Growth in Soviet's G.N.P.," *New York Times,* sec. 1, p. 1, col. 1, December 26, 1982; "Standard of Living Is Found to Be Increasing Rapidly in Khrushchev's Russia," *New York Times,* sec. 1, p. 1, col. 3, September 13, 1959.

7. Barry, "Soviet Housing Law," 11–12; Morton, "Housing Quality," 97, 100; "Soviet Jails Mayor and 28," *New York Times,* sec. 1, p. 2, col. 7, May 20, 1964; "Soviet Paper Tells of Housing Scandal," *New York Times,* sec. 1, p. 2, col. 3, January 19, 1963; Barry, "Soviet Housing Law," 12; "Soviet Police Chief Would Bar Drinkers from New Housing," *New York Times,* sec. 1, p. 15, col. 8, July 4, 1964.

8. "Exile says Soviet Shackles the Arts," *New York Times,* sec. 1, p. 15, col. 1, January 6, 1948.

9. Morton, "Contemporary Soviet City," 7, and "Housing Quality," 95; Barry, "Soviet Housing Law," 2–3; Hedrick Smith, *The Russians,* rev. ed. (New York: Ballantine Books, 1976), 98; "City Housing Lag in Soviet Marked," *New York Times,* sec. 1, p. 6, col. 1, September 12, 1954; Gwertzman, "U.S. Survey"; Smith, "In Soviet."

10. Barry, "Soviet Housing Law," 7; "City Housing Lag"; Nadezhda Mandelstam, *Hope Against Hope: A Memoir,* trans. Max Hayward (New York: Modern Library, 1999), 280; "Space Pilot Rises in the World," *New York Times,* sec. 1, p. 7, col. 2, April 18, 1961; V. F. Koliazin, ed., "*Vernite mne svobodu!*" [Give me back my freedom] (Moscow: Medium, 1997), 145; Morton, "Housing Quality," 100.

11. Edward Braun, *Meyerhold: A Revolution in Theater* (Iowa City: University of Iowa Press, 1995), 302–3; Antonina Pirozhkova, "Years at His Side [1932–1939] and Beyond," *Canadian Slavonic Papers/Revue canadienne des slavistes* 36, nos. 1–2 (March–June 1994): 217; Elena Bonner, *Mothers and Daughters,* trans. Antonina W. Bouis (New York: Vintage Books, 1993), 265, 285, 321.

12. Norton D. Dodge and Murray Feshbach, "The Role of Women in Soviet Agriculture," in *Soviet and East European Agriculture,* ed. Jerzy F. Karcz (Berkeley:

University of California Press, 1967), 265–302; reprinted in Beatrice Farnsworth and Lynne Viola, eds., *Russian Peasant Women* (New York: Oxford University Press, 1985), 255; Barry, "Soviet Housing Law," 3; Gertrude E. Schroeder, "Rural Living Standards in the Soviet Union," in *The Soviet Rural Economy,* ed. Robert C. Stuart (Towota, NJ: Rowman and Allenheld, 1984), 250; Morton, "Housing Quality," 98.

13. Seymour Topping, "Soviet Family Realizes Dream: A Room to Live in All by Itself," *New York Times,* sec. 1, p. 19, col. 1, December 11, 1960; Mervyn Matthews, "The New Inequality," in *The Stalin Revolution,* ed. Robert V. Daniels (Boston: Houghton Mifflin, 1997), 159; Smith, *The Russians,* 98, 102; Barry, "Soviet Housing Law," 2–3; Morton, "Housing Quality," 96; Middleton, "Class Distinction"; Sheila Fitzpatrick, *Everyday Stalinism: Ordinary Life in Extraordinary Times: Soviet Russia in the 1930s* (New York: Oxford University Press, 1999), 141.

14. Aleksandr Solzhenitsyn, *Cancer Ward,* trans. Nicholas Bethell and David Burg (New York: Bantam Books, 1969), 339–40.

15. Eugenia Ginzburg, *Within the Whirlwind,* trans. Ian Boland (San Diego: Harcourt Brace Jovanovich, 1982), 202.

16. Ginzburg, *Within the Whirlwind,* 314.

17. Middleton, "Class Distinction"; "Standard of Living"; Ginzburg, *Within the Whirlwind,* 204; "Exile Says."

18. Ginzburg, *Within the Whirlwind,* 393.

19. Ginzburg, *Within the Whirlwind,* 333, 393–94.

20. Hangen, "Soviet Expands"; "Soviet Ulcers Laid to Crowded Homes," *New York Times,* sec. 1, p. 7, col. 2, July 22, 1962; Smith, "In Soviet," Morton, "Contemporary Soviet City," 7; Raymond H. Anderson, "Long Wait to Wed Is Urged in Soviet," *New York Times,* sec. 1, p. 5, col. 1, July 4, 1966; Topping, "Soviet Family;" Morton, "Housing Quality," 112.

21. Grose, "Co-op Home"; Smith, "In Soviet"; Barry, "Soviet Housing Law," 14–15; Morton, "Housing Quality," 110; Smith, *The Russians,* 99.

22. Theodore Shabad, "Discount Stores Opening in Soviet," *New York Times,* sec. 1, p. 1, col. 1, p. 6, col. 1, December 16, 1964; Smith, "In Soviet."

23. Barry, "Soviet Housing Law," 3–5; Shabad, "Discount Stores"; Smith, "In Soviet"; Morton, "Contemporary Soviet City," 9; Mandelstam, *Hope Against Hope,* 285.

24. Osgood Caruthers, "Soviet Estonia Is Found a Land of Many Private Homes," *New York Times,* sec. 1, p. 14, col. 4, October 1, 1959.

25. Smith, *The Russians,* 50; *Soviet Union—A Country Study,* ed. Raymond E. Zickel (Washington, D.C.: Federal Research Division, Library of Congress, 1989); Schroeder, "Rural Living Standards," 250.

26. Aleksandr Solzhenitsyn, *Matryona's Home,* in *The Norton Anthology of World Masterpieces,* ed. Maynard Mack et al., expanded edition, vol. 2 (New York: W. W. Norton, 1995), 2309.

27. Editor's note in *The Norton Anthology of World Masterpieces,* 2311; Andrei Amalrik, *Involuntary Journey to Siberia,* trans. Manya Harari and Max Hayward (New York: Harcourt Brace Jovanovich, 1970), 149; Roy D. Laird and Ronald A. Francisco, "Observations on Rural Life in Soviet Russia," in *Contemporary Soviet Society: Sociological Perspectives,* ed. Jerry G. Pankhurst and Michael Paul Sacks, 149–50 (New York: Praeger, 1980); "Standard of Living"; Solzhenitsyn, *Matryona's Home,* 2306–8.

28. Helmut Altrichter, "Insoluble Conflicts: Village Life between Revolution and Collectivization," in *Russia in the Era of NEP: Explorations in Soviet Society and Culture,* ed. Sheila Fitzpatrick, Alexander Rabinowitch, and Richard Stites (Bloomington: Indiana University Press, 1991), 193; Alexander Vucinich, "The Peasants as a Social Class," in *The Soviet Rural Community: A Symposium,* ed. James R. Millar (Urbana: University of Illinois Press, 1971), 320; Amalrik, *Involuntary Journey,* 148.

29. Amalrik, *Involuntary* Journey, 149–50; Robert Conquest, *Agricultural Workers in the USSR* (London: Bodley Head, 1968), 119–20; Hangen, "Soviet Expands."

30. Morton, "Contemporary Soviet City," 7; Middleton, "Class Distinction"; Vladimir Voinovich, *The Anti-Soviet Soviet Union,* trans. Richard Lourie (San Diego: Harcourt Brace Jovanovich, 1986), 102–8.

31. Smith, *The Russians,* 98–101.

32. "You May Beg, Borrow or Rent: It's Dacha Time Again in Moscow," *New York Times,* sec. 1, p. 2, col. 3, August 17, 1977; Smith, *The Russians,* 48–55; Morton, "Housing Quality," 102, 104–6, 111; Christopher S. Wren, "Sakharov, Seeking a New Apartment in Moscow, Finds a Tangle of Red Tape Barring the Door," *New York Times,* sec. 1, p. 3, col. 4, March 4, 1977; Smith, "In Soviet."

33. Morton, "Contemporary Soviet City," 7, 9; Smith, "In Soviet"; Peter H. Juviler, "The Soviet Family in Post-Stalin Perspective," in *The Soviet Union Since Stalin,* ed. Stephen Cohen, Alexander Rabinowitch, and Robert Sharlet (Bloomington: Indiana University Press, 1980), 119.

34. Francis X. Clines, "Off the List, Into a Lean-To: A Hammer Beckons," *New York Times,* sec. 1, p. 4, col. 3, November 18, 1989.

8

Health care and Health problems

The Soviet government pioneered the concept of a national health service with free medical care for all citizens, a right proclaimed in their constitution. On July 18, 1918, Lenin created the People's Commissariat of Health of the Russian Republic. Nikolai Semashko, the first Commissar of Health, led this massive undertaking. Revolution, civil war, famine, mass migrations, and incursions of soldiers, together with long-standing, widespread conditions of poor hygiene, poverty, illiteracy, and primitive living conditions, produced raging epidemics. Scabies (a contagious itchy skin disease), malaria, syphilis, smallpox, cholera, typhus, and tuberculosis were common contagious diseases. Cholera and typhus epidemics erupted in 1918; between 1918 and 1920 there were more than six million cases of lice-spread typhus, a disaster that prompted Lenin to remark, in his address to the Seventh Congress of Soviets: "Either lice will defeat socialism or socialism will defeat lice." In these early days of Bolshevik power the average life expectancy in Russia was 30 years, a statistic that put Russia about 150 years behind England and America.

From its founding the Ministry of Health focused on preventive medicine through vaccination, personal hygiene education, and easy access to free basic health care. The government in the 1920s published eye-catching cartoon posters exhorting citizens to get vaccinated, bathe often, use soap, avoid alcoholic drinks, quit smoking, and be alert for their small children's safety, particularly during spring cleaning when industrious housewives left windows wide open. However, there was always much greater emphasis on delivering medical care and education to urban workers than to peasants, and Moscow gave the central Asian republics especially short shrift in medical services. Even at the end of the Soviet era most central Asian hospitals did not have heat, running water, or indoor plumbing.[1]

During the years immediately following the October Revolution, large numbers of physicians died from epidemic diseases and many others fled the country. Thousands of new doctors were needed, and fast, so the government turned to a source of plentiful cheap labor: women. Before the 1917 Revolutions medical schools had been all but closed to women, but now on government orders the medical schools opened welcoming doors to them. Because many of these women were poorly educated, academic standards were compromised so that students could pass their courses and quickly get to work as low-level government employees. Professors who protested the changes were likely to be brutally silenced, as the medical-educational machinery continued to grind out legions of doctors (1,255,600 in 1988, compared with 612,000 that year in the United States). Most of these medical foot soldiers were female.[2]

WOMEN IN SOVIET MEDICINE

In 1946, 8 out of 10 medical students were women. In the 1970s, 72 percent of doctors were women, and they earned on average about two-thirds of the average factory worker's salary. In the 1980s a general practitioner was paid about 130 rubles a month, 40 more than a hospital orderly, and less than a bus driver's salary of 200 rubles. A doctor without a wage-earning husband would likely have hard times, especially if she had children. With or without a co-breadwinner, women doctors shouldered all the same household responsibilities as other working women, since it was not customary for men to help carry out these chores. Such "double shifts" made life particularly exhausting for women doctors, especially those who struggled to keep up with the latest developments in their field. In his novel *Cancer Ward*, Aleksandr Solzhenitsyn captured the Soviet doctor's dilemma in the character of Dr. Lyudmila Dontsova. As she travels home from work after a long day, Dontsova, a highly respected radiologist, slowly and with great difficulty tears her thoughts away from her patients and tries to focus on the time-consuming tasks of a wife and mother:

Home was her responsibility, and hers alone, because what can you expect from men? Her husband and son, whenever she went to Moscow for a conference, would leave the dishes unwashed for a whole week. It wasn't that they wanted to keep them for her to do, they just saw no sense in this repetitive, endlessly self-renewing work.[3]

In social prestige Soviets apparently ranked doctors on the same level with schoolteachers (rather than above them as in the United States and other Western countries). If women were the infantry troops of Soviet medicine, men were the officers. By the mid-1960s however, the proportion of male to female doctors was beginning to change; more men than women were entering medical schools, and these men were intent on having a lifestyle closer to their Western European and American counterparts. To achieve that standard, male students took advanced classes and training (beyond the six years required for an ordinary doctor) in order to become specialists and professors of medicine, and to land important posts in large city hospitals, research institutes, and medical schools. That sort of position guaranteed higher salaries, city residence, and respect. Besides being male, possessing a Party card and having excellent connections greatly improved chances of being admitted for advanced training and reaching the higher echelons of medicine.[4]

Feldshers and nurses were on the lowest rung of trained medical personnel. Feldshers, 75 percent of whom were women (*fel'dsheritsy*, sing. *fel'dsheritsa*) were paramedics with two and a half years' training, sometimes with a specialization in such fields as emergency care, midwifery, or public health (monitoring conditions in factories, giving first aid). After the revolution there was an attempt to eliminate feldshers because of their brief preparation, but that initiative quickly vanished, and instead the number of feldshers steadily increased. In the late 1970s, there were 500,000 such medical assistants in the Soviet Union. Feldshers could continue their medical education; Solzhenitsyn's Dr. Dontsova began her career as a feldsher-midwife. Perhaps feldshers could take comfort in the fact that they also were not at the very bottom of the health care profession. That space was reserved for nurses, virtually all of whom were women.[5] Nursing was not respected, and like other Soviets who toiled in low-paying service jobs, nurses tended to be bossy and rude to those they were supposed to be helping. They often seemed more interested in making sure patients observed hospital rules than in providing professional care and comfort. For some women nursing was a stepping-stone to becoming a *fel'dsheritsa*.[6]

EXPENSES

Whether people were counseled or treated by specialists, general practitioners, feldshers, or nurses, the care was, according to the law, free of charge. Furthermore, all citizens were legally entitled to free medical care whether in a hospital, in an outpatient clinic, or at home being visited by a medical professional. Nevertheless, it was customary to bribe doctors and other medical personnel with money, gifts, or services in order to get better care, a more qualified doctor, or "private" medical services (e.g., services provided "off the books" in the doctor's or patient's home, or in a clinic after regular hours). Many doctors felt it was more dignified to receive noncash gifts from their patients. Such bribes covered a range of scarce or expensive consumer items, including but not limited to food—especially meat—and clothing. A doctor in Riga, the Latvian capital city, helped a young stationery clerk get a private medical abortion for the bargain price of 10 rubles in exchange for two hard-to-find typewriter ribbons. The doctor's wife regularly received free meat at a collective farmers' market in exchange for her husband's ongoing treatment of the butcher's chronic endocrinological condition. In the 1970s it was customary to tip a doctor who made a house call 4 rubles, plus the cost of her round-trip taxi ride. In case of emergencies, however, payment was not expected. Hospital nurses and orderlies had to be bribed to perform such basic tasks of patient care as changing sheets, providing (and promptly emptying) a bedpan, or dispensing painkillers, especially if they knew the patient could pay. Even meals might not be available without a bribe. Soviet patients understood this and generally came into a hospital with plenty of rubles to distribute among hospital personnel. The amount patients paid unskilled and semiskilled hospital personnel "under the table" (*na levo;* literally, "on the left") was not much—a few rubles per day—and affordable for most. Sometimes, however, when lower-income patients or relatives wanted to assure the services of a highly regarded surgeon, hundreds of rubles might be required, plus extra tips for amenities such as antibiotics, a private or semiprivate room, and more intensive caregiving than was usual in a Soviet hospital ward, they could feel a financial pinch. One infant taken to a Moscow children's hospital in 1988 at first shared a room with 12 other children, but because his grandmother knew "how to talk to people the right way" a private room materialized.[7]

PRIMARY CARE: POLYCLINICS

Polyclinics were all-purpose health clinics. With their examining rooms and (in larger cities and towns) staffs of nurses, general practitioners, internists, and specialists, polyclinics were the first stop in the medical care system. People were assigned to a district polyclinic based on where they lived, but many had "closed" access to another clinic in addition to the district facility. For example, the Ministry of Health and other ministries had their own polyclinics, as did universities and factories of more than 4,000 workers, or, in small, dangerous enterprises like mining, as few as 2,000 workers. Smaller factories were staffed by feldshers rather than by physicians. Policemen, military personnel, railroad workers, Party members, members of the ultra-prestigious Academy of Sciences, and the artistic and intellectual elite all had access to special closed networks of clinics and hospitals that were superior to ordinary district facilities. Large cities had specialized outpatient clinics such as women's clinics and clinics for certain diseases or organs, and first-aid posts in subway stations and other public places. In rural areas, depending on location, polyclinics had fewer examining rooms and fewer doctors, or only a feldsher.[8]

At a city clinic people first saw a general practitioner (*vrach*) or internist (*terapevt*), who might refer the patient to a clinic specialist for further diagnosis and treatment. Officially, patients could not choose a doctor, but determined patients could manipulate the system through bribes and connections or by finding out which doctors worked what hours, and then appear for treatment or advice during their chosen doctor's shift. It was not uncommon for patients to wait at least two hours, perhaps as much as half a day to see a doctor, and then have only 7 to 10 minutes of the doctor's time, part of which was taken up with the paperwork she had to fill out for each patient. People could and often did visit the different clinics they had access to—neighborhood, workplace, and perhaps a third at a hospital—for the same complaint. Soviet citizens, especially those of working age, tended to consult with doctors more often than did people in other parts of the industrialized world, perhaps because people were legally entitled to time off to see a doctor.[9]

Free house call service was also part of the medical care system. Staff doctors at regional clinics and hospital outpatient departments rotated this duty, visiting patients within their service area, especially those with chronic ailments, the elderly, and the dying. Besides being an important and convenient service for invalids, home visits, which were eight times more frequent in cities than in the countryside, helped free up hospital beds in perpetually overcrowded urban hospitals. Since hospitals were crowded and were not supposed to exceed a certain number of inpatient deaths, the house call service made it convenient for administrators to stay within their quota by sending dying patients back home, listing them as "deteriorations" rather than "deaths." Certainly for many patients dying at home among familiar faces and surroundings was preferable to death in a packed, impersonal hospital ward.[10]

EMERGENCIES

In or near a city people could summon an ambulance by dialing 03 from home or make a free 03 call from any public telephone. The call was answered by a clerk (who might be a nurse) at the city's central ambulance dispatching station. She would ask the name, address, and phone number of the caller and what the problem was, writing that information on a card. If the emergency was dire, the clerk put a red stripe on the card, then sent it to a dispatcher along a conveyor belt. The dispatcher noted which substation was closest to the source of the call and checked a large control board to keep tabs on how many ambulances were available and where. In Moscow, Leningrad, and a few other big cities, the best ambulances were reserved for true crises and were specialized according to the emergency: heart attacks, strokes, poisonings, and psychiatric cases. These specialized ambulances carried a feldsher and a doctor who had 10 months' special training in emergency medicine.

If the desk clerk thought the call was not urgent, she often gave instructions over the phone for home remedies or transferred the call to a doctor who decided whether an ambulance was necessary. If the doctor decided the case was not critical, he could send an emergency doctor to make a home visit (this service was available only in a few large cities) or (especially in chronic cases) tell the caller to contact his or her local polyclinic for a house call. In the late 1970s, Moscow, Leningrad, and Kiev had the best ambulance systems and they often, but not always, provided prompt service. In rural areas, where doctors were scarce, it was more likely that only a feldsher would be riding the ambulance; perhaps she would have had special emergency training, perhaps not. In Irkutsk, a major Siberian city in south-central Siberia, the ambulance that arrived to transport a visiting American to the local hospital had trouble starting and had no medical equipment except what was in the feldsher's bag. Whatever means were used—ambulance, emergency home service, or house call service—the doctors when they arrived were expected to diagnose and decide on the spot whether to transport the patient to a hospital. Even though the state provided a range of free or at least inexpensive medical services, there were many who doubted the quality of care. For these people, the government also provided an option, at least in some cities.[11]

FEE-FOR-SERVICE POLYCLINICS

Although the regular polyclinics were free, there were also government-run paying polyclinics where, for a modest fee, patients could get the services of doctors presumably more highly qualified than the doctors in a free clinic. In 1980 there were around 130 paying polyclinics in the Soviet Union, where patients could choose their doctor, were more likely to find the specialists they needed, did not have to wait as long, and were treated more considerately than in free clinics. The fee-for-service system included a number of psychiatric clinics where patients might get better treatment than at the free mental health facilities. Whether or not paying clinics were truly superior, there may have been a certain placebo effect in the patients' belief that "you get what you pay for." However, the most flourishing fee-for-service medicine was almost always conducted illegally.[12]

PRIVATE PRACTICE, LEGAL AND ILLEGAL

Soviet physicians and dentists were allowed to hang out their shingles, but legal, open private practice was not widespread because private doctors were subjected to very high taxes, intense government oversight, and even housing restrictions. In *Cancer Ward* Solzhenitsyn describes one such rare holdout: an old-fashioned self-employed physician who practices from his home office despite the fact that "the neighborhood was full of spies from the tax office." Solzhenitsyn's Dr. Oreshchenkov is everyone's nostalgic dream of an elderly doctor, straight out of a Norman Rockwell painting. Kindly, wise, ambitious only to alleviate suffering, he has earned his social prestige from grateful patients and cares not for luxuries, advanced degrees, or government awards. He has been able to keep his private practice only because he saved the lives of influential people and their relatives and because his practice was located in Uzbekistan, which "was more easygoing."[13]

Illegal private practice was the rule. Doctors and dentists saw patients in the patient's or the doctor's home or at public clinics after hours, charging fees for the service. In the late 60s, such covert charges ranged from 5 or 10 rubles for in-hospital procedures or homeopathic consultation to 500 rubles for treatments by a senior specialist for a venereal disease. Patients often exchanged goods and services, as well as rubles, for private care.[14]

SANATORIA

Workers were entitled to time at a sanatorium, a combination of country rest home, hospital, and vacation resort where people with chronic illnesses, real and imagined, could at minimal or no cost to themselves get away from their daily routines and be pampered. In 1978 there were 2,277 sanatoria and 1,170 rest homes and boardinghouses linked to various medical care facilities. Individual sanatoria generally specialized in a certain disease or family of diseases: gastrointestinal problems, high blood pressure and heart-related problems, diabetes, hypertension, kidney stones. Special sanatoria for children focused on rheumatic fever and respiratory infections. Before the Revolution such rest home–therapeutic resorts were favorite getaways only wealthy people could afford. With the 1919 Decree on Therapeutic Areas of Nationwide Importance, the Bolsheviks made popular resort areas accessible to workers and peasants. In 1960, the Council of Ministers of the USSR gave 80 percent of sanatoria over to trade unions (*profsoiuzy*), which then distributed a limited number of sanatorium tickets (*putevki*) to their members. Typically a worker interested in a sanatorium ticket—and what worker would not be?—had to first get a medical evaluation, and then perhaps negotiate and finagle for the most attractive sanatorium. Some locations were far more alluring than others; most people preferred to go south rather than north in the winter, for example. Lower-paid workers paid little or nothing for their sanatorium stay. While higher-salaried employees such as midlevel administrators did pay a modest amount, the highest-ranking directors of enterprises and the highest level of Party officials had cost-free exclusive access to their own especially luxurious sanatoria. People regarded sanatorium treatment as both vacation time and serious medical therapy. In the late 1970s a standard 24-day sojourn at the city sanatorium at Ufa (an industrial town in the southern Ural mountains) cost 120 rubles, or $186.00, of which trade unions paid 90 rubles and the patient the rest. There were 25 doctors on the Ufa sanatorium staff for the 450 patients who came there to eat tasty large meals and receive various therapies and advice on how to live a healthier life. Upon arrival patients were assigned a small, brightly painted double room. Their medical history was reviewed, and they were given a treatment program. A typical daily schedule would likely call for morning exercises, mud baths, mineral baths, heat treatments, and well-balanced meals. Mud-bath therapy meant that heated mud was applied to the affected area only: neck, arms, legs, or back. For mineral baths patients soaked in large bathtubs for 30 minutes, showered, then rested for an hour. The routine began at 8:00 A.M. with a short exercise session led by a physical therapist. Then patients were off to breakfast in a large, airy dining hall. Like all meals breakfast was attractively prepared and plentiful. Special diets (low salt, low fat, etc.) were served depending on a person's medical needs. Patients were on doctor's orders to drink *kumiss,* a popular, very sour-tasting drink made from fermented mares' milk and believed to be good for various ailments, including tuberculosis. "I have all my patients drink it three times a day," the assistant director of the Ufa sanatorium proclaimed. "For ulcer patients I use it more often." Other popular therapies at the Ufa and other sanatoria included megavitamin injections, drinking alkaline soda water, herbal remedies such as compresses of hot olive oil applied to the small of the back for treatment of migraine headaches, and nettle and burdock leaves "wrapped around arthritic fingers and tied across sprained backs." Patients received pine-scented oil massages, lay under heat lamps, submitted to mustard plasters, and consulted with a doctor every fourth day.[15]

Because of their status as political undesirables, the poet Osip Mandelstam and his wife, Nadezhda, had been forced to live in poor health and poverty for years, with no permanent home. When in 1938 the Union of Soviet Writers unexpectedly offered them a voucher for two months at a rest home (a type of sanatorium) they gratefully accepted. Installed in a comfortable separate cottage in an isolated country resort and well fed, they were lulled into almost forgetting their constant fear of arrest. Only the seeming impossibility of getting transportation to the nearest town made them uneasy. "You don't think we've fallen into a trap, by any chance?" the poet asked his wife. But, treated like "guests of honor," they convinced themselves otherwise. One morning, however, the couple were awakened by a knock on their door. Two military men, accompanied by the rest home doctor, had come to take away the poet.[16]

For lower and middle-class workers the demand for sanatorium tickets far exceeded the supply: in 1986 less than 20 percent of the population were able to enjoy a stay at a resort facility.[17]

MEDICAL CARE FOR THE ELITE

The Fourth Department of the Ministry of Health operated special medical accommodations throughout the Soviet Union that were exclusively for the Communist Party elite—top Party officials, directors of large enterprises and scientific institutions, famous creative artists. The network included clinics, hospitals, and sanatoria. Fourth Department facilities had technology and equipment not available to other citizens, whether Party members or not.

The higher up the sociopolitical pyramid, the more comfortable, respectful of personal privacy, and personalized the care and the more up-to-date the technology. Ordinary citizens might get no more than 10 minutes of a doctor's time at a district polyclinic, but members of the Academy of Sciences and their spouses were entitled to check themselves into the academy's hospital for two or three weeks for their yearly physicals. At the very peak of the health care pyramid, scattered across the USSR, in all Soviet cities, were medical facilities of all kinds that were open only to the *crème de la crème* of Party elite and their families, who did not pay for their medical care extras.[18]

Medical services for topmost Party officials differed from those of other closed networks (clinics and sanatoria reserved for the military and for railroad workers or workers in huge factories, for example) in that they offered the very best-equipped clinics and hospitals. If blood tests could not be done in the USSR, samples were flown to a lab in Helsinki, Finland, and back to Moscow; drugs and equipment not available in the USSR were imported from abroad. For these favored few, specialists might be imported to consult or to operate. But class distinctions did not end at the top. Even within the ultra-elite special clinic in the Kremlin, there were distinctions according to rank. Deputy ministers and below were seen in private cubicles, but special examining rooms with carpeted floors, bookcases, leather couches, and heavy red drapes on the windows were reserved for ministers. Meanwhile, most hospitals struggled to acquire basic equipment, not surprising since in the 1970s less than 1 ruble per day per patient was allocated for everything a patient needed, while hospitals for the privileged received up to 15 rubles per day per patient.[19]

MEDICAL SHORTAGES

Even the commonest household medicine cabinet staples were hard to find: bandages, absorbent cotton, thermometers, iodine. Hospitals resorted to desperate measures to get needed supplies. Bandages were reused; one hospital turned to appropriating the cotton artificial snow from a New Year's display; many doctors, including those who had ambulance duty, relied on their personal connections for life-saving medicines like insulin for diabetics or potassium for regulating heart rhythm, and medications for high blood pressure. X-ray machines and film, incubators for premature babies, stethoscopes and otoscopes (instruments for examining ears) were chronically in short supply or not available. Equipment that could be purchased was usually outdated, poorly made, and sometimes unworkable. In a pediatric intensive care ward in Samarkand, one of five incubators was working in 1990, but only now and again. There was no sterilizing equipment in the ward, and the only automatic respirator was made for adults.

A one-year-old boy, hooked up to the respirator by means of a makeshift adapter, was lying on a card table because there were not enough cribs. "This [hospital] is one of the best places," an Uzbek doctor declared. "Still we have only our hands and our heads to work with." The widespread shortage of disposable hypodermic syringes in hospitals and clinics and failure to sterilize needles threatened the health of the whole population in many ways and contributed to the rising incidence of AIDS in the Soviet Union. In late 1988 unsterilized needles used in a children's hospital in the Kalmyk Autonomous Republic caused up to 41 children and eight mothers to become infected with AIDS. In January 1989 there was an outbreak of AIDS among 10 children in a pediatric ward in Volgograd. Soviet authorities traced the disease to a child in a hospital in a nearby city. That child's blood had been drawn by a reused, unsterilized needle that had passed the (undiagnosed) illness on to other children in the ward. Still without a correct diagnosis, these HIV-positive children were eventually transferred to the Volgograd hospital children's ward, where once again unclean needles carried the disease to more young patients.[20]

An 11-month-old boy at a Moscow children's hospital had an incision above one eye stitched up with silk thread because that was all that was available. When the stitches were removed, "blood gushed all over his face," the child's mother recalled. The doctor informed her that if she had wanted better suture material she "should have supplied it herself." The lack of vascular sutures meant that a nine-year-old boy who had injured his leg in a tractor accident had to undergo a leg amputation because the needed surgical sutures were not available. A surgeon near the East Siberian city of Khabarovsk had to operate with his bare hands because of a delay in production of rubber gloves. In the 1980s only one-fourth as many respirators were produced as were needed, and a third of them were broken. Even those that "worked" were so shoddily made that they tended to deliver either too much or too little ventilation. Outpatient clinics and hospitals also lacked common equipment for diagnostic testing, so that treatment was based on the educated guesses of primary care doctors and specialists rather than on such standard equipment as X rays, CT scans, and blood tests. In the late 1970s in all of Irkutsk, there were no gastroscopes—a common piece of medical equipment that enables a doctor to look inside a patient's stomach. In mid-1988 the country needed about 1,000 more operating tables. There was little in the way of disposable equipment such as scalpels, catheters, syringes, and rubber tubing. Needles had to be resterilized after each use, rendering the needle points rough. As an American doctor observed,

Finding a vein is like trying to cut a tomato with a dull knife. Even with initial success, the coarse needles will rapidly tear through the vein wall and stop [a blood transfusion]. The tubing is sticky after repeated heatings and the blood frequently clots.

Hospital administrators had to deal with shortages as best they could. If one hospital was low on sutures, for example, but had extra supplies of syringes, doctors in another hospital might agree to an exchange. For this reason doctors routinely ordered more medical supplies than they needed, in hopes of having extras to trade. There was also a black market. In Moscow for the price of 100 rubles one could get a packet of 10 disposable needles "home-delivered by underground medical entrepreneurs."[21]

Nevertheless, talented, devoted doctors could and often did overcome these obstacles, delivering seriously ill patients back to health. Solzhenitsyn's autobiographical novel *Cancer Ward*, closely based on his experience as a cancer patient in a Tashkent hospital, is a song of praise to his doctors. Overworked, underpaid, and toiling in conditions dangerous to their own health, Solzhenitsyn's cancer specialists saved his life.

Obstetrics and gynecology were near the top of Soviet medical priorities from 1918, just below care of military and industrial workers. After all, women were the bearers and nurturers of future workers and soldiers. The Soviet government had provided (by the late 1970s) 250,000 hospital beds for childbirth, 25,000 clinics where women could go to get Pap smears, routine gynecological examinations, abortions (when legal), and prenatal care. One out of 20 doctors were obstetrician-gynecologists, and all their maternity services as well as routine physicals and Pap tests, were free. Abortions, available on demand, cost five rubles ($7.75 in the late 1970s), except where necessary for the mother's health, in which case there was no charge. Expectant mothers were supposed to visit a maternity clinic 14 to 17 times during pregnancy. Ninety-eight percent of all births occurred in hospitals, according to Soviet statistics. Nevertheless, other factors dimmed this rosy picture.[22]

Women's clinics and maternity wards in the 1980s lacked such basic modern equipment as fetal heart monitors, ultrasound units, and other equipment for monitoring labor and delivery. Consequently, thousands of newborns died who might otherwise have lived. In the Russian Republic alone poorly trained doctors may have caused some 600 to 700 deaths every year of women who were in childbirth or who had recently undergone abortions.[23]

MATERNITY

The government provided women's clinics where pregnant women could get their monthly checkups, official permission for 112 days of maternity leave (starting in the seventh month), or abortions and other gynecological services. Typically, when a woman visited such a clinic, there was a long wait in line, perhaps an hour or more, just to get an admission card to the clinic. Eventually she was shown into a doctor's office, where she was questioned about any problems and given her vitamins, advice, and orders for ultraviolet treatments to insure she got enough vitamin D. When labor began, an ambulance was called and eventually, up to an hour later, the ambulance arrived with a midwife on board. The ambulance took the expectant mother to a maternity hospital or maternity ward, whose conditions were likely to be a "horror." In theory a pregnant woman with Rh-negative blood who lived in Moscow was entitled to be hospitalized at one of the three special maternity clinics for women with that condition, so they and their offspring could be specially cared for. In practice, admission depended on *blat* (connections), not blood type. Even at these special facilities, however, the sanitary conditions were abominable. "I couldn't believe how dirty the place was," a young woman recalled, shuddering at the memory of the "flies stuck to all the light fixtures" and her feeling that "Everything was slimy."[24]

At this special clinic, whose routines were typical of many other maternity wards, the expectant mother changed into a hospital gown and slippers, gave her clothes to her husband or parents, and kissed her relatives goodbye. In accordance with Soviet hospital sanitation rules, they could not accompany her into the hospital ward, much less into the labor or birthing rooms, nor were they allowed to wait in the hospital to find out how things were going. Women in labor might be required to walk up flights of stairs to get to an assigned room, to sit and wait in a corridor, or to trudge to some other part of the hospital and labor there until a short time before delivery, whereupon they might be expected to walk back to the delivery room. The expectant mother whose connections got her into the Moscow maternity hospital for Rh-negative women found herself in a delivery room with 12 other patients in "pandemonium, all of them screaming in pain and using the most ferocious Russian curse words." Generally when pains increased the laboring woman was told to breathe deeply and given a small, one-time injection of painkiller. Official medical policy, influenced by the government-approved Russian psychologist Ivan Pavlov, regarded childbirth pain as a reflex controllable by mental attitude. Soviet medical dogma about childbirth pain led to the popular "Lamaze method" (named after the French obstetrician Fernand Lamaze) of "natural childbirth," a system of prenatal training in deep breathing, supportive coaching, physiology lectures, and psychological awareness that is still current in the United States and Western Europe. The crucial difference between Soviet-style natural childbirth and the Lamaze method is that deep breathing, auto-suggestion, and minimal or no anesthesia for normal births were legally required for all Soviet maternity wards and maternity hospitals; women who preferred painkillers to deep breathing, or for whom the breathing and psychological suggestions were ineffective, did not have the option of receiving more anesthesia than the small amount allotted by government decree. Lamaze's own ideas (e.g., presence of a close friend, spouse, or partner as coach, prenatal training sessions) were not incorporated into Soviet prenatal care. During labor and delivery, a midwife simply wiped her patients' foreheads and kept tabs on her charges. After the baby was born it was immediately taken from its mother, and to guard against infections, no contact between mother and child was allowed for the first 24 hours. Women stayed in the hospital for 10 days following childbirth. The special Moscow maternity hospital for Rh-negative women had a single bathroom with one cold-water faucet for all the new mothers, a luxury compared with conditions in country hospitals that often did not have any running water.[25]

INFANT MORTALITY

From 1951 to 1971, infant mortality statistics steadily improved. In 1950, 80.7 of every 1,000 children born died before they reached their first birthday. Twenty years later, infant mortality had decreased to 24.7 deaths per 1,000 live births, a significant improvement but still behind the United States and other developed countries. The USSR stopped publishing their infant mortality statistics in 1974, a sign that the downward trend had been reversed. American scholars estimated the rate to be 31 deaths per thousand in 1976, and the increase appeared to be Union-wide. Possible causes might be increasing numbers of Soviet women addicted to alcohol and cigarettes, which can cause low birth weight and many other life-threatening problems for the affected newborns, and lack of medical resources (such as neonatal intensive care units) and technology (miniature respirators, etc.) to save at-risk newborns. These technologies by the 1970s were becoming common in the United States and other developed countries. By contrast, Moscow had one hospital with special equipment for premature babies; no other hospitals had special equipment beyond "simple nurseries." In addition, breastfeeding was difficult for those Soviet women who had full-time jobs. A 1978 study in Daghestan (an autonomous Russian republic on the Caspian Sea) found that only one-third of infants were breastfed; the others drank formula. This was problematic given the frequent shortages of formula and absence of preparations for children who needed a special mixture. Finally, severe air and water pollution increasingly took their toll on children's health and lives (see "Other Public Health Problems," below).[26]

The Kirghiz, Tajik, Turkmen, and Uzbek republics had 22 percent of the Soviet Union's births and 39 percent of infant deaths. Their infant mortality rate was nearly twice the average for the whole Soviet Union and among rural people, more than twice the average. Respiratory and intestinal tract diseases killed infants up to five times more often in Central Asia in 1987 than in the Soviet Union as a whole. In Turkmenistan the official infant mortality rate was 54.2 per 1,000 live births, 10 times higher than in most Western European countries. In Turkmenistan's poorest areas infant mortality was even higher: 111 per thousand births. Those were the official numbers; according to Moscow officials, Central Asian republics underreported infant mortality rates by as much as 60 percent. There were several forces working against infants in this region: environmental pollution; inadequate medical facilities, including incompetent and insufficient numbers of medical workers; cultural bias toward very large families, with little or no government support for family planning and birth control education; and Central Asian women's reluctance or inability to seek prenatal care from medical professionals. In 1991 the new Minister of Health for Turkmenistan pointed out that "especially in the countryside, women only come to the hospitals to give birth." But for poor Turkmen women getting to a hospital could be almost impossible. A man whose family of seven lived in a two-room mud hut on the outskirts of Ashkabad, the capital, described the conditions surrounding the death of one of his children soon after it was born: "No one has phones here, and there are no hospitals or doctors around. I ran two or three kilometers [one to two miles] to the pay phone and called. It looked like the baby was dying—or was dead already, maybe—and it took the doctors more than an hour to get here. By then the child was dead."[27]

CONTRACEPTION

Soviet men generally did not consider themselves responsible for birth control. In the mostly Islamic central Asian republics, particularly in rural areas, women were encouraged to stay at home, avoid using abortion or birth control of any sort, and to have at least five or six children, preferably males. Most Russian women, on the other hand, had and were expected to have outside jobs; in the late 1970s, over 68 percent of Soviet women over 16 juggled full-time jobs and complete household responsibilities, burdens more likely to be alleviated by a retired grandmother than by a husband. Among Russians the main contraceptive techniques were the rhythm method, withdrawal (some believed the latter method could make a man mentally ill), and a trip to the local gynecological clinic for an abortion. Other methods of contraception (condoms, creams, jellies, pills) were unpopular. Diaphragms were made in only one size, so they were not effective for every woman. By the late 1970s, more women were becoming interested in using IUDs (intrauterine devices) as an alternative to frequent abortions, but the supply outstripped demand; urban women had to place their names on waiting lists for an IUD. In the 1970s birth control pills produced in Hungary were available mainly on the black market since the USSR was only just beginning to manufacture them. The government officially discouraged women from using the pill because of possible dangerous side effects. Since user-friendly woman-controlled birth control was not available for most women, those who got pregnant but preferred not to carry the fetus to term turned to low-cost legal medical abortions.[28]

ABORTIONS

An estimated 16 million abortions were done in the USSR in 1980, or 40 percent of the number of abortions performed worldwide. The average

Soviet woman had six abortions, though some had many more than that. An Odessa woman told William Knaus that her mother had had 24 abortions. All abortions were prohibited immediately after the October Revolution but made legal in 1920, on the grounds that illegal abortions were tremendously dangerous to women's health. In 1936 abortions were again outlawed except for women with certain physical or mental problems, and this remained in force until 1955. In the 1940s, a Leningrad gynecologist claimed that approximately 70 percent of women in hospital gynecology wards were the victims of infections incurred as the result of illegal abortions. A common method for self-inducing abortion during the period from 1936 to 1955 was to push a heavy armoire around a room for as long as one could before dropping from fatigue, so that the miscarriage, if it happened, would look spontaneous. If that tactic succeeded, a woman might go to a gynecology clinic to get "cleaned out," and she would not have to worry about being reported to the authorities by clinic personnel.

After 1955 abortion was available on demand during the first 12 weeks of pregnancy. After 12 weeks, a woman could have the operation legally only if it was medically necessary. The most common method of abortion was by scraping or aspirating the womb. No tranquilizers were given beforehand; local anesthesia was used during the procedure, and the patient might be kept in the hospital for two or three days after. Illegal abortions were infrequent when they were easily and legally available in a government clinic, but occasionally women did have illegal medical abortions when they wanted the procedure done with more privacy and comfort.[29]

MEDICAL CARE FOR RETIREES

Medical care was free for pensioners as it was for workers. Since there were virtually no nursing homes elderly people remained at home and depended on their children, other relations, and visits from a local house call doctor to help them in their old age. During the 1960s and early 1970s the government established geriatric rooms for the elderly at a few larger city clinics. In these facilities older people were given more time with an internist than usual: 30 minutes for the first visit, 15 to 20 minutes for each follow-up, compared with the usual 7 to 10 minutes per patient. Elderly people liked the geriatric rooms; nonetheless, the number of such places decreased from 134 to fewer than 100 in the late 1970s. In contrast to the situation in the United States, Soviet citizens over 75 were less likely to be hospitalized than those who were younger, a situation that may in great part have been caused by hospitals' reluctance to admit very elderly patients. On the other hand, during any given year the "young old" (mainly in their 60s) were more than three times as likely to be hospitalized as the average person.[30]

Soviet citizens age 50 and up were more likely to seek medical care from home visit doctors, including ambulance doctors, than were their younger compatriots. With regard to ambulance service, however, the elderly were second-class citizens because emergency medical personnel had definite instructions to take care of young patients first. For that reason people who telephoned for an ambulance often hid the fact that the call was on behalf of an old person. The elderly were frequently treated as throwaways at local polyclinics also. One woman weepingly related to a journalist how she had with difficulty dragged herself to the clinic and waited in line only to be asked by the doctor, "Why are you here? I don't even have time to examine the younger patients." The Soviet Union had about 1,500 old-age homes (called "homes for labor veterans") in 1979, with some 360,000 residents. By 1986 the number of nursing home residents had decreased to 327,000 with 90,000 on waiting lists, and an unknown number who needed to enter but had not applied because of the small chance of getting in. One observer described the old-age homes as "warehouses," dilapidated and lacking in the most basic physical and psychological comforts, an extreme last resort for the frail elderly.[31]

FOLK MEDICINE, OFFICIAL AND UNOFFICIAL

Perhaps because modern pharmaceuticals and up-to-date-equipment for diagnosis and treatment were scarce and of poor quality Soviet doctors frequently used old-fashioned discredited remedies such as hot mustard plasters (thin squares of strong-smelling paper that when applied to a patient's back and chest leave large red marks) and "cupping" (the application of small heated glass cups to the back or chest; the rim of the heated glass causes suction against the flesh, producing large black-and-blue bruises). Doctors often prescribed herbal remedies as well as homeopathic medications (homeopathic medicine is based on the theory that diseases can be cured with tiny doses of drugs that would cause those same disease symptoms in a healthy person). There were seven homeopathic pharmacies in Moscow in the 1970s. Some sick people sought relief completely outside the official health care network by visiting folk medicine practitioners like the *znakharki*, women who prepared potions and claimed the ability to whisper diseases away. Health care reform legislation in 1969 aimed at banning those with no medical training from practicing medicine or dispensing medications.[32]

HOSPITALS

Despite the many outpatient facilities—polyclinics, house call doctors, on-the-spot ambulance treatment, emergency house calls, folk medicine and homeopathic remedies—Soviets entered hospitals early and often. As a result, most Soviet city hospitals were overcrowded. Metal beds were jammed together within hospital wards and often overflowed into the hallways. The maximum amount of time patients could stay in a hospital

was decreed by law, according to the illness (10 days following an appendectomy, childbirth, or gallbladder surgery, two weeks for a hysterectomy,
eight weeks for a heart attack), and most patients stayed the maximum
whether they really needed to or not. In addition, clinic doctors were more
likely to send their patients to a hospital than most American doctors
were: in the 1970s, one out of four Soviet citizens was hospitalized each
year. The average hospital stay in the early 1980s was 15 days, compared
with 5 in the United States. Often a long confinement was necessary
because of inefficiencies that could stretch the minutes needed for a routine test or exam into a week or more.[33]

City people ill enough to be referred to a hospital by a polyclinic doctor
were expected to arrive by ambulance; country folk got themselves to the
hospital however they could, and sometimes the jour-
ney was long and painful. Solzhenitsyn's Kostoglotov   **In the Hospital**
(the author's slightly fictionalized self-portrait) is found
one night at a Tashkent hospital, lying on the floor, wet, muddy, in pain,
and exhausted from his long journey. As happened to many such new
arrivals, he is given first a bench to sleep on and then a place on a staircase
landing until a bed becomes available.[34]

Often Soviet hospitals were housed in prerevolutionary buildings not
originally intended as hospitals. Many old mansions, former government
buildings, even prisons, in the case of some psychiatric hospitals, served
as hospitals without being remodeled for their new purpose. Inside such a
structure, such as the Botkin Hospital in Moscow, one would see high ceilings, spacious hallways, and rooms with large windows. These once elegant structures were frequently dilapidated and short on plumbing and
sewage facilities. Upon entering the hospital, a patient would be met by a
doctor in charge of interviewing new patients. This doctor had the responsibility of assigning a diagnosis (ulcers, appendicitis, heart attack), generally by questioning the patient about symptoms but without the help of
medical tests, and entering that diagnosis on a "sick list." The diagnosis
determined the number of days a patient would be allowed to take off
from work. (Workers were paid their normal salaries as long as they were
within their official number of sick leave days, whether in the hospital or
at home). At the end of the official sick leave patients would have to go
back to work, bringing with them certification from the hospital. Those of
working age who were discharged as invalids got documents excusing
them from returning to work. In most cases, the admitting doctor's initial
diagnosis, even if unsupported by testing, would be accepted by the doctor assigned to treat the patient.[35]

New patients at the Botkin Hospital were sent to a room where they
removed their clothes and deposited clothing, identification, and money
into a paper bag. Then they were handed a sheet to cover themselves and
told to climb onto a stretcher for a trip to the X-ray department for a chest
X-ray. From there the patient was brought to his room, again on a

stretcher, since wheelchairs were not available. Hospital wards in Soviet cities generally contained from 6 to 12 or 14 beds, often pushed together so that one could not walk between them. The room would be pungent with a certain "musky, sweet, slightly nauseating odor of old urine and damp sheets." Beds had a single thin mattress, a small pillow, and no privacy curtain; next to the bed, if space allowed, might be a battered metal night-stand.[36]

The women's wards at Botkin were more cheerful, with flowers on many nightstands, a TV viewing area (the men's wards had a bedside earphone that was wired into a Moscow radio studio), and newer, cleaner bathrooms than in the men's areas. In fact, the men's toilet facilities at Botkin, one of Moscow's best hospitals, were "primitive." One floor had only three seatless toilets for 76 men and no toilet paper—patients had to provide their own copies of *Pravda* or other newspapers. Unsanitary conditions were only worsened by the common medical practice of giving enemas not only as preparation for tests but also as standard treatment for many illnesses and complaints. At Botkin men patients lay on a couch in the toilet room, receiving the enema from a woman who used the same equipment for all, rinsing the nozzle in soapy water after each application. The few toilets frequently broke down from constant use and overflowed, forcing patients to step through a smelly, sticky mess on the toilet room floor. Still, the Botkin Hospital was not the worst facility in the USSR.

At best a camaraderie developed among the patients in the multi-bedded rooms—they helped, comforted, and scolded each other. At worst patients as well as hospital personnel might behave harshly toward patients who inconvenienced them by doing things like constantly moaning or vomiting during the night. One Russian journalist claimed that lucky patients with relatives or friends to nurse and feed them ignored their less fortunate ward-mates at holiday times when hospital personnel took off. Newcomers to a hospital ward were quizzed by roommates wanting to know the new patient's illness, medical history, treatment plan, and physicians and surgeons past and present. They weighed the information, comparing it with their own knowledge and experiences, and offered their medical opinions. After the questions newcomers were given important advice about bedsheet changing, toileting, bathing, tipping personnel, and so on.[37]

Once a day a staff doctor wearing a tall white starched hat and white lab coat conducted rounds, spending a few minutes with each patient, but even the most devoted hospital staff at Botkin observed the six-and-a-half-hour working day of all Soviet hospitals. After 3 P.M. only a small staff remained for emergencies. The short shifts undoubtedly benefited the mainly female staff of doctors, nurses, and orderlies, who still had hours of shopping, cooking, and cleaning ahead of them.[38]

Soviet medical custom emphasized the dangers of infection brought into the hospital from outside rather than the threat of infection from

within. Probably for that reason, visiting hours were often **Hospital**
limited to one period per week (except in some but not all **Sanitation**
pediatric wards, where mothers were allowed to stay with
their children around the clock if they wished). Hospitals required visitors
to put cloth "booties" over their shoes and to remove or put cloth coverings over their coats. Visitors were not allowed to place reading material
on a hospital bed, sometimes were prohibited altogether from bringing
books and newspapers from outside, and were told not to sit down on a
hospital bed. New mothers were not allowed to visit with the baby's
father or other relatives or friends while they were in the hospital, except
through a glass barrier. It was not unusual to see women leaning out
maternity ward windows, waving at their husbands. These practices
probably originated in earlier Soviet times when lice-borne epidemics
raged and measures were taken to prevent people from bringing lice into
hospitals. On the other hand, inside the hospital not enough attention was
paid to basic precautions like washing hands and sterilizing cloths and
instruments. Too often containers with intravenous solutions were left
open or capped only with a piece of gauze. Hospital personnel not
assigned to a particular surgery blithely strolled in and out of operating
rooms while surgery was in progress. Women "cleaned out" after miscar-
riages or abortions often had these routine procedures under nonsterile
conditions in which operating room personnel wore neither masks,
gowns, nor head coverings and did not use sterile towels. In at least one
case, the physician performing a curettage (scraping of the uterus) had
only one hand gloved, picking up the surgical instrument (curette) with
her bare hand. A Russian medical scientist who had an appendectomy in
Kharkov in "an ordinary district hospital" complained that "the place was
so dirty that you cannot imagine it.... I got an infection and so did the others. I saw one man die in my presence because of [the unsanitary condi-
tions]." In 1987 in Tajikistan, 240 out of 325 hospitals lacked plumbing
outside the operating rooms, and a complete lack of plumbing was a fact
of life in many rural health care facilities. In the late 1980s more than a
fourth of all rustic hospitals had no sewage disposal facilities, two-thirds
had no hot water, half had no running water, and 17 percent had no water
supply at all.[39]

At Botkin patients ate in a small dining room; there were supposed to be
special menus geared to their illnesses, but in fact the food was the same
for all and varied little, if at all, from day to day. Many
were able to supplement the skimpy hospital fare with **Hospital Food**
food brought in by relatives, although food packages
might be stolen or rifled before they reached their destination. Supper for
the patients of Solzhenitsyn's *Cancer Ward* was "a rectangular rubbery
suet [animal fat] pudding with yellow jelly on top."[40]

In Lithuania, one of the Baltic republics the Soviet Union annexed during the summer of 1940, hospital quality came much closer to that of the

United States and other developed countries. For example, the Kaunas Eye Hospital, which opened in 1977, was light, bright, cheerful, "spotlessly clean," and completely financed by a private organization, the Society for the Blind. Although the Kaunas hospital owned some modern equipment, it still lacked standard apparatus such as the laser equipment American ophthalmologists would have considered necessary for their work. The Moscow Research Institute for Micro Eye Surgery, under the directorship of its founder, Svyatoslav Fyodorov, was blessed with highly advanced equipment, modern facilities, and very competent personnel. Fyodorov, an internationally famous eye surgeon, invented radial keratotomy (a method of correcting nearsightedness through surgery) and pioneered the implantation of artificial lenses in human eyes as well as a "conveyor belt" high-volume method of performing routine eye operations. His deserved fame earned him a place in the Soviet elite class along with the clout to demand and receive the best for his institute. Because Soviet health care was free to foreigners as well as citizens, patients came from around the world to be operated on by Fyodorov himself, the surgery often being part of a two-week package tour. Ordinary Soviets needing treatment at Fyodorov's hospital had to have a referral from their local polyclinic and would have to wait six months to a year for admission.[41]

RURAL MEDICINE

Except for those with the highest grade average, the law required new doctors to work for two years in the countryside or smaller towns. But most medical school graduates did not want to work in rural areas even temporarily, and often found ways to avoid the boot camp of village hospitals and clinics. Consequently, the doctor–patient ratio was much higher in cities than in rural areas. During the Stalin era it was not unusual for medical care in Siberia and Central Asia to be in the hands of doctors and nurses serving out sentences as "enemies of the people." If they survived they practiced medicine where they found themselves, whether in prison camps or in forced residence near the camp in which they had served their time. Within the gulag, women were recruited as nurses from the female prison population without regard to previous training or experience. For prisoners a job in the camp hospital was a treasure because it meant indoor work and enough food to sustain life. Eugenia Ginzburg, a prisoner in Siberian camps and former Kazan University lecturer in literature, was saved from freezing and starvation by the happy accident of meeting a prisoner-doctor who had been friendly with a relative of hers in Leningrad. The doctor got her a job as nurse in a home for prisoners' children and she "[o]nce again...[gave] death the slip." Her beloved husband, Anton Walter, arrested because of his German descent, was a devoted doctor-prisoner who ministered to his patients in and out of camps during his Siberian imprisonment. In 1952 Aleksandr Solzhenitsyn was a prisoner in a camp in Ekibastuz, northern Kazakhstan, and was about to be operated on in the prison hospital (where all the doctors were prisoners) for a fast-growing tumor in his groin. The day before the writer's operation the camp surgeon was sent to a different camp, and Solzhenitsyn had to wait almost two weeks for the arrival of another prisoner-surgeon, who removed a cancerous lymph node. Because the prison hospital had no laboratory, sections of Solzhenitsyn's tumor were sent to Omsk (some 250 miles north) for analysis. Solzhenitsyn was not informed about the results of the lab tests, nor was he offered any follow-up or further treatment while he was a camp inmate. He finally was treated for a recurrence of the cancer but only because he battled an indifferent bureaucracy for the right to travel to a Tashkent hospital. Where no doctors could be found (or forced) to practice, a district was served by a feldsher.[42]

In 1980 a logging village of 30 small log cabins, wooden sidewalks, and dirt roads, about 150 miles north of Irkutsk, boasted a restaurant, grocery store, and small hospital. This hospital, a little wooden building with 20 beds and two doctors, was the only medical care for the district's 2,000 people. In winter it could be reached only by a small aircraft the doctors used for emergencies. Unless there was something like a flu epidemic, the hospital usually had three or four of its beds occupied at any given time. Heavily cultivated areas of the USSR had bigger hospitals built for collective farms.[43]

PHARMACEUTICALS

As with other consumer goods, production and distribution of pharmaceuticals was very inefficient. Patients had to pay for prescription drugs, except for those prescribed in hospitals; vitamins for children and pregnant women; and drugs for chronic illnesses like tuberculosis, schizophrenia, and epilepsy. Drug retail prices were relatively low, but people often could not find prescribed medications or found them with difficulty, or paid high prices on the black market. Urban drugstores sold some common remedies like Vikalin, which was the only available Soviet antacid preparation. Unlike American antacids, which are pleasantly colored, flavored, and buffered, Vikalin was a brown, extremely bitter pill.

Soviet pharmacies sold many herbal preparations such as anise seeds, which were mixed with honey and water to relieve gas; dill seeds, sold in green envelopes, for heartburn; chamomile tea for ulcers; and *kumiss* for digestive problems. In the Siberian city of Kemerovo in 1989 one could find only bottles of leeches and jars of aspirin on the pharmacy shelf.[44]

DOCTOR–PATIENT RELATIONSHIPS

Patients might reject a doctor's prescription or other method of treatment and try to find help elsewhere, but it was considered rude to openly question her judgment. Too often patients were processed in a hurried, impersonal, assembly-line fashion. As with other service providers in the Soviet economy, health workers' jobs did not depend on satisfied customers. As if to prove this, a hospital in the heavily polluted Urals town of Berezniki, where an unusually high number of children had blood infections, posted a list of "Mothers' Duties" in its children's ward. The list ended with the warning that mothers who disobeyed would "be ordered off the premises."[45]

Doctors did not feel obligated to explain their treatment plan in detail to the patient, present alternatives, or be truthful about the seriousness of a patient's illness. People sometimes had major surgery without being informed about what had been done to them. "I think they cut out part of my stomach," a woman in Ufa said, "but I'm not sure. The doctor never told me."

"Generally speaking, we don't have to tell our patients what's wrong with them, but if it will make you feel any better, very well, it's lymphoma."
    "You mean it's not cancer?"
    "Of course it's not."[46]

With psychological preparation and sedation gastroscopy can be an easy and quick procedure but was a source of intense fright and discomfort for nonsedated, unprepared Soviets. Gastroscopy at the Botkin Hospital was usually done without any advance explanation or sedation; shocked patients screamed and struggled against having a long black tube "about the thickness of a small garden hose" inserted down their throats into the esophagus and stomach. Like patients in other parts of the world, Soviet health care consumers often complained about the deterioration of the doctor–patient relationship, nostalgically recalling a golden age when they got more personal, sympathetic attention. One middle-aged factory worker complained that most doctors "don't even bother to ask your name." Soviet patients always faced the possibility that their assigned doctor had been admitted to and graduated from medical school through bribery and had no professional skills, not even basic ones.[47]

American-style malpractice lawsuits were unheard of. People could bring a lawsuit against a doctor, but only to remove the license to practice, not for a money award.

DENTISTRY

Dental care was crude by Western standards. Painkillers were used sparingly and teeth were often pulled rather than fixed. A privately paid dentist in 1980 could get 150 rubles for "extensive repairing and filling done with local anesthetics." A patient wanting gold fillings had to bring his own gold. Like doctors, dentists accepted gifts in kind or cash. A

Moscow woman who could knit got good dental work, and her dentist received a nice sweater.[48]

PSYCHIATRY AND "PUNITIVE MEDICINE"

The first criminal codes enacted after the Bolshevik Revolution set forth the principle that the criminally insane should not be punished as common criminals but could be committed and treated against their will in mental hospitals. Before the October Revolution and also during the early revolutionary period, labeling political enemies or dissenters as insane and committing them to mental hospitals occurred, but rarely. It was not until the late 1930s that the government began a systematic policy of committing "enemies of the people" to mental institutions dedicated to that purpose. Such places, known as "special psychiatric hospitals" (hereafter, SPHs) were used to confine political prisoners and the criminally insane. Political prisoners might also find themselves forcibly committed to an "ordinary psychiatric hospital" (OPH) for the nonviolent mentally ill. Before 1960 many politicals preferred being sentenced to a mental hospital rather than to a camp. Hospital conditions, though bad, were "oases of humanism" compared to prison camps, and even into the 1950s prisoners in mental hospitals sometimes enjoyed a freedom of speech unknown on the outside. Torture as a means of manipulating hospital inmates' behavior is known to have been practiced in the 1950s but was not as widespread as it became starting in the 1960s. It was often hospital policy to put only one "political" in a ward with violent patients, leaving the dissenter at their mercy.[49]

In a typical SPH the windows were small and barred, often covered outside with a blind. Wards were extremely crowded, with little or no space between beds. Sanitation was abominable, especially where inmates were routinely kept tied to their beds. Inmates might be allowed a bath and change of bed linen once every 10 days. Access to toilets might be restricted either routinely or as a means of punishment. In some places food was dispensed through "a trough in the door"; in others inmates ate together in a mess hall. Either way, if the rules allowed, inmates relied on food packages sent from home to get enough calories, though the contents were liable to be stolen. Inmates were allowed to send out letters only twice a month; all letters were read by a censor before being mailed and could become part of the inmate's file. Both incoming and outgoing letters were liable to be confiscated. Visits were generally allowed once a month for two hours, but only from relatives. Hospital authorities regulated what subjects could be discussed with visitors. SPHs officially allotted an exercise period of one-and-a-half or two hours once a day.

Inmates were disciplined by being prevented from having visitors, sending and receiving mail, and exercising. They were also disciplined through torture. It was not unusual for patients to be savagely beaten, whether by

the common-criminal orderlies or by high officers in the hospital administration. Often "insubordinate" inmates (the insubordination was often simply complaining or, in the case of politicals, refusing to recant their views)
were controlled through medical measures, such as being forced to take certain drugs or having their regular dosages increased. The purpose was to
cause physical or mental pain, or both. In the case of political dissenters,
drugs were administered to force them to admit their wrongdoing or confess to being insane, or as punishment for being troublemakers. A favorite
"treatment" was giving unusually high doses of aminazin, a drug ordinarily used for controlling symptoms of such severe mental illnesses as
schizophrenia, paranoia, and manic depression. Patients were not tested
beforehand for possible negative reactions to the medication, even though
aminazin can cause grotesque involuntary body and facial movements that
may not disappear when a patient is taken off the drug. Aminazin has other
dangerous side effects: it can cause irregular heartbeat and can intensify ailments a patient already has.

While forcibly confined in a psychiatric hospital at Kaluga, the dissident
biochemist Zhores Medvedev met a middle-aged man imprisoned for past-
ing up handwritten complaints about the local Party Committee. Diag-
nosed with "poor adaptation to the conditions of the social environment,"
the complainer was administered "two powerful depressant drugs" that the
doctors promised would "change the basic structure of his psyche."
Another inmate, about 24 years old, incarcerated for criticizing the Komsomol (Communist youth league) for being too bureaucratic, was said to suffer from "reformist delusion" and for three months had been undergoing
"periodic insulin shock." Other punishments for politicals and their mentally ill ward-mates included being strapped to a bed for hours or days. The
"wet-pack" treatment consisted of wrapping victims tightly in strips of wet
canvas that tightened as they dried, causing horrible pain.[50]

SPHs were run by the secret police and Ministry of the Interior rather
than by the Ministry of Health, which administered the OPHs. SPH orderlies were convicted criminals who often abused patients, and many of the
SPH psychiatrists, including all department heads, were commissioned
officers in the secret police. Some of the supposed psychiatrists were secret
police operatives with no psychiatric training, and many nurses as well
worked directly for the police. In the 1970s the government turned to these
"psychiatric" methods for repressing approximately 1 in 10 dissenters, so as
to avoid court trials and unwanted publicity from the Western press.[51]

At the Serbsky Institute of Forensic Psychiatry in Moscow, accused dis-
senters were often examined by KGB (Committee for State Security, the
name of the secret police, 1954–1991) psychiatrists. Psychi-
The   atrists would find that the accused had committed crimes
Commitment   against the state because of mental illness (schizophrenia
Procedure for   was a favorite diagnosis). This "expert" testimony was
Dissenters   presented in court without the defendant being present,

and judges then ruled that the prisoner needed hospitalization. Political prisoners were committed to mental hospitals for "criminal" behaviors such as leaving—or trying to leave—the country; publishing abroad or self-publishing their work in the USSR; "anti-Soviet agitation and propaganda"; openly demonstrating religious belief; and espousing political or cultural self-determination for one of the USSR's republics or ethnic groups. A woman who complained to the prosecutor's office, a young man who announced his intention of quitting the Party, a Lithuanian engineer who refused to participate in building a monument to the Soviet war dead unless the state also memorialized the victims of Stalin's terror, young "hippies," religious believers, and draft dodgers were among those who served time in mental hospitals. Few psychiatrists protested this degradation of their profession; those who did risked losing their jobs and their freedom. Dissenters dispatched to OPHs had a chance of getting more humane treatment than in SPHs, although the physical conditions of OPHs were unsanitary and overcrowded, the food scanty and distasteful, and the personnel often badly trained and self-serving. Dedicated, humane psychiatrists at OPHs were limited in how far they could go to protect dissenters.[52]

Just as the new Bolshevik government focused its health care services on disease prevention, it directed its health care system toward avoiding mental illness. Patients with mental problems usually went first to their local polyclinic to consult with a physician. If the doctor thought it necessary, the patient was sent on to see a psychiatrist at the district psychiatric clinic, each of which served about 50,000 people.

Psychiatric Services for the Genuinely Ill

Emphasis was on outpatient treatment. Though some mental health clinics did have small inpatient facilities where patients could be confined for a short time, psychiatrists were supposed to avoid hospitalizing patients if at all possible. Some clinics had day care facilities, their patients being sent home in the evening. Work therapy was favored for treatment and cure of psychiatric problems, so most patients participated in an industry-related workshop attached to their clinic, manufacturing or assembling a variety of goods for which they were paid a small salary plus an invalid's pension. This kind of therapy was also used in mental hospitals, although "the patients dislike it"—a psychiatrist reported—"because it is primitive and monotonous, and they do it under duress." Mental patients, including the retarded, who were too disabled to go to work were given piecework to do at home. Whether in a clinic or in a hospital setting, Soviet psychiatry offered very little in the way of personal or group "talk therapy."[53] Patients who could no longer function in the community were most likely to be admitted to the nearest regional psychiatric hospital for treatment, although some general hospitals also had psychiatric units. There were also prison psychiatric hospitals and psychiatric colonies. The latter, for patients who needed long-term care, tended to be in the countryside where patients worked the land.

Managers of enterprises had the right to begin commitment proceedings for any of their workers, by means of a formal psychiatric evaluation. A relative or doctor could also request such an evaluation. Until 1960, articles in the criminal code stated that doctors and psychiatrists could be punished as criminals if they committed someone to a mental hospital without good reason, and these regulations made it possible for people to appeal a commitment through the courts. In the 1961 criminal code, however, those provisions were left out; people who thought they or a relative had been unjustly committed had no recourse in the court system. They had to begin a lengthy process of appealing to the various levels of the health care bureaucracy, beginning with the lowest regional level and if necessary, continuing right to the top, the USSR Ministry of Health.[54]

Upon entering an ordinary psychiatric hospital most patients, like patients in Western mental hospitals, were given drug treatment and counseling until their acute symptoms diminished. Sometimes patients had insulin coma treatment (rarely used in the West), which consisted of administering enough insulin to put the subject into a coma and then bringing the patient out of his coma. The regimen was applied several times over several weeks. Soviet psychiatrists also used electroshock therapy and sleep therapy (long periods of drug-induced sleep). Brain surgery such as prefrontal lobotomy, which destroys part of the brain, a method used in the West before effective drug therapy was available, was banned in the Soviet Union.[55]

ALCOHOLISM AND OTHER PUBLIC HEALTH PROBLEMS

Russians have been called "the hardest-drinking people on earth," and what they drink most is straight vodka, store-bought and homemade (*samogon*). The history of Russian vodka-drinking culture—which affects mainly the Russian, Ukrainian, and Byelorussian peoples—reaches back into the late fifteenth or early sixteenth century. Widespread alcohol addiction was one of the Soviet Union's toughest health problems and remains so in the three republics today. In the late Soviet period, alcoholism was called "the third disease" because it followed cancer and cardiovascular diseases as a leading cause of death. In the 1960s the government stopped publishing statistics on the amount of alcohol consumed per person nationwide, but the USSR apparently led the world in per capita consumption of hard liquor (drinks with an alcohol content of 40 percent or more). It was estimated that Soviets consumed slightly more than eight liters per person per year, about twice that of persons in the United States. Between 1940 and 1980, when the Soviet population grew 25 percent, Soviet alcohol consumption increased 600 percent. Western scholars estimate there were at least 20 million alcoholics in the USSR in 1987. The Russian male custom of drinking large amounts of hard liquor quickly on an empty stomach caused many deaths from acute alcohol poisoning. *Samogon* was probably the deadliest drink because like all moonshine it was made without controls over ingredients or alcohol content. In the 1970s excessive drinking may have caused over half the 370,000 to 400,000 deaths from "accidents, trauma, and poisonings."[56]

In 1985, during the period of glasnost (openness), Mikhail Gorbachev, the Party's leader, publicly acknowledged the crippling effect alcoholism had on his country's economy, health, and family life. He imposed an antidrinking campaign that featured, among other things, a significant reduction in alcohol production and marketing, and a national antialcohol campaign. Gorbachev's war on alcoholism collapsed in 1988 in the face of fierce popular opposition and loss of tax revenues; in fact, people were drinking more than ever.[57]

There are an unusual number of situations in Russian life that call for drinking: when meeting or leaving others, as a substitute for food when hungry, a follow-up to food when full, a cold-weather warmer-up, a warm-weather cooler, a stimulant when sleepy, a sedative when wakeful. Life's events, big and small—births, deaths, weddings, payday, a new apartment—are occasions for a man to drink himself into a stupor. Rural weddings, birthday parties, and other celebrations often last several days, with heavy drinking a must for the male guests. Not participating or drinking moderately is seen as insulting and unmanly. Alcoholism, once regarded as a man's prerogative, has become more common among women, though they generally begin drinking at a later age (30 to 40) and in the privacy of their homes. Men start imbibing in their teens or even earlier and are not embarrassed to stagger around in public, alone or in groups of three (*na troikh*), having split the cost of a bottle among themselves. Fathers offer liquor to their small sons. Later, as teenage factory workers, these same boys might accompany older workers on payday drinking sprees. Often when people try to quit drinking they are pressured by friends and relatives to fall off the wagon. In the Soviet era, people could always get liquor, on credit if necessary, even though consumer goods and basic grocery items were chronically hard to find.[58]

Sometimes habitual drunkards were arrested and sentenced to "compulsory treatment" in the "treatment labor" divisions of prison camps, under the supervision of the secret police. If sentenced to a camp, the alcoholic inmate had to work, and the cost of room, board, **Treatment** and any treatments were deducted from his pay. If committed to a psychiatric hospital, medical care was free, and the patient got sick-leave pay and may or may not have been required to participate in "work therapy." Sometimes alcoholic patients were placed in ordinary hospitals while they underwent treatment. For the very short term, police-run sobering-up stations were widely used in almost every sizable city and town. Militia picked up drunkards off the streets and kept them in a drunk tank overnight. Prisoners had to pay a fine when they were released, and the police reported them to their employers. In 1979, between 16 and 18 million people (12 to 15 percent of the Soviet urban adult population) had been detained in sobering-up stations, but they were just the tip of the iceberg of USSR alcohol abusers. In the first place, rural areas were unlikely to have sobering-up stations, or special hospital treatment facilities. Second, many drunks were locked up in regular police stations, or because of serious accidents or alcohol poisoning ended up in general hospitals rather than police stations. The first Soviet self-help organization for alcoholics, Alcoholics Anonymous, was introduced in Moscow in 1987.[59]

Child and spousal abuse, deaths caused by drunken driving, inability to work, and diseases of the liver and pancreas were some of the damaging effects of alcoholism. A 1971 survey showed that 6.5 to **Effects of** 6.8 percent of women listed their husband's alcoholism **Alcohol Abuse** as the reason for having abortions. In the countryside **on Daily Life** most divorce actions were brought by women, and of these over 40 percent cited their husband's alcoholism as grounds for divorce.[60]

OTHER PUBLIC HEALTH PROBLEMS

The Party's attention to preventive medicine produced improvements in certain areas of public health. Through vaccination, widely accessible pre- and postnatal care, improved personal hygiene, and health education, such contagious diseases as smallpox, syphilis, gonorrhea, typhus, cholera, tuberculosis, whooping cough, diphtheria, and polio were either stamped out or greatly diminished. Infant mortality fell from 275 deaths per thousand in 1913 to 130 in 1930. However, vaccination programs were not systematic and focused on city rather than rural residents and on those who were living in the city legally rather than illegally. A smallpox outbreak in 1960 prompted the government to vaccinate seven million people in seven days. It was not until 1987, when Gorbachev's glasnost policy shed light on the state of Soviet health care, that the government acknowledged some hard facts. Statistics for the 1970s and 80s showed rising infant mortality; falling life expectancy, especially for men; increases in infectious diseases, including sexually transmitted diseases; and many new cases of tuberculosis among children and teenagers. Statistics also showed that in 1986 Soviet citizens of working age were dying mainly of cardiovascular disease, accidents, poisoning, trauma, cancer, and lung disease. Suicides also took a heavy toll—officially counted in 1987, they numbered 19.1 per 100,000, one of the highest suicide rates in the world.[61] Many of the deaths from cardiovascular illnesses would have been prevented if medical equipment for angioplasty and bypass surgery had been as available in the USSR as in the West. Widespread addiction to cigarette smoking also took its toll. A 1987 survey showed that more than 70 million people smoked, or about 25 percent of the population.

Smoking, drinking, and lack of exercise (exercise for its own sake is an idea that has still not taken hold in the former Soviet republics) are self-inflicted health dangers. By the 1970s it was becoming increasingly evident that people, including millions of children, were getting seriously ill and dying from ecological disasters perpetrated in Moscow. Probably the greatest threat to a Soviet citizen's life and physical well-being was the ecological damage that followed the regime's drive to industrialize the country and create a massive cotton belt in Central Asia, at any and all cost. To an extent unprecedented in the West, Soviet citizens increasingly became victims of ferocious pollution that poisoned their air and water and in some regions greatly diminished or wiped out valuable sources of nutritious fruit, vegetables, and fish.

The Aral Sea, on the border between Kazakhstan and Uzbekistan, not long ago was larger than Lake Huron and sustained rich fisheries. In 1960 it had 26,000 square miles of seabed, but by 1990 nearly half of that had become desert. Now the Aral Sea is on the verge of extinction, killed off by the Soviet government's decision to turn the region into a colossus of cotton production by draining the Aral's feeder rivers for irrigation. The diverted river waters carried ever-increasing amounts of chemical runoff from cotton fields heavily overtreated with fertilizers, pesticides, and herbicides, poisoning most of the groundwater that served more than 35 million people. Children who worked in the cotton fields often drank irrigation water poisoned by chemicals; babies took in toxic substances with their mothers' milk. By 1989 the radically diminished sea was three times saltier than it had been in 1961. Giant dust storms from the desertified salt seabed carried millions of tons of sand and salt into surrounding areas, causing throat cancers and respiratory and eye diseases. Even without sandstorms, people who lived in the Soviet cotton belt were poisoned by the everyday air they breathed, especially if they had worked in the fields since childhood. In 1974 the Nobel Prize–winning physicist and political activist Andrey Sakharov told the world that Uzbek schoolchildren used as field hands were having respiratory problems from exposure to herbicides. In Tajikistan it was apparently not uncommon to repeatedly expose child fieldworkers to aerial spraying of chemical defoliants. Consequently, the infant mortality rate in Kara-Kalpak (in northwestern Uzbekistan) reached twice the Soviet average; maternal mortality rates there tripled from 1984 to 1989. This mortality rate resulted not only from poisoned air and water but also from the severe malnutrition that took place when poor peasants were forced to raise cotton, a crop they themselves did not profit from and could not eat. As the land became ever more sterile, officials ordered peasants to give up their personal garden plots and trees to cotton production. In 1990 the newspaper *Komsomol'skaia Pravda* published evidence that children in Turkmenistan were dying of starvation even "before they are born."[62]

The adverse effects of environmental pollution were not limited to the cotton belt. Moscow offered the best health care facilities available in the

USSR, but infant mortality rates toward the end of the Soviet era were two to three times higher there than in other Soviet capital cities. In 1989 more Moscow residents died than were born. Poisoned air from car emissions and industrial pollutants was a likely contributor to Muscovites' drop in life expectancy, which in 1990 fell 10 years below what it had been in 1970, placing Moscow 70th in life expectancy among the world's 90 largest cities. Very many Soviet cities were environmentally unhealthy places to live and raise children, but the poster child for a poisoned industrial city was Kemerovo, "a smoky inferno of chemical, metallurgical, and mining enterprises" on the Tom River just east of Novosibirsk. Kemerovo's children had unusually high rates of respiratory illnesses as well as urinary tract and kidney infections. In one especially badly polluted city district the frequency of mental retardation was over twice that found in a "cleaner neighborhood" on the opposite bank of the river. *Washington Post* journalist David Remnick wrote that everywhere in Kemerovo, "the air was thick with gas," while near Kemerovo's mines the leaves on trees were covered with gray dust. A pond filled with toxic waste was used by city workers to dispose of dead dogs, which soon disintegrated, bones and all. The rising incidence of mental retardation in Kemerovo reflected a national problem. From 1975 to 1990 the number of births of the mentally retarded increased "more than twice as fast in the USSR's big cities as in the countryside."[63]

The Soviet Union's most spectacular ecological disaster occurred on April 26, 1986, when a nuclear reactor of the Chernobyl power station (north of Kiev) twice exploded and released huge amounts of toxic radioactive material into the air. Direct results of that accident are still being felt; some 2,500 died, hundreds of thousands were displaced, tens of thousands were disabled, and the toll is still rising. The Ukrainian government does not have enough money to cope with the medical expenses and needs of Chernobyl's victims, past, present, or future.[64]

Although the USSR emerged from World War II a "superpower," its health care system in many respects more closely resembled that of a developing third-world country. Its medical care was free (more or less) but of low quality compared with Western countries. Although the Soviet Union could boast more hospitals, clinics, and doctors than any other country in the world, its physicians were poorly trained and its health network lacked basic modern equipment and comforts. Its hospitals were dilapidated and unsanitary, its citizens short-lived.[65]

NOTES

1. Michael Kaser, *Health Care in the Soviet Union and Eastern Europe* (Boulder, CO: Westview Press, 1976), 40; William A. Knaus, *Inside Russian Medicine* (New York: Everest House, 1981), 76–77. This chapter on Soviet medicine is highly

indebted to Knaus's book; Murray Feshbach and Alfred Friendly Jr., *Ecocide in the USSR: Health and Nature under Siege* (New York: Basic Books, 1992), 37–38, 80–85; David E. Powell, "Aging and the Elderly," in *Soviet Social Problems*, ed. Anthony Jones, Walter D. Connor and David E. Powell (Boulder, CO: Westview Press, 1991), 173, 178; Tricia Starks, "Health Care Propaganda and Programs in 1920s Moscow," paper delivered at the University of Illinois Russian and East European Center's Summer Research Laboratory, June 19, 2001.

2. Knaus, *Inside Russian Medicine*, 77–78, 81, 84; Powell, "Aging and Elderly," 175.

3. Aleksandr Solzhenitsyn, *Cancer Ward*, trans. Nicholas Bethell and David Burg (New York: Bantam Books, 1969), 92.

4. Knaus, *Inside Russian Medicine*, 92–93, 97, 100; David K. Shipler, *Russia: Broken Idols, Solemn Dreams* (London: Futura Publications, 1983), 218, 221–22; Alan Bookbinder, Olivia Lichtenstein, and Richard Denton, *Comrades: Portraits of Soviet Life* (New York: Plume, 1986), 85, 97; Kaser, *Health Care*, 64–65; Nigel Grant, *Soviet Education* (Baltimore: Penguin Books, 1964), 115.

5. Kaser, *Health Care*, 58; Knaus, *Inside Russian Medicine*, 255–57; Grant, *Soviet Education*, 115.

6. Knaus, *Inside Russian Medicine*, 131.

7. Mark G. Field, "Soviet Urban Health Services: Some Problems and Their Sources," in *The Contemporary Soviet City*, ed. Henry W. Morton and Robert C. Stuart (Armonk, NY: M.E. Sharpe, 1984), 132, 142, 146–47; Shipler, *Broken Idols*, 218–19; Kaser, *Health Care*, 64; Sydney Bloch and Peter Reddaway, *Psychiatric Terror: How Soviet Psychiatry Is Used to Suppress Dissent* (New York: Basic Books, 1977), 46–47; "Provision of Medical Care," and "Declining Health Care in the 1970s and 1980s," in *The Soviet Union: A Country Study*, http://lcweb2.loc.gov/cgi-bin/query/D?cstdy:1:./temp/frd_DmZq::, and http://lcweb2.loc.gov/cgi-bin/query2/r?frd/cstdy:@field[DOCID+su0180]; book version: Raymond E. Zickel, ed., 2d ed. (Washington, DC: Library of Congress, 1991), 269–78; Knaus, *Inside Russian Medicine*, 135–36; Feshbach and Friendly, *Ecocide*, 211.

8. Field, "Soviet Urban," 135; Knaus, *Inside Russian Medicine*, 120, 220; Kaser, *Health Care*, 39–40.

9. Knaus, *Inside Russian Medicine*, 220–21, 224; Field, "Soviet Health Problems and the Convergence Hypothesis," in *Soviet Social Problems*, ed. Anthony Jones, Walter D. Connor, and David E. Powell (Boulder, CO: Westview Press, 1991), 86; Bloch and Reddaway, *Psychiatric Terror*, 45.

10. Knaus, *Inside Russian Medicine*, 259, 271; Solzhenitsyn, *Cancer Ward*, 57–58; Elena Bonner, *Mothers and Daughters*, trans. Antonina W. Bouis (New York: Vintage Books, 1993), 6.

11. Hedrick Smith, *The Russians*, rev. ed. (New York: Ballantine Books, 1976), 96; Knaus, *Inside Russian Medicine*, 20, 229–30, 233; Bonner, *Mothers and Daughters*, 3, 6; *Country Study*, "Provision of Medical Care," http://lcweb2.loc.gov/cgi-bin/query/D?cstdy:1:./temp/frd_DmZq::.

12. Field, "Soviet Urban," 148; Knaus, *Inside Russian Medicine*, 331.

13. Solzhenitsyn, *Cancer Ward*, chapter 30, "The Old Doctor."

14. Kaser, *Health Care*, 66; Knaus, *Inside Russian Medicine*, 330.

15. Knaus, *Inside Russian Medicine*, 242–49; *Country Study*, "Provision of Medical Care," http://lcweb2.loc.gov/cgi-bin/query/D?cstdy:1:./temp/frd_DmZq::.

16. Nadezhda Mandelstam, chapter 76, "The Accomplice," and chapter 78, "The First of May," in *Hope Against Hope* (New York: Modern Library, 1999).

17. *Country Study*, "Provision of Medical Care," http://lcweb2.loc.gov/cgi-bin/query/D?cstdy:1:./temp/frd_DmZq::.

18. Knaus, *Inside Russian Medicine*, 299; Elena Bonner, *Alone Together*, trans. Alexander Cook (New York: Alfred A. Knopf, 1986), 13–14; Field, "Soviet Urban," 135, and "Soviet Health Problems," 86.

19. Field, "Soviet Urban," 135–36; Bloch and Reddaway, *Psychiatric Terror*, 46.

20. Field, "Soviet Urban," 138, 144–45; Knaus, *Inside Russian Medicine*, 21, 28–29, 107, 137; Shipler, *Broken Idols*, 217, 221; Feshbach and Friendly, *Ecocide* 82, 211; Solzhenitsyn, *Cancer Ward*, 83; *Country Study*, "Declining Health Care in the 1970s and 1980s," http://lcweb2.loc.gov/cgi-bin/query2/r?frd/cstdy:@field[DOCID+su0180].

21. Field, "Soviet Urban," 144–45; Knaus, *Inside Russian Medicine*, 23–24, 110, 128; Shipler, *Broken Idols*, 217; Powell, "Aging and Elderly," 179; Feshbach and Friendly, *Ecocide*, 211–12.

22. Knaus, *Inside Russian Medicine*, 197–98, 201, 203; *Country Study*, "Provision of Medical Care."

23. *Country Study*, "Declining Health Care in the 1970s and 1980s," http://lcweb2.loc.gov/cgi-bin/query2/r?frd/cstdy:@field[DOCID+su0180].

24. Knaus, *Inside Russian Medicine*, 193–94; Feshbach and Friendly, *Ecocide*, 209–10.

25. Feshbach and Friendly, *Ecocide*, 210; Knaus, *Inside Russian Medicine*, 195, 203–5; *Country Study*, "Provision of Medical Care," http://lcweb2.loc.gov/cgi-bin/query/D?cstdy:1:./temp/frd_DmZq::.

26. Knaus, *Inside Russian Medicine*, 203–4, 206–8, 212–14; Feshbach and Friendly, *Ecocide*, 273; *Country Study*, "Declining Health Care in the 1970s and 1980s," http://lcweb2.loc.gov/cgi-bin/query2/r?frd/cstdy:@field[DOCID+su0180].

27. David Remnick, *Lenin's Tomb: The Last Days of the Soviet Empire* (New York: Vintage Books, 1994), 205–6; Feshbach and Friendly, *Ecocide*, 213.

28. Knaus, *Inside Russian Medicine*, 196, 198–99.

29. Knaus, *Inside Russian Medicine*, 201–2; Greta Bucher, "'Free, and Worth Every Kopeck,'" in *The Human Tradition in Modern Russia*, ed. William B. Husband (Wilmington, DE: Scholarly Resources, 2000), 179–80, 182.

30. Knaus, *Inside Russian Medicine*, 270–71; Powell, "Aging and Elderly," 181.

31. Powell, "Aging and Elderly," 181–82; 184–85.

32. Powell, "Aging and Elderly," 179; Kaser, *Health Care*, 44; Bookbinder et al., *Comrades*, 85; Knaus, *Inside Russian Medicine*, 37.

33. Knaus, *Inside Russian Medicine*, 106–7, 123, 343; *Country Study*, "Provision of Medical Care," http://lcweb2.loc.gov/cgi-bin/query/D?cstdy:1:./temp/frd_DmZq::.

34. Knaus, *Inside Russian Medicine*, 117 ff; Solzhenitsyn, *Cancer Ward*, 61–63; *Country Study*, "Declining Health Care in the 1970s and 1980s," http://lcweb2.loc.gov/cgi-bin/query2/r?frd/cstdy:@field[DOCID+su0180].

35. Knaus, *Inside Russian Medicine*, 121–22; Bloch and Reddaway, *Psychiatric Terror*, 458; Field, "Soviet Health Problems," 78, 80; Solzhenitsyn, *Cancer Ward*, 112.

36. Knaus, *Inside Russian Medicine*, 117, 121–22, 127; Drew Middleton, "Class Distinction in Russia Depicted," *New York Times*, sec. 1, p. 2, col. 2, December 3, 1948; Sozhenitsyn, *Cancer Ward*, 8.

37. Solzhenitsyn, *Cancer Ward*, 8; Knaus, *Inside Russian Medicine*, 124–25, 133–34; Field, "Soviet Urban," 142; Middleton, "Class Distinction," 2:2, Bookbinder et al., *Comrades*, 86–87, Bloch and Reddaway, *Psychiatric Terror*, 46.

38. Knaus, *Inside Russian Medicine*, 125; Solzhenitsyn, *Cancer Ward*, 42–53.

39. Knaus, *Inside Russian Medicine*, 21, 132–33, 138, 142; Feshbach and Friendly, *Ecocide*, 81, 211; Field, "Soviet Health Problems," 78, 80; Middleton, "Class Distinction," 2:2; Powell, "Aging and Elderly," 178; *Country Study*, "Declining Health Care in the 1970s and 1980s," http://lcweb2.loc.gov/cgi-bin/query2/r?frd/cstdy:@field[DOCID+su0180]; Smith, *The Russians*, 94–95.

40. Field, "Soviet Urban," 143; Solzhenitsyn, *Cancer Ward*, 13.

41. Knaus, *Inside Russian Medicine*, 115; Bookbinder et al., *Comrades*, chapter 6, "Doctor in Moscow."

42. Knaus, *Inside Russian Medicine*, 255, chapter 14, "Solzhenitsyn's Cancer—A Case History;" Eugenia Ginzburg, *Journey into the Whirlwind* (New York: Harcourt, Brace, and World, 1967), 414–16, and *Within the Whirlwind* (San Diego: Harcourt Brace Jovanovich, 1982).

43. Knaus, *Inside Russian Medicine*, 252–54.

44. Knaus, *Inside Russian Medicine*, 119, 128, 329; Field, "Soviet Urban," 144, 148; Remnick, *Lenin's Tomb*, 226.

45. Field, "Soviet Urban," 141, and "Soviet Health Problems," 84; Knaus, *Inside Russian Medicine*, 127; Feshbach and Friendly, *Ecocide*, 212.

46. Solzhenitsyn, *Cancer Ward*, 47.

47. Knaus, *Inside Russian Medicine*, 100, 127, 134; Solzhenitsyn, *Cancer Ward*, 47; Remnick, *Lenin's Tomb*, 231; Field, "Soviet Health Problems," 85.

48. Knaus, *Inside Russian Medicine*, 330, 363; Bookbinder et al., *Comrades*, 86.

49. Bloch and Reddaway, *Psychiatric Terror*, 49, 51, 57; Harvey Fireside, *Soviet Psychoprisons* (New York: W.W. Norton, 1979), 135; *Country Study*, "Provision of Medical Care," http://lcweb2.loc.gov/cgi-bin/query/D?cstdy:1:./temp/frd_DmZq::.

50. Bloch and Reddaway, *Psychiatric Terror*, 200–201, 218; Fireside, *Soviet Psychoprisons*, 140, 144–49; Zhores Medvedev and Roy A. Medvedev, *A Question of Madness: Repression by Psychiatry in the Soviet Union*, transl. Ellen de Kadt (New York: Vintage Books, 1971), 140.

51. Knaus, *Inside Russian Medicine*, 288; Fireside, *Soviet Psychoprisons*, 143.

52. Fireside, *Soviet Psychoprisons*, xvi–xvii, 138, 140–43; Andrea Lee, *Russian Journal* (New York: Vintage Books, 1984), 93; Bloch and Reddaway, *Psychiatric Terror*, 189–91.

53. Bloch and Reddaway, *Psychiatric Terror*, 38–39, 460; *Country Study*, "Provision of Medical Care," http://lcweb2.loc.gov/cgi-bin/query/D?cstdy:1:./temp/frd_DmZq::.

54. Bloch and Reddaway, *Psychiatric Terror*, 39; Knaus, *Inside Russian Medicine*, 292; Medvedev and Medvedev, *Question of Madness*, 105–6.

55. Bloch and Reddaway, *Psychiatric Terror*, 41.

56. Alexander Solzhenitsyn, *Matryona's Home*, trans. H. T. Willetts, in *The Norton Anthology of World Masterpieces*, expanded edition, vol. 2, ed. Maynard Mack (New York: W.W. Norton, 1995), 2321; Michael Wines, "Tippling Russians," *New York Times*, May 20, 2001, national edition, sec. 1, 24; Knaus, *Inside Russian Medicine*, 276–77; *Country Study*, "Declining Health Care in the 1970s and 1980s," http://lcweb2.loc.gov/cgi-bin/query2/r?frd/cstdy:@field[DOCID+su0180];

Vladimir G. Treml, "Alcohol Abuse and the Quality of Life in the Soviet Union," in *Quality of Life in the Soviet Union,* ed. Horst Herlemann (Boulder, CO: Westview Press, 1987), 153–55, and "Drinking and Alcohol Abuse in the USSR in the 1980s," in Jones et al., ed., *Soviet Social Problems,* 119.

57. Kate Transchel, review of *Russia Goes Dry* by Stephen White, in *Canadian-American Slavic Studies* 32, 1–4 (Spring–Winter 1998): 445–46; Sydney Schultze, *Culture and Customs of Russia* (Westport, CT: Greenwood Press, 2000), 68–69.

58. Walter D. Connor, "Alcohol and Soviet Society," in *Slavic Review* 30, no. 3 (September 1971): 573–75, 582–84; Treml, "Alcohol Abuse," 158; Schultze, *Culture and Customs,* 69; Knaus, *Inside Russian Medicine,* 278.

59. Connor, "Alcohol and Soviet Society," 584–85; Bloch and Reddaway, *Psychiatric Terror,* 460; Treml, "Alcohol Abuse," 157; Transchel, review, 446.

60. Kaser, *Health Care,* 46; Susan Bridger, "Soviet Rural Women: Employment and Family Life," in Beatrice Farnsworth and Lynne Viola, eds., *Russian Peasant Women* (New York: Oxford University Press, 1992), 287–88.

61. Knaus, *Inside Russian Medicine,* 86; Powell, "Aging and Elderly," 175; Kaser, *Health Care,* 52; *Country Study,* "Declining Health Care in the 1970s and 1980s," http://lcweb2.loc.gov/cgi-bin/query2/r?frd/cstdy:@field[DOCID+su0180], "Mortality and Fertility," http://lcweb2.loc.gov/cgi-bin/query/D?cstdy:1:.temp/~frd_03R0::.

62. Remnick, *Lenin's Tomb,* 205; David MacKenzie and Michael W. Curran, *Russia and the USSR in the Twentieth Century,* 4th ed. (Belmont, CA: Wadsworth/Thomson Learning, 2002), 387–88; Feshbach and Friendly, *Ecocide,* 73–75, 77–78.

63. Feshbach and Friendly, *Ecocide,* 9–11; Remnick, *Lenin's Tomb,* 226.

64. MacKenzie and Curran, *Russia and USSR,* 388–89; "Kto ukral chernobyl'skie den'gi," *Novyi svet* , December 17, 2001, 2.

65. Field, "Soviet Health Problems," 80; Powell, "Aging and Elderly," 179.

9

Education

HISTORICAL BACKGROUND

In the mid-nineteenth century, the imperial government began to promote literacy among the lower classes. In 1864, it created local elected rural councils, called zemstvos, which set up and managed primary schools (grades 1–4, ages 7–10) and other social programs for peasants. The Orthodox Church and the Ministry of Education, distrustful of the semi-democratic zemstvos and what their schools might be teaching, each established primary schools. In 1897 some 20 to 30 percent of the empire's population were literate, a statistic that rose to 40 percent by 1914. At that time, there were 108, 280 elementary schools in Russia, up from 20,000 in 1870, and the Duma (parliament) was laying plans for all children to have a four-year education by the mid-1920s. Still, progress was slow, especially among peasants and women and in the empire's Asian territories.[1]

Beyond the government- and church-sponsored efforts, peasants struggled on their own to achieve literacy—especially for their sons—by creating and paying for primary schools. In the 1880s, there were several thousand such peasant-run schools. The imperial government never made school attendance compulsory, however, and peasants' devotion to their children's education had its limits: in 1911 about 88 percent of rural children in primary schools dropped out before finishing the four-year course. As for higher education, which was almost entirely state run, there were a few universities for the children of the nobility and wealthy upper class, and business and technical schools for the middle and lower middle classes. Nor did policy makers envision equal educational opportunity for all social classes and ethnic groups. The imperial government only wanted its masses to be more useful workers and soldiers. As for Jewish students, the government strictly limited their enrollment in secondary and higher education.[2]

From the start, the Bolsheviks' educational vision was very ambitious. The new government's Commissariat (ministry) of Education, from 1917 to 1929 under the direction of Anatoly Lunacharsky, quickly laid plans to provide the huge, mostly dirt-poor and illiterate population with free, universal, coeducational, compulsory (from age 7 to age 17), education, with equal opportunity for higher education. The dream, set back by the devastating consequences of war and revolution, was not realized in Lunacharsky's lifetime, however. The Commissar's efforts were stymied by extreme shortages of schoolroom space, books, and equipment. Children used pieces of coal or chalk to write on cooking pans, boards, their desks, the school's stove, or pages ripped from old journals. Teachers, always on pitifully low salaries, were expected to devote many unpaid hours per week to social work. In rural areas, a single teacher might well have to teach all grade levels in a one-room schoolhouse without heat or plumbing. Throughout the 1920s, the pupil absentee and dropout rate was very high: in 1926 the average schoolchild finished with only 2.77 years of education. Nevertheless, by that same year literacy was up to about 51 percent of those age nine and older.[3]

In February 1919, Lunacharsky oversaw the creation of remedial schools for workers (*rabfaki*). Located in or near factories, *rabfaki* gave basic instruction in reading, writing, and arithmetic and usually had an affiliation with a university or some other institution of higher education. Nikita Khrushchev was among the millions of workers who attended the *rabfaki*. The last such school closed in October 1941. For peasants, who tended to have even less book learning than urban workers, the government established schools called *likbezy*, "circles for the elimination of illiteracy."[4]

From its beginnings in 1917 into the early 1920s the Commissariat of Education experimented with and encouraged a variety of progressive educational methods aimed at developing and educating the "whole child." Lunacharsky envisioned an educational environment in which children worked cooperatively in groups without the constraints of tests, grades, or textbooks. Academic subjects such as literature, math, and science would be studied not as separate disciplines, but in the context of "themes" like farming and other national and local concerns. These liberal ideas included generous amounts of time devoted to creative arts, and class discussions rather than lectures. Children were to venture frequently outside schoolroom walls into their community as observers and helpers. Corporal punishment was prohibited, and parents and children were to have a strong voice in running their school.[5]

At the university level, the Commissariat mandated similar experiments: there were orders to abolish the traditional lecture method of presenting information; all classes were to become "laboratories" of political discussion; anyone (except members of "exploiting" classes) could go to college without having to show a high school diploma or even registering, and students could graduate without having to take finals. Doctors, construction engineers, and other "professionals" without real qualifications were loosed upon the country while established universities and other higher-education institutions were deluged with academically unqualified students. New institutions of higher education with questionable credentials sprang up around the country. Then, in response to educational chaos and public resentment, the pendulum began to swing back. In 1922 the government ordered all college-level students to officially register; those without a high school certificate could register only at *rabfaki*, not at universities; exams were restored for those preparing for professions; graduates once again received diplomas; many newly created universities closed down.[6]

At the primary and secondary school levels, Lunacharsky's reforms were not widely or systematically carried out by teachers and principals, who far preferred a traditional "3 Rs" approach with regular classroom hours, schoolbooks, lectures, dictation, memorization, and homework. Parents were also hostile to the unfamiliar methods of progressive education. Under Stalin, school management, teaching methods, and curricula were hauled back under central authority and educational experiments were officially squelched. Teaching returned to the traditional European system: formal exams; strict, regimented classroom atmosphere; authoritarian teachers; centrally prescribed courses of study; lectures; much memorizing; compulsory homework; a five-point grading scale; and school uniforms. The uniforms were "bus-driver gray" pants and jacket, white shirt and peaked cap for younger boys; dark dresses, with dark pinafores (switching to white pinafores for special occasions) with white collars and big white hair bows for primary school girls. Older boys and girls wore blue uniforms with white shirts and the red neckerchief of the Young Pioneers youth club.[7]

The constitution of 1936 guaranteed everyone the right to an education, but for many that entitlement ended after fourth grade, when children had to pass rigorous exams in order to continue. But it wasn't just the exams that forced children, especially rural children, out of school. Many factors were working against them and their teachers. During the famines of the 1930s, rural children and teachers suffered from hunger and starvation. Children's farm labor was needed and exploited. After Stalin's death in 1953, the government abolished the fourth grade winnowing exams and raised the number of compulsory school years to eight. Especially in the countryside, however, school administrators often allowed their charges to drop out before eighth grade.[8]

In the mid-1930s Stalin decreed that children of "alien social elements" (the former priesthood, nobility, "bourgeoisie," prosperous peasants, and

political arrestees) should be admitted to schools, but severe discrimination against them continued. At about the same time, thousands of teachers were among those arrested, deported, or killed during the Great Terror
of the 1930s. During World War II, an untold number of teachers died and
some 82,000 schools were destroyed. Despite the catastrophes, by 1939 the
literacy rate was 81 percent, up from 51 percent in 1926, and by the mid-
1960s, illiteracy was probably at most 5 to 10 percent (many classified as
literate had completed four years or less of school). In 1940 low tuition
fees—discontinued in 1956—were introduced for students in the upper
grades of secondary school and university-level students.[9]

GENERAL PHILOSOPHY OF SOVIET EDUCATION

Soviet educational philosophy and law rejected the concept of "track-
ing" schoolchildren according to intellectual ability. All except those with
severe mental or physical handicaps were to cover the same curriculum at
the same pace. IQ tests were banned from 1936, when the Party's Central
Committee denounced them, and were never again used in Soviet schools.
Officially, intellectual ability was the result of, and modifiable by, environment; all normal children had the same innate ability to keep up with the
core curriculum and their peers. If a child fell behind, it was assumed (officially, at least) that the cause was not mental deficiency but laziness, bad
parenting, or poor teaching. Diagnoses of mental retardation were done
by observation rather than testing. Abler students were encouraged to
help slower ones; those who failed were supposed to repeat grades until
they passed or aged out of school. Official policies were often transformed
in the real world, however, especially because principals and teachers
were pressured to keep their failure rates low. In his novella *Matryona's
Home*, Aleksandr Solzhenitsyn, who had been a rural math teacher,
describes a thoroughly lazy, smug schoolboy who "hadn't even mastered
his decimals and didn't know one triangle from another." Thanks to the
school's determination to keep up appearances, the boy is promoted each
year, though he does no homework and mocks his teachers.[10]

Preschools were neither compulsory, available to all children everywhere in the USSR, nor free of charge, though they were cheap, with fees
based on income. There were two kinds of day care: nurseries for children
three to six months to three years, and kindergartens for ages four through
five or six. Preschools were set up and run by factories, farms, soviets, or
various government agencies. In cities these facilities were usually open
from seven or eight in the morning until six or seven at night, and slightly
over half operated during the usual workweek of six days. Others were
open five days a week. By 1965 approximately 22.9 percent of Soviet children (most of them living in cities) attended nurseries or kindergartens.
After the mid-60s, nursery facilities for rural infants and toddlers more
than doubled but still did not meet the demand. By the mid-1980s one in

four rural prekindergarten children were in day care, but these were mainly children three to five, since most women, urban and rural, preferred to keep their children below three years old at home with a trusted caregiver. Most preschools were open all year, but some farm nurseries operated only spring through fall, when women worked in the fields. Nurseries and kindergartens were supposed to provide a healthy environment with good supervision, food, rest, arts activities, and playtime. For kindergartners there might be some basic preparation for reading, writing, and counting. Ideally, the staff included a doctor, nurses, and at least one teacher with college-level training in early childhood education. However, most preschool teachers had trained in a high school vocational course and were not college graduates.[11]

Soviet kindergarten teaching discouraged children's native creativity. Kindergartners were encouraged to produce "creative" work as identical as possible to all the other children's artwork. In one kindergarten, for example, when the children drew daisies, the flowers were placed identically on their paper, with the same number of petals, "in the same colors and with the same three leaves on the stem." At another kindergarten, walls were covered with pictures drawn by three-year-olds, all of whom had drawn children either doing calisthenics or drinking milk, subjects the teacher had chosen for them. Copied from models, the pictures were unusually precise for three-year-olds' artwork. Once a month, however, the tots were allowed to draw whatever their hearts desired.[12]

Preschoolers were expected to participate in the same activities at the same time. "It would only confuse a child to see the person next to him doing something different," one teacher explained. Even in kindergarten, political indoctrination was heavy, reinforced by the youth groups (Octobrists, Young Pioneers, and Komsomol). Stalin disappeared as an object of worship after 1956, but there was still "Uncle Lenin," whose flower- and ribbon-bedecked classroom shrines often portrayed him dandling children on his knee.[13]

THE GENERAL ACADEMIC SCHOOL

Compulsory schooling increased from four years (beginning at age seven, 1930s to early 1950s) to nine years (beginning at age six in the 1980s). Throughout the Soviet period the backbone of the educational system was the general academic school. From 1918 to 1934, classes were organized in groups (*gruppy*) according to children's academic preparedness rather than age. After May 1934, the system returned to age grouping (*klassy*), and pupils studied all subjects with one classroom teacher until grade four or five. Then they were ready to begin "incomplete secondary education" (approximately equivalent to junior high), at which point each subject had its own teacher and students met each day in a "homeroom" group that remained the same from year to year. Most college-bound stu-

A kindergarten class in Khabarovsk, 1965. Children ages one and a half to seven lived there, going home to their parents on Wednesdays and weekends. Reproduced from the Collections of the Library of Congress, LC-U9-14379-328550 #28A.

dents stayed in their general academic school for two or three years of senior high (called "complete secondary education"). Other options were to transfer to a two- or three-year vocational or, more academically oriented, technical program, with a possibility of taking college exams at graduation, or simply to leave school at age 14 or 15 and go to work, perhaps studying part-time for high school equivalency credit. The last two or three years in a technical program trained students to be preschool and elementary school teachers, librarians, feldshers (paramedics), nurses, and technicians. Most children of the urban *intelligentsiia* (educated people who earn a living using their minds rather than their hands) took the traditional path: graduation from a "complete secondary" general academic school followed by college[14] entrance exams.[15]

SPECIAL SUBJECT SCHOOLS

Toward the end of the Soviet period, more and more general academic schools turned themselves into "special subject" schools that focused on one academic discipline, such as the study of a foreign language, math, physics, chemistry, computer science, or other sciences, with study often beginning at the elementary level. At the secondary level, this kind of magnet school was called a *lycée* or *gimnaziia*. Admission was often very competitive because these were schools urban professionals wanted their children to enter—graduates had the best chances of admission to the most prestigious colleges, plum jobs, and foreign travel. Most special-subject schools were day schools sponsored by universities and research institutes, but a few, mainly physics-mathematics boarding schools, were not just sponsored, they were administered, by the university or research institute where the pupils would eventually enroll.[16]

Children with handicaps that prevented them from entering main-stream schools attended special schools run by the Ministry of Health. Education for the mentally and physically impaired improved somewhat after World War II, but in general the government failed the handicapped, young and old, whether they were disabled genetically, from war wounds, or some other cause. In 1988, of 147,400 preschools, about 1,600 were special facilities for the handicapped.[17]

CURRICULUM

Students in general academic schools studied nineteenth-century classic Russian writers as well as officially approved Soviet and foreign writers. Foreign language instruction, which children were required to begin in fourth or fifth grade, continued throughout their junior high and high school years. Most schools offered only one foreign language, generally English (the most commonly taught foreign language), though German (the most commonly taught language before World War II), French, Spanish, Chinese, or Hindi were sometimes taught. The official curriculum mandated an impressive array of courses in math and sciences, but the quality of courses depended on a school's location and population. The intelligentsia were more likely than workers and peasants to demand high-quality education for their children, to live in districts with superior schools and teaching, and to provide an educationally rich home environment. Older grade-school children were required to take "social studies," a study of Marxist-Leninist theory. Those who continued to higher education, whatever their school or specialization, had to take courses and pass exams in ideas about history, history of the Communist Party of the Soviet Union, and principles of political economy, all taught from the Marxist point of view, as were literature, geography, language, and even the sciences, fine arts, physical education, and so on.[18]

Every student was supposed to get training in practical work and become familiar with the adult working world, a goal that waxed and waned depending on the educational policy of the moment. For Khrushchev, the intertwining of academic and practical work was so important that in 1958 he decreed that high school graduates had to work for two years before being allowed to apply for college entrance, a decree revoked in 1964 when he fell from power. Khrushchev also raised the number of school hours devoted to work training. Education for the workplace included both classroom talk about different kinds of jobs (in lower grades) and in middle grades, courses like wood shop, metal shop, and electronics for boys and domestic arts like sewing and cooking for girls. At the senior high level, students might spend four hours a week practicing an employment skill, often in a real workplace. Time was also set aside for gym classes and field trips, but traditional academic subjects were always the main focus of general schools. Students interested in athletic competition could join a local after-school sports club, if one was available. These clubs fielded teams for regional and national competitions and provided coaches to spot exceptionally talented young athletes. Schools did not provide such teams.[19]

LANGUAGE POLICY IN NON-RUSSIAN REPUBLIC SCHOOLS

In non-Russian republics the primary language for teaching was the native language of the area, so that education was available in as many as 60 languages, with Russian introduced as a second language in second grade. In non-Russian cities with a mixed ethnic population there were sometimes both Russian and native language schools. Since fluency in Russian was a pathway to social advancement, and Russian-language schools were often considered superior to native-language schools, even non-Russian parents sometimes chose Russian schools for their children. Still, in the Central Asian republics, lack of Russian fluency did not prevent people from getting university degrees.[20]

BOARDING SCHOOLS

In the 1920s, the government established boarding schools as a way of sheltering and educating thousands of homeless children displaced by war, revolution, and civil war. Some educators saw boarding schools as great social equalizers, raising and educating together children of different backgrounds. But most parents far preferred raising their offspring, relinquishing them only if the boarding school was a prestigious one for the unusually gifted. Nevertheless, Khrushchev, harking back to social melting pot ideals of the 1920s, enthusiastically built many new boarding schools, especially in the countryside. His plan was for children to board during the week, returning home only on weekends. But burdened though Soviet mothers were, and crowded as their living spaces were, there were few takers. On the other hand, after-school programs, where available, were a welcome alternative for most working mothers. In the late Soviet period fewer than 2 percent of children were enrolled in boarding schools, and those who did enroll were mainly from rural areas with no local high schools. Other boarders might be children who, because of conditions at home, had problems attending a regular day school.[21]

CONTINUING EDUCATION AND PART-TIME EDUCATIONAL PROGRAMS

Adult education was important. In the 1980s more than half of those studying for diplomas and degrees from vocational-technical schools, general education secondary schools, universities, and professional institutes were studying part-time. Continuing education also included formal and informal short courses, refresher courses, lectures, and TV and radio programs for professional and personal development. Part-time programs for school dropouts enrolled mainly the socially and educationally disadvantaged and had to cope with problems that plague such endeavors. A history teacher described how he and other teachers at a workers' dormitory went around begging "the pupils to come downstairs one flight—to class." A night-school teacher complained about the "demoralizing" effect of beginning class with only one student present and having a few others straggle in late, in the midst of "the most poetic moment" of his lecture. Part-time schools sometimes ignored absences and invented grades. An official investigation in 1980 showed rampant corruption in the part-time program—enrollment figures greatly inflated in order to meet quotas and the wholesale graduation of uninterested, absentee students who had been pressured to enroll. Some professions, such as medicine, did not offer part-time programs.[22]

RELIGIOUS INSTRUCTION

The Soviet constitution mandated complete separation of church and state. There was no religious instruction or worship in schools, and there were no parochial schools, with the exception of a few officially approved, church-run seminaries for training Orthodox priests. It was a teacher's duty to detect and be ready to combat religious beliefs transmitted to young children, often by *babushki* (grandmothers). Many people were sent to the gulag for trying to give their children formal religious schooling.[23]

THE CLASSROOM

Pupils sat in pairs behind desks fixed to the floor in rows facing the teacher. Children stood when their teacher entered or left the room and while answering a question or reciting from memory. They were expected to listen to their teacher quietly with arms folded and raise a hand for permission to speak. Although Soviet children were generally well behaved in class, like children anywhere they were exuberant and unruly when the teacher wasn't looking. Behind their teacher's back, Hedrick Smith's children reported, boys threw spitballs, flew paper airplanes, immersed girls' braids in inkwells, and smoked in the boys' restroom; girls jabbed the teasing boys with sewing needles. Teaching methods were conservative and emphasized listening to lectures and memorizing. Instructors generally began each lesson by reviewing the previous lesson, going over homework, and calling on students to recite their assigned memorizations. Individual students were called on to give answers to very specific lesson-based questions, or go to the blackboard to work out a problem. The performance was graded for its quality. New material, introduced with a lecture, was next on the agenda. After lecturing, the teacher asked students questions to check whether they had understood. This was also an opportunity for the students to ask questions. Afterward, the teacher might summarize her lecture and show how the day's lesson was related to previous information. There was little leeway for mistakes or nonconformity, no matter how trivial. Notes had to be recopied from the blackboard into students' notebooks exactly as the teacher had written them, even with exactly the same indentations and underlining. Children were expected to wait until recess or some other class break to sharpen a pencil, get a drink of water, or go to the bathroom. The class ended with the day's homework assignment. A homework load of four hours each day was common, though some parents and educators thought that was asking too much of children. Other after-school work included helping teachers clean the school, or that might be a job only for the teachers. One high school teacher described her school's janitorial routine: when classes were over for the day, the cleaning lady handed out supplies and equipment (soap powder, mops, pails, brushes, brooms) to teachers and then supervised their work. When the job was done, Auntie Masha, the cleaning lady, reported to the principal those teachers she felt had not pulled their weight, recommending that the shirkers "get a good dressing-down."[24]

COEDUCATION

Boys and girls attended primary and secondary schools together until 1943. In that year the government issued a decree ordering males and females to be educated separately after preschool in big cities. A 1954 decree restored coeducation to all regions of the USSR, to all subjects except physical education and "domestic science" classes, and to all educational facilities except military schools.[25]

The grading system, from 1944, was on a five-point scale. Before that, students were graded "very bad, bad, average, good, and very good," and later, "unsatisfactory, satisfactory, good, and excellent." Under the five-point system, good students expected to get fours or fives. A three meant passable but mediocre; a two was a seriously low mark reserved for problem students such as those who refused to do their homework. One, the rock-bottom lowest grade, "a sort of [educational] equivalent of the death penalty," was rarely given. Pressures on teachers to change twos to threes made the two almost extinct and made the five-point system really a three-point scale, with three being the "compulsory" mark for failing students. Thus grade inflation and pressures against students' repeating course work allowed the government to point with pride to a system of public education that graduated nearly all students and raised the expectations of more and more teenagers who had completed high school. Nevertheless, at least some former Soviet students remember how they anxiously brought home their grade record books for parents' weekly signatures. Those who did receive a two knew they were in serious hot water with parents and school officials alike, and possibly faced repeating a grade level. Competition for admission to college-level study became ever fiercer, since places in higher education did not keep up with the increasing number of high school graduates with college ambitions.[26]

SCHOOL DISCIPLINE AND PUNISHMENTS

The one-to-five scale was also used to grade children for conduct. Official educational policy did not allow corporal punishment, and apparently it was rare, although an American journalist reported that elderly women day care and kindergarten workers did spank their charges. But most teachers and school administrators relied on nonphysical means of discipline: scoldings, being kept after school to do extra work, suspension from the Young Pioneers, lowering the student's conduct mark, expulsion from school, pressure on parents. Separating a young child from the rest of the group, a punishment often used for kindergartners, could cause a misbehaver "to cry as if he had received a beating." School authorities made it clear that classroom discipline was not just the teachers' responsibility. From kindergarten onward, children were often reminded that each one must work hard not only for personal achievement but also for the greater glory of their class, school, and country.[27]

Teachers were supposed to make home visits to discuss a child's progress and problems, but classrooms were crowded (perhaps 40–50 students) and educators had their own children and households to tend to. At parent-teacher meetings, a regular feature of school life, teachers publicly identified and scolded parents whose children misbehaved or did inferior work. For the most part, parents (it was mainly mothers who attended these sessions) meekly accepted the teachers' tongue lashings. "You know," one teacher scolded a father, while other parents quietly looked away, "it isn't the boy who is guilty [of chronic tardiness]. It is the parents. It is your responsibility as a father to see he is on time. Please look after it." Many Soviet classrooms relied on "institutionalized tattling": a child was appointed as the teacher's watchdog for his or her row, reporting on tardiness, uncleanliness, fighting, failure to do homework, and other violations of classroom order. Sometimes the teacher assigned better students to help weaker ones with classroom work and homework. Evidently children tended to lose their enthusiasm for these jobs as they got older and faced increasing peer pressure against tattlers and teacher's pets.[28]

Even in the best schools, instructors commonly winked at cheating, or even helped students cheat, a tradition that survived the fall of the Soviet regime. Teachers might place weaker students next to brighter ones during tests, "[n]ot every time, of course, but when it mattered and as long as it was not too obvious." Children whose parents had influence and connections, including pupils with a parent who taught at their school, were immune from failure. Inflating grades was an effective way for teachers to dodge criticism for their students' poor performance.[29]

EXPENSES FOR GENERAL EDUCATION (PRIMARY AND SECONDARY)

In 1940 low tuition fees were charged for senior high school students as well as college students, though exceptions were made for hardship cases, students with outstanding grades, and servicemen's children. After 1956 no tuition fees were charged for students in any primary or secondary schools, but parents did have to pay for textbooks and other materials, uniforms (which mothers sometimes sewed), and inexpensive hot lunches. Those whose parents could not afford to pay were helped by a school fund.[30]

Textbooks had to agree with the current Party line and thus became obsolete when Party policies changed. From grade school through graduate studies, there was often a scramble to rewrite textbooks. Teachers also underwent periodic reprogramming in order to reflect policy changes. That was accomplished through refresher courses.[31]

SCHOOL CALENDAR

First graders began with four hours a day, five or six days a week. By the time children were in eighth grade an extra hour had been added to their school day, with five to six class periods a day. For upper-level students, classes lasted 45 minutes, with 10- to 15-minute breaks between. The academic year began on September 1 (when children arrived bearing bouquets of flowers for their teacher) and lasted between 34 and 38 weeks, depending on grade level. There were various brief holidays and a longer winter break, after which schools reopened in late to mid-January or early February, running until mid- or early June.

A typical day began at 8 A.M., unless the school operated in shifts. The youngest children were collected by a parent or other caregiver at noon; the rest stayed until two. Some schools might have just a morning snack break of juice and a container of jam, but no lunch break. At others, school cafeterias provided plain but nourishing food at little or no cost to students and teachers.[32]

We get a sense of the school life of a bright, lively Russian teenage girl, Nina Kosterina, through the diary she kept from 1936, when she was 15, to

1941, the year she was killed as a partisan fighting the invading German army. Tensions before important exams; feverish studying; loving friendships and bitter quarrels with friends; adoration of a wise, kind, woman teacher; loathing of a male teacher who pursues her; parties and club activities; and holiday festivals are all recorded in her journal. Even after her father's arrest, Nina could find satisfaction and even joy in her daily life at school.[33]

But Nina's cousin Irma, both of whose parents were arrested during the purges as "enemies of the people," was sent to a children's home. Conditions in the majority of these homes were atrocious, with rundown facilities, poorly trained teaching staff, abusive caretakers, inadequate food and clothing, and fellow inmates who were young criminals. There children would be exploited as unpaid laborers or sexually abused. Many infants and toddlers were sent to overcrowded, unsanitary, understaffed facilities near their mothers' prison camps. In these places, neglected children failed to develop normal verbal skills and social behavior, if they survived at all. "Luckier" children, like Galina Rykova and her sister, children of "enemies," were deposited at institutions that provided access to decent education as well as adequate care and living conditions. Galina and her sister were able to adapt and lead a relatively normal life. Along with non-"enemy" inmates and children of the local village, they went to school and played sports; Galina even joined the Komsomol.[34]

EDUCATION IN THE COUNTRYSIDE

As in other areas of Soviet life, educational quality and opportunities were much lower in the country than in cities and towns, whether because of poor teaching, understaffing, inadequate physical plants, lack of necessary equipment and supplies, or overcrowding. Because education and Party membership were the two main roads up the social ladder, inferior rural schools made it difficult for country children to get ahead. Village schools were sometimes abandoned, leaving children with no schooling if their parents could not afford to transport them elsewhere (until 1965 such transportation had to be financed by parents).[35]

Rural schoolchildren were often used as a source of free field labor—so-called vocational training—that kept them out of school. A Kirghiz high school principal complained in a letter to *Pravda* that between 1977 and 1981, his students had never begun the academic year before November. Teacher turnover was high in villages because, despite government incentives, teachers did not want to commit their own lives and their children's to the isolation, primitive conditions, poor housing, and other deprivations of rural life. Country girls who were accepted at a city teacher-training institute generally did not care to return. However, remote Stalin-era schools often benefited from the skills of highly educated political prisoners serving out sentences of exile and in need of a salary.[36]

According to a Soviet survey of 1967, only 26 percent of kolkhozniks (collective farmers) had a secondary or higher level of education, compared to 44 percent of other working-class people. The disparity between the educational levels of children of the urban intelligentsia and farmworkers was even wider. Khrushchev tried to even out the playing field by starting an "affirmative action" program that reserved most college-level places for applicants with at least two years of working experience in industries and farms. Also under his leadership, state and collective farms could send workers off for specialized education, at farm expense. After completing their education, workers were obligated to return to their farms. These policies began to be withdrawn even before Khrushchev fell from power and were abolished after his fall in 1964. Farms could still opt to finance their workers' further education, but in fact villagers who emigrated to cities mostly took the menial jobs city people scorned. Even when it came to specialized training in agricultural sciences, village schoolchildren were at a disadvantage compared with their city counterparts. In 1961, for example, only a third of students admitted to Soviet higher agricultural schools came from farm families.[37]

WOMEN'S EDUCATIONAL DISADVANTAGES

In principle, but not fact, Soviet men and women had equal access to education. The influences of culture and preference affected urban as well as rural children in their life's choices, but culture and tradition probably had the strongest effects in the far-flung, isolated villages. About the same number of boys as girls were enrolled in school in town and country until senior high school. At that point, there were 6 percent fewer girls enrolled in rural as compared to urban areas. In Muslim regions, many girls, especially in rural areas, married young and dropped out of school. In the Uzbek Republic in 1955, in grades 8 to 10, girls made up 48 percent of urban but only 26 percent of rural enrollments.[38]

EDUCATION AND SOCIAL CLASS

Children of the Soviet elite received the best education and professional opportunities because they lived in important cities with superior schools and had parents with connections. In addition, expensive private tutoring, which was not illegal but was out of reach of most workers' and farmers' families, helped applicants get into the better schools. It was common for students at a particular university or institute, who had known each other all their lives, gone to the same schools, shared desks, sat in the same homeroom for years, and grown up in families whose parents socialized with each other, to marry among themselves, often when their college studies were almost finished.[39]

Social-economic segregation according to neighborhood was not as pronounced as in American cities, but Soviet cities did have their rough workers' districts and upscale neighborhoods clustered around universities and research institutes. Parents who belonged to the intelligentsia wanted to live near the best high schools rather than in blue-collar districts where schools were likely to be poorly equipped and staffed. City teachers often chose long commutes to better schools rather than assignments in worker neighborhoods closer to home.[40]

The widespread educational policy of *shefstvo* (sponsorship) also helped determine an urban school's prestige. Each general academic school had to be sponsored by an enterprise, organization, or farm. There was supposed to be interaction, including social events and job site visits, between the enterprise's employees and the school's students. Middle-class parents preferred to see their offspring hobnobbing with professorly role models rather than with, for example, department store clerks and chose their schools accordingly.[41]

INFORMAL EDUCATION

Youth organizations were linked to the school system and through regular meetings were able to exert peer pressure on unruly or otherwise nonconforming children. A misbehaving child would be the subject of discussion at such meetings, often with the culprit present. Troublesome students might find themselves caricatured on the classroom wall newspaper, or ostracized, or on the receiving end of other kinds of peer pressure. These state-sponsored organizations, which in some respects resembled the Boy Scouts or Girl Scouts, were part recreational and part a means of molding children to be useful, obedient, and loyal members of Soviet society. There were three levels, based on age: Octobrists accepted children ages 5 to 9 and were the most informal. The children learned nursery rhymes and other songs and games. There was no particular pressure to join and no reason to fear being expelled. Next were the Young Pioneers, to which the great majority of schoolchildren ages 10 to 14 or 15 belonged. The impressive initiation rite might be held in a school, factory, sumptuous Pioneer Palace, former nobleman's mansion, or decrepit rural cabin. Children recited a promise to love their country and follow the precepts of Lenin and the Communist Party. When the ceremony was over, each child sported a new red neckerchief and a badge with the motto "Always ready." Children did not have to belong to the Pioneers to participate in their recreational and educational activities, but most nonmembers were those who had been suspended or expelled for bad behavior. Young Pioneers were supposed to be trained to be good citizens, have good manners, revere Lenin and Stalin, and learn some basic military drills. Their activities included sports, nature studies, singing, dancing, drama, summer camps, and hobby groups.[42]

The Komsomol—Young Communist League—was an organization for youth approximately 14 to 28 (age boundaries changed from time to time), so that members included not only high schoolers but also college students, young professionals, military personnel, and skilled and unskilled workers. At first it was an elite organization, like the Party, but over the years, membership became more or less mandatory. Like the other two youth organizations, the Komsomol was controlled by the Party. There was no initiation ceremony and no uniform; emphasis was on political work and theory. The Komsomol's structure, with its local primary organizations, district or city-level committees, and All-Union Congress and Central Committee in Moscow, closely paralleled that of the Communist Party, and about 75 percent of new Party recruits came out of the Komsomol, including many top Party leaders like General Secretary Mikhail Gorbachev.[43]

HIGHER EDUCATION

There were two main types of higher education: universities and institutes. Universities (more than 70 in the 1980s) were located in big cities and generally had higher prestige than institutes, although there were important exceptions. Universities focused on theoretical rather than applied fields of study, offering a wide range of academic subjects. Far fewer students were enrolled in universities than in institutes. Each university had several "faculties" (schools) subdivided into "chairs" or departments, and offered courses of study in natural sciences and math, social and political science, humanities, and law. Institutes (numbering about 800 in the 1980s) were professional schools for future physicians, teachers, engineers, agriculturalists, and foreign studies specialists. Other higher education institutes included art and music conservatories and military academies. Institutes enrolled more than 75 percent of all college-level students.[44]

Students chose their majors when they applied to a faculty or institution, rather than after two years or so into a general liberal arts curriculum as is usually done in the United States. Once they were admitted, required courses beyond the major were usually only classes on Marxism-Leninism and foreign languages. Very few electives were allowed, and they could be taken only as overloads. The number of students accepted in courses of study depended on the government's projection of how many workers were needed in given areas. For that reason there were always many more openings in practical specialties like engineering than in the liberal arts, and graduates were virtually guaranteed work in their specialization.[45]

College admission requirements were based on high school graduation and grades, plus the score on a standardized, competitive, all-day examination given once a year in the summer. Generally, applicants took entrance exams in Russian language and literature; a foreign language;

fields related to their major; and, if the application was to a non-Russian republic, the republic's native language. Exams were both written and oral, graded on a five-point scale, with total possible scores varying from 25 to 40. Grading standards were higher for some colleges than for others, depending on location, field of study, and prestige. For example, it was easier to gain entrance to law school in Dushambe (previously Stalinabad, in the Tajik Republic) than in Leningrad or Odessa.[46]

Applicants also had to have a recommendation from a high school official or employer. In some cases a family's social status or connections could tip the scales, or bribery might play a part, according to Soviet newspaper reports. In the 1970s the rector (head) of the Tbilisi Medical Institute was convicted of taking hundreds of thousands of rubles in bribes from eager parents. For several years he had operated a fee-based no-fail system—oral exams facilitated by question cards with attached answers, and written exams completed and corrected.[47]

It was common for high school graduates to choose an institution according to their chances of being accepted rather than their interest in a particular field. Applicants who had graduated from general academic high schools could end up with menial work if they did not get into college.[48]

In the 1920s and early 1930s, students from worker and peasant families were supposed to be given priority in college admissions, with a restrictive quota applied against those from the pre-Revolutionary middle classes and nobility. In practice, however, most offspring of the intelligentsia did continue to higher education, while most from the lower classes did not get past the primary grades. Other factors, such as ethnicity, also weighted the scales for or against students. Although official Soviet policy proclaimed equal opportunity for all groups, Jewish students knew they had to be especially outstanding in order to gain entrance to the best universities and institutes. Despite the obstacles, Soviet Jews managed to maintain a high level of educational achievement. Being a native speaker of a non-Russian language could also be a serious obstacle to acceptance at the best schools. The student body at Moscow State University was fairly homogeneous, with few students from ethnic minorities. Most freshmen were Great Russians, the dominant population of Moscow and of central European Russia. Freshman students newly arrived from the countryside—the boys in ill-fitting suits of synthetic material and the girls with beribboned coiled braids—stood out like sore thumbs and were disparaged by urban classmates who mocked them as hicks: "They gawked at everything [in the university cafeteria], and then they started to gobble the food—tough meat and watery soup—as if it was the best thing they'd eaten in their lives."[49]

Qualified students might be rejected because they or relatives were in political disfavor. In late July of 1939 Nina Kosterina, who described herself as "an ordinary girl" five months out of high school and as she then thought, "five minutes away from being a college student," recorded in her diary her struggle to gain admission to Moscow's Institute of Geology. First there were exams to study for. In her diary entries she berates herself for studying "only six or seven hours a day, which is very little." In the end she received the 30 total points required for entrance, but instead of being admitted to the institute, the director telephoned her, asking about her father and uncles who had been arrested. Nina, ever mindful of her "Komsomol honor," answered honestly and was rejected for admission to the institute on the grounds that there was not enough dormitory space, even though she lived in Moscow and so did not need a dorm room. She found herself among the many promising students her age who had been "turned into lepers" because of their parents. At the time, such bright but politically tainted young people were often ordered to study at colleges far distant from the USSR's most desirable cities. Nina was dispatched by train to Baku (the capital of Azerbaijan) and almost a month after she arrived was rejected by the Baku college, again because of her father's arrest. After she returned to Moscow, her mother, a woman with "flinty strength" of character, sent a letter to Stalin.

On what basis…are they violating the principle that you have proclaimed yourself: "The son is not responsible for his father"?

Shortly thereafter, Nina was admitted to the Moscow Institute of Geology and awarded a scholarship, despite having missed two months of classes. When Elena Bonner's application to the journalism department of Leningrad University was rejected because she was the daughter of "traitors to the homeland," she successfully applied to a Leningrad teacher's college. One reason she chose that particular institute was because it offered night classes—she had to work to support what was left of her family.[50]

As far as sheer numbers were concerned, higher education blossomed under the Soviet government. Institutions of higher education rose from 105 in 1914, mostly in the major cities of European Russia, to 766 spread across the USSR in 1959. The number of students enrolled in higher education institutions in that same period rose from 127,400 to 2,150,000, with almost 3 million students by the mid-1960s and 5.3 million in the 80s, with 60 percent full-time students. In the 1980s, about 650,000 full-time students were admitted to higher education institutions every year, out of a much larger pool of applicants. Under the Soviets, the numbers of male and female students became nearly equal. Only students age 35 and under were admitted to full-time undergraduate and graduate schools. There was no age limit for part-time students.[51]

Tuition was free. Students paid a negligible amount to stay at a student dorm if they could not live at home. Most received stipends as long as they made satisfactory progress in their studies. Stipends varied accord-

ing to year (freshman, sophomore, etc.), major, and qual-   Cost of Higher
ity of scholarship and were generally inadequate to pay   Education
for the necessities of life, so students depended on part-
time jobs and help from their families to survive. Most
joined the student trade union, which cost 2 percent of their monthly grant
but entitled them to discounts at concerts, movies, and other entertainment.[52]

The academic year was divided into two semesters, the first beginning on
September 1 and ending in mid-December. The spring semester started in
early February and ended in late May or early June.
University-level students were expected to shoulder a   Structure of
heavy course and homework load. Students often   Academic Year,
attended class or labs six hours a day, six days a week,   Length of Study,
with some weeks set aside each year for students to   Course Loads
write theses and do practical work in their fields. Read-
ing assignments tended to be unrealistically heavy, even for very devoted
students. As in elementary and high schools, by far the main teaching technique at the college level was lecturing, with little or no opportunity for students to enter into a freewheeling classroom discussion of ideas. All
students had to take courses, and pass exams, in Marxist-Leninist political
theory and the history of the Communist Party in the Soviet Union.[53]

The oldest, biggest, and most prestigious Russian university is Moscow
State University (founded 1755), with its Stalin era "titanic," tiered, gray
and red granite 32-story dormitory-classroom main building in Moscow's
Lenin Hills. Built in 1949–1953, the monstrous "wedding cake" was constructed in part by prison labor.

Seen from a distance, it suggests a Disney version of a ziggurat; its central spire, like
the Kremlin towers, holds a blinking red star. Inside, as in a medieval fortress, there
is everything necessary to sustain life in case of siege: bakeries, dairy store, a fruit
and vegetable store, a pharmacy, a post office, magazine kiosks, a watch-repair
stand—all this in addition to classrooms, and student rooms, and cafeterias…. As I
climb the endless stairs and negotiate the labyrinth of fusty-smelling hallways, I feel
dwarfed and apprehensive, a human being lost in a palace scaled for giants.[54]

Typical student quarters in the Lenin Hills building would be a *blok*—a
tiny suite of two green and beige 6- by 10-foot rooms, with a miniscule
entryway and "a pair of cubicles containing, between them, a toilet, a
shower and washstand, and several large, indolent cockroaches." These
rooms, generally occupied by four to six students, were furnished with
chairs, tables, bookcases, beds, and a radio permanently wired into Radio
Moscow. The radio could be turned down but not off.

Students at Moscow State might wake up to the radio's morning exercise program, shower, dress, and walk over to the university's outdoor
track for a morning run or physical education class. Afterward, they could

get breakfast in one of the high-ceilinged, dully painted cafeterias, "filled with spotted black Formica tables and dozens of sleepy students." Breakfast choices were kasha (a cooked grain cereal resembling cream of wheat) with butter, and beef in various forms and combinations: in chunks with potatoes, chopped with potatoes, or ground with fried egg and potatoes. For drinks there were kefir (a fermented milk drink) or tea with sugar. Scattered through the cafeteria were small buffets that sold other breakfast staples: sausage, cheese, or fish sandwiches; jellied meat; hard-boiled eggs; cookies topped with whipped cream. Thus fortified, the students were ready for the day, and for their classes.[55]

Students were regularly evaluated through written and oral exams, essays, and lab work. At the end of the program they had to present a

Evaluation

diploma thesis or, for students in applied fields, a diploma project. The whole second semester of the final year was usually set aside for students to finish their diploma work. Then they had to make an oral defense of their diploma essay or project before an academic committee. If the defense was successful the diploma was awarded with or without "distinction," depending on the committee's opinion of the overall quality of the student's work during the entire course of his or her college study.[56]

Sports and Other Extracurricular Activities at the College Level

Physical education courses were compulsory for all first- and second-year students. Instead of fraternities and sororities, students belonged to "circles": groups that focused on a particular hobby or interest. Many students liked to attend movies and concerts as well as

date and debate, stroll in the park, joke, sing and dance, study hard or loaf, complain a lot, and cheat occasionally...They frequently read clandestine literature...view[ed] [banned] abstract art in private [and listened to] "decadent jazz."[57]

Another popular entertainment was simply gathering in a dorm room with friends to listen to pirated American pop music, talk, sing, smoke, and drink vodka and beer. At Moscow State, party noises included the sound of glass shattering. Alcohol was banned in dorms, so to destroy the evidence students routinely flung empties out the window. The following dawn, *babushki* cleaning crews swept up the glassy mess.[58]

In his novel *The First Circle*, Aleksandr Solzhenitsyn described the student life of one of his characters, Simochka, a technician who was lucky because "no one [at work] made demands on her knowledge in her special field. Not only she but many of her girlfriends had graduated without any such knowledge." Simochka and her fellow students found there was no time to study even had they wanted to. Because they were required to spend two or more months in the fall to help harvest potatoes, they had to make up the time with 8 to 10 hours per day of lectures in addition to the obligatory twice-weekly political meetings and indoctrination sessions. Add that to the demands of partying, and what was a fun-loving co-ed to do? Faculty were also pressed for time, and as much under pressure not to fail students as Simochka's high school teachers had been. No professor wanted to face the wrath of administrators for whom "there are no bad pupils, only bad teachers." Therefore, Simochka and her girlfriends regularly cheated, hiding answers

in those sections of female clothing denied to males, and at the exams they pulled out the one they needed, smoothed it out, and turned it into a worksheet...The examiners did not try to trip the students up but, in fact, attempted to get them through the examination with as good results as possible.

As their courses neared their ends, Simochka and her friends realized with a feeling of despondency that they did not like their profession, and, in fact, found it a bore.[59]

POSTGRADUATE WORK ASSIGNMENTS

After graduation, students were allowed a month's vacation before beginning their mandatory two- to three-year work assignments. From 1928 to 1991, the law required college graduates to repay the country for their education by accepting an assignment in their special field. When new graduates arrived at their job sites, they were assigned housing and reimbursed for travel expenses. By this requirement the state hoped to supply less popular areas with badly needed professionals. In 1985, 98 percent of all new graduates who had been full-time students were given job assignments. But getting these newly minted specialists to follow through on assignments was another matter. Generally the best students got first choice of jobs. Many graduates, such as married couples who would be separated and those with health problems or dependent relatives, were exempted from being sent away from home. Others managed, whether through good connections, bribery, or sheer determination, to squeeze themselves into those loopholes. Staying close to the comforts of family and home was important, especially if home was in a city. Graduates from Moscow were especially reluctant to leave for fear of permanently losing their residency permits. Many graduates failed to turn up at their assignments or quit long before their time was up, knowing they would probably not be punished, especially if they had under-the-table support from someone with clout. Purposely getting oneself fired was another method of cutting short an unwanted assignment. Sometimes assignees who did report for work were turned down because the enterprise had no job for them in their specialty, could not provide housing, had asked for more specialists than they really needed, or did not want someone from a particular geographic region or ethnic group. Rather than turn down an assigned specialist flat, managers frequently, albeit illegally, gave unwanted graduates menial jobs or failed to provide them with an apartment, hoping the newcomer would disappear, sooner rather than later. On the other hand, many bosses were glad to (illegally) hire needed specialists who had fled an assignment elsewhere. The job assignment program (called *raspredelenie*) sometimes led young people onto weird paths. In *The First Circle,* Solzhenitsyn describes how young Simochka and nine of her fellow Institute of Communications Engineers graduates, not qualified for any scientific work, are inducted wholesale into the secret police, given the rank of lieutenant, and assigned to a secret scientific laboratory, whose scientists are political prisoners forced to work on voice-identification technology. Whether or not the assignment was as morally tainted as Simochka's, *raspredelenie* offered virtually all new graduates a shelter from menial work. When in the 1980s the program started to fall apart, students were at liberty to find their own jobs, if they could, and thousands could not.[60]

GRADUATE DEGREES

There were two graduate degrees for those who continued their studies after the *diplom* (undergraduate degree): first, the candidate of sciences (*Kandidat nauk*), which can be roughly compared to the M.A. or M.S. in the United States, then, the doctor of sciences (*Doktor nauk*), approximately equivalent to a Ph.D. People generally worked in their specialties for two or three years before applying to graduate school. The candidate of sciences degree usually required three additional years of study and an original research project, plus an oral exam at the end of the program, when the degree candidate (*aspirant*) had to defend the project before an examining committee. The government gave generous grants to those who entered full-time graduate school, but many chose to remain in the workforce and study part-time. Very few attained the extremely prestigious doctor of sciences, which was awarded only after graduate students had achieved candidate of sciences, worked in the specialty for several years, published original research, and defended it before an academic committee.

NOTES

1. David MacKenzie and Michael W. Curran, *Russia and the USSR in the Twentieth Century,* 4th ed. (Belmont, CA: Wadsworth/Thomson Learning), 82; Nigel Grant, *Soviet Education* (Harmondsworth, England: Penguin Books, 1964), 18–19; David Lane, *Politics and Society in the USSR* (New York: Random House, 1971), 488; John M. Thompson, *A Vision Unfulfilled: Russia and the Soviet Union in the Twentieth Century* (Lexington, MA: D.C. Heath, 1996), 86–87.

2. Thompson, *Vision Unfulfilled,* 87; Lane, *Politics and Society,* 488; Vadim Medish, *The Soviet Union,* 3rd ed. (Englewood Cliffs, NJ: Prentice-Hall, 1987), 199; MacKenzie and Curran, *Russia and the USSR,* 27.

3. Thompson, *Vision Unfulfilled*, 185; Larry E. Holmes, "Soviet Schools: Policy Pursues Practice, 1921–28," *Slavic Review* 48, 2 (Summer 1989): 240–41, nn. 28, 29, 30; MacKenzie and Curran, *Russia and the USSR*, 188.

4. Woodford McClellan, *Russia: The Soviet Period and After,* 3rd ed. (Englewood Cliffs, NJ: Prentice-Hall, 1994), 75.

5. Lane, *Politics and Society*, 491; Gail Warshofsky Lapidus, "Educational Strategies and Cultural Revolution: The Politics of Social Development," in *Cultural Revolution in Russia, 1928–31* ed. Sheila Fitzpatrick (Bloomington: Indiana University Press), 84, 85, 94, 102.

6. McClellan, *Russia: Soviet Period,* 81; Sheila Fitzpatrick, "The "Soft" Line on Culture and Its Enemies: Soviet Cultural Policy, 1922–1927," in *Slavic Review* 33, no. 2 (June 1974): 274.

7. Holmes, "Soviet Schools," 234–53; Thompson, *Vision Unfulfilled,* 186; Lane, *Politics and Society*, 491; McClellan, *Russia: Soviet Period,* 81; Grant, *Soviet Education,* 21; Medish, *Soviet Union,* 199; Alan Bookbinder, Olivia Lichtenstein, and Richard Denton, *Comrades: Portraits of Soviet Life* (New York: New American Library, 1986), 23–24; Hedrick Smith, *The Russians,* revised and updated edition (New York: Ballantine Books, 1977), 196; "Education," in *Soviet Union: A Country Study,* http://lcweb2.loc.gov/cgi-bin/query/D?cstdy:1:./temp/~frd_W61D; the very useful table of contents, which has links to all of the chapters and sub-chapters, including "Education," is accessible at http://lcweb2.loc.gov/frd/cs/sutoc.html. The *Country Study* is also available from the U.S. Government Printing Office, 2nd ed., 1991.

8. Susan Jacoby, *Inside Soviet Schools* (New York: Hill and Wang, 1974), 23; Lewis Siegelbaum and Andrei Sokolov, *Stalinism as a Way of Life: A Narrative in Documents* (New Haven: Yale University Press, 2000), 359–63.

9. Richard B. Dobson, "Soviet Education: Problems and Policies in the Urban Context," in *The Contemporary Soviet City* ed. Henry W. Morton and Robert C. Stuart (Armonk, NY: M. E. Sharpe, 1984), 115; Grant, *Soviet Education,* 21–22; Thompson, *Vision Unfulfilled,* 284; Siegelbaum and Sokolov, *Stalinism,* 408–13.

10. Dobson, "Soviet Education: Problems and Policies," 163; Grant, *Soviet Education,* 43–44, 91; Medish, *Soviet Union,* 203; Lane, *Politics and Society,* 496; Aleksandr Solzhenitsyn, *Matryona's Home,* in *The Norton Anthology of World Masterpieces,* ed. Maynard Mack et al., expanded edition, vol. 2 (New York: W. W. Norton, 1995), 2317.

11. Susan Bridger, "Soviet Rural Women: Employment and Family Life," in *Russian Peasant Women,* ed. Beatrice Farnsworth and Lynne Viola (New York: Oxford University Press, 1992), 283; Grant, *Soviet Education,* 78–81; Norton D. Dodge and Murray Feshbach, "The Role of Women in Soviet Agriculture," in *Russian Peasant Women,* 255–56; Lane, *Politics and Society,* 491–93; Bridger, *Women in the Soviet Countryside* (Cambridge: Cambridge University Press, 1987), 157; Medish, *Soviet Union,* 202; Grant, *Soviet Education,* 78.

12. Jacoby, *Inside Soviet Schools,* 66.

13. Jacoby, *Inside Soviet Schools,* 66, 173; Smith, *The Russians,* 213–16.

14. Here and elsewhere, I use "college" as an all-purpose synonym for Soviet higher education, including the two main kinds: the universities, and institutes collectively known as *VUZy.*

15. Siegelbaum and Sokolov, *Stalinism,* 439, n. 23.

16. Erika Popovych and Brian Levin-Stankevich, *The Soviet System of Education: A PIER World Education Series Special Report* (Washington, DC: American Association of Collegiate Registrars and Admissions Officers, Association of International Educators, 1992), 11, 14; Dobson, "Soviet Education: Problems and Policies," 165; Lane, *Politics and Society,* 497; Grant, *Soviet Education,* 35, 81–82.

17. Grant, *Soviet Education,* 45; McClellan, *Russia: Soviet Period,* 192; Popovych and Levin-Stankevich, *Soviet System of Education,* 11.

18. Medish, *Soviet Union,* 205; Grant, *Soviet Education,* 25–26.

19. Grant, *Soviet Education,* 38–39; Popovych and Levin-Stankevich, *Soviet System of Education,* 10–11; Dobson, "Soviet Education: Problems and Policies," 172.

20. Medish, *Soviet Union,* 197; Dobson, "Soviet Education: Problems and Policies," 164; Mobin Shorish, review of *Inside Soviet Schools,* in *Slavic Review* 34, no. 4 (December 1975): 839.

21. Anna Kisselgoff, "In the Ural Mountains, Youngsters Who Dare to Dream," *New York Times,* August 9, 2000, sec. B 3, cols. 1–5; Grant, *Soviet Education,* 97; Seymour M. Rosen, *Education and Modernization in the USSR* (Reading, MA: Addison Wesley, 1971), 69; Jacoby, *Inside Soviet Schools,* 25, 134, 149.

22. Medish, *Soviet Union,* 214; Dobson, "Soviet Education: Problems and Policies," 166–67.

23. Grant, *Soviet Education,* 28–29; Jacoby, *Inside Soviet Schools,* 29.

24. Grant, *Soviet Education,* 84, 103–4; Smith, *The Russians,* 200, 219–21; Dobson, "Education and Opportunity," in *Contemporary Soviet Society,* ed. Jerry G. Pankhurst and Michael P. Sacks (New York: Praeger, 1980), 123; Popovych and Levin-Stankevich, *Soviet System of Education,* 17; Jacoby, *Inside Soviet Schools,* 122–23; also see Dora O'Brien, *From Moscow: Living and Teaching among the Russians in the 1990s* (Nottingham, England: Bramcote Press, 2000), 99–100.

25. Medish, *Soviet Union,* 198–99; Lane, *Politics and Society,* 491; Holmes, "Soviet Schools," 162; McClellan, *Russia: Soviet Period,* 191–92; Grant, *Soviet Education,* 42–43.

26. Friedrich Kuebart, "Aspects of Soviet Secondary Education: School Performance and Teacher Accountability," in *Quality of Life in the Soviet Union,* ed. Horst Herlemann (Boulder, CO: Westview Press, 1987), 86–87; Elena Bonner, *Mothers and Daughters* (New York: Vintage Books, 1993), 118; O'Brien, *From Moscow,* 38; Grant, *Soviet Education,* 57; the subject of grades was discussed at length in August 2002 in the H-Net Russia History list (H-Russia@H-NET.MSU. edu).

27. Grant, *Soviet Education,* 57; Lane, *Politics and Society,* 500; Jacoby, *Inside Soviet Schools,* 64.

28. Smith, *The Russians,* 197, 216–18; O'Brien, *From Moscow,* 2; Jacoby, *Inside Soviet Schools,* 126.

29. O'Brien, *From Moscow,* 38, 99; Sydney Schultze, *Culture and Customs of Russia* (Westport, CT: Greenwood Press, 2000), 47; Smith, *The Russians,* 221, 218.

30. Dobson, "Education and Opportunity," 120; Rosen, *Education and Modernization,* 41; John Gunther, *Inside Russia Today* (New York: Harper and Brothers, 1957), 256; Grant, *Soviet Education,* 85.

31. Grant, *Soviet Education,* 26, 35, 37.

32. Grant, *Soviet Education,* 82; Medish, *Soviet Union,* 202–3, 205–6; Popovych and Levin-Stankevich, *Soviet System of Education,* 10; Bookbinder et al., *Comrades,* 24–26; Smith, *The Russians,* 219; O'Brien, *From Moscow,* 97.

33. Nina Kosterina, *The Diary of Nina Kosterina,* trans. Mirra Ginsburg (New York: Crown, 1968); Larry E. Holmes, *Stalin's School: Moscow's Model School No. 25, 1931–1937* (Pittsburgh: University of Pittsburgh Press, 1999).

34. Corinna Kuhr, "Children of 'Enemies of the People' as Victims of the Great Purges," *Cahiers du monde Russe* 39 (January–June 1998): 211–14; Eugenia Ginzburg, *Within the Whirlwind* (San Diego: Harcourt Brace Jovanovich, 1981), 5–7; Siegelbaum and Sokolov, *Stalinism,* 391–405.

35. Bridger, *Women in the Soviet Countryside,* 157; Smith, *The Russians,* 208; Schultze, *Culture and Customs,* 48.

36. Robert Conquest, *Agricultural Workers in the USSR* (London: Bodley Head, 1968), 123–24; Alexander Vucinich, "The Peasants as a Social Class," in *The Soviet Rural Community: A Symposium,* ed. James R. Millar (Urbana: University of Illinois Press, 1971), 314. Stephen P. Dunn, "The Soviet Rural Family," in *The Soviet Rural Community,* 330–31; Gertrude E. Schroeder, "Rural Living Standards in the Soviet Union," in *The Soviet Rural Economy,* ed. Robert C. Stuart (Towota, NJ: Rowman and Allenheld, 1984), 252–53; Medish, *Soviet Union,* 198; Bridger, *Women in the Soviet Countryside,* 162–63; Jacoby, *Inside Soviet Schools,* 40–41.

37. Conquest, *Agricultural Workers,* 123; Dobson, "Education and Opportunity," 118, 173; Dunn, "Soviet Rural Family," 330; Demitri Shimkin, "Current Characteristics and Problems of the Soviet Rural Population," in *Soviet Agricultural and Peasant Affairs,* ed. Roy D. Laird (Lawrence: University of Kansas Press, 1963), 86; Stephen L. Solnick, *Stealing the State: Control and Collapse in Soviet Institutions* (Cambridge, MA: Harvard University Press, 1999), 132.

38. Dodge and Feshbach, "Role of Women," 256; Dunn, "Soviet Rural Family," 331.

39. Lane, *Politics and Society,* 507; Dobson, "Education and Opportunity," 129; Medish, *Soviet Union,* 211.

40. Smith, *The Russians,* 208–9; Dobson, "Soviet Education: Problems and Policies," 164.

41. Dobson, "Soviet Education: Problems and Policies," 165.

42. Grant, *Soviet Education,* 58, 64–69; Kosterina, *Diary,* 48–49; Medish, *Soviet Union,* 200; McClellan, *Russia: Soviet Period,* 81; M. K. Dziewanowski, *A History of Soviet Russia and its Aftermath,* 5th ed. (Upper Saddle River, NJ: Prentice-Hall, 1997), 127.

43. McClellan, *Russia: Soviet Period,* 81; Solnick, *Stealing the State,* 60–67, 101; Medish, *Soviet Union,* 109.

44. Medish, *Soviet Union,* 207; Dobson, "Soviet Education: Problems and Policies," 120, 157–59.

45. Grant, *Soviet Education,* 38, 117, 112; Medish, *Soviet Union,* 207–8, 210–11; Dobson, "Education and Opportunity," 119–20.

46. Grant, *Soviet Education,* 118; Kosterina, *Diary,* 131.

47. McClellan, *Russia: Soviet Period,* 245; Bookbinder et al., *Comrades,* 13.

48. Solnick, *Stealing the State,* 138; Andrea Lee, *Russian Journal* (New York: Vintage Books, 1984), 35.

49. Jacoby, *Inside Soviet Schools,* 154–55; Lee, *Russian Journal,* 36.

50. Kosterina, *Diary,* 124, 127–28, 135–38; Bonner, *Mothers and Daughters,* 325.

51. Medish, *Soviet Union,* 207; Grant, *Soviet Education,* 108–9; Lane, *Politics and Society,* 503.

52. Medish, *Soviet Union,* 208; Bookbinder et al., *Comrades,* 16.

53. Grant, *Soviet Education,* 119–24.

54. Lee, *Russian Journal,* 3.

55. Lee, *Russian Journal,* 6, 11.

56. Dobson, "Education and Opportunity," 119; Grant, *Soviet Education,* 124; Medish, *Soviet Union,* 208.

57. Rosen, *Education and Modernization,* 94–95.

58. Lee, *Russian Journal,* 13.

59. Aleksandr I. Solzhenitsyn, *The First Circle,* trans. Thomas P. Whitney (New York: Harper & Row, 1968), 24–25.

60. Solnick, *Stealing the State,* 125, 129–36, 144, 157, 174; Medish, *Soviet Union,* 208, 213; Grant, *Soviet Education,* 124–27; Bookbinder et al., *Comrades,* 16.

10

The Arts[1]

HISTORICAL BACKGROUND

The history of the arts in the Soviet Union is a history of lethal repressions that extended and refined the censorship apparatus of the tsars. Lenin's 1905 article "Party Organization and Party Literature," the Bible of Soviet arts policy, spelled out the idea that literature

cannot be at all an individual affair independent of the proletariat as a whole. Down with non-party writers!...Literature must necessarily and inevitably become an inextricable part of the work of the Social-Democratic Party. Newspapers must become the organs of the various party organizations. Publishing houses and storerooms, bookshops and reading rooms, libraries and book concerns of all sorts—must all become Party enterprises subject to its control.[2]

After the October Revolution, the Bolsheviks moved quickly to control the arts. On November 9, 1917, Lenin issued a decree giving supervision of all arts activities to the newly formed Commissariat (later Ministry) of Education (*Narkompros*), headed by Anatoly Lunacharsky. In January 1918, perhaps the first instance of censorship in the Soviet era occurred with the shutdown of a Yiddish newspaper, *Togblat*, the seizure of its equipment, and the arrest of its publisher and editor.[3]

Despite repressions, the period between the 1905 revolution and 1917 provided an interlude of comparative liberalization, when artists and audiences looked forward to the construction of a more humane society in which all talented people, regardless of social or religious heritage, could freely innovate. This optimism was accompanied by an eruption of revolutionary experimentation in the arts. The Russian avant-garde became active and pathbreaking in every artistic arena: photography, film, book design (including typography), architecture, painting, sculpture, literature, literary criticism, music, and theater. It was, moreover, a time of wonderful mingling of artistic genres. Poets no longer thought of themselves just as poets, but as poets–directors–artists–actors. One of the best examples (among many) of such a border crosser was the poet–poster artist–playwright–actor Vladimir Mayakovsky, who, hounded by vicious and unrelenting official criticism of his work and haunted by a failed love affair, committed suicide in 1930 and was then officially sanctified by the government. Stalin declared it a crime not to honor Mayakovsky's work.

In the theater, directors, poets, painters, architects, and musicians shared their talents and enlarged their artistic horizons. This interaction among artists was embodied by the Futurist opera *Victory Over the Sun* (1913), a product of the collaboration of Mikhail Matyushin, a painter-musician who composed the music; the Futurist poet Alexey Kruchyonykh, who wrote the libretto; and the artist Kazimir Malevich, who designed the abstract sets and costumes, the most sensational and fascinating part of the production. But theatrical innovation was not limited to Moscow and St. Petersburg. Some of the pioneering director Vsevolod Meyerhold's earliest dramatic experiments were carried out at the very beginning of the century in places like Vitebsk and Tiflis.

A 1919 decree brought all theaters under government control; in 1922 orders were issued to censor scripts and monitor performances. Nevertheless, for another decade or so luminaries such as Meyerhold, Les Kurbas, Solomon Mikhoëls, Sergey Radlov, Sergey Eisenstein, Alexander Tyshler, Alexander Tairov, and many others kept Soviet theater at the apex of world drama. Encouraged by an ideology that emphasized bringing art and literacy to the masses, artists also experimented with book design and content. Among the masters in this art form were the painter-photographers Alexander Rodchenko and El Lissitzky, whose exhibitions and designs were popular at home and abroad.[4]

During the same period, writers experimented with redefining the forms, uses, and meanings of language. A group of writers tried to move poetry into the realm of abstract art, as many photographers, painters, and composers were doing in their media. Kruchyonykh and his fellow avant-garde poet Velimir Khlebnikov created what they called *"zaumnyi iazyk* (transrational, trans-sense, or transmental language). In his highly experimental landmark poem "Incantation by Laughter" (*Zaklyatie smekhom,* 1908–1909) Khlebnikov broke through the envelope of ordinary language by taking the root of a common word—*laugh* (Russian *sme*)—and playing around with it. By attaching a variety of prefixes and suffixes to the root, he created new "words" (or wordlike sounds) like "Hlaha! Loufenish lauflings lafe," that attempt to communicate the very heart and soul of laughter itself.[5]

Kruchyonykh, Khlebnikov, and Mayakovsky were among the rebellious young poets who belonged to a politically and artistically radical movement called Futurism. Among the Futurists, Mayakovsky's varied poetic gift turned out to be the most brilliant and enduring. He read his warlike, even terroristic poetry to large, spellbound audiences. In "Left March" (1918) he urges people to let revolutionary guns do the talking—but he also created enduring love lyrics in which the poet offers to transform himself from a volcano to "a cloud in trousers."[6]

Women were strongly represented among avant-garde painters and designers of the 1910s and 20s. Among them were Alexandra Exter, Natalia Goncharova, Lyubov Popova, Olga Rozanova, Varvara Stepanova, and Nadezhda Udaltsova. Together they made important contributions to Russian, and world, modern art. Like their male colleagues, they painted in a variety of styles, from folk art to Cubism, and did not restrict themselves to easel painting; they experimented in a variety of artistic genres: stage settings, textiles, and other media. Also like their male counterparts, those who did not die young or emigrate were stifled.[7]

The New Economic Policy (NEP) period (1921–1928) was from its beginning a time of fearfulness among artists. The poet Nikolay Gumilyov, accused of participating in a counterrevolutionary conspiracy, was executed in 1921 as an "enemy of the people and the worker-peasant revolution." In the same year the Symbolist poet Alexander Blok languished and died while Lenin and Lunacharsky considered whether he ought to be allowed to leave the country for medical treatment. The secret police were everywhere and artists had good reason to be afraid. In 1927, the visiting German writer Walter Benjamin wondered why Moscow audiences responded so indifferently to Meyerhold's remarkable stage version of Nikolai Gogol's *The Inspector General*. Benjamin concluded that the cause was simply fear that an opinion—pro or con—might turn out to be "incorrect."[8]

The New Economic Policy Period

In 1923 centralized control of dramatic works, musicals, and film was handed over to the newly born Glavrepertkom (Central Repertory Committee), which was an arm of Glavlit (Main Administration for Literary and Publishing Affairs), established in 1922 as a subdepartment of the Commissariat of Education, to "liquidate literature directed against Soviet construction." Both Glavlit and Glavrepertkom were eyes and ears for the secret police, and like them reported to the ideological department of the Central Committee. Drama censorship was considered especially crucial because of the strong, immediate, and emotional impact plays could have on audiences, and the difficulty of absolutely controlling every moment of every performance.

In 1929 Stalin removed the relatively liberal Lunacharsky from his position as head of the Commissariat of Education. Lunacharsky's successor, Andrey Bubnov, led the mid-1930s campaign against avant-garde art,

The 1930s oversaw the closing of the Moscow Art Theater's experimental studio (1936), and increased the number of banned productions. He and his wife were arrested in 1937 and shot the following year. While it is not surprising that politically independent art movements were suppressed early on, beginning in 1930 even the most loyal artists and arts organizations, such as LEF and VAPP (acronyms for Left Front of the Arts and All-Union Association of Proletarian Writers, respectively) got the axe. Some members of Oberiu, an extremely avant-garde group of writers, were put on trial in 1931 for their unconventional style. Modernist poets with quirky styles began hiding their real creations and earning their living as translators, screenwriters, playwrights, librarians, and children's book writers, although "safe" work did not necessarily protect anyone from arrest. The quality of Soviet theater and other arts began a steady decline under intensifying censorship and fear. The theatrical pioneers either met violent ends or were permitted to stay alive, to thrive or not as producers of mediocre work encased in traditional, easily understandable forms.[9]

In 1932, the Party's Central Committee, with Stalin's backing, adopted a crucial resolution that mandated bringing all writers into a single organization—the Union of Soviet Writers. The establish-
Artists' "Unions" ment of similar "unions" for other artistic groups soon followed. This forced reorganization of artists' leagues closed the last door between an artist and his or her intellectual freedom. Without union membership, artists and writers were not allowed to publish or exhibit their work, much less enjoy the other perks that came (or at least were promised) with membership: a chance for decent housing and medical care, city residency, country vacations, first-class education for their children, and old-age pensions. Stalin allowed non-Party artists to join the unions, which most did.[10]

SOCIALIST REALISM AND FORMALISM

The concept of Socialist Realism, first proposed by Stalin in 1932, was publicly introduced as the officially preferred artistic style at the First Congress of Soviet Writers in Moscow (August 17–September 1, 1934). The idea was presented in a speech by Stalin's spokesman, Andrey Zhdanov, and was soon used as a wide net to snare all arts, including painting, sculpture, film, theater, and music. As interpreted by Stalin's regime and after, Socialist Realism demanded a "realistic," easily understood, optimistic picture of Soviet life and the future of the Soviet Union. Socialist Realism was therefore not so much an artistic style as it was a means of control. Those artists and writers who did not conform to the officially approved style were labeled "Formalist." Originally an important philosophy of literary criticism that began about 1914–1915 in Moscow and St. Petersburg, Formalists were not interested in using the arts for political purposes. But during Stalin's regime the label "Formalist" was applied to all artists and varieties of art (including music and music criticism) that did not conform to the officially approved style. Even some scientists and teachers were attacked as Formalists. The label could ruin people's careers; push them into poverty; and even lead to arrest, imprisonment, and execution.[11]

During World War II, writers and other creative artists were expected to produce works radiating patriotism and hostility to the enemy. Even some previously banned or imprisoned writers, such as Anna Akhmatova and Nikolai Erdman, were tolerated and allowed to publish as long as their efforts served the cause. After the war censors returned to repressing works and artists that diverged from Socialist Realism and other aspects of Party policy. Zhdanov denounced such national treasures as Mikhail Zoshchenko, Anna Akhmatova, and Boris Pasternak, calling them "anti-Soviet, underminers of Socialist Realism, and unduly pessimistic." Sergey Eisenstein and the composers Sergey Prokofiev and Dmitry Shostakovich were accused of "neglect of ideology and subservience to Western influence." Although Zhdanov died in 1948, the cultural purges he spearheaded continued beyond Stalin's death in 1953. Targeted artists were made to suffer in a variety of ways. Whether or not they were actually arrested, the constant fear of arrest and for the safety of their loved ones crippled the lives of many.[12]

By the beginning of 1936, the young composer Shostakovich was a highly regarded artist whose groundbreaking opera, *Lady Macbeth of the Mtsensk District* (premiered 1934), was popular and critically successful at home and abroad. But because Shostakovich's music was not to Stalin's taste, on the morning of January 28, **Socialist Realism** *Pravda* (one of the main newspapers) announced that **and Music** the composer was a "formalist"; in other words, an outcast. The first newspaper article, "Muddle Instead of Music" (January 28), savaged his *Lady Macbeth* and accused it of Formalism and other political crimes. Equally guilty of political-artistic blunders, according to the article, were all other avant-garde composers as well as music critics who praised their work. For Shostakovich's friend and mentor, Vsevolod Meyerhold, the article took an especially ominous turn by equating Formalism with "Meyerholdism." *Lady Macbeth* was quickly pulled from the repertoire and did not reappear until after Stalin's death. Shostakovich withdrew his *Fourth Symphony* (1935–1936) from a planned performance in case authorities might object to it also, but even that precaution did not satisfy Stalin's wrath against Shostakovich's music (of "quacks, grunts, and growls"), other avant-garde composers, and music critics who approved their work. Soon there appeared yet another *Pravda* offensive, "Falsehood in Ballet" (February 6), this one aimed at Shostakovich's music for the ballet *The Bright Stream* (1934), which was hastily canceled. Finally, as if to prove that Formalist dissonance was everywhere, *Pravda* published

"Cacophony in Architecture." Meetings organized for the purpose of denouncing targeted colleagues were part of a ritual that often preceded arrest. After the *Pravda* articles, there were three days of denunciations of Shostakovich, sponsored by the Moscow Union of Composers. Many arrests of composers and music critics followed, though Shostakovich himself was not among them.[13]

Throughout the Soviet period, the government continued to control the arts through the media, especially the press, by means of hostile reviews that slandered not only the targeted artist's talent, but that person's character and patriotism as well. After Stalin's death, negative reviews or other evidences of official displeasure were generally not lethal; rather, they were warnings that an artist, writer, or musician who wandered too far from official cultural policies, or showed dissatisfaction with the government, could face a prison term, domestic or foreign exile, or withdrawal of perks. As the director Yury Lyubimov said to a friend after his sudden dismissal—in 1984—from the post of chief director of the Taganka Theater: "I have to thank them for not shooting me like Meyerhold."[14]

THE CASE OF VSEVOLOD MEYERHOLD

The closing of the State Meyerhold Theater in early 1938 was also preceded by a furious denunciation in *Pravda*, "An Alien Theater" (1937), as well as by an official proclamation accusing the theater of being bourgeois, Formalist, a distorter of classics, antiartistic, defamatory of Soviet reality, foreign to Soviet art, and failing in its duty to mount a special production to celebrate the 20th anniversary of the October Revolution. This barrage foreshadowed Meyerhold's arrest in 1939; three weeks after Meyerhold's detention, his wife and leading actress, Zinaida Raikh, was stabbed to death in her home, presumably by government agents. Her imprisoned husband was tortured hideously, severely beaten on the most sensitive parts of his body with a club, and forced to drink his own urine and to sign a confession (of having committed fantastic espionage crimes) with his unbroken right hand. Then he was convicted by a closed military court and quickly disposed of in the Lubyanka prison's basement killing room. Within the USSR, no one dared to speak or write publicly about the great director for 15 years, and he was nearly forgotten in the West, a colossal affront to theater history. Meyerhold's circle of colleagues, friends, and acquaintances was riven by betrayals, terror, arrests, extorted confessions, and violent deaths. In a brave act of defiance, Eisenstein preserved some of Meyerhold's papers by hiding them in the walls of his *dacha*.[15]

SELF-CENSORSHIP

Through these and hundreds of other campaigns of terror against artists was born the most powerful method of censorship: the fear-driven self-censorship that made artists commit their work to oblivion before it was ever submitted to a government official or audience of any sort. The pervasiveness of self-censorship and the harnessing of art to state service makes it impossible to know all the treasures that were sacrificed by those who could say, with Mayakovsky, "I have stepped on the throat of my own song." Under the weight of this terror, the brilliant art born in Russia at the beginning of the century collapsed entirely or was entrusted to the precarious custody of memory, or hidden for decades in every sort of cache: pots, pillowcases, walls.

NONPERSONS

By making people afraid even to speak to each other about banned artists, by airbrushing the "nonpersons" out of photos, removing their works from public access, and expunging them from encyclopedias and other publications, Stalin attempted to purge even the memory of an artist's life and work. This fate befell not only artists and intellectuals, however. Millions of loyal Communists, including most Old Bolsheviks, among them many who had achieved political power and glory, also violently disappeared from the world and from print. The government printing authority regularly mailed owners of *The Great Soviet Encyclopedia* notices about entries to razor out. When the secret police boss, Lavrenty Beria, fell from power and was executed, encyclopedia owners were sent an article on the Bering Strait with instructions to paste it over the entry on Beria.[16]

ARTISTS AS WITNESSES

Artists dealt with the ongoing terror in various ways. Some, like Meyerhold (who himself served on a theater censorship committee) and Eisenstein, cooperated with the regime, accepting its honors and special privileges, while still preserving their singular art. Other loyalists were not successful in keeping both their unique voices and their jobs. There were a few, like the poets Anna Akhmatova and Osip Mandelstam, who at harrowing personal cost never aligned themselves with the regime, and more and more as the terror progressed went beyond self-centered lyrics to poetry that witnesses, protests, and condemns. One result of this commitment was Akhmatova's lyric cycle "Requiem," published in the West (1963–1964), in which the poet describes life under terror. In a brief introduction to the poem, Akhmatova explains her impetus for writing it. While standing "in the prison lines of Leningrad," along with many other women hoping for news of imprisoned loved ones or attempting to send a parcel from home (Akhmatova's son was among those arrested), a woman "with bluish lips" recognizes her and asks Akhmatova if she can "describe this." The poet answers that she can, which brings a kind of joy to the other woman: "something that looked like a smile passed over what had once been her face."[17]

Other poets also recorded the persecution. Anna Barkova, before her arrest in 1934, wrote poems that commented sardonically on the artistic-political situation and complained about the "poets" who fawningly created lines to rhyme with Stalin. She also noted how poets struggled to find rhymes for "tractor." Her criticism of Soviet reality was implicit in such strategies as rhyming "bad" (*plokho*) with "epoch" (*epokha*), or "tears" (*slezy*) with *kolkhozy* (collective farms). In other poems she openly announced her disillusionment with the Revolution she once supported, reproached herself and other idealists for their naivete, and called her century "sick" because "It betrayed our hopes/ It mocked our love/ It promised us victories and gave us new despots." Her lyrics pointed out that perpetrators and victims were often one and the same.[18]

Writers who seemed to have quit writing were as much objects of suspicion as those who produced the "wrong" kind of work. Besides, most artists and writers crave an audience. Osip Mandelstam attempted to harmonize his public silence and his private beliefs by reading his satirical poem about Stalin's "cockroach mustaches" and "jackboots" to a small group of friends. As it turned out, one of the listeners was an informer.[19]

Mandelstam perished in a prison transit camp in 1938, thereby merging his fate with that of other "enemies of the people" arrested by the millions. The last group from the arts community to be executed at Stalin's personal command, in 1952, had links to the Jewish Anti-Fascist Committee. The dictator's campaign against thinking human beings took various forms: physical, economic, and psychological, but even during the worst times, some creative art continued, albeit secretively, and some unusual poetry written during the Stalin years was published abroad.

"THE THAW" AND AFTER

Censorship liberalization followed almost immediately after Stalin's demise in March 1953. Olga Berggolts declared her right to record her inner life without regard to the social usefulness of her writing. A newspaper critic attacked the heavy-handed chauvinism of Soviet film. The composer Aram Khachaturian publicly condemned the government's meddling with music. A literary journal, *Novyi mir* (New World), under its editor Alexander Tvardovsky, published stories that ignored the easy patriotism and hopefulness of Socialist Realism to focus on some harsh realities of Soviet life. Other early "thaw" works attacked Stalinism and self-aggrandizing bureaucrats. In February 1956, First Secretary Nikita Khrushchev made a (well reported) "secret speech" to the 20th Party Congress, in which he denounced Stalin's crimes. In 1961, after the 22nd Party Congress, Khrushchev led a "de-Stalinization" campaign that made it possible for Soviets to speak and write more freely. Many writers killed in

Stalin's terror campaigns were "rehabilitated" beginning in the late 1950s. Their works were published, and others were allowed to write positively about them. But tolerance was turned on and off at the government's will, and crackdowns on artists, writers, and other intellectuals continued.

Prison and torture remained a government option, but physical terror against creative intellectuals took second place to other means, the main one being ejection from one's union or academic institution and the resulting loss of privileges. Celebrities might be forced out of the country and not allowed to return, as happened with the Nobel laureate Solzhenitsyn, who in 1975 was arrested and put on a specially chartered plane to West Germany. In other instances the government simply waited until troublesome artists went abroad before snatching away their citizenship and right to return.

In the 1960s and 70s, Andrey Voznesensky, Bella Akhmadulina, Yevgeny Yevtushenko, Vladimir Voinovich, and Alexander Solzhenitsyn were among the brightest lights of the younger generation of writers. Sometimes poetry readings were held in soccer stadiums, to accommodate all the fans. Solzhenitsyn's novel *One Day in the Life of Ivan Denisovich*, a portrayal of prison camp life that Khrushchev in 1962 had personally approved for publication, quickly sold out, but copies were shared about. In the same year, however, Khrushchev visited a small Moscow abstract art exhibit, pronounced the works to be "dog shit," and warned the artists, "Gentlemen, we are declaring war on you." Two weeks later, meeting with artists and writers, Khrushchev announced that the Party would decide what forms of artistic expression were permissible. According to Voznesensky, most writers and other artists ignored these warning signals, believing Khrushchev was dedicated to liberalization "in his heart." "We continued to have faith in Khrushchev," Voznesensky recalled, "and we continued to look to him for protection." They were in for a shock.[20]

In March 1963, Khrushchev spoke at a Kremlin meeting devoted to a new official policy on the arts. While Khrushchev's watershed "secret" 1956 speech seemed to open the door to a freer society, his public outburst at the 1963 meeting slammed the door shut. In the course of the meeting, Khrushchev made ominous references to traitors in the audience, singling out Voznesensky as the main target of his fierce abuse, and in closing spoke well of Stalin. Voznesensky fled Moscow to hide in the countryside. A fellow poet publicly demanded that Voznesensky and certain other writers be sentenced to death as traitors, even though producing illegal art had been downgraded from "counterrevolutionary activity," a capital offense, to "anti-Soviet agitation and propaganda," which carried sentences of long prison terms, forced exile abroad or within the USSR, or both.

After Khrushchev's fall in 1964, there was yet another official tightening up, beginning with the arrest (for "parasitism") and trial of the poet Joseph Brodsky, whose work, though not political, did not conform to offi-

cial requirements. The year 1966 saw the trials of the writers Yuly Daniel
(pen name, Nikolai Arzhak) and Andrey Sinyavsky (pen name, Abram
Terts) for publishing anti-Soviet material abroad. Brodsky, Daniel, and
Sinyavsky all served time in prison camps; the latter two also had to
endure internal exile. And the art itself was punished: in 1974, in a
Moscow suburb, the government used bulldozers to crush an outdoor
exhibition of modernist art, but at least the painters survived.[21]

THE CENSORSHIP PROCESS

Throughout the Soviet period, the censorship apparatus had many
bureaucratic levels, each of which had to judge a submitted work and
then, if it was approved at that level, pass it on up to the next
Theater   office. Although the procedures changed in their details over
time, the basic process remained the same. For example, a playwright who hoped to have a play staged first submitted the script to
Glavlit, then waited for a later interview with a censor, at which time the
writer would be told what revisions were necessary; submit the revisions
in triplicate; wait for approval; and have the script returned, pages sealed
in wax, with the number of authorized pages written on it by hand and a
note stipulating the maximum number of copies allowed. These copies
could be made only at a special office designated for that purpose. Then
the author had to submit the play to Glavrepertkom censors. If the play
was approved by Glavrepertkom, the playwright brought copies to the literary directors of various theaters. A literary director interested in the
script would probably ask the writer for more revisions. If the play cleared
the literary director and had the approval of a theater's chief director
(often a genuine artist rather than a mere Party functionary), the playwright would be required to give a reading for the theater's artistic council. At this point, the council could refuse the play, accept it as it was, or
order revisions. If the council approved the play, Glavrepertkom still had
to be petitioned for permission to allow rehearsals. If permission was
granted, that still was not the end of the vetting process, which continued
until the very eve of public performance, and often beyond. The (theoretically) final hurdle was the closed dress rehearsal for members of
Glavrepertkom as well as the artistic council, author, director, and
designer. If a show was banned at dress rehearsal, great expenditures of
time, money, and energy were down the drain. If the council gave its
thumbs-up at the dress rehearsal, a nervous bureaucrat or censorship
committee could pull the play from the repertory at any time after its
opening. Indeed, the more popular the play, the greater the likelihood this
would happen. The Taganka Theater's tremendously successful play *The
Poet Vladimir Vysotsky* (1981), for example, was finally given permission to
be staged, but only twice a year; nevertheless, it was banned after a few
performances.[22]

Film censorship began even before writers were hired, because scripts had to conform to official demands for certain themes, such as village life, Lenin's (and earlier, Stalin's) life, Soviet industry, and various national occasions and celebrations. After a writer was hired and **Film** the script written, it had to pass through some 17 to 20 "editorial" (censorship) committees. When "editors" were finished with a script, the work emerged radically pruned of politically incorrect material. Soviet screenwriters had a joke to describe their situation: "What is a telephone pole?" "A telephone pole is an edited pine tree." After the censorship boards had done their work, the film was carried off to private showings for higher-level civilian and military censors. If a film passed this scrutiny, it was returned, with a panoply of certifications and stamps, to its director. The government determined how many copies of the movie were to be made and where it could be shown. As with painters and photographers, filmmakers could not point their cameras anywhere they pleased. It was forbidden to film tall landmarks, military personnel, landscapes near a military base or weapons factory, and scenes of everyday life that showed Soviet reality in a bad light. In one of his movies, Andrey Kuznetsov recalled, censors discarded a scene in which the hero meditated about life and death. The censors' rationale was that "Soviet people are too positive to dwell upon death!" For some mysterious reason, calendars showing the actual date of filming were also off-limits. After Khrushchev's denunciation of the "cult of personality," all previous Soviet films with Stalin portraits had to be doctored to eliminate the offending pictures.[23]

Sergey Eisenstein's fruitless struggle in the 1930s to produce a politically acceptable version of *Bezhin Meadow* and Tarkovsky's later, ultimately successful battle to show his *Andrei Rublev* in the Soviet Union illustrate the relative but still very constricted liberalization after Stalin. *Bezhin Meadow* was made and remade for the censors but was never allowed to be shown, even though the director was a world-famous filmmaker. In 1935, when *Bezhin Meadow* was about 60 percent finished, Boris Shumyatsky, the head of the Central Administration of Cinematography, stole it away in order to view it himself and show it to other leading members of the Soviet film industry, as well as to Party elite. This resulted in such heavy criticism of the work that the director had to start over practically from scratch, hiring a new screenwriter (Isaac Babel, soon to be arrested and shot) and new actors. But in March 1937, Shumyatsky once again decreed that work on the film be stopped. It was attacked in the press; meetings were organized specifically for condemning the unfinished movie very few had been allowed to see. Many film workers (including Eisenstein himself) were called on to speak at those meetings. A few brave souls defended Eisenstein and the film, spoke ambiguously, or called in sick. Eisenstein was allowed to continue in his profession, but Shumyatsky was arrested and executed in 1938. Because of a 1941 bombing raid, only a few stills remain of *Bezhin Meadow*. This was not to be

Eisenstein's last brush with the censor, however. He had planned a trilogy on the life of Tsar Ivan the Terrible. Part one, completed in 1944, won a Stalin Prize for its portrayal of Ivan's dynamic leadership. Perhaps Stalin saw his own portrait therein. He may have also recognized himself in part two, which shows Ivan's advancing paranoia and extraordinary violence. Whatever the reasons, part two was banned and not shown until 1958, 10 years after Eisenstein's death. Part three was never made.[24]

Andrey Tarkovsky's renowned film *Andrei Rublev,* set in the early fifteenth century, is about Russia's most famous icon painter. The work had its premiere in 1967 but was banned from further screening. Censors objected to it in part because it showed Russians in a light as bad as, or worse than, that of their enemies, the Turks. Maybe that was the reason Soviet authorities considered the film "too depressing" for USSR audiences. The authorities eventually approved its being sold abroad, and it was unofficially entered in the Cannes Film Festival, receiving the International Critics Prize. The internal ban on *Andrei Rublev* was lifted in 1971, when it was allowed showings in Moscow's suburbs, albeit with only word-of-mouth publicity. The movie theaters showing the film were packed. Tarkovsky was fortunate in being able to present all of his five feature-length movies, a success won at the cost of an ongoing struggle against censorship.

In other cases as well, diplomatic compromises with censors sometimes ended in the production and domestic distribution of worthwhile films, including Grigory Chukhrai's masterpieces, *Ballad of a Soldier* (1959) and *The Clear Sky* (1961). Chukhrai well knew how to delicately balance social criticism with praise for his country's accomplishments. Nevertheless, his movies about vulnerable human beings struggling to survive in an often cruel society brought him into conflict with authorities who threatened to expel him from the Party. Once when Khrushchev fell asleep during a screening of the Italian film *8 1/2*, Chukhrai was ordered not to award it the Moscow Film Festival's grand prize. His refusal to cave in, Chukhrai said, resulted in his being refused permission to travel abroad for several years. The struggle against censorship was a struggle many filmmakers (and their potential audiences) often lost. Worthwhile movies were shelved, or so compromised by censorship they were no longer artistically significant. At the Fifth Congress of the Union of Soviet Cinematographers, in May 1986, union members, emboldened by Gorbachev's glasnost, voted out their repressive first secretary, as well as the union's entire secretariat, and elected a leader more in tune with the liberalizing times.[25]

During glasnost film directors and screenwriters had more freedom to move away from Socialist Realism and show realistic, even negative, aspects of Soviet life. They also began to include explicit sex scenes, which had been strictly taboo before. The first movie with explicit sex was Vasily Pichul's *Little Vera* (1988). It not only flouted the Soviet ban on frank sexual imagery, but it also dared to show working-class life in a grimy industrial city, a dysfunctional family, aimless unhappy youth, pointless sexual adventures, and an unhappy ending. In other words, *Little Vera* was a complete rejection of the cheap optimism, positive heroes, and easy moral judgments of Socialist Realism. After *Little Vera* Soviet directors tended to include sex scenes no matter what. A Soviet critic commented, "It is as if someone calls out the command 'undress!' and the hero obediently strips off in every second or third frame, even if this has nothing to do with the action on screen." In some of those films, sex was used as social commentary; for example, to show how it was the only entertainment in otherwise dreary lives. As often as not, however, erotic scenes were simply a way to make a film more profitable when state subsidies dried up.[26]

"How can we know the dancer from the dance?" asks the poet W. B. Yeats. Unlike Yeats, Soviet censors did not wrestle with that distinction. The professional and personal life of Maya Plisetskaya, the Bolshoi Ballet's longtime prima ballerina and one of the twentieth century's greatest dancers, illustrates both the cruelties of life **Dance** under Stalin and the "lesser purgatories" of the post-Stalin years in which there was less fear for one's life. Like the Russian serf artists of previous centuries, performers (even in the best of Soviet times) were "always forced to beg—to travel, to prepare new works, to be paid fairly." Plisetskaya's father was arrested and executed in 1937, possibly because, as a mine director, he had hired a friend who had been Trotsky's secretary; her mother was taken away to a Kazakhstan prison camp for wives of "enemies of the people." The parental taint was never washed away, despite her great fame and many official honors. Whether because of her family history or her defiant personality, or both, for six years she was not allowed to travel with her troupe when they went abroad. Being banned from foreign travel could be a personal catastrophe. Dancers lived to tour abroad, because the small amounts of hard currency they earned in the West could mean the difference between comfort and misery at home. "And if you couldn't go on a tour and had to stay in Moscow," Plisetskaya explains, "you might as well put your teeth on a shelf, curse yourself, be jostled in a bus filled with sweaty people, and listen to your wife's weeping rebukes." When she was permitted to travel abroad, the secret police urged her to encourage Robert Kennedy's interest in her. Plisetskaya remained a Soviet citizen, but the great dancer Mikhail Baryshnikov, denied opportunities to experiment and innovate, defected to the West, as did Rudolf Nureyev and Natalia Makarova. As with others who chose or were forced to emigrate, Baryshnikov and Nureyev were obliterated from USSR arts history and regarded by many of their Soviet countrymen as "shameful traitors."[27]

According to the Party, there were basically two kinds of music: "relevant" and "irrelevant." "Relevant" works were those with officially acceptable accompanying words, so that anyone could know the ideas the music was supposed to express. Contemporary Soviet music with no text,

Music   such as a sonata or a symphony, was "irrelevant," and even
                when not banned, serious obstacles were set up that made it dif-
ficult, if not impossible, to get the piece performed. When music was performed without words, it was the reviewer's job to inform readers about
the work's political implications. Since the only way for any Soviet artist
to earn a living and be allotted special privileges was to get commissions
from the state, composers wrote music for government-approved words.
Music with politically incorrect text would have to be tailored and
adjusted. There were instances in which music was changed to accommodate new words, or chunks of music with offending words were simply
amputated. Sometimes it was enough just to change the title of a work, as
when Rimsky-Korsakov's *Easter Overture* became *Radiant Holiday.* If the
offending words remained, they could be a serious obstacle to performance within the Soviet Union. Shostakovich's *Thirteenth Symphony,*
which includes a choral rendition of Yevtushenko's poem *Babi Yar* (about
the massacre of Kiev Jews during World War II), was unofficially banned
in the Soviet Union for many years.

Although a certain degree of creative freedom was allowed to a few
famous Soviet composers, such as Shostakovich, Khachaturian, and
Kabalevsky, most younger Soviet composers were forced to write their
cutting-edge compositions "for the drawer," circulating printed copies of
their "irrelevant" works or performing them only among a select group of
trusted friends and colleagues. Sometimes, to impress the rest of the
world, the government sent outstanding music by young Soviet composers to international music festivals, while performance of those same
compositions was not allowed within Soviet borders.

Works by contemporary foreign composers might be performed if the
composer had demonstrated a pro-Soviet bias, but those who left the
Party or otherwise showed hostility to Soviet policies were classified as
"bad" composers; their works were not performed.

Soviet conservatories emphasized the classics and did not encourage an
interest in experimental modern music. Upon graduation each musician
was given an "artist's certificate" good until the date stamped, which
listed the works he or she was allowed to perform. Nonetheless, thanks to
radio and recordings, music lovers kept up with developments in the
music world.

Music censors were often accomplished musicians with conservatory
degrees. Besides censoring compositions, they also scrutinized lectures
about music. Anyone who planned such a lecture had to first prepare a
copy for the censors, who reviewed it and informed the author how it had
to be revised. Lecturers planning to talk about Tchaikovsky, for example,
might be advised to mention that Lenin heard the composer's *Sixth Symphony* in London and liked it. Just as plays had censors in the audience to
check the actual performance, those who spoke in public about music
knew that censors would be listening to insure the talk conformed to the

one they had okayed. Every concert organization also had its "music editor" whose function was to meet with musicians ahead of a concert to ensure the program would be ideologically acceptable, and that the musicians had permission to perform it.[28]

The official path through the censorship bureaucracy was labyrinthine and slow, but as in all other areas of Soviet life, there were alternate routes via personal connections. A patron with clout could ignore the decisions of underlings; give permission to get a new composition performed; or secure a favorite pianist a *dacha,* superior medical care, or an apartment with space for a piano. Top Party bosses who liked to patronize the arts and artists expected something worthwhile in return, such as the reflected glory of celebrity or the ability to get children, however untalented, into a conservatory. Maya Plisetskaya's relatives were honored Soviet artists; their prestige could not save her father, but it did rescue her mother from the gulag and exile in a dusty Kazakh town.

Goskomizdat (State Commission for Publishing Houses, Printing Plants, and the Book Trade) was the agency responsible for book publishing decisions and had the power to allocate paper, which was also a means of control. From the 1960s **Book Publishing** until the end of the regime, writers and their friends had two main ways of circumventing state censorship: typing, copying, and circulating their own works (*samizdat*), or sending them abroad for publication (*tamizdat*).

OTHER ARTISTIC PRODUCTIONS

Amateur theater ensembles were popular. They had a heyday in the 1920s, when, with government blessings, the numbers of such groups, used as delivery systems for political propaganda as well as social and moral preaching and teaching, bal- **Amateur Theater** looned. Amateur groups went into decline under the repressions of the 30s, gathered new strength during the Khrushchev era, declined again with the cultural-political crackdown of 1968, and experienced a rebirth of talent and energy in the early 70s. The troupes might or might not be led by professional theater people or have one or more professional performers among them. It was very unlikely, however, that an amateur actor would be able to cross over into professional status without formal training and certification from a theater institute. Tickets to amateur performances were usually free; if there was a charge for admission the money typically went to the organization (university, factory, club) that sponsored the ensemble rather than to the acting group. Sometimes the director and less often the designer got a tiny wage. The ensemble might share space with other amateur groups or find themselves an unused space. Because amateurs were less monitored by censors and less influenced, or fettered, by the acting "rules" and other conventions of formal training schools, they were freer to innovate if they chose to, and some did, calling their ensemble a "studio," a label that implies experimentation. Most commonly, however, amateurs strove to look like the "real thing," producing pale imitations of professional shows.

During the Gorbachev era, amateur studio theaters in Moscow presented a wide range of plays: classics of world literature, a dramatic version of the American novel *Jonathan Livingston Seagull,* and unusual plays by contemporary young Soviet writers such as Lyudmila Petrushevskaya's *Cinzano.* Many of the Moscow studio groups consistently performed at a high level of quality and often had more devoted fans than seats to accommodate them. Playgoers appreciated the enthusiasm they missed in professional theaters, though they also complained about the discomforts of a jerry-rigged, undermaintained theater space. "The water...drips for real between the fourth and fifth rows," commented a group of students about a studio production of Bulgakov's *Molière.* Increasingly during the Brezhnev and Gorbachev eras, amateur theaters provided comment books for audiences as well as the opportunity to stay after the performance to discuss a play with its company. Because amateur theatricals were shoestring operations, fans often pitched in to help out in various ways, a show of volunteer community support that was not offered to professional theaters. People donated time; talent; materials; and, though it was illegal, money to help their favorite group survive. But with the approach of glasnost in the mid-1980s, that picture began to change. The small amateur groups, whose staples had been social criticism and protest, found themselves competing for audience attention in the face of a freer press, and ever more kinds of entertainments.[29]

ART AND ARTISTS IN THE GULAG

KVcH, or Cultural and Educational Section, was part of the vast Soviet concentration camp system. Because guards and other camp personnel liked to buy paintings and painted rugs, prisoner painters could sometimes make some money or get other advantages that might mean the difference between life and death. "On the whole," the ex-prisoner Solzhenitsyn remarks, "[painters] could make out in camp." Poets often composed by memorizing their work, since written poems would have been destroyed if found and the writer severely punished. For prose writers, the situation was almost hopeless, for who can memorize an entire novel, or even a short story? "There were just no prose writers in camp," Solzhenitsyn recalls, "because there were not supposed to be, ever.... From the thirties on, everything that is called our prose is just the foam from a lake which has vanished underground."[30]

Camp commanders vied for the best, most professional ensembles of prisoner actors, directors, set designers, and so on. For the prisoner-artists, this meant a slightly more comfortable but highly insecure existence. An actor's slip of the tongue, a singer's sour note, a dancer's stumble was a personal affront to the commander and so could lead to days in a punishment cell, banishment to dangerous hard labor, transportation to the dreaded Kolyma zone of northern Siberia, or any combination of these—punishments the prisoner might not survive. Solzhenitsyn, who for a time belonged to a prisoner drama group, describes their pitiful, humiliating situation as "serf" performers owned by the camp commander:

The worthless Lieutenant Mironov, if he had found no other distractions and entertainments in Moscow on a Sunday evening, could come to camp [drunk] and give orders: "I want a concert in ten minutes."...And in a trice we would be singing, dancing, and performing on the brilliantly lit stage before an empty hall, in which the only audience was the haughty dolt of a lieutenant and [three] jailers.[31]

In 1991, the American journalist Adam Hochschild interviewed a woman named Yulia who had grown up in the Kazakhstan city of Karaganda, the administrative center for numerous prison camps in its region. Yulia recalled that as a child she had sometimes gone to the theater in Karaganda, never realizing that "all the performers were prisoners."[32]

Most artists who remained unarrested churned out hack work, doing what they had to in order to survive and enjoy a standard of living and gentility unavailable to most Soviets. Amazingly, classic art, too, was produced all along, albeit at great human cost. In literature, the Soviet period produced (to name a few of the best known) Osip Mandelstam, Boris Pasternak, Aleksandr Solzhenitsyn, Mikhail Bulgakov, Anna Akhmatova, Marina Tsvetaeva, Isaac Babel, Vladimir Mayakovsky, Alexander Blok, Sergey Yesenin, Boris Pilnyak, Mikhail Sholokhov, Ilya Ilf and his cowriter Yevgeny Petrov, Mikhail Zoshchenko, Vasily Grossman, Varlam Shalamov, and Nadezhda Mandelstam; in architecture, there were Vladimir Tatlin's extraordinary designs and those of the Vesnin brothers; in the visual arts, the Supremacist, Futurist, and Constructivist movements and the artists who fueled them had worldwide influence. Among their inheritors was Ernst Neizvestny, a sculptor whose abstract style Khrushchev had reviled and who emigrated West in 1974. Ironically, Neizvestny was chosen to sculpt Khrushchev's tombstone, a powerful image in metaphoric black and white.

In music, the works of Aram Khatchaturian, Sergey Prokofiev, Dmitry Shostakovich, and other less famous but highly talented composers survived despite persecution. In the 1920s and into the early 30s, Soviet theater, under the leadership of brilliant directors like Vsevolod Meyerhold, Yevgeny Vakhtangov, Sergey Radlov, Les Kurbas, and Solomon Mikhoëls, was at the cutting edge of world theater. They were the precursors of later Soviet world-class directors such as Yury Lyubimov, all succeeding in no small part because they had outstanding performers and set designers to work with. During and after the Stalin era, classic films were made only to be suppressed on government orders. In the late 1980s the world began to see powerful, heretofore banned Soviet films such as *The Commissar, Repentance, Agony, Andrei Rublev,* and *My Friend, Ivan Lapshin.* Of course no amount of reform could bring back movies (whether fictional or documentary) whose negatives had been destroyed on official orders or whose development had been squelched before filming ever began.[33]

POPULAR CULTURE AND FOLK ARTS

Most people, left to their own devices, chose pop and folk art rather than the "high" arts. Old Bolsheviks and intelligentsia distrusted commercialized popular art (music halls; pulp fiction, including romantic novels, science fiction, adventure and detective stories; etc.) and failed to appreciate the richness of folk art forms. But attempts to replace folk and pop art with their own idea of serious or socially relevant art met with a stone wall of disinterest. Most citizens were not looking for intellectual challenges or political education. They wanted a thumping good story, hearty laughter, tears, and a happy ending. They preferred to look at paintings that told a story they could understand, with (in the words of H. H. Munro) "generous help from the title." Soviet art was never creatively free, but many writers, composers, painters, and filmmakers learned how to infuse popular and folk genres with "red" themes. Readers gobbled up pulp fiction with Soviet action heroes who keenly outwitted capitalist villains. People also read nineteenth-century classic Russian novels and government-approved Western popular fiction (such as the novels of Jack London and Upton Sinclair). They flocked to Soviet, Western, and especially American movies that gave them the entertainment and escape they enjoyed: *Tarzan, The Mark of Zorro, The Thief of Baghdad,* and Charlie Chaplin movies were among American features beloved by Soviet audiences. Western books and movies were never completely banned; the government imported and distributed some American and other Western books and movies that showed capitalism in a bad light.

Popular music and dance, much of it of foreign origin, created an on-again, off-again struggle between what people wanted to hear, sing, and move to and what their government deemed morally proper and politically safe. Jazz, rock, tango, and other exotic music that encouraged "the swaying of female bottoms" set off censorial alarm bells, but Soviet society also had its composers who wrote popular, officially acceptable melodies from patriotic hymns to love songs. The easily memorized words and hummable tunes were embraced by the population and endlessly repeated. Nevertheless, there was always tension between the state's fear of losing control and the people's wish to create and receive art according to their heart's desire.[34]

NOTES

1. Parts of this chapter are taken from material I previously published in *Enemies of the People: The Destruction of Literary, Theater and Film Arts in the Soviet Union in the 1930s*, ed. Katherine B. Eaton (Evanston, IL: Northwestern University Press, 2002), and *Censorship: A World Encyclopedia*, ed. Derek Jones (Chicago: Fitzroy Dearborn, 2001).

2. V. I. Lenin, "Party Organization and Party Literature," *Dialectics* 5 (1938), 3.

3. Arlen V. Blium, *Evreiskii vopros pod sovetskoi tsenzuroi: 1917–1991* (St. Petersburg: St. Petersburg Jewish University, 1996), 29.

4. Mikhail Deza and Mervyn Matthews, "Soviet Theater Audiences," *Slavic Review* 34, no. 4 (December 1975): 716–18; Gail H. Roman, "The Ins and Outs of Russian Avant-Garde Books: A History, 1910–32," in *The Avant-Garde in Russia*, ed. Stephanie Barron and Maurice Tuchman (Cambridge, MA: MIT Press, 1980), 102, 106.

5. Velimir Khlebnikov, *Collected Works*, vol. 3, *Selected Poems*, ed. Ronald Vroon, trans. Paul Schmidt (Cambridge, MA: Harvard University Press, 1997), 30; Victor Terras, *A History of Russian Literature* (New Haven, CT: Yale University Press, 1991), 407, 441; *The Cambridge History of Russian Literature*, ed. Charles A. Moser (Cambridge, England: Cambridge University Press, 1989), 435.

6. "Left March" and "A Cloud in Trousers," trans. Herbert Marshall, in *Mayakovsky* (New York: Hill and Wang, 1965), 99, 129.

7. Michael Kimmelman, "Sisters for a Time in Revolution," *New York Times*, September 8, 2000, B29, 33; "Exile Says Soviet Shackles the Arts," *New York Times*, January 6, 1948, 15.

8. Archival documents concerning the trial and sentencing of Gumilev are reprinted in Zakhar Dicharov, *Raspiatye: Pisateli-zhertvy politicheskikh repressii*, vol. 1 (St. Petersburg: "Severo-Zapad," 1993), 192–210; Vitaly Shentalinsky, *Arrested Voices: Resurrecting the Disappeared Writers of the Soviet Regime*, trans. John Crowfoot (New York: Martin Kessler Books, 1993), 234–35; Walter Benjamin, *Moscow Diary*, ed. Gary Smith, trans. Richard Sieburth (Cambridge, MA: Harvard University Press, 1986), 11–13.

9. Alexander Gershkovich, "Censorship in the Theater," in *The Red Pencil: Artists, Scholars, and Censors in the USSR*, ed. Marianna T. Choldin and Maurice Friedberg (Boston: Unwin Hyman, 1989), 267; Herman Ermolaev, *Censorship in Soviet Literature: 1917–1991* (New York: Rowman and Littlefield, 1997), 7; Arlen V. Blium, *Za kulisami "Ministerstva Pravdy": Taina Istoriia Sovetskoi Tsenzury 1917–1929* (St. Petersburg: Akademicheskii Proekt, 1994), 9, 105; Steven Richmond, "'The Eye of the State': An Interview with Soviet Chief Censor Vladimir Solodin," *Russian Review* 56 (October 1997): 581–90; Irene E. Kolchinsky, "The Last Futurists: 'Nebyvalists' and Their Leader Nikolai Glazunov," *Slavic and East European Journal* 43, no. 1 (1999): 174–75.

10. Denis Babichenko, *"Schast¢e literatury"*: *Gosudarstvo i pisateli 1925–1938. Dokumenty* (Moscow: Rosspen, 1997), 121; T. M. Goriaev, comp., *Iskliuchit vsiakie upominaniia . . . : ocherki istorii sovetskoi tsenzury* (Minsk: 1995), 3.

11. Terras, *History of Russian Literature*, 517. Besides Roman Jakobson (1896–1982), other notable Formalists included: Viktor Shklovsky (1893–1984); Boris Eikhenbaum (1816–1959); Boris Tomashevsky (1890–1957).

12. "Revelations from the Russian Archives. Attacks on Intelligentsia: Renewed Attacks," Library of Congress Special Exhibit; lcweb.loc.gov/exhibit/archives/ intro/html; Max Hayward, *Writers in Russia: 1917–1978,* ed. Patricia Blake (San Diego, CA: Harcourt Brace Jovanovich, 1983), 254–55, 260–61.

13. Harlow Robinson, *Sergei Prokofiev. A Biography* (New York: Viking, 1987), 316; V. A. Kumanev, *30-e gody v sud'bakh otechestvennoi intelligentsii* (Moscow: Nauka, 1991), 206–7; see also " Diary of Lyubov Vasilevna Shaporina," in *Intimacy and Terror: Soviet Diaries of the 1930s,* ed. Veronique Garros, Natalia Karenevskaya, and Thomas Lahusen, trans. Carol A. Flath (New York: New Press, 1995), 381.

14. Quoted in Gershkovich, *The Theatre of Yuri Lyubimov: Art and Politics at the Taganka Theater in Moscow* (New York: Paragon House, 1989), 170.

15. Gershkovich, *Lyubimov,* 39–40; David Remnick, *Lenin's Tomb* (New York: Vintage Books, 1994), 34.

16. See also David King, *The Commissar Vanishes: The Falsification of Photographs and Art in Stalin's Russia* (New York: Metropolitan Books, 1997).

17. Translated by Judith Hemschemeyer, in *The Norton Anthology of World Masterpieces,* vol. 2, ed. Maynard Mack et al., expanded edition (New York: W. W. Norton, 1995), 1880–81.

18. Translated by Katharine Hodgson in *Enemies of the People,* ed. Katherine B. Eaton, 25.

19. "We live, hardly sensing our country below us," translated by Victor Terras in *Enemies of the People,* ed. Katherine B. Eaton, 82.

20. Emily Johnson, "Nikita Khrushchev, Andrei Voznesensky, and the Cold Spring of 1963: Documenting the End of the Post-Stalin Thaw," *World Literature Today* 75, no. 1 (Winter 2001): 31–33; John M. Thompson, *A Vision Unfulfilled: Russia and the Soviet Union in the Twentieth Century* (Lexington, MA: D.C. Heath, 1996), 392–93; *Censorship: A World Encyclopedia,* s.v. "Thirty Years of Moscow Art."

21. Terras, *History of Russian Literature,* 509; Johnson, "Khrushchev, Voznesensky," 33; *Censorship,* s.v. "Thirty Years."

22. Mark Zaitsev, "Soviet Theater Censorship," *Drama Review* 19 (June 1975): 119–28.

23. Martin Dewhirst and Robert Farrell, eds., *The Soviet Censorship* (Metuchen, NJ: Scarecrow Press, 1973), 107–11; 117–20.

24. Peter Kenez, *"Bezhin lug* (Bezhin Meadow)," in *Enemies of the People,* ed. Katherine B. Eaton, 113–26.

25. Michael Wines, "Grigorii Chukhrai," *New York Times,* October 30, 2001, A17; Dewhirst and Farrell, *Soviet Censorship,* 113; *Censorship: A World Encyclopedia,* s.v. "Andrei Tarkovskii"; Leo Hecht, "Glasnost in Film in Retrospect," *Slavic and East European Performance* 21, no. 3 (Fall 2001): 65–68.

26. Lynne Atwood, "Sex and the Cinema," in *Sex and Russian Society,* ed. Igor Kon and James Riordan (Bloomington: Indiana University Press, 1993), 64–66, 71, 73.

27. *I, Maya Plisetskaia,* foreword by Tim Scholl, trans. Antonina W. Bouis (New Haven: Yale University Press, 2001), xi–xiv, 360–61; Richard Eder, "The Ballerina of the Century Recalls Soviet Oppression" (review article), *New York Times,* October 23, 2001; Jennifer Dunning, "Stepping into the Worlds of Three Great Dancers" (review article), *New York Times,* July 31, 2002.

28. Dewhirst and Farrell, *Soviet Censorship,* 96–106.

29. Susan Costanzo, "Reclaiming the Stage: Amateur Theater-Studio Audiences in the Late Soviet Era," *Slavic Review* 57, no. 2 (Summer 1998): 398–402, 405–7, 417–23.

30. Aleksandr Solzhenitsyn, "The Destructive Labor Camps," vol. 2, part 3, *The Gulag Archipelago 1918–1956: An Experiment in Literary Investigation,* trans. Thomas P. Whitney (New York: Harper and Row, 1975), 486–87, 488, 489.

31. Solzhenitsyn, "The Destructive Labor Camps," 501.

32. Adam Hochschild, *The Unquiet Ghost: Russians Remember Stalin* (New York: Penguin Books, 1995), 73.

33. *Censorship: A World Encyclopedia,* s.v. "Russia: The Shelf."

34. Richard Stites, *Soviet Popular Culture: Entertainment and Society since 1900* (Cambridge, England: Cambridge University Press, 1992), 37–49; Thompson, *A Vision Unfulfilled,* 229.

11

Mass Media, Leisure, and Popular Culture

It was difficult for most people to get tickets to classical music, ballet, and theater performances at prestigious Moscow and Leningrad theaters. Those cities offered the widest range of entertainments, but across the USSR people had to have connections to see top-notch performances wherever they were being staged. Among Soviet citizens, only high-ranking Party, secret police, and other government officials or highly respected intellectuals such as prominent writers and scientists would be assured of getting in. The best of the hugely popular circuses and puppet shows were also likely to be booked out of the reach of ordinary citizens. Other tickets—purchased in advance with hard currency—went to foreign tourists on package tours. Theaters always withheld some tickets for each performance, just in case someone at the top (for example, a Politburo or Central Committee member) suddenly telephoned ahead or turned up to see the show. Such extremely high ranking authorities were assured a VIP box seat and champagne reception. Important but less well connected persons could usually get seats by bribing key theater workers with Western clothing, ballpoint pens, cosmetics, fine soaps and chocolates, Cognac, and other luxuries. Between acts, the upper crust promenaded inside the lobbies of the best theaters, happy to see and be seen by their peers.[1]

As in other areas of Soviet life, people in certain professions were in a good situation to swap their skills for whatever they wanted, and prized tickets were often payment for private surgery, dental work, and the like. In any case, not all shows were "hot tickets" beyond the reach of the masses; city dwellers without "pull" could attend productions staged by

A circus performance, 1967. Reproduced from the Collections of the Library of Congress, LC-L9-67-3337-328553, #30A.

touring companies from the provinces. And millions could enjoy performances broadcast on radio and TV.

Connections not only got theater tickets, but also moved one to the head of lines waiting to enter premier art museums like Moscow's Tretyakov Gallery or Leningrad's Hermitage Museum. Of course, ballet, classical music, art, and theater were not everyone's favorite entertainments, and people enjoyed many other pastimes.[2]

FAVORITE LEISURE ACTIVITIES

Visiting was a popular amusement. People expected friends and relatives to drop by, freely and often, just to chat and sometimes to create impromptu parties, especially when a special event like a birthday or holiday provided an excuse. Young adults loved to stroll with friends; older men whiled away the time playing dominoes, cards, and chess. Drinking vodka; gardening; working on stamp and badge (*znachok*) collections; reading; dancing; enjoying long-drawn-out feasting with friends and relatives, usually at home, but sometimes in a restaurant; listening to the radio, watching TV, and going to the movies were also favorite diversions. Many Soviets gambled regularly, especially on government-sponsored lotteries, of which each republic had its own. The main lottery for the Russian Republic in the late 1970s offered around 12,000 consumer goods, everything from cars to vacuum cleaners. Winners could take the prize or

Winter fun in Sokolniki Park, Moscow, 1955. Reproduced from
the Collections of the Library of Congress, Lot 740 #41.

its value in cash. People bought lottery tickets from kiosks; winning numbers were published in newspapers and, in the case of one very popular
weekly lottery (Sportlotto), also announced on TV.

Millions loved warm- and cold-weather outdoor activities in the
countryside and urban parks: swimming, sunbathing, picnicking, hiking,
year-round fishing, and skiing. Hunting and gathering wild edible plants,
especially mushrooms, was a hobby for many Russians and Ukrainians
who spent their weekends riding trains and buses to woodlands, where
they could stalk the wild mushroom. They carried with them all manner
of containers: baskets, buckets, bags, hats, kerchiefs. Sometimes groups
chartered buses that served as both transport and overnight lodging,
where people slept or chatted and drank tea or vodka until sunrise. Oth-

ers slept in village train stations or camped in the woods, ready to forage at dawn, hoping to get ahead of other hunters. Enthusiasts had their special secret hunting grounds; others tried their luck in any convenient stand of trees, intent as much on socializing and picnicking as on bagging trophy mushrooms. As with other outdoor activities, Russians liked to spend the entire day at it, coming home completely and pleasantly exhausted, feeling they had earned their steam bath, glasses of vodka, and pickled mushroom snacks from the previous year's hunt. For children it could mean precious time spent with parents and other family members, sometimes the stuff of bittersweet memories after loved ones disappeared in Stalin's purges.

Father loved to bring the family out to gather mushrooms and then to roast shashlyk [pieces of lamb on skewers] in the deserted, silent woods. We would load ourselves with supplies and board the train. Then get off at any spot that pleased us. Whether we'd find mushrooms or not did not worry anyone. The main thing was the fire and the shashlyk. In the evening, tired, sleepy, we'd barely manage to get home, and straight to bed.[3]

Mushroomers (*gribniki*) prided themselves on their ability to distinguish benign from fatal fungi, and the government published books, pamphlets, magazine articles, and charts on different species. Still, every year some unfortunate mushroom eaters sickened and sometimes died. Cleaning, cooking, or pickling the catch was usually women's work. Mushrooming was such a popular recreation that even in cities mushroom hunters might be seen searching the ground on median strips or in parks.[4]

Like mushrooming, steaming oneself in a bathhouse (*banya*) was a favorite inexpensive way for men and women to spend leisure time. People believed steam-induced sweating was healthy and even cured diseases by flushing out dirt through the pores. Banyas, like sanatoria, had their pleasant, dependable rituals. Upon entering and paying, customers were handed a rough sheet to drape toga-style around their bodies. Then they rented a *venik*, a leafy bundle of birch twigs (like a little broom) that they used to slap themselves and each other in order to help open their pores. Steam was created by throwing water on the bath's hot brick walls. In the men's section of a Moscow *banya* anyone who had just entered the steam room was by custom duty-bound to throw more buckets of water against the bricks, if asked to do so. Some bathers preferred splashing mugs of beer or small amounts of eucalyptus essence against the bricks, for a pleasant scent. Men and women came to the *banya* as much to relax and socialize as to get clean or improve their health. When they had had enough of the steaming ritual, bathers went to a changing room, where they continued to relax. Men liked to chat about women, recent soccer or hockey games, "where to find [scarce] goods, or how to keep young in old age." Other men sat a bit apart from the others, reading or playing dominoes. Many brought food to munch on in the changing room, favorites being sardines, bread with salami, and dried salty fish for snacking on with the beer they ordered from an attendant. A trip to one's favorite *banya* was supposed to be unhurried—at least two or three hours; that was part of the enjoyment.[5]

Those with access to a *dacha* (a country cottage, cabin, or shack) looked forward to retreats there. Most dachas had a small plot of land that could be gardened for pleasure, practicality, or both, yielding a food supply against future shortages and high prices. In 1986 Sergey Starnovsky and his wife purchased a 10th of an acre (the maximum allowed at the time) a one-hour commute by bus, trolley, train, and foot from their home in Chita, Siberia. The couple built with their own hands a plain log cabin with a *banya*. Having a *dacha*, albeit a very humble one surrounded by other cabins on tiny plats, was both emotionally and economically impor-tant to city dwellers, the great majority of whom lived (and still live) in gloomy, vast concrete low-rise apartment complexes. For the Starnovskys, time spent at their cabin meant both tough manual labor (gardening, pick-ling, preserving, maintenance work) and joyful vacations. They loved to first unwind in their *banya*, then cool off in the nearby river. Their other country pleasures included watching beautiful sunsets and seeing their children enjoy the delights of rural life.[6]

Millions of Muscovites (Moscow residents) who did not have dachas escaped summertime heat and humidity by taking a trolley bus to bodies of water and wooded areas just outside the city. One of the most popular hot-weather escapes was Serebryany Bor (Silver Forest) on a sandy shore of the Moscow River. In summer the beach was crowded with sun wor-shippers of all ages, from young lovers to grandmothers hovering over their small grandkids. People sat on wooden benches; played cards; drank beer or lemonade; and picnicked on newspaper-wrapped dried fish, sar-dines, and boiled eggs. If the seedy-looking food stand was open (which happened infrequently) they could buy snacks, drinks, and Russian ciga-rettes (an "inch of strong, sweet tobacco at the end of three inches of hol-low cardboard tubing") there. Besides being used as fish wrapping, newspapers also came in handy for fashioning triangular paper sun hats. While some people frolicked in the water or napped, others played volleyball or table tennis, or rowed rented boats. Moscow residents also enjoyed Gorky Park of Culture and Rest, an amusement park and nature preserve. Gorky Park was and still is an extremely popular place for indi-viduals, families, and groups of friends to pass the time: they stroll; swim; socialize; play chess; row; ride a Ferris wheel and other rides; and partici-pate in winter sports, including team ice and snow sculpture competitions and sledding.[7]

Sanatorium vacations in a rural setting were highly coveted, inexpen-sive treats for those fortunate enough to get reservations through their trade union or by other means. A typical day in a sanatorium near Riga, Latvia, included rising at 7:30 A.M.,

Relaxing on the Dnieper, near Kiev, 1965. Reproduced from the Collections of the Library of
Congress, LC-U9-14393-328550 #5.

group morning exercises, breakfast, medical treatment, a prescribed walk on the
beach [apparently patients did not go in the water without permission]...lunch, a
free hour...quiet hour...afternoon tea, [group] cultural activities or excursions,
supper...evening walk...show or concert...yogurt at 10 P.M.... lights out at 11.[8]

Entrance doors were locked at 11 P.M. When asked what would happen if
a patient returned after lights out, the spa's doctor acted as though he did
not understand the concept.[9]

 Rural people had fewer opportunities for diversions common to city
life—going to a drama or movie theater, listening to or playing music,
dancing, socializing, watching TV, reading, and so
forth. Villages (like cities) had clubs intended as places
for the community to meet and have recreational fun,
but rural programs and facilities were frequently a big
disappointment. "It's boring in our village," a young
woman from the Ryazan area complained, "especially in the evenings."

**Leisure
Activities among
Peasants**

There's nowhere to go dancing or meet people of your own age even though we do have a club with a tape recorder, two radios and a television set. Everything except the television is locked up. They bring a film show once a month and we have to be thankful for that.[10]

Because of poor transportation facilities and mud- or snow-choked roads, even short distances could thwart a fun night out. The same bored girl commented that a neighboring village club had "dances, concerts, and new films nearly every week...[but] you often can't get there, especially in the evenings, as they're 7 or 8 kilometres [4–5 miles] away. So that's how we live!" With or without the help of a club, young singles in rural areas spent most of their free time outside their homes, socializing with friends and relations. Once they got married they spent most of their leisure at home, especially after they had children. Rural men were much more likely than women to spend their spare time reading, watching TV, or listening to the radio. Women everywhere had much less free time than men and tended to spend their daily two hours or so of free time visiting or hosting friends and relatives, or not doing much of anything. Watching TV, once sets became common in the countryside, became the most popular leisure activity, especially among young people, who spent about seven more hours watching TV than city people did. Despite the allure of video, however, time spent reading also increased over the years as more and more country people became literate and the number of rural libraries increased. Some villages had small bookshops where people liked to buy novels and children's books, as well as magazines that focused on the interests and daily lives of farm people: *Krest'yanka* (The Peasant Woman) and *Sel'skaya zhizn'* (Rural Life).[11]

The idea that a woman's spare time ought to be spent usefully at home prevented many country women from participating in or even learning athletics, including swimming and bicycling. A 28-year-old peasant woman said she had some free time in winter to ski, which she loved to do, but was afraid of being shamed by her neighbors as someone who shirked her household duties. A stableman on a state farm noticed that not many girls had joined the farm's new riding club (though they did ride horses on the sly) because people thought horseback riding "indecent [for women] and bad for their health." With or without customary prejudices against female athletics, time was women's toughest opponent. After farmwork, household chores, and child care, there was no time left for recreation.

In town or country, birthdays were occasions for throwing a big party. Guests brought birthday presents as well as a hostess gift such as a bouquet of flowers (an odd number for good luck), chocolates, or wine. Hosts tried to provide a memorable many-course feast. A birthday or other occasion might also be celebrated in a restaurant, though Soviets did not eat out often. The best restaurants required advance reservations, were geared to serve large parties, or were only for foreigners and the highest elite. One or two people by themselves were liable to be ignored. Popular restaurants were most accessible to those with special "pull." Just as some could obtain scarce groceries discreetly at the back of a store, so might preferred customers enter a prestigious restaurant through the back door, while the front door perpetually bore a sign reading "closed" or "full." Even in the best public restaurants service was likely to be slow and inept, the food lukewarm, the menu limited, and not everything listed would actually be available.[12]

New Year's Festivities

New Year's Eve and New Year's Day substituted for pre-Revolutionary Christmas festivities. People bought presents or cards to give or exchange on New Year's Eve, prepared a festive meal, bought (or sometimes poached) a fir tree and decorated it with ornaments and colored lights. Trucks brought thousands of small skinny pines (*yolki*) from state tree farms to city market places. The satirist Vladimir Voinovich wrote about complications that befell an ordinary man when he attempted to provide his wife and daughter with a New Year tree. Starting out early in the evening, the story's hero ends up waiting three hours in line; is arbitrarily handed a balding, scrawny, lopsided tree; loses the receipt needed to prove it was legally obtained; is stopped by the militia and hauled into a cellar room at a police station; waits two hours for his case to be heard; is dismissed with a warning; and without his tree, finally returns home at midnight only to discover that his daughter's new boyfriend is the very militiaman who arrested him. The new boyfriend has brought them a New Year tree that looks familiar. His daughter cools his rage by pointing out their good luck: "If someone else had taken [the tree]," she argues, "he would have given it to *his* girlfriend and then we'd be here without any tree at all."[13]

Those who could not get real trees, however stunted and sickly, made do with branches or plastic imitations. City centers also had decorated New Year trees (in Moscow a huge lighted tree was set up in the Kremlin). At New Year's parties children's presents were distributed by adults dressed as old, white-bearded *Ded Moroz* (Grandfather Frost) in a fur-trimmed robe. By the 1980s, Grandfather Frost was popular around the USSR even where frost was rare. He was often accompanied by a lovely young *Snegurochka* (Snow Maiden) with her long blond braid and fur-trimmed blue dress. On New Year's Eve Grandfather Frost and his Snow Maiden even made house calls (for a few rubles). Quickly and surreptitiously they collected toys from parents and then dispensed those toys to the family's children. By New Year's Eve most toy shop shelves were sold out. People tried to obtain East German toys because they were better made than Soviet ones, which tended not to work, to quickly fall apart, and sometimes to be rather dangerous. Adults snapped up toy tool kits and used them instead of the real tools they could not find in shops.

New Year's Eve usually meant the biggest and best feast of the year. In Moscow many people went to Red Square to join masses of other

New Year Tree celebration in the White Column Hall of the Palace
of Pioneers in Leningrad, 1955. Reproduced from the Collections
of the Library of Congress, Lot 7401 #36.

champagne-bearing celebrators to welcome the New Year. When the
Spassky Tower clock struck midnight everyone toasted the New Year and a
band played the national anthem, the *Internationale.* Fireworks lit the sky.
After that, people celebrated at their home or someone else's. Others stayed
home with guests, ate and drank, and watched the Kremlin celebration on
TV. Customarily the partying lasted many hours into the New Year.[14]

In the later Soviet period, the big parades on Red Square in Moscow on
May 1 (May Day or International Labor Day) and November 7 (anniversary of the Bolshevik Revolution) were closed to the
general public except for those who were part of the   **Official Holidays**
show or had special invitations. The events, which
people could watch on TV, consisted of mighty displays of heavy military

equipment such as planes, rockets, and tanks. Thousands of brightly cos-
tumed gymnasts performed in sync, marching and tumbling, stopping
momentarily in front of Party leaders whose review stand was on top of
the Lenin Mausoleum. When they paused there, they looked up to the
leadership and shouted, "Glory to the Communist Party of the Soviet
Union! Glory! Glory! Glory!" As in religious processionals of pre-
Revolutionary times, marchers carried images aloft, but instead of the
Holy Family and saints, the icons were of Party leaders. Even though
ordinary people could not attend the celebrations as spectators, they were
often required to participate as representatives of their workplaces. A government worker told Hedrick Smith that in his mother's time it was considered an honor to march in the November 7 and May Day parades, but
by the 1970s, participation was "just a duty they impose on people," and
some tried to wriggle out of parade duty by getting medical excuses.
Elena Bonner remembers the 1937 May Day festivities with a mixture of
bitter irony and warmth. She was 15 and in love with one of her classmates, and her parents had not yet been arrested. The whole school
marched in the demonstration.

There [was] music blaring out of the loudspeakers, flags fluttering, and smiling
people on the sidewalks. A group of teenagers with big paper poppies walked past
me, laughing....
    Many people attended the parade in those days. And I think that everyone, and
not just the schoolchildren, had a good time.[15]

"I was fully certain," Bonner recalls, "that not only I but everyone marching with me, waving flags and banners and artificial flowers, carrying
heavy posters, and shouting slogans fiercely, were all thrilled to see [Party
leaders] on the right wing of the Mausoleum." They seemed "familiar, like
friends or family." March 8, International Woman's Day, was marked by
women and girls being given gifts, cards, flowers, and candy. Some husbands took over the household chores for that day.[16]

POP CULTURE

Since the end of the 1950s, foreigners had been bringing Western pop
music, newspapers, and magazines into the USSR, and these found their
way into the black market, mainly in major cities like Moscow, Leningrad,
Tallin, Riga, and Lvov. By the early 1960s, the demand for Western pop
music was so high and so outstripped supplies of equipment for duplicat-
ing records and tapes that fans ingeniously made crude copies of records
with used X-ray film (bought cheaply from hospitals and clinics). A small
hole was cut in the center of the film, edges were rounded off with scis-
sors, and, using special equipment, the grooves were cut. Music fans
called such copies "ribs" after the images on the film. In the 1960s the Bea-

tles, though banned in the USSR, became both musical and spiritual gurus for young Soviets, and many a "rib" preserved their (pirated) music. The cost of a Beatles recording was high: a month's salary for a black market record or tape and the risk of arrest for listening to a Beatles performance.

By 1969 in Moscow alone there were several thousand amateur rock bands. At first authorities did not go out of their way to control amateur rock shows, but after some Leningrad fans rioted at a 1967 concert, Leningrad amateur guitar-vocal groups had to get authorization before appearing in public. In 1969 the state tried to co-opt such groups by inviting them to become, in effect, government employees whose performances had to be officially approved. With their superior state-supplied equipment and numerous gigs, particularly in smaller towns and cities where they had no competition, these official rock bands enjoyed much popular success. There were notable holdouts, however. Boris Grebenshchikov, leader and songwriter of the nonofficial rock band Aquarium, became a kind of cult figure for many Soviet youth, his Leningrad home a place of pilgrimage. Staircase walls leading up to his eighth-floor communal apartment were covered with pilgrims' graffiti: "Boris you are life," "We cannot survive without you." Signatures beneath the graffiti revealed the writers' hometowns—thousands of miles away from Leningrad. Youngsters waited patiently just to touch his hand.

Prominent poets like Yevgeny Yevtushenko, Andrey Voznesensky, and Bella Akhmadulina, reading from their own work, filled indoor arenas, and young adults loved them.[17]

As Western contacts, even before glasnost, punched more and more holes in the "iron curtain" that had surrounded Soviet culture, ever more Western youth fads poured through—besides rock there was Zen, heavy metal, break dancing, among others. In the 1970s and 80s as Western technologies became increasingly accessible, young people liked to gather in a friend's apartment or room to watch and swap music videos. Videocassettes and VCRs usually had to be purchased on the black market since not many were produced in the Soviet Union. An urban youth culture, spurred by the more liberal atmosphere of perestroika, began to grow. It was based on traditional free-time activities, including heavy drinking, but with some new wrinkles. Hard drugs, for example, were increasingly supplementing vodka. Marijuana (called *travka* or *plan*) was well known among Soviet youth even before the 1980s.

Young artists unaffiliated with any official organization exhibited their creations on busy public thoroughfares. Rock musicians, singers of folk and prison camp ballads, and poets also got together in public and private to entertain themselves and others without state permission. At last Soviet life had homegrown hippies, nonconformists, and dissidents who refused to have their heroes prepackaged and spoon-fed to them. One of the most electrifying among the artistic nonconformists, a true "angry young man," was the hugely popular actor, poet, songwriter, and singer Vladimir

Vysotsky. Vysotsky's ballads, all the rage and officially banned, were protests against official corruption; class privilege; the horrors of the gulag, war, and poverty. After he died in 1980 at the age of 42, Vysotsky became a kind of cult figure; on the anniversaries of his death thousands visited his grave.[18]

By the beginning of the 1980s it became possible to turn a room or apartment into a workshop for creating tape cassettes. Now the music of famous groups could be easily distributed around the country, even though under Leonid Brezhnev's regime (1964–1982) most forms of rock were officially banned. Official intolerance intensified under Yury Andropov (General Secretary 1982–1984), who personally hated and mistrusted rock. The effect of the crusade was to energize the radical rock community. And over the next few years the prospects for freer expression seemed to grow. By early March 1985 both Andropov and his successor, Konstantin Chernenko, were dead. Mikhail Gorbachev, the new Party leader, was about to introduce "openness" (glasnost). But popular culture never became truly free. The government always feared that rock groups and their fans would easily get out of control, so although the militia and KGB (secret police) allowed the rock community to exist, it was always being watched, regulated, and suppressed. Musicians and fans were subject to arbitrary arrests; concerts were broken up and equipment confiscated. As a song by the Leningrad group Televizor (Television) ruefully noted, even though Soviet youth were allowed to break-dance and "be happy sometimes," they were always being watched by secret policemen with "cement" in their eyes.[19]

Hard-eyed KGB men were not the only threats to rockers and other Western-oriented youth. *Lyubery* were a gang of teenage hoodlums from Lyubertsy, a working-class suburb 12 miles southwest of Moscow, who from the early 1970s roamed around looking for victims. Anyone with "chains...dyed hair or [who] brings shame on our country...anyone who looks or acts as a protester" was fair game for *Lyubery* violence, according to one 16-year-old gang member. Or, as another gang member declared, "We come [into Moscow every night] to beat up punks, hippies, heavy metal and break-dance fans." *Lyubery* stayed away from drugs, alcohol, and nicotine; practiced bodybuilding, boxing, martial arts, and weight training; and dressed in a unique costume: white shirt, thin black tie, and baggy checked trousers. Thus dressed, they liked to stalk city streets with their hands behind their backs. Early in 1987 *Lyubery* were blamed for beating up Jewish "refuseniks" (those who had unsuccessfully applied for permission to emigrate) and Western journalists. In many cases these gangs seemed to have the tacit approval and even the protection of police. There were similar lower-class suburban gangs in other Soviet cities, sometimes directed by embittered *Afgantsy* (Afghanistan war veterans), sometimes by professional thieves, who commuted into cities to terrorize and rob. The media reported on their transgressions or did not, depending on orders from above. Other Soviet hoodlums turned their frightening attention to spectator sports, especially soccer.[20]

SPECTATOR SPORTS

Before the Revolution, the Russian Empire lagged behind the developed world in spectator sports. The largely peasant population usually lacked leisure time for watching or participating in sports, although some peasants did skate, ski, and take part in traditional games such as *gorodki*, a kind of bowling, and *lapta*, a baseball-like pastime. In the northwest of the empire, near Tver and Pskov, peasants played various games that resembled football, usually at local festivals. There were no admission charges for spectators or special training for participants. By the time of the Revolution, organized pay-to-watch sport was still in its early stages; most city workers sent their extra money, if they had any, back to their families in the villages. Besides, after a typical 12- to 14-hour workday, with few days off, they had little time to go to a stadium to watch others play games.[21]

Although the state selected, groomed, and supported male and female prize-winning athletes in a variety of sports, in everyday life there never were more than three significant spectator sports: soccer (football), basketball, and ice hockey—all games played and watched by men. There was little popular or state interest in women's sports and probably no overwhelming interest in spectator sports in general. A burst of enthusiasm in the late 1960s and early 70s flattened out as the economy worsened. Outside the arenas people were waiting in longer and longer lines to obtain food for their families.

Since games usually started as early as six-thirty, there was little or no time to return from work, grab a bite, and then go out to the stadium. In the midst of society's gloom, journalists and fans complained that one did not have a feeling of "holiday"...at a game.[22]

Sometimes, however, an exciting game offered some people a fleeting escape from the dreary struggles of daily life. As the eminent Soviet sportswriter Leonid Trakhtenberg proclaimed after a suspenseful 5–4 game between two of the USSR's best soccer teams (Spartak and Central Army Sports Club),

Is there anything to be particularly joyful about, as goods disappear from the shelves of stores and the press of our daily problems becomes greater?...We can stand the suffering of no meat or flour, but, without this kind of [soccer], we cannot live.[23]

From the 1970s violent behavior by players, fans, or both was an intermittent problem but one that was becoming more frequent and severe, especially at soccer games. Those events often turned into excuses for fan violence, whether on the grounds of nationalism and ethnic loyalty or simply because mobs of soccer hooligans (*fanaty*) wanted to riot and shed blood. Apparently more interested in fomenting violence than in seeing their team win, *fanaty* attacked players, coaches, and referees before, during, and sometimes after games, traveled to contests in large groups, trashing trains and hotels en route, and in one case robbed and beat elderly people who crossed their path. Police often did not intervene and when they did, made few arrests.[24] News about ugly incidents was tightly controlled by the Soviet government.

MASS MEDIA

There had been severe controls on the press since the time of Peter the Great, who personally founded the first Russian newspaper, *Vedomosti* (Official Reports). The last 10 years before the 1917 Revolution saw a loosening of press censorship restrictions: some expression of differing political opinions was allowed, and there were occasional exposures of corruption in high places. There was a brief "thaw" in 1917, under the short-lived Provisional Government, but following the wishes of Lenin who advocated total control of the press, press freedom was quickly killed off after the October/November Revolution. Within days after seizing power, before they established a secret police agency or an army, the Bolsheviks issued their first press censorship decree (November 9, 1917), banning all non-Socialist newspapers. By the early 1920s Bolshevik authorities had eliminated all non-Bolshevik newspapers, nationalized printing presses, and radically tightened press censorship. From then until the fall of Soviet Communism, media were managed by a government bureaucracy that included the special censorship office, *Glavlit*. Everything that appeared in any of the media anywhere in the USSR had to be first approved by *Glavlit*'s censors, who were part of the staff in all editorial offices. Like all writers, journalists were expected to save time and trouble by censoring themselves before submitting material.[25]

The government and Party published newspapers in about 60 languages, and most appeared six days a week. The two most important and prestigious national papers, *Pravda* (Truth), newspaper of **Print Media** the Central Committee of the Communist Party of the Soviet Union, and *Izvestiya* (News), newspaper of the Soviet government, were issued every day. Readers bored with their dry, predictable reporting would get only more of the same if they turned to other Soviet papers. Like all other Soviet periodicals, *Pravda* and *Izvestiya* were inexpensive and could be bought at newsstands or by subscription. In addition, these two national papers were posted in sidewalk displays and at workplaces so that anyone could read them for free. The USSR also published thousands of journals and magazines, some national, some regional, including professional and literary journals, magazines for hobbyists, journals of social commentary, and humor magazines. There were publications targeted for children, farmers, farm women, young people, military personnel, sports fans, trade associations, and more. Western newspapers, which provided more interesting and generally more accurate coverage, were not available to most people.

The state did not publish periodicals devoted to crime and crime detection, sex, pornography, religion, or the occult. Of course, forbidden subjects could be found in foreign print media, but no foreign publications were sold except in a few foreigners-only hotels. To borrow foreign publications from libraries, people had to show they needed the material for officially approved research projects. Tight controls on who could travel abroad and for how long, as well as rigid surveillance of foreign tourists within the country, helped keep information under wraps. Some news did circulate out and then back in. Foreign journalists stationed in the USSR fed news not only to their own countrymen, but also to radio broadcasters like Voice of America and the BBC, which in turn beamed information into the USSR, thus keeping Soviets up-to-date about certain events in their own country and the outside world.

The government kept a long list of subjects journalists either were not allowed to report or had to delay reporting on: news about disasters in the USSR, such as plane crashes and natural disasters; work-related injuries; morale in the military; special payment and treatment for athletes; these were but a few of many taboo subjects. In early July 1972 fires raged on thousands of acres near Moscow, but not until a month later did newspapers inform people about the origin of the blue haze that had engulfed the city.[26]

More than 1000 firefighters, including planes, paratroopers and entire military units had joined the battle.... Yet most of the press printed practically nothing, and *Pravda*, the Party's flagship newspaper, ran not a word.[27]

A friend of Hedrick Smith's told him about a young woman from Central Asia who flew from Karaganda to Moscow to take entrance exams for Moscow State University. When after two weeks her family did not hear from her, her father flew to Moscow to find her. In Moscow he discovered she had not taken the exams, and no one knew anything about her. He began making the rounds of police stations. Finally the police advised him to check with the airport police, who confided that his daughter had died in a plane crash en route to Moscow. The accident had not been mentioned in any media, and the police made him promise to keep quiet about the tragedy. Such secrecy and failure to report important information fed wild rumors and endangered people's lives, as when in 1974 the press failed to report a Jack the Ripper–style murderer stalking Moscow streets. With only rumor to go on, one murderer was transformed, in people's imaginations, into 500 escaped psychopaths roaming the city. After 1985, editors had more freedom to publish articles on previously taboo subjects. In 1989 *Sovetskii sport* (Soviet sport) revealed that the number of dead in a 1982 sports arena trampling was 340, rather than a little over a dozen, as news reports had originally implied. The 1982 accounts also failed to mention that it took ambulances 30 minutes to arrive.

The danger to human life posed by the lack of a free press was horrifyingly demonstrated in 1986 with the Chernobyl, Ukraine, nuclear power plant explosion of April 26. While Swedish instruments picked up the increased airborne radiation and Swedish news media reported on it, the Soviet government and its news media for three weeks suppressed, denied, or minimized what could have been life-saving information for thousands of victims. In the meantime millions continued to live in the area, breathing deadly air and drinking toxic water and milk, while children continued playing in contaminated soil.[28] Censorship of information from Chernobyl showed that despite Gorbachev's glasnost campaign, the government's habit of suppressing bad news had not disappeared.

Local papers might give regional tragedies passing mention, but they mainly reported on good events and good people in the area. Criticisms and concerns that did get published usually appeared in the form of letters to the editor and contributions from local residents who sent in stories from their regions. In either case, only lower-level bureaucrats were the objects of criticism. No one dared criticize top leaders unless they were out or on their way out. Like plane crashes, earthquakes, and nuclear disasters, the personal lives of VIPs and stories about their families were rarely reported in newspapers and other media.[29]

Because the media's purpose was to promote official policies and keep everyone in line politically, consumers of Soviet radio, print media, and TV, especially Party members, generally knew how to read between the lines—what to ignore, what deserved attention. In his novel *Cancer Ward*, set shortly before and after Khrushchev's denunciation of Stalin's terror policies, Aleksandr Solzhenitsyn shows how Pavel Rusanov (a Party hack who had willingly helped carry out Stalin's purges) reads newspapers:

He regarded newspapers as a widely distributed instruction, written in fact in code; nothing in it could be said openly, but a skillful man who knew the ropes could interpret the various small hints, the arrangement of the articles, the things that were played down or omitted, and so get a true picture of the way things were going.[30]

Thus reading and decoding, Rusanov gets a shock: *something* earth-shaking has happened at the highest level—and it does not bode well for him.

It was set in quite small type and would have had no significance for the uninitiated, but to him it shrieked from the page. It was an unprecedented, impossible decree! The whole membership of the Supreme Court of the Soviet Union had been changed.[31]

Soviet journalists were not encouraged to be objective in their reporting; their jobs depended on presenting the official point of view and on following Party policies. All reporters, editors, and broadcasters were government employees who belonged to the Union of Soviet Journalists and were expected to join the Party or Komsomol. They were well paid by Soviet standards. A lucky few were appointed foreign correspondents with one of the two government news agencies—TASS (Telegraph Agency of the Soviet Union) and *Novosti* (News), which had correspondents around the world. Some of the information they collected was for government use only, some for the Soviet reading public.

During World War II, news reports became more oriented toward "human interest" stories that boosted morale and patriotism. A favorite device was the publication of personal letters supposedly exchanged between frontline soldiers and their loved ones at home. Because these letters followed a certain formula—love for motherland and mother, desire to wreak vengeance on the enemy, exhortations to be brave, readiness to die for the cause, and so forth—it is not known whether those letters were genuine or written by newsroom staffers. There is no reference in the Soviet-published personal letters to such things as the price of potatoes or the problems of surviving from day to day, concerns that were universal in home-front letters taken from Soviet soldiers by their German captors. In contrast, home-front letters published in the Soviet press expressed such sentiments as this one from a wife to her soldier husband:

My beloved!...Probably you're sleeping very little now. And sharing makhorka [low quality tobacco] with your friends and remembering us—me, your little boy, your ChTZ [Chelyabinsk Tractor Works].[32]

Soviet newspapers had few pages and a small number of advertisements and want ads. There were no comic strips, but there were political cartoons, at least one per issue. Besides the government-approved news (good things happening in the USSR vs. bad things happening in the United States and other capitalist countries), there were sometimes also short poems.

Articles for rural women generally did not address their day-to-day problems of overwork or their husband's reluctance or failure to help out. Instead, peasant women's magazines glorified housewifery along with child and husband tending. A common sort of feature article would be an interview with a high-achieving career woman who revealed that her duties as wife, daughter, and mother were at least as important as her career. Rural women were urged to

Newspaper and Magazine Articles Aimed at Rural Women

put their families first, indulge and be forgiving to their husbands, be happy cooks, prepare tasty meals, and show interest in their husbands' work. The husband in turn was advised to thank his wife "for an ironed shirt, or when she pointed out a magazine article that related to his work, he should say 'Clever girl, Tamara, thank you!' "[33]

Most Soviet newspapers, whether national or local, sometimes or often reported on sports but did not carry regular sports sections. *Pravda* and *Izvestiya* carried a few results every day and occasion-

Sports Reporting   ally an article. *Komsomolskaya Pravda* (the Komsomol newspaper), *Trud* (Labor), and *Sovetskaia Rossiia* (Soviet Russia) gave much space to sports, but serious fans read sports periodicals, and above all *Sovetskii sport*, called *Krasnyi sport* (Red Sport) from 1924 to 1946. *Sovetskii sport* was popular and respected for its honesty and accuracy. Of course, government officials always made the final decisions about what would be published in it, requiring, for example, that important speeches by Party leaders appear on its front page, whether or not the speeches had anything to do with sports.[34]

In July 1918 the Bolsheviks monopolized the fledgling radio stations and in the mid-1920s began beaming revolutionary messages around the

Wired and   world, via shortwave. Inside the USSR broadcasts were
Wireless Radio   a means for the government to extend its messages to millions of people, many illiterate, across a vast empire. There were programs on a variety of subjects, aimed toward different audiences, including children, in over 70 languages. In the 1920s and early 30s most people got their programming through radios wired directly into broadcasting stations. In the earlier years, farms, factories, apartment buildings, and village centers had such radios hanging from poles, amplified by loudspeakers. Later, people had their own radios wired straight from their living space to studios in downtown Moscow. By law almost every building in Russia and much of the USSR had to be wired for government radio. Though there were local exceptions, until the 1960s most wired-speaker systems offered only one station whose programming ranged from fine arts to boring propaganda to sports play-by-plays. Under Brezhnev listeners were offered a choice of two or three government stations, including (in 1964) a station—Radio *Maiak* or Lighthouse—teenagers loved because, besides news and commentary, it broadcast foreign pop music. By the 1950s, more and more citizens were enjoying their own wireless sets and receiving domestic and foreign broadcasts on AM, FM, medium-wave, and shortwave bands.

The more people acquired radios that could pull in foreign stations, the more the government tried to prevent people from listening. At various times, authorities threatened to arrest listeners, jammed broadcasts, confiscated radios, prohibited the manufacture of shortwave radios inside the USSR (eventually such radios were produced), and tried to pressure foreign governments to stop broadcasting to its citizens. Nevertheless, depending on where they lived, Soviets with the right kind of radios could tune in to regular programs from various Western European countries as well as programs beamed to them from Radio Free Europe/Radio Liberty, the Voice of America, England's BBC, and West Germany's *Deutsche Welle*.[35]

There were 10,000 sets in 1950, and almost 3,000,000 in 1958. In the 1960s factories began mass-producing TVs priced in a range most people could afford, so that by the 1980s tumbledown peasant cottages that still had no indoor plumbing sported rooftop antennas that connected their world to "the biggest television transmission system in the world."

Television

In Russia in the late 1950s TV stations broadcast for about four hours a day and more than half the shows were live. Movies were then about 40 percent of the programming. Besides movies, programming in the 50s and later included exercise programs, music, news, drama, concerts, ballet, children's programs, film clips of bountiful harvests, productive factories, and government officials at public functions. Sex and homegrown violence were not depicted. For most of the Soviet period there were few commercials; when they appeared they were stodgy promotions of consumer goods not necessarily available to viewers. By the mid-1980s, when most households owned at least one TV and state factories began producing VCRs, only two TV channels were broadcasting across the whole country, from Vladivostok to Kaliningrad: First Program, for the most important news and cultural events, and Second Program, for less important shows. Moscow had two more channels broadcasting several hours a day, one for adult education, the other for sports. Minority republics and important regional centers like Leningrad or Novosibirsk had local programming for a few hours a week, featuring mainly folklore and folk dancing. Images of Soviet happiness and success contrasted with films of a troubled capitalism (horrors of the Vietnam war, strikes, unemployed workers, homeless people, race riots, and the like).

During the Gorbachev era, the government kept its monopoly on broadcasting, and much of the old dullness persisted. But there were changes, including glitzier news programs that began to embrace Western-style "infotainment" along with some real news and investigations of previously taboo subjects. There were also rock music; MTV; talk, game, and fashion shows; and beauty contests. In addition the fierce cold

Television and Glasnost

war stereotypes of the evil capitalist West were softened as viewers were allowed a wider, more balanced range of pictures and stories of American and Western European politics and everyday life. Even some portentous events of 1989—the collapse of Soviet satellite countries' governments and demolition of the Berlin Wall—were covered honestly and quickly. At the same time news programs were reined in when it came to broadcasting stories about social and political upheavals at home, such as when the Soviet military violently suppressed peaceful demonstrators in Georgia in

April 1989, the occupation of Azerbaijan in 1990, and the Lithuanian seces-
sion movement later that year.

In the twilight of the Soviet Union the most popular TV program was a
weekly Friday night one-and-a-half to two-hour magazine show, *Vzglyad*
(Glance). It shocked and delighted Soviet viewers by presenting Western
rock stars; interviewing Gorbachev and his wife, Raisa, or KGB agents and
Afghanistan veterans; and comparing Soviet and American armies. Its
speedy format kept each segment down to six or seven minutes. At first
much of it was live and unrehearsed, but government censorship eventually dampened its early spontaneity. One night's extraordinary program,
anchored in very untraditional style by young men "slouching in easy
chairs and dressed in jeans and windbreakers," jumped from man-on-the-
street interviews to a Soviet rock group to a political report from Bulgaria
to bits on Michael Jackson, American wilderness, radiation sickness at
Chernobyl, Soviet drug addicts, alcoholics, prostitutes, corrupt police, a
violent right-wing group's raid on a Moscow Writers' Union meeting, and
AIDS in the USSR and its relation to filthy hospital conditions, especially
in maternity wards. The news program also showed horribly graphic
films of war carnage in Afghanistan, the brutal "gang rapes and psychological browbeating" (*dedovshchina*) new recruits suffered, and other quick
news bytes interspersed with pop entertainment, including Soviet rock
groups. In addition *Vzglyad* presented evidence of the 1940 Katyn Forest
massacre of thousands of Polish army officers by Soviet secret police.
Their biggest "hot potato," however, was a reporter's suggestion that the
Lenin Mausoleum on Red Square be removed and Lenin given a traditional burial next to his wife. As with other bold programs that made their
appearance in the liberalized atmosphere of the late 1980s, *Vzglyad*
increasingly fell under official control. Politically sensitive segments—
including a comedian's impersonation of Gorbachev (planned for September 1, 1989)—were cut back, delayed, or banned outright. In December
1990 *Vzglyad* was canceled after airing a program about Foreign Minister
Edward Shevardnadze's resignation.

Three daring Leningrad TV programs reached viewers in northwest
Russia and the Baltic republics. *Pyatoe koleso* (Fifth Wheel) debuted in
spring 1988. Aired twice a week in two-hour segments,
Leningrad   it specialized in in-depth documentaries on current
Television and   events, social problems, and Russian history: mistreat-
Glasnost   ment of children in a police-run orphanage, problems
                      faced by returning Afghan veterans, Leningrad's poor
and disabled, testimonies of Stalin's victims. *Pyatoe koleso* also aired a
frightening interview of a Stalin executioner, an old man living in poverty.
He demonstrated how he had shot victims in the back of the head at close
range and then described how he and other guards "later stripped the
corpses of jewelry and gold fillings." "You'd put some sort of spirit, alcohol, on the gums, and the teeth came out easier." After dark "trucks with

crates marked MEAT or VEGETABLES or FURNITURE would pull up to the crematorium and dump the bodies in the fire. The place where they finally buried the bones and ashes was paved over a few years ago," the old man said. Even though such broadcasts were unprecedented in their truthfulness compared with pre-glasnost journalism, censorship was still alive. Among program segments banned outright were one on mass graves in Minsk, and one that revealed discrepancies between Gorbachev's private and public statements. *Pyatoe koleso*'s most controversial programs dealt with perks allotted to Leningrad's Party elite, as when a reporter and a cameraman climbed the high walls of country villas to show viewers the luxury enjoyed by Party bigwigs (including in some cases separate servants' houses). After that program, and two on graft, censorship tightened. *Shest'sot sekundov* (600 Seconds)—a very popular Leningrad TV program—was a 10-minute sensationalistic nightly news show. Its anchor, Alexander Nevzorov, was a former movie stuntman and church choir singer turned "full-tilt ambulance chaser."

He can cover thirteen news bits in ten minutes. His topics range from how rotting meat is ground into sausages at a Leningrad factory, to how radioactivity emanates from old Soviet helicopters in a children's park, to a trip to the morgue to report on the tragic suicide leap of a woman and her two small children.[36]

Some critics saw Nevzorov not as a courageous harbinger of a more open society, but as a tool of secret police and other forces opposed to perestroika. They believed his sensationalism was intended to make people long for the good old days of law and order, and that certain lurid reports encouraged people to despise homosexuals more than any other groups, "including prostitutes and drug addicts."

The third important Leningrad TV news program reflecting glasnost was *Obshchestvennoe Mnenie* (Public Opinion), which began broadcasting in early 1987. It was a three-hour call-in show that featured experts debating important current events, live on-the-street interviews of ordinary people, and call-in opinions on various contemporary issues. Among other topics, people discussed the death penalty, alcoholism, the economy, Leningrad's unhealthy water, empty shops, and perestroika. One night a caller asked how perestroika was possible when Gorbachev and members of the Politburo could not even agree on what the word means. Because the question implied disagreement at the top, a taboo subject, the show's anchor barely managed to save her career, and the program's format lost a bit of its daring.

GENERAL EFFECTS OF GLASNOST ON THE MEDIA

Despite constraints, TV journalists at the end of the Communist era felt excited and energized; at last they could begin to do their jobs. Though still shadowed by censorship, greater freedom for media journalists made it possible for striking workers and others to bring their grievances and demands to the attention of the general public as well as to bureaucrats high and low. It became more difficult for the government to eliminate strikes and other rebellions and dispose of troublemakers secretly, or to quash the independent radio and TV (including homemade cable) broadcasters that proliferated. Still, even in its last months the government resorted to repression. In early 1991, as Soviet authority was about to topple, Gorbachev forbade truthful broadcasting or writing about violent antigovernment demonstrations in Lithuania, including reports that tanks had crushed demonstrators (14 were killed). TV news broadcasters who dared contradict the official version of events in Lithuania were fired, reports about Boris Yeltsin, Gorbachev's main political opponent, were heavily censored, and some newspapers suddenly found it hard to get newsprint.[37]

NOTES

1. David K. Willis, *Klass: How Russians Really Live* (New York: Avon Books, 1987), 69, 71–74; Hedrick Smith, *The New Russians* (New York: Random House, 1991), 150.

2. Willis, *Klass*, 73–75; Mikhail Deza and Mervyn Matthews, "Soviet Theater Audiences," *Slavic Review* 34, no. 4 (December 1975): 719, 729–30.

3. Nina Kosterina, *The Diary of Nina Kosterina*, trans. Mirra Ginsburg (New York: Crown Publishers, 1968), 178–79.

4. Michael Binyon, *Life in Russia* (New York: Pantheon, 1983), 71–72, 78–79, 88–90; Richard Stites, *Russian Popular Culture: Entertainment and Society Since 1900* (Cambridge, England: Cambridge University Press, 1992), 207–8; Hedrick Smith, *The Russians*, rev. ed. (New York: Ballantine Books, 1976), 155.

5. Smith, *The Russians*, 156–59.

6. Michael Shipley, "Russians Balance Work, Play at Summer Cottages," *Dallas Morning News*, April 12, 2001, 14A.

7. Binyon, *Life in Russia*, 81–82; Walter G. Moss, *A History of Russia, vol. II: Since 1855* (New York: McGraw-Hill, 1997), 347–48.

8. Hedrick Smith, *The Russians* (New York: Ballantine Books, 1976), 358.

9. Denis J. B. Shaw, "Achievements and Problems in Soviet Recreational Planning," in *Home, School and Leisure in the Soviet Union*, ed. Jenny Brine, Maureen Perrie, and Andrew Sutton (London: George Allen & Unwin, 1980), 197–98; Smith, *The Russians*, 358–59.

10. Quoted in Susan Bridger, *Women in the Soviet Countryside* (Cambridge, England: Cambridge University Press, 1987), 176.

11. Bridger, *Women*, 166–76.

12. Binyon, *Life in Russia*, 70–71, 73–75; Smith, *The Russians*, 160, 165; Sydney Schultze, *Customs and Culture of Russia* (Westport, CT: Greenwood Press, 2000), 71.

13. Vladimir Voinovich, "The New Year's Tree," in *The Anti-Soviet Soviet Union*, trans. Richard Lourie (San Diego: Harcourt Brace Jovanovich, 1986), 88–94.

14. Binyon, *Life in Russia*, 76–78; Schultze, 51–53.

15. Elena Bonner, *Mothers and Daughters*, trans. Antonina W. Bouis (New York: Vintage Books, 1993), 291–93.

16. Smith, *The Russians*, 356–57, 379; Schultze, 53–54, 68; Bonner, *Mothers and Daughters*, 292–93.

17. Paul Easton, "The Rock Music Community," in *Soviet Youth Culture*, ed. Jim Riordan (Bloomington: Indiana University Press, 1989), 47–50; Tanya Frisby, "Soviet Youth Culture," in *Soviet Youth Culture*, 3–4; Bill Carter, "McCartney Finds Fans 'Back in the U.S.S.R.,'" *New York Times*, sec. 2, p. 1, col. 7, September 18, 2003.

18. Easton, "Rock Music," 71; Stites, *Russian Popular Culture*, 198–99; Frisby, "Soviet Youth Culture," 6–8, 13; Raymond E. Zickel, ed., *Soviet Union: A Country Study*, 2nd ed. (Washington, DC: Federal Research Division, Library of Congress, 1991), 393–94.

19. Easton, "Rock Music," 53, 61–62, 76; Catherine Evtuhov and Richard Stites, *A History of Russia: Peoples, Legends, Events, Forces Since 1800* (Boston Houghton Mifflin), 451.

20. Jim Riordan, "Teenage Gangs, 'Afgantsy' and Neofascists," in *Soviet Youth Culture*, 122–39.

21. Robert Edelman, *Serious Fun: A History of Spectator Sports in the USSR* (New York: Oxford University Press, 1993), viii, 27.

22. Edelman, *Serious Fun*, 206.

23. Quoted in Edelman, *Serious Fun*, 206.

24. Edelman, *Serious Fun*, 204–5, 208–11, 213.

25. Vadim Medish, *The Soviet Union*, 3rd ed. (Englewood Cliffs, NJ: Prentice-Hall, 1987), 221–22, 234; Joseph Gibbs, *Gorbachev's Glasnost: The Soviet Media in the First Phase of Perestroika* (College Station: Texas A&M University Press, 1999), 5.

26. Medish, *Soviet Union*, 221–25, 227–28; 232–34, 237, 241–42.

27. Smith, *The Russians*, 459–61.

28. Smith, *The Russians*, 459–63; Edelman, *Serious Fun*, 199; Zickel, *Soviet Union*, 378–79.

29. Jeffrey Brooks, "The Press and Its Message: Images of America in the 1920s and 30s," in *Russia in the Era of NEP: Explorations in Soviet Society and Culture*, ed. Sheila Fitzpatrick, Alexander Rabinowitch, and Richard Stites (Bloomington: Indiana University Press), 232.

30. Aleksandr Solzhenitysyn, *Cancer Ward* (New York: Bantam, 1969), 207.

31. Solzhenitysyn, *Cancer Ward*, 208.

32. Quoted in Lisa A. Kirschenbaum, "'Our City, Our Hearths, Our Families': Local Loyalties and Private Life in Soviet World War II Propaganda," *Slavic Review* 59, no. 4 (Winter 2000): 830.

33. Susan Bridger, "Soviet Rural Women: Employment and Family Life," in *Russian Peasant Women*, ed. Beatrice Farnsworth and Lynne Viola (New York: Oxford UP, 1992), 285.

34. Edelman, *Serious Fun*, xi–xii, 198–99.

35. Medish, *Soviet Union*, 222, 228–29; Michael Wines, "Moscow Journal. Wired Radio Offers Fraying Link to Russian Past," *New York Times*, October 18, 2001, sec. 1, 4; Zickel, *Soviet Union*, 382.

36. Smith, *New Russians*, 153–54.

37. Smith, *New Russians*, 149–70; Medish, *Soviet Union*, 229–31; Gibbs, *Gorbachev's Glasnost*, 18–19; Schultze, 95; Igor Kon, "Sexual Minorities," in *Sex and*

Russian Society, ed. Igor Kon and James Riordan (Bloomington: Indiana University Press, 1993), 100, 107, 154; Gladys D. Ganley, *Unglued Empire: The Soviet Experience with Communications Technologies* (Norwood, NJ: Ablex Publishing Corporation, 1996), 76–78; Scott Shane, *Dismantling Utopia: How Information Ended the Soviet Union* (Chicago: Ivan R. Dee, 1994), 149–81.

12

Religion

The Soviet Union was the first modern state to promote atheism as official policy. Article 52 of the 1977 Soviet constitution repeated earlier guarantees of freedom of religion and conscience, and separation of church and state. It also reaffirmed the right of atheists to promote their views—a right not granted to religious groups. That omission gave the state license to ban religious outreach activities. Also, since Party and government were entwined, and the Party was openly antireligious, constitutional promises of freedom of worship had no force. Criminal laws also blocked religious freedom. For example, it was a crime to involve minor children or anyone else in religious ceremonies or activities that might be harmful to their health. These were handy laws that could be applied whenever the state wanted to prevent fasting, baptism, Sunday school classes, bar mitzvah ceremonies, circumcisions, and so on. For example, an official objection to baptism was that it is unhealthy to bring an infant into a drafty church and sprinkle cold water on its bald little head.

Being openly religious blocked people's chances for career advancement since believers were barred from Party membership. All denominations had to get official permission for such things as opening, closing, or repairing houses of worship; resolving problems with local authorities; and organizing religious conferences. Repressions waxed and waned; although the state never forbade religion, worshippers were always aware of their government's hostility.[1]

Many old Russian Orthodox churches, including Leningrad's St. Isaac's and Kazan cathedrals, and churches within Moscow's Kremlin were turned into museums, including "museums of atheism," where people could go to see the terrible things religion had done. Valuable church property was carted away to state museums, sold abroad for hard cash, or simply vanished. Sometimes church property was recycled for new uses, as when bells were used to summon peasants to work rather than to worship or melted down for industrial use. Moscow's Cathedral of Christ the Savior was dynamited in 1931 in order to build in its place a palatial government building, meant to be the world's largest building, topped by "the world's largest Lenin…pointing the way to the future, with the world's largest index finger, 15 feet long." But in what some believers regarded as a sign from God, the ground beneath the church was too soft to support such a huge structure. The site remained a ditch until Khrushchev in the 1960s made it into the world's largest outdoor public swimming pool. The clouds of vapor arising in winter from the heated water only proved, to some at least, the pool's hellish origin. But for others, such as "secret" Baptists, it furnished a place for new converts to be discreetly baptized. As unsuspecting Muscovites swam, the Baptists "prayed and dunked." Similarly, St. Petersburg's Church of St. Peter and Paul, first built by Peter the Great for Lutherans of that city, was closed by government decree as a place of worship in the 1930s, used for several different warehouse purposes, and in the 1960s converted to an indoor city swimming pool, a purpose it served for 30 years.

In 1926 the visiting German writer Walter Benjamin described in his diary Moscow's Our Lady of Kazan Cathedral, with its "gloomy" anteroom just right for hatching "the shadiest deals, even pogroms, should the occasion arise." He went on to picture "the actual place of worship."

It has a few small stairs in the background that lead up to the narrow, low platform on which one advances past the pictures of saints. Altar upon altar follows in close succession, each one indicated by the glimmer of a small red lamp…. Those portions of the wall…not hidden by [very large] pictures are covered in luminous gold. A crystal chandelier hangs from the cloying, painted ceiling.[2]

Benjamin observed how worshippers approached an icon (painting of a saint or deity), crossed themselves, kneeled, touched their foreheads to the ground, crossed themselves again, and proceeded to the next icon. When worshippers approached smaller, glass-covered icons on stands, they bowed and kissed the picture instead of crossing themselves. Benjamin was disconcerted to find that some stands held invaluable antique icons side-by-side with cheap mass-produced pictures.

When the state introduced a continuous workweek, eliminating Sunday as a day of worship and rest, many believers met for Sunday evening services after work. The government countered such efforts by substituting secular rituals and holidays for religious rites, including those that mark life's transitions: birth, marriage, death. The secular version of infant baptism was a naming ceremony: the baby, flanked by two family friends, received a certificate and the friends promised to be the child's "moral guardians." Civil weddings, which were the norm, were sterile affairs done in assembly-line style at a government office (called by its acronym, ZAGS) where people went to register marriages, births, and deaths. In response to people's craving for beauty and ritual to mark life's transitions, the government eventually provided more ornate "wedding palaces," but the basic approach was the same. A clerk (often a woman), standing beneath a portrait of Lenin, read a brief statement, rings and kisses were exchanged, and the couple exited to make way for the next bride and groom. Despite the rather colorless ceremony, many couples arrived formally dressed, with the bride wearing a traditional elaborate white wedding dress and veil and carrying flowers. Couples who wanted the lengthier Orthodox wedding ritual with its processions, incense, candles, wedding crowns, icons, and chanting might arrange for a church wedding, though many kept such weddings secret to protect their careers.[3]

RECIPE FOR RUSSIAN EASTER *KULICH*
(USING A BREAD MACHINE)

(Makes one 1 $\frac{1}{2}$-pound loaf)
1/2 cup milk/ 1/3 cup water/ 1 tsp. vanilla extract/ 2 tbsp. butter, cut up/ 1 large egg/ 1 tsp. salt/ 3 cups bread flour/ 1/3 cup chopped candied fruits and peels drained of syrup, plus a few more for decoration/ 1/3 cup coarsely chopped almonds, toasted/ 2 tbsp. sugar/ 1 1/2 tsp. finely shredded orange peel/ 1 1/2 tsp. finely shredded lemon peel/ 2 tsp. active dry yeast or bread machine yeast.

Recommended cycle:

Basic/white bread; light or medium/normal color setting.
Add all ingredients except icing to bread machine pan in the order suggested by the manufacturer, adding fruits and peels and almonds with flour. Stand the cooled loaf upright and spread a thick coating of the almond icing over the dome, allowing the icing to run down the sides. Place reserved candied fruit or a single (non-pesticide-treated) red rose in the center of the dome.

Almond icing:

Stir together 1/2 cup sifted powdered sugar, 1/4 tsp. almond extract, and enough milk (2 to 3 tsp.) to make icing of thick, spreadable consistency.[4]

After the ceremony, city couples traditionally got into a black car decorated with streamers and rings and a doll or teddy bear attached to the front and toured the town with wedding party members in tow, stopping at various points of interest to have their pictures taken. For many, it was mandatory to deposit the wedding bouquet at a famous local gravesite. Tombs of unknown soldiers, the Lenin-Stalin mausoleum, Tolstoy's grave

Moscow, 1925. A crowd lines up to view Lenin's embalmed body. Behind the tomb is the Kremlin, and at left, the Cathedral of St. Basil. There were always long lines waiting to enter the tomb. Reproduced from the Collections of the Library of Congress, LC-USZ62-101129.

at his estate, *Yasnaya polyana*, were popular stops. The writer Vladimir Voinovich regarded the postnuptial grave visit as a weird state-promoted substitute for religious rites.

Finally there was a grand feast at a restaurant or at the bride's home. Then as now, guests shouting "Bitter!" repeatedly raised vodka-filled glasses to the bride and groom, whereupon the couple kissed to make the drinks "sweet," and guests duly gulped them down. The couple got a few days off work for their honeymoon but did not necessarily travel since the partying might continue for days.

Christmas and (especially) Easter remained important holidays for Soviet Christians, whether or not they were particularly religious. At Easter bakeries stocked *kulich*, a traditional yeast-risen, cylindrical, high-domed coffee cake, and *paskha*, an unbaked cheesecake filled with candied fruit and nuts that is eaten along with the *kulich*.

The *kulich*, which is supposed to be tall, even towering, is sliced hori-zontally in rounds, and then (if necessary) in halves and quarters, with the top round being saved as a kind of lid to put atop leftover cake. Slices are placed on a platter along with slices of *paskha,* or the *paskha* may be placed on top of the *kulich. Paskha,* which means "Easter," was officially called "spring cake" in order to downplay its religious associations. People who wanted to prepare their own *paskha* and *kulich* struggled to find enough eggs, butter, cheese, and other necessary ingredients. Also at Easter, people dyed eggs reddish brown by boiling them with onion skins or (especially in Ukraine) followed ancient tradition by painting them with tiny, exquisitely detailed, colored geometrical designs. Elderly women, the mainstay of Russian Orthodox worshippers, brought homemade bread and cakes to church to be blessed. It was also customary to visit family graves before Easter. Relatives of the departed went to the graves to "tidy up": paint the railings that customarily encircle each grave, clip grass, pull weeds, and clean the stone crosses with their inset photos of the deceased. On the actual memorial day, families put flowers, Easter eggs, and sometimes even small glasses of vodka on the graves.

In the city of Vladimir, on Easter eve in the early 1970s, authorities organized an outdoor dance for young people, in hopes of distracting them from services at the Cathedral of the Assumption. But Orthodox churches and services are a sensory feast—of sparkling color, music, the fragrance of incense, and gorgeous icon and wall paintings, which contrasted with the grayness of everyday Soviet life. By 11:30 P.M., the pewless church was packed with worshippers standing shoulder to shoulder for the lengthy service. When priests and worshippers emerged from the church for the traditional candlelight procession they were quickly engulfed by young people who, the dance over, had broken through restraining police lines in an effort to enter the church. Officially, the police were stationed outside the cathedral to protect worshippers from harassment by nonbelievers, but the youth who managed to push their way into the cathedral were obviously not there to make trouble, but rather to wonder at, and even tape record, the ceremonies and music.[5]

Despite decades of repression, many Soviets continued to regard themselves as followers of one or another of the empire's array of religious traditions. Christianity and Islam had the most followers. Christians belonged to a variety of denominations, of which the Russian Orthodox Church, Russia's pre-Revolutionary state church, had the most followers. There were also significant numbers of Roman Catholics, Baptists, and other Protestant sects, especially Evangelical Christians. About 90 percent of Soviet Muslims belonged to the Sunni denomination, who supported an elected caliph. The rest, mostly Azerbaijani, were Shiites who supported an hereditary caliph as their leader. Judaism also had many believers. Other religions with a smaller number of faithful included Buddhism, Lamaism, and shamanism.[6]

The *Russian Orthodox Church* before the Revolution was subsidized by the country's treasury, under state control, and was the royal family's religion. Seventy percent of the empire's population were Russian Orthodox.

In its pre-Revolutionary heyday the church was a major economic and social force. It was a huge landowner, owned a third of all the empire's primary schools, and housed 95,000 monks and nuns in over a thousand cloisters. A decree of January 1918 announced the separation of church and state, mandated withdrawal of all government financial support from the Russian Orthodox Church, and seizure of its property.

In a secret letter to the Politburo of March 19, 1922, Lenin personally ordered a campaign of terror against Russian Orthodox clergy and supporters who were trying to prevent the government from confiscating valuable objects from churches. In that letter, Lenin urged that Russian Orthodox priests and their "bourgeois" followers be smashed "with utmost haste and ruthlessness." During the first five years after the Revolution the Bolsheviks executed 28 Russian Orthodox bishops and over 1,200 Russian Orthodox priests. Many others—clergy and parishioners— were imprisoned, exiled, or both. Besides the lives lost, seminaries were closed and church publications banned. In 1927, Metropolitan Sergii (the church's de facto leader) tried to save his church by declaring it subservient to the government, a tactic that earned him many bitter enemies, inspired the growth of an underground church movement, and failed to restrain the Party's ferocious attacks against Orthodoxy. By 1933 only 100 Moscow churches out of 600 in the early 1920s remained open. By 1941 only 500 of about 54,000 churches active in the country before World War I were still open. Several thousand Orthodox had been executed by the late 1930s.[7]

ILLEGAL UNDERGROUND CHURCH MOVEMENTS BASED ON THE RUSSIAN ORTHODOX CHURCH

Although no religion was spared, a fierce antireligious campaign begun in 1929 intensely targeted Russian Orthodox underground groups and split-offs from the mainstream church. Most known leaders of the Orthodox underground were arrested that year, but people found ways to continue worshiping. Sometimes priests traveled secretly to visit groups of believers; sometimes laymen conducted services, often from memory. Occasionally people got together outdoors and conducted services under a special tree or at a spring thought to be holy. The atmosphere of secrecy caused many believers to split from the mainstream church into sects that strayed far from doctrines and rituals of the original church. Through World War II and for several years after, many small underground branches of Russian Orthodoxy merged into two larger movements, the True Orthodox Church and the True Orthodox Christians.

The *True Orthodox Church* was the closest in spirit, traditions, and rituals to the Russian Orthodox Church. At least through the 1940s, it had sufficient priests, secretly trained and ordained, though they probably had a very limited supply of bishops. For most laypeople who had grown up in

Moscow, Red Square. St. Basil's Cathedral, Russian Orthodox, 1959. Reproduced from the Collections of the Library of Congress, LC-U9-2816-328-550 #29.

the church, services in the True Orthodox Church were not significantly different from traditional Russian Orthodox rituals. Where people had a choice between attending Russian Orthodox services and attending those of the True Orthodox Church, they often chose the latter. Its Achilles heel was that very resemblance to its parent: it depended on a trained priesthood to hold services. When in the early 1950s authorities began arresting its priests, the True Orthodox Church nearly vanished. When their priest was arrested True Orthodox Church members often became True Orthodox Christians.[8]

The *True Orthodox Christian movement* was most popular where people had no access to an active Russian Orthodox church and clergy. They welcomed itinerant priests (or men claiming to be priests) who came their way, but if none appeared a layperson (likely to be an elderly woman drawing from her memory) conducted services and might also preach a sermon. Though each congregation was a small secret "cell," detention of individual members did not necessarily destroy the nucleus. True Orthodox Christians survived the 1950s campaign to stamp out underground religion and during the severe antireligious campaign of the 1960s True Orthodox Christians went even deeper underground, organizing themselves into larger secret networks across the USSR. But they were not the most radical of the underground breakaway movements.

True Orthodox Christian Wanderers renounced their links to society and destroyed their official documents, including internal passports, to live a secret religious life of hiding or wandering. Their clandestine lives included a secret postal system, codes, signals, false names, and papers. True Orthodox Wanderers had networks across the country, even their own system of elementary and secondary religious schools. The Wanderers were one among many mystical groups that sprang up in the north Caucasus, Central Asia, and Siberia, irritating authorities because they rejected participation in official Soviet life, met in secret, looked to their own chosen leaders for moral guidance, raised money to support their own causes, and defied the government's often severe persecution.

CHANGING SITUATION OF THE RUSSIAN ORTHODOX CHURCH DURING WORLD WAR II AND AFTER

Metropolitan Sergii spearheaded the church's decision to help the Soviet war effort. Under Sergii's leadership, the church distributed anti-German, pro-Soviet propaganda, raised funds, and formed a special organization to look after war orphans. Taking care of its own interests at the same time, the church leadership supported the government's anti–Roman Catholic Church campaigns. In return for those efforts about 20,000 churches were allowed to reopen; parish priests were allowed to safeguard church property and carry out other church-related duties. Membership rose; and distribution of religious publications was once again allowed. This born-again alliance between the government and the Russian Orthodox Church continued postwar (with an interruption in 1954) until 1958–1959 when Khrushchev launched a harsh antireligious campaign directed mainly against Judaism and Christianity, a campaign that continued after he fell from power. In 1961 parish priests were again deprived of control over church property, and there was a new wave of church, seminary, and monastery closings. As in the past, and as with other officially registered religions, prominent churchmen and lay members went to prison and were often replaced by cooperative priests and senior clergy. Antichurch tactics included placing secret police agents in congregations to observe and inform, allowing "hooligans" to disrupt services, increasing taxation on churches, demanding that churches make certain repairs and then denying them the needed materials, prohibiting Sunday School classes, banning minors from attending services, separating children from religious parents, arrest, exile, imprisonment, and occasionally the death penalty.[9]

At the same time, in the 1960s, 70s and 80s, there was a growing resistance to government domination of religion, a resistance that paralleled a rising tide of political dissidence and national hopes for independence. When Gorbachev became head of state, religious tolerance took some wobbly steps forward. The Soviet leader began working toward greater lenience for religious institutions and beliefs and in 1988 started returning churches to worshipers, but the process could be maddeningly slow. In 1989 three thousand parishioners from Ivanovo signed a letter of complaint about the overcrowding of their town's one Russian Orthodox Church, the Preobrazhensky Cathedral. On holidays the cathedral was jammed to capacity: the crush of the crowd caused a number of injuries, including fractures and concussions. Red tape prevented another church in town, which had been used for storage, from being returned to the congregation. "Nobody is openly harassing us," the letter writers pointed out, "but at the same time our problems are not being solved. Are half-baked measures really democracy?" In the end the church was not returned to its faithful until some went on a hunger strike and an influential magazine defended their actions.[10]

Roman Catholic believers lived mostly along the western borders of the USSR. Their church represented a special danger to the state because its leader, the Pope, resided outside the country and so was not under the government's thumb. The fact that millions of the USSR's Roman Catholics lived in Lithuania and Ukraine made authorities uneasy about possible links between the religion and independence movements. Clergy were arrested, seminaries were closed, and as with other religions, there was secret police infiltration of the church. By 1926 there were no bishops left in the country, and by 1941 only two of the 1,200 Roman Catholic churches that had existed before the Revolution were still active. Persecution of Lithuanian Catholics receded after Stalin died, intensified under Khrushchev's antireligion campaign, and continued under Brezhnev's leadership.[11]

The Uniate Church (also called the *Greek Catholic Church, Ukrainian Catholic Church,* or *Eastern Rite Catholic Church*) was established in 1596 when many Orthodox clergy and parishioners decided to recognize the Pope's authority while preserving most Eastern Orthodox rituals. Because this church became identified with Ukrainian nationalism, the Soviet regime was very hostile to it. In 1941 Soviet authorities arrested many Ukrainian Uniate priests, whom they either killed outright or deported to Siberia. In 1945 the government arrested and deported to prison camps (where most died) its metropolitan archbishop and all of its bishops, along with hundreds of clergy and laypeople active in the church. In 1946 the remaining priests were forced to forswear their ties with Rome and allow their church to become subordinate to the Russian Orthodox Church. However, the Ukrainian Catholic Church continued as an underground religion and continued to be a focal point for Ukrainian hopes of having a separate nation.[12]

Autocephalous (self-governing) Orthodox Churches appointed their own metropolitans without consulting authorities from other Orthodox Churches. The Ukrainian Autocephalus Orthodox Church separated from the Russian Orthodox Church in 1919 and soon attracted Bolshevik suspicions for the same reason the regime was hostile to the Uniate Church: fear that it was nurturing a Ukrainian independence movement. By 1936, the UAOC had almost vanished under state repression but became active again when the Germans occupied Ukraine during World War II, a fact that must have further alienated Stalin, who repressed it again in 1944 along with the Byelorussian Autocephalous Orthodox Church. Thousands of Ukrainian and Byelorussian Autocephalous priests were shot or sent to labor camps. Lay believers were also persecuted.

The Georgian Orthodox Church is another Eastern Orthodox autocephalous church. It was combined with the Russian Orthodox Church in 1811 but regained its independence in 1917 (after the Revolution). However, the Russian Orthodox Church did not formally recognize its independence until 1943. As with some other Soviet religions, it enjoyed a temporary respite from persecution during World War II, in return for supporting the war effort. But as soon as the war was over, tight controls were resumed. The Georgian Orthodox Church had around 2,100 churches in 1917, a number reduced to 200 in the 1980s, and they were banned from ministering to followers outside the Georgian Republic.

The Armenian Apostolic Church was the pre-Revolutionary national church of Armenia, and the Soviet government allowed it to continue as such, at the same time confiscating its property; harassing its clergy and believers; and setting tight limits on the number of churches, seminaries, and monasteries. Most Armenians belonged to the Apostolic Church, and many nonbelievers supported it as part of their national heritage.

JUDAISM

The status of Soviet Jews was complicated by official ambiguity about whether Judaism was primarily a religion or a nationality. On the one hand, the state, as well as the general population, regarded Jews as belonging to a particular nationality, and in the space for "nationality" on internal passports, and other official papers, a believing or nonbelieving person of Jewish heritage would have "Jewish" inscribed, while non-Jews were recorded as being from a certain geographical area, such as "Estonian" or "Azerbaijani." Jews of mixed parentage could choose for themselves at age 16 how they wanted to be listed on their passports, and very many, with their parents' encouragement, chose to inscribe themselves as belonging to a geographic nationality. The label "Jewish" could be a formidable handicap for young people trying to make their way in the Soviet world. Because nationality was the fifth "point" (or item) in internal passports, people often derogatorily referred to Jews as "fifth pointers."[13]

Until the early 1970s, the Jewish population of the USSR was larger than that of Israel and second only to that of the United States. By 1980, because of emigration (starting in the late 1960s) and assimilation, the USSR's Jewish population had dropped to third place. In 1989 most of the Soviet Union's 1.4 million Jews lived in the Russian Republic, the Ukrainian Republic, and the Byelorussian Republic. Jews were also a large minority in the Moldavian Republic and Central Asia (mainly in Uzbekistan and in Tajikistan, where they spoke a dialect of the Tajik language). There was a unique community of Georgian Jews, whose first language was Georgian and whose ancestors may have settled there in the first centuries A.D. For some reason, there was relatively less repression of Georgian Jews' religious activities. In 1979 almost half the synagogues in the USSR were in Georgia, and they were more successful in preserving their customs and religious rites than were other Soviet Jewish communities. There was also a community called Mountain Jews living mainly in Daghestan and Azerbaijan. They spoke Tat, a Persian dialect. Although Mountain Jews maintained religious beliefs identical with mainstream Orthodox Judaism, they assimilated some customs from the Islamic majority around them, such as covering their synagogue floors with carpets. For traditional Mountain Jews, life revolves around the demands of religious observance, the patriarchal family, and clan.[14]

Violence against Jews was a regular feature of life under the tsars, a phenomenon that did not disappear after the Revolution, even though the Bolsheviks offered Jews equal opportunity to join the mainstream of Russian life and banned anti-Semitism in all its forms. At the same time Bolsheviks were as hostile toward Judaism as they were to other religions. In 1919 the state swept away Jewish councils that had traditionally maintained synagogues and supervised social and spiritual good works within Jewish communities. Newly established Jewish sections within the Party had the job of producing propaganda against Judaism and rabbis, among other responsibilities. After the Revolution, hundreds of thousands of Jews eagerly grasped the opportunities offered them to integrate into and contribute to Russian/Soviet life. Many achieved important, even key positions in higher education, art, and science. In government, Jews such as Leon Trotsky, Grigory Zinoviev, Lev Kamenev, Lazar Kaganovich, and Maxim Litvinov held some of the highest Party positions. Yiddish, the first language of most East European Jews, was allowed to have a "renaissance" with, by the 30s, more than 1,200 Yiddish schools and university departments of Jewish studies. There were also a number of Yiddish newspapers and several artistically important Yiddish theaters. Stalin's 1930s purges of top Party leaders, however, severely and permanently limited Jewish participation in high levels of government. Jews remained prominent in the arts to the end of the USSR, but by the mid-1930s cultural life was crippled by the state's meddling with and even terrorizing artists and art critics. Although Lenin detested anti-Semitism, Stalin, Khrushchev, and other Party leaders had no such qualms. As Stalin aged, his hatred for Jews seemed to grow ever more virulent. During the 1920s and into the late 1940s, aspects of Jewish culture, such as a few Yiddish publications, were allowed to continue and even (as in the case of Yiddish theater in the 1920s and 30s) to flourish. But overall the regime systematically destroyed Jewish religious observance and culture, eventually suppressing written and spoken use of Yiddish and Hebrew. Most of the 5,000 synagogues in existence at the time of the Revolution were closed under Stalin; by 1964, synagogues were down from about 400 at the beginning of Khrushchev's antireligious campaign to 60 or less. But the greatest suffering of Soviet Jews came during the first several months of World War II, when invading Germans murdered about 2.5 million of them, often with help from other Soviet ethnic groups and Romanians who were Germany's allies.[15]

The threat to Jewish lives did not end with the German defeat. Official persecution of Jews and other groups waxed and waned according to shifting policies. Hitler's surprise attack in 1941 meant a cooling off of persecution of Jews, whose international connections were useful for the war effort. But when German forces besieging Stalingrad were vanquished in February 1943, Stalin smelled victory and began going after the Jews in his domain. Many suddenly lost their jobs, no matter how devotedly they had labored for state and Party. Shortly after the Stalingrad victory a newspaper editor was ordered to fire the Jews on his staff. The editor, David Ortenberg, replied, "It has already happened," and proceeded to list nine war correspondents who had been killed at the front. "I can add one more...myself," Ortenberg said as he walked out the door. Toward the end of his life Stalin began a vendetta against prominent Jews. In 1948 Solomon Mikhoëls, a prestigious actor-director and leader of the Soviet Jewish community's support for the war effort, was murdered in a staged "traffic accident." Two weeks later, his murderer was secretly given a high government award (the Order of Lenin) "for exemplary execution of a special assignment from the government." That was just stage one. Arrests of Yiddish-language writers, other prominent Jews, and in some cases their close relatives soon followed. The actor Benjamin Zuskin was snatched, heavily sedated, straight out of his hospital bed and deposited in prison. When he awakened the next day he was still in his hospital gown. Coerced confessions led to more arrests. Most of the arrested Jewish cultural leaders were executed; others, including hundreds not well known, were also murdered outright or perished in prisons and labor camps. The arrests occurred at about the same time that Yiddish writers' organizations, theaters, and journals were being closed down across the country.[16]

In 1952, in what came to be known as the Doctors' Plot, several prestigious Jewish doctors were arrested, among them the chief physician of the Red Army during the war and a pediatrician who tended to the offspring of high officials. Perhaps to deflect foreign charges of an anti-Semitic campaign, Stalin's personal physician, who was not Jewish, was also arrested. These doctors were charged with conspiring with Zionist organizations and the United States to murder high military officers, as well as Kremlin officials and their children. Stalin's death in March 1953 saved seven of the nine doctors and may have saved Soviet Jews from widespread trials, executions, and massive deportations to Soviet Asia.

With a few exceptions, by the later Soviet period most Jews were unofficially barred from careers in diplomacy, political journalism, the military, and high Party posts. There were quotas in publishing (only so many Jewish authors allowed per year) and science (highly qualified scientists were rejected for research positions on the grounds that "we already have enough Jews"). Khrushchev insisted that such discrimination was for the Jews' own good, so as not to engender resentment in the hearts of others. It became increasingly difficult for Jews to be accepted to prestigious universities. Yelena Mandel, a Jewish woman brought up as an atheist, had been an A student all her life but was cautioned not to try to enter Moscow State University. However, in the 1970s, when she was 18, she applied to the university's history department.

The examination commission was clearly and explicitly trying to knock me down. They had to work hard, because I did know a lot.... They asked me question after question, until finally they asked me something I couldn't answer; then, triumphantly, they gave me a grade of B. I was not accepted to the university. This was the kind of thing that happened to all the Jews.... Of course, it felt bad not to be accepted—especially because the Department of History that year had accepted one of the worst students in my high school class.[17]

Nevertheless, Soviet Jews tended to be high achievers, especially in arts and sciences, despite the obstacles, and (compared to Russians, for example) were more likely to have higher education.

Anti-Jewish policies, along with the wish, of some, to live in a homeland of their own or just to escape the hardships of Soviet life, impelled Jewish dissidents to demand that the government actually enforce the human rights promised in the Soviet constitution, including the right to leave. While worldwide publicity, diplomatic considerations, and support groups helped Jewish emigration go forward, there were, beginning in the 1970s, harsh crackdowns on selected Jewish would-be emigrants and their relatives, as well as on Armenians, Lithuanians, Ukrainians, and others who tried to get exit visas.

Envy of Jews' ability to emigrate intensified Russian anti-Semitism, but it also motivated people to acknowledge Jewish roots and relationships.

People joked about a man named Abramovich who applied to emigrate and was called to the Office of Visas and Registration (OVIR) for questioning by a KGB officer. The officer asks Abramovich why, as a professor with all the benefits of Soviet privilege—a private apartment, summer cottage, and a car—he would want to leave. Abramovich protests that he does not wish to leave, but his wife, children, mother-in-law, aunts, and cousins want to go, and he is his family's only Jew.

"Refuseniks," Jews who had applied to emigrate but were refused exit visas, were in a bad situation. Having applied to leave, they were fired from their jobs and thereafter remained jobless or stuck in low-level work.

THE JEWISH AUTONOMOUS REGION OF BIROBIJAN

In one of Soviet history's odder twists, the state attempted to give its Jews a "homeland" far from civilization as they knew it. In 1928 the government chose an area of East Siberia, close to China, to be a secular, socialist Jewish homeland and a place to settle impoverished Ukrainian and Byelorussian Jews. Although the idea was publicized as a Jewish homeland where Jewish pioneers would learn to be collective farmers, Jewish immigration there was actually meant to provide the government with manpower to exploit the area's rich resources and maintain a Soviet presence on the Chinese border. Non-Soviet Jews came too, enticed by Moscow's promise to help them build a "Zion" in the USSR. "My grandfather told me how people were standing in line to get here!" a Birobijan man recalled. "So many came, including my whole family, to get something better." Between 1928 and 1938, about 40,000 Jews settled in Birobijan, becoming almost one-fourth of the area's population. Jews in Europe and North America, including Albert Einstein, sent money, supplies, and "pioneers." But help from abroad was insufficient, and the promised help from the state never materialized. For many the dream quickly turned into a nightmare. At journey's end, people found themselves stranded. Families with no experience in farming, building construction, farm management, or land draining were on their own in an inhospitable region of bitterly cold winters and mosquito-ridden summers. There were no barns, no livestock, and no proper tools or equipment for farming. In the early years of Birobijan, people lived in tents, shabby barracks, or roofed-over holes in the ground. New arrivals sometimes had to sleep outside, waiting for tents to arrive or barracks to be built. Most families with the wherewithal to leave—left. Others had to stay and tough it out as best they could, some forced into begging and prostitution to survive. As soon as emigration to North America, Israel, or Germany became possible in the 1970s, Birobijani Jews, many of them from families that had long since hidden or forgotten their Jewish roots, scrambled to document their Jewish heritage in order to leave the Jewish Autonomous Region and the USSR.[18]

PROTESTANT DENOMINATIONS

An official government report of 1929 described the Sunday night meetings of Evangelical Christians near the city of Smolensk. The congregation met in an "old, dark, dirty, sooty hut. The furnishings—a table and benches." About 80 congregants read and sang "various prayers from the Gospel." Most of the worshippers were middle-aged, female, and probably working class: farmers, construction workers, and other unskilled laborers. The report concluded, "All these [Protestant sects] do counterrevolutionary work…and spread various counterrevolutionary rumors."[19]

Before World War II the number of Protestants was relatively few, but the faith grew quickly after the war, especially among Evangelical Christians and Baptists (known collectively as ECB). In 1944 the government started an official Protestant organization, the All-Union Council of Evangelical Christians-Baptists, in order to control them. For that reason, many Protestant groups refused to join the council, while others that did join eventually left. In the 1960s there was a major split in the council, after which an unofficial group formed, calling itself the Council of Churches of the ECB. Under Khrushchev the government pushed to dissolve congregations not affiliated with the All-Union Council as well as to destroy many that were. Protestant faithful generally had to confine themselves to worship services and were very limited in their outreach opportunities, whether proselytizing, teaching their own parishioners, or publishing religious literature.[20]

Protestants who refused to register with the government held secret meetings in homes or in secluded places outdoors, formed clandestine "cells," and published religious material on hidden presses; some groups opposed military service. Many paid for their defiance with long prison sentences. Soviet Baptists, most of whose converts came from the Russian Orthodox Church, tended to be strict in their lifestyle. They avoided alcohol and tithed (gave a 10th of their income to the church). Generally Soviet Baptists belonged to the less-well-educated class of society. Women who wanted their menfolk to stop drinking were often attracted to the Evangelical message. In the early 1980s a British journalist described his impression of a Baptist gathering—it was a scene that in basic respects had not changed since 1929: the setting was cheerier, the congregation larger, but the plainness and earnestness of the gathering remained the same.

There is none of the mystery and ceremony to be found in Orthodox churches. Hospitality is warm but frugal compared with the banquets I have enjoyed in the residences of Orthodox bishops: and the involvement of the community in its beliefs is much more full-time: as I sat under the trees in the grounds of one prayer house, eating vegetable soup from trestle tables together with 300 others after Sunday morning service, a singer sang hymns and read from the Gospels while the community listened with serious attention.[21]

Lutherans, who mainly lived in Latvia and Estonia, were the second-largest Protestant group (about 850,000 in the 1970s). During Khrushchev's antireligion campaign Baltic Lutherans lost around half of their churches.

ISLAM

In the late Soviet period about 55 million people called themselves Muslims, a number of believers second only to those who followed Russian Orthodoxy. Most Muslims lived in Central Asia, though important enclaves existed in the Caucasus and other parts of the country. As with other religions, the state limited the number of places of worship and the amount of religious activity. From the early 1920s, the government tried to ward off a movement toward religious and cultural unity among its Muslim citizens by creating six separate Muslim republics: Uzbekistan, Tajikistan, Turkmenistan, Kyrgyzstan, Kazakhstan, and Azerbaijan. The state permitted mosques in most of the bigger cities of Central Asian republics and the Azerbaijan Republic, but their number slipped from 25,000 in 1917 to about 500 in the 1970s, to about 400 in the mid-1980s, with only two madrasahs (Muslim religious schools), which produced about 60 graduates annually. As with the finest Russian Orthodox churches, the state appropriated the most beautiful mosques, turning them into museums. In 1989, at the twilight of Soviet power and under the influence of Gorbachev's more liberal policies toward religion, some government-closed mosques were given back to Islamic believers.

Soviet Muslims comprised a wide variety of ethnic groups: Turks (Azerbaijanis, Uzbeks, Tatars, Uygurs, etc.), Iranians (Tajiks, Ossetians, Kurds, Baluchi), Caucasians (Avars, Lezgins, Tabasarans), and some smaller groups. About 50 million Soviet Muslims spoke a Turkish language; most others spoke a Persian dialect. Adding to this diversity was the fact that some were city people while others were newly settled nomads or still followed a nomadic or seminomadic life. Some educated Muslims could communicate with each other in Russian, but most were not fluent in that language, a circumstance that was a big obstacle to advancement in Soviet society.

Muslims are expected to carry out the "five pillars of the faith": recitation of the creed that "There is no god but God [Allah], and Mohammed is his prophet," daily prayer, charitable donation to the poor (*zakat*), fasting during the Islamic ninth month of Ramadan, and pilgrimage to Mecca (the *hajj*). Fortunately for Soviet Muslims, Islam also recognizes that one does what one can; circumstances may not always allow completing all five requirements. Permission to travel to Mecca was doled out at the rate of about 20 Muslims per year, and the privilege was allotted only to high-level religious dignitaries. *Zakat* was forbidden. Observant or not, most Soviet children of Muslim parents thought of themselves as Muslims, but those who felt freest to openly practice their religion were pensioners with no jobs or careers to worry about. For Muslim students and employees, as for other citizens, open religiosity could put education and career at risk. Nevertheless, Muslim rituals such as circumcision, Ramadan fasts, religious marriages, and burials were widely practiced. The early 1980s saw some lifting of state controls. A few new mosques opened; it became possible for a handful of young men to go to Cairo or Damascus to study to become clergy; some Islamic monuments were being restored at state expense. Unofficial Muslim congregations began meeting in teahouses and homes, often led by a self-taught mullah. Some of these unofficial groups began leaning toward Sufism, a mystical branch of Islam. Soviet Sufis joined secret societies called *tariquas* and practiced their religion clandestinely. Members ran underground religious schools and underground mosques in people's homes. As a substitute for the forbidden *hajj*, they organized pilgrimages to the graves of local heroes.

RELIGION IN THE RUSSIAN COUNTRYSIDE

In the 1920s the villagers in Tver Province began electing their village priest themselves rather than accepting a priest imposed on them by the church. Since Russian Orthodox priests are expected to marry, one criterion for choosing a new priest was the size of his family; a priest with several children would be difficult for villagers to support. After the election, the new priest was given a plot of land to grow food. Peasants were supposed to apply to the state for use of a church, robes, and whatever else was wanted for religious services, since these things officially belonged to the state.

Reflecting the government's campaign to stamp out religious belief and observances, provincial newspapers published articles that lectured peasants on the primitive and pagan origin of Christian beliefs and church holidays, the huge sums of money given over by poor peasants to the church, and priests' shady dealings. Since illiteracy was still rampant in the 1920s, colorful posters of sly priests trying to dupe peasants supplemented the printed word. Despite the campaign, religious practices persisted, in part because people believed bad things would happen to them if they abandoned their traditional religious and semireligious rituals. An unbaptised child was bound to die; a civil rather than church wedding would doom a couple to bad luck; livestock not blessed by a priest would not thrive. Even peasant Party members were loathe to take such chances with supernatural powers, especially since many rural believers saw no boundaries between Orthodox religion, pre-Christian beliefs, magic, and witchcraft. Witches were exorcised, for example, during the Feast of the Protection of Mary, so that they could not destroy the grain harvest. The novelist Aleksandr Solzhenitsyn's simple, saintly, but "heathen" peasant heroine Matryona believed that "you mustn't go into the garden on the feast of St.

John or there would be no harvest next year. A blizzard meant somebody had hanged himself."

If you pinched your foot in the door, you could expect a guest. All the time I lived with her I didn't once see her say her prayers or even cross herself. But, whatever job she was doing, she began with a "God bless us," and she never failed to say "God bless you," when I set out for school.

Like most country people, Matryona keeps icons (sacred paintings) in a corner of her house, but she fails to light the traditional lamp in front of them, "except for the vigil of a great feast or on the morning of a holiday."[22]

Russian Orthodoxy had many religious holidays that endured and remained popular in the countryside: Christmas; Easter; Whitsun; New Year's; Epiphany; various feasts of the Virgin Mary; and feasts of saints Elias, Michael, John the Baptist, and Nicholas. Some of these were celebrated for several days. In addition to the general Russian Orthodox feast days and holidays there were local celebrations. The yearly calendar for the Christian peasants of Tver Province had more than a hundred feast days and holidays. Most feast days, such as the feast of the Blessed Virgin Mary in the spring, occurred before planting or after harvest and so did not disrupt farmwork. But other holidays came at times when workers were needed on state and collective farms, which tended to give officials a dim view of peasants' merrymaking.

Feast days were very different from ordinary days. On a typical Orthodox feast day in the 1920s, a peasant family left their home early in the morning, rode in a horse-drawn cart to the nearest village church for the service, then loitered with other peasants to chat, gossip, and discuss local problems. After services on special local feast days, the priest visited each house in his parish. In the Russian village of Gradobit, peasants performed a ritual cleansing every year. All went down to the river, took off their outer clothing, immersed themselves in the water, and then removed their undershirts. Clothing left lying on the riverbank often disappeared into the hands of less prosperous neighbors.

Residents of Gadyshi observed the Orthodox Church doctrine of fasting before taking communion. From the morning of the holiday until returning home from church, no one ate or drank. After that point, customs varied according to the holiday. If it was a "high" feast day, housewives began preparing for the festivities days before, in part by thoroughly cleaning their houses. The family's men brewed beer by building a fire outside the house and even carried the water (the only time peasant men carried water, as this was considered woman's work) needed for the brewing process. Besides water, the brew contained malt, rye, barley flour, and hops. Family, friends, and neighbors stood around, tasted, and commented on flavor and quality. Every village family, from highest to lowest, was expected to brew beer for important feast days. Peasants of some localities were also accustomed to home distilling a liquor made of corn and potatoes called *samogon*. Depending on the amount of distillation, the alcohol content of this popular beverage was anywhere from 25 to 70 percent. Although the government banned home brewing and distilling, it was always a losing battle, especially since local police joined in the drinking. Peasants invited friends and relatives from their village and other villages to partake of the feast, so people started coming by the family's hut (*izba*) after church.

Upon entering the hut . . . the guests blessed themselves before the icon, toasted the host, and were served appetizers. During the dinner which followed, everyone ate from a common bowl. Between eight and nine courses were served. Especially when guests were present, the host sought to show off his possessions.[23]

Not long after this meal, visitors were invited to share two more meals, in the afternoon and in the evening. Young people met for strolling in the village's main street. The day ended with singing, dancing, and drunkenness. The next day, men continued drinking, and drunkenness led to violence: brawls, fistfights, rapes, and murders. Such behavior is reflected in the Russian proverb "What a sober man has in his head, a drunk has in his fist." During a festival in the village of Marfino in 1926, two men raped a girl on a public road in the presence of several young people and adults, but no one tried to help her. Many of the witnesses refused to appear in court, and those who did appear gave testimony that protected the rapists, who were never punished. No local government official or agency advocated on the girl's behalf.

Holiday celebrations, religious and otherwise, were often seen as a time to settle old scores: a reporter for a Tver Province peasant newspaper, who happened to cross paths with family enemies, had his skull bashed in on New Year's night. The perpetrators were known but not punished, thanks to the cooperation of their fellow villagers. That August in the same locale, during the multiday Feast of the Holy Savior, the chairman of a village council was jumped and severely beaten by the men of a family who held a grudge against him. Again onlookers did nothing to help, and in court the victim was declared at least 50 percent responsible for his own beating, although he was the only one hurt. Religious feast days seemed to allow a kind of violent behavior, accelerated by alcohol, that was less acceptable at other times. The area around Rzhev had a special feast day on a Sunday in May, in which women, who were otherwise expected to be subservient to their male relations, were allowed to be bosses for a day and take the traditional male holiday roles. Women brewed *samogon*, got together for eating and drinking, drank too much, sang dirty songs, screamed obscenities at each other, and brawled. In the evening the husbands (those sober enough) "plucked their stray wives out of the gutter," as the local village newspaper put it, brought them home, and once again ruled their households.

The state invented politically correct holidays as substitutes for the old religiously based ones with their drunken sprees and violence. People were encouraged and often required to observe International Women's Day in March, International Labor Day and Journalism Day in May, International Cooperation Day in early July, Harvest Day in mid-October, and the anniversary of the October Revolution. At such times the government decreed parades, decorations, and lectures on uplifting subjects such as current economic and political problems. Schools offered special activities for students; for the grown-ups there were exhibits focusing on the latest agricultural methods and equipment, all culminating in an evening of theater and (if available) movies. Moreover, the Party wanted the festivities to be organized by authority figures: teachers, technical specialists, leaders of village soviets, party cells, and komsomols. These were celebrations manufactured for the peasants, rather than homemade by the peasants themselves.[24]

The state of religious worship during the Soviet years reflected the society as a whole. Freedom of worship, along with other civil liberties, existed on paper, but not in fact. While many believers struggled to live according to the highest moral principles of their faith, even in the face of suffering and death, many others, including clergy, cooperated with authorities in spying on and hunting down those the state saw as its enemies. With the fall of the Soviet regime, religious intolerance fueled by self-serving economic considerations, nationalism, and ethnic hatreds was unleashed, but so were the humanitarian, charitable impulses religion can sow in people's hearts.

NOTES

1. Jerry G. Pankhurst, "Religion and Atheism in the USSR," in *Contemporary Soviet Society: Sociological Perspectives,* ed. Jerry G. Pankhurst and Michael Paul Sacks (New York: Praeger, 1980), 183; Susan Bridger, *Women in the Soviet Countryside* (Cambridge: Cambridge University Press, 1987), 177; Harvey Fireside, *Icon and Swastika: The Russian Orthodox Church under Nazi and Soviet Control* (Cambridge, MA: Harvard University Press, 1971), 10; Michael Binyon, *Life in Russia* (New York: Pantheon, 1983), 227.

2. Walter Benjamin, *Moscow Diary,* ed. Gary Smith, trans. Richard Sieburth (Cambridge, MA: MIT Press, 1986), 51.

3. Sheila Fitzpatrick, *Stalin's Peasants: Resistance and Survival in the Russian Village after Collectivization* (Oxford, England: Oxford University Press, 1996), 42; Diane Koenker and Ronald D. Bachman, eds., *Revelations from the Russian Archives: Documents in English Translation* (Washington, DC: Library of Congress, 1997), 436 (note: this material has also been available online, as a link from the Library of Congress Web site, and I have used both sources); Richard Lourie, "Moscow," *New York Times Magazine,* part 2, *Sophisticated Traveler,* September 29, 2002, 30–33, 70–71; David K. Shipler, *Russia: Broken Idols, Solemn Dreams* (New York: Times Books, 1983), 265–77; Dennis Shasha and Marina Shron, eds., *Red Blues: Voices from the Last*

Wave of Russian Immigrants (New York: Holmes and Meier, 2002), 6; Jake Bowman, "Lutherans Work to Turn a Swimming Pool Back into a Church," *St. Petersburg Press* (1995), www.friends-partners.org/oldfriendsspbweb/lifestyl/136/lutherans.html

4. Adapted slightly from *Fleischmann's Yeast Bread Machine Favorites* (Des Moines, IA: Meredith Publishing Services, 1995), 62, or online at www.breadworld.com/recipes/recipedetail.asp?id = 85; for making *kulich* by hand and for *paskha* recipes, see Helen Papashvily and George Papashvily, *Russian Cooking* (New York: Time-Life Books, 1969), 58–59.

5. Binyon, *Life in Russia,* 238; Hedrick Smith, *The Russians* (New York: Ballantine Books, 1977), 578–79.

6. *Soviet Union. A Country Study. Religious Groups in the Soviet Union* http://lcweb2.loc.gov/cgi-bin/query/r?frd/cstdy:@field[DOCID+su0127].

7. *Revelations from the Russian Archives: Anti-Religious Campaigns, http://lcweb. loc.gov/exhibits/archives/html*; William C. Fletcher, "World War II's Effects on Religion: Church-State Relations," in *The Impact of World War II on the Soviet Union,* ed. Susan Linz (Totowa, NJ: Rowman & Allenheld, 1985), 92–94, 95–98; Koenker and Bachman, *Revelations,* 434, 436; *Country Study,* "Policy Toward Nationalities and Religions in Practice," http://lcweb2.loc.gov/cgi-bin/query/r?frd/cstdy: @field [DOCID+su0128].

8. William C. Fletcher, "Religious Dissent in the USSR in the 1960s," *Slavic Review* 30, no. 2 (June 1971): 299, 303–4, 306.

9. Pankhurst, "Religion and Atheism," 194; Bridger, *Women,* 177.

10. Christopher Cerf and Marina Albee, eds., *Small Fires: Letters from the Soviet People to Ogonyok Magazine 1987–1990* (New York: Summit Books, 1990), 149–51.

11. *Soviet Union. A Country Study.* "Policy Toward Nationalities."

12. *Revelations.* In this chapter I have made heavy use of the following *Country Study* sections: "Ukrainian Catholic Church," http://lcweb2.loc.gov/cgi-bin/query/r?frd/cstdy:@field[DOCID+su0125]; "Policy toward Nationalities and Religions in Practice," http://lcweb2.loc.gov/cgi-bin/query/r?frd/cstdy: @field [DOCID+su0128]; "Orthodox," http://lcweb2.loc.gov/cgi-bin/query/r?frd/cstdy:@field[DOCID+su0120]; "Ukrainian Autocephalous Orthodox Church," http://lcweb2.loc.gov/cgi-bin/query/r?frd/cstdy:@field[DOCID+ su0122]; "Georgian Orthodox Church," http://lcweb2.loc.gov/cgi-bin/query/ r?frd/cstdy:@ field[DOCID+su0122]; "Armenian Apostolic Church," http:// lcweb 2.loc.gov/cgi-bin/query/r?frd/cstdy:@field[DOCID+su0123]; "Jews," http://lcweb2.loc.gov/ cgi-bin/query/r?frd/cstdy:@field[DOCID+su0113]; "Protestant," http://lcweb2. loc.gov/cgi-bin/query/r?frd/cstdy:@field[DOCID+su0126]; and "Muslim," http:// lcweb2.loc.gov/cgi-bin/query/r?frd/cstdy:@field[DOCID+ su0127]; Pankhurst, "Religion and Atheism," 184–85.

13. Binyon, *Life in Russia,* 245; Smith, *The Russians,* 636, 653.

14. www.haruth.com/JewsGeorgia.html; Frank Brown, "Mountain Jews Struggle to Keep Culture Intact," *Chicago Tribune,* November 22, 2002, 6.

15. Smith, *The Russians,* 642–43; Fletcher, "Religious Dissent," 300.

16. Joshua Rubenstein, introduction to *Stalin's Secret Pogrom: The Postwar Inquisition of the Jewish Anti-Fascist Committee,* ed. Joshua Rubenstein and Vladimir P. Naumov, trans. Esther Wolfson (New Haven: Yale University Press, 2001), 2, 35, 42, 44, 52, 62; Jeffrey Veidlinger, *The Moscow State Yiddish Theater: Jewish Culture on the Soviet Stage* (Bloomington: Indiana University Press, 2000), 270–72.

17. Shasha and Shron, *Red Blues,* 62–64; see also Binyon, *Life in Russia,* 240–47; Smith, *The Russians,* 633–35, 640–41, 643; M. K. Dziewanowski, *A History of Soviet Russia and its Aftermath,* 5th ed. (Upper Saddle River, NJ: Prentice Hall, 1997), 339–40.

18. Colin McMahon, "Promise of a Homeland in Russia. Jewish Republic Struggles to Retain Identity," *Chicago Tribune,* sec. 1, p. 1, col. 4, April 7, 2001; Robert Weinberg, *Stalin's Forgotten Zion. Birobidzhan and the Making of a Soviet Jewish Homeland: An Illustrated History, 1928–1996* (Berkeley: University of California Press, 1998), 20–28 (page numbers are to the electronic version).

19. Merle Fainsod, *Smolensk under Soviet Rule* (Boston: Unwin Hyman [1958] 1989), 438.

20. Pankhurst, "Religion and Atheism," 188.

21. Binyon, *Life in Russia,* 240.

22. Aleksandr Solzhenitsyn, *Matryona's Home,* in *The Norton Anthology: World Masterpieces,* vol. 2, expanded edition, ed. Maynard Mack et al. (New York: W. W. Norton, 1995), 2315.

23. Helmut Altrichter, "Insoluble Conflicts: Village Life between Revolution and Collectivization," in *Russia in the Era of NEP,* ed. Sheila Fitzpatrick, Alexander Rabinowitch, and Richard Stites (Bloomington: Indiana University Press, 1991), 197.

24. Helmut Altrichter, "Insoluble Conflicts: Village Life Between Revolution and Collectivization," in *Russia in the Era of NEP,* ed. Sheila Fitzpatrick, Alexander Rabinowitch, and Richard Stites (Bloomington: Indiana University Press, 1991), 195–205.

glossary

Afghan war—Soviet armed forces invaded Afghanistan in 1979, installing a puppet Marxist government but finding much stiffer resistance than anticipated. The invasion led to disastrous human losses on both sides; the Soviet military pulled out of Afghanistan in early 1989.

animism—The belief that inanimate objects and natural phenomena (e.g., trees, rocks, fire) have souls.

Autocephalous churches—Self-governing Orthodox churches that appoint their own **metropolitan**s.

babushka—An old woman; a grandmother.

banya—Bathhouse; steam bath.

beryozki **(sing.,** *beryozka*)—Special shops carrying a variety of quality goods, where foreign tourists, diplomats, foreign correspondents, and a few privileged Soviets with Western money ("hard currency") could shop in a relatively pleasant environment.

besprizorniki **(or** *besprizornye*)—Literally, "neglected ones"; the millions of children who, in the decade following the October Revolution, were made homeless by revolution, civil war, and famine and wandered the USSR in gangs.

black market—An illegal buyer-seller transaction that usually involves goods bought from an entrepreneur looking to make a profit.

blat **(***po blaty***) (pull),** *nalevo* **(on the left),** *po znakomstvu* **(through an acquaintance)**—Terms indicating use of one or more of the following—

influence, networking, bribes, personal favors, "pull," and so forth—that helped someone obtain consumer goods, services, or special privileges. Such transactions did not always involve money.

Bolsheviks—At a 1903 conference of the Russian Social Democratic Workers' Party, Lenin's followers achieved a brief majority and used the occasion to name his faction "majority men," or Bolsheviks. Lenin's opponents took the name "minority men," or Mensheviks, and the split among Social Democrats became permanent.

borshch—Soup prepared in a variety of ways, but often with beets as the main ingredient.

bourgeois/bourgeoisie—See **capitalism/capitalist.**

caliph—The spiritual and civic leader of the Islamic community.

capitalism/capitalist—Capitalism is the economic system that encourages ownership of private property and depends on privately owned, profit-making businesses (a free market economy); a capitalist is a person who participates in that system. According to Marxist thinking and Soviet ideology, capitalist economies, controlled by wealthy capitalists (bourgeoisie, sing. bourgeois), ruthlessly exploited workers.

Central Committee—The highest Party organization when a Congress was not meeting. The Politburo (Political Bureau), called the Presidium from 1952 to 1966, was the Central Committee's executive committee—the Party's highest policy-making and executive body.

Civil War—The 1918–1920 war between the Bolsheviks and their supporters against the very diverse White forces.

cold war—The series of post–World War II hostilities, diplomatic tensions, and confrontations short of actual warfare that characterized the relationship between the United States and the Soviet Union.

collective farm (*kollektivnoe khoziaistvo, kolkhoz***)**—A "cooperative" farm whose workers (*kolkhozniki,* kolkhozniks) were managed by state-appointed leaders, with state-determined production goals.

collectivization—The seizure of privately owned farms, buildings, livestock, and the like, and placement of farm families and seized property onto state farms and collective farms.

commissar—Term used for a government minister, 1917–1946. Also, the political officer attached to each military unit whose duties at various times included political indoctrination, battlefront fighting, and even (until 1940) military decisions.

Commonwealth of Independent States—December 21, 1991, successor to the USSR.

communal apartment (*kommunalka,* **pl.** *kommunalki***)**—A single apartment divided into separate rooms for multiple families who share kitchen, bath, and toilet.

communism/communist—An economic system and ideology that promotes government ownership of all important industries, and in its extreme form prohibits all private enterprise and private land ownership and is coupled with the belief that within such a system, government and its bureaucracies will "wither away" while goods and services are distributed justly among all citizens.

Communism/CPSU (Communist Party of the Soviet Union)—One who believes in the communist economic system. A card-carrying, dues-paying member of a national Communist party, or of the Communist Party of the Soviet Union. Established in 1898 as the Russian Socialist Democratic Labor Party, the CPSU was the Soviet Union's only legal political party and oversaw the state bureaucracy.

comrade—A fellow socialist or communist; in the USSR used as a way of addressing someone: "Comrade Ivanov," or "Comrade Political Instructor," for example.

Congress of People's Deputies—The first (1989) USSR parliament, with some democratically elected representatives; disbanded in 1991.

Congress of the Communist Party of the Soviet Union (CPSU)—The Congress, composed of delegates from around the country, met approximately, but not necessarily, every five years, mainly to rubber-stamp plans and policies decided by the ruling Politburo.

constitution—Document that is supposed to set forth the basic laws and principles governing Soviet society. There were four such constitutions: 1918, for the RSFSR; 1924, the first USSR constitution; 1936, the "Stalin constitution"; and 1977, the "Brezhnev constitution." Soviet constitutions set forth many praiseworthy civic ideals but never actually hindered the powers of the state or Party.

dacha—A summer house or cabin in the country.

dedovshchina/gruppovshchina—The brutal hazing of new military recruits by their slightly older colleagues; attacks on enlisted men of one ethnicity by those of another.

dictatorship of the proletariat—The idea that after capitalism is overthrown, workers will take the lead in suppressing their bourgeois exploiters.

Doctors' Plot—The January 1953 arrests of prominent physicians (mostly Jewish) on charges they had killed two top Soviet leaders—Andrei Zhdanov and Alexander Shcherbakov—and were conspiring with American intelligence and a Jewish organization to murder a number of top military officers plus other government leaders and their children. Charges against the doctors were dismissed in 1953, some weeks after Stalin's death. Of the nine arrested, seven survived their imprisonment; two had died from torture.

East Slavs—Slavic peoples who became known as Russians, Ukrainians, and Byelorussians and whose languages belong to the East Slavic branch of Indo-European languages.

February Revolution—The February (March 8–16, New Style) 1917 revolution that overthrew Tsar Nicholas II and the Russian monarchy.

feldsher—A physician's assistant or paramedic who often practiced alone in rural areas where no physicians were available.

First Secretary—See **General Secretary (secretary-general).**

five-year plans—USSR economic goals that the State Planning Committee (*Gosplan*) established for five-year periods. Once plans were established, they became law and were expected to be fulfilled.

Formalism (Formalist)—Artists and writers who did not conform to the officially approved style, Socialist Realism, were labeled Formalist, which had nothing to do with the original Formalist movement in literary criticism that began around 1914–1915. Eventually the term was applied to all art and artists suspected of cultural-political nonconformity, as well as to suspect teachers and scientists.

General Secretary (secretary-general)—The title of the head of the Communist Party of the Soviet Union (CPSU) Secretariat, chairman of the Politburo, and leader of the Soviet Union. The title was changed to First Secretary in 1953, was used by Khrushchev and then Brezhnev until 1966, and then was changed back to General Secretary.

glasnost—Openness; a word used during Gorbachev's 1980s leadership to describe government policy of allowing more open debate and less censorship.

Gosplan—Acronym for State Planning Committee. See **five-year plans.**

Great Patriotic War—The name the Soviets gave to World War II (1941–1945).

Great Terror—The period from about 1934 to 1939 when millions of Soviets were arrested, tortured, imprisoned, deported from their homelands, or executed for imaginary crimes against the state. The Terror was sometimes random and sometimes aimed at certain political, ethnic, or professional groups; no one was safe.

gulag—Acronym for Main Directorate of Corrective Labor Camps. Established in 1930, the Soviet network of slave labor camps where political prisoners and common criminals served their sentences.

hooligan (*khuligan*)—A person (usually a teenager or young adult) who, according to the criminal code, intentionally violates "public order in a coarse manner...expressing a clear disrespect for society."

intelligentsia—People who belonged to the upper levels of Soviet society and were well-educated, cultured people, intellectuals, white-collar workers (but not mere clerks), professionals, members of the arts community; those who earn a living using their minds rather than their hands.

internal passport—Identification issued by both the imperial and Soviet governments that people had to always carry and produce on demand. The purpose of internal passports was to control the movements of citizens within the country. Until 1976, kolkhozniks were not issued internal passports.

izba—A peasant's small hut, cottage, or cabin.

Jewish Anti-Fascist Committee—Established in 1942 as one of several Soviet organizations that campaigned for moral and financial support, at home and abroad, in the fight against Germany. In 1948–1949 25 leading members of the Soviet Jewish community, some of whom had been active in the Anti-Fascist Committee, were arrested, tried on trumped-up charges, and (in the case of 24 of them) executed in 1952.

kolkhoz/kolkhoznik—See **collective farm.**

Komsomol—Established in 1918, the youth organization for older teenagers and young adults approximately 14–28; a stepping-stone to Party membership.

Kremlin *(Kreml')*—The medieval fortress section of many Russian cities. In Moscow the Kremlin contained the heart of Soviet power: government office buildings, medical facilities, and residences for the USSR's top leaders and their families.

Kronstadt rebellion—The 1921 failed revolt by sailors at the Kronstadt naval base against the Bolshevik regime.

kulak—A prosperous independent farmer; a negative term the Bolsheviks applied to any peasant who owned his own land and livestock and hired one or more workers to help him. Eventually the Bolsheviks called any peasant who opposed collectivization a kulak.

kumiss—Fermented mare's milk; the Kazakh national drink.

kvas—Sour beer made by pouring water over rye bread and allowing the bread to ferment.

labor book *(trudovaia knizhka)*—The management-provided record every worker had to carry. In it was listed previous employment, work qualifications, and misbehavior.

labor-day or work-day *(trudoden')*—A method of measuring farmwork done by collective farmers (kolkhozniks, *kolkhozniki*) in order to determine wages. Each labor-day equaled the amount of work done in one day to finish a certain job. Some assignments (e.g., driving a tractor) earned workers more labor-days than others (e.g., hoeing weeds). After Stalin's death, kolkhozes gradually moved toward paying their workers defined salaries and benefits.

left, leftist, Left Opposition—A leftist is a person or group that leans toward socialism; in Soviet history the term was often used negatively to indicate people who were too politically radical to be of use to the Party or the country. In early Party history, the more radical Party members were called the Left Opposition.

Lend-lease/Marshall Plan—A U.S. World War II foreign aid program that, beginning in 1941, supplied the USSR and other Allied countries who fought the Axis powers (Germany, Japan, and Italy) with billions of dollars' worth of war *matériel*. Postwar, the United States offered the USSR Marshall Plan aid, a program announced in June 1947 for the reconstruction of Europe, but Stalin refused.

Marxism/Marxist—Socialist ideology of the German philosopher Karl Marx (1818–1883) that emphasizes material and economic factors in social development and identifies history as a struggle between haves and have-nots, a history moving toward a classless and stateless utopia.

Mensheviks—See **Bolsheviks.**

metropolitan—In the Orthodox Church, the head of the church for a certain geographical area, headquartered in a large city.

militia—Regular police, as opposed to secret police.

mujahideen (**sing.,** *mujahid*)—Afghan rebels who resisted the Soviet invasion of Afghanistan called themselves *mujahideen*, "holy warriors."

New Economic Policy (NEP)—Begun in 1921 by Lenin, NEP allowed peasants to sell their produce on the open market; it also allowed small private businesses to operate. In 1929 Stalin shut down NEP and demanded complete collectivization of agriculture and elimination of **kulak**s.

New Style—Refers to the more astronomically correct Gregorian calendar introduced by Pope Gregory XIII in 1582 that replaced the Julian (or Old Style) calendar named for Julius Caesar, which had been introduced in 46 B.C. By the time of the November 7 Revolution most of the Western world was using the Gregorian calendar; the Russian Empire, however, had not adopted it. On February 1, 1918 (Old Style), the Bolsheviks substituted the New Style calendar for the old one, omitting 13 extra days that had accumulated since 325 A.D. February 1 became February 14. The Russian Orthodox Church, like other Eastern Orthodox Churches, continues using the Old Style calendar.

October Revolution—The Bolsheviks overthrew the **Provisional Government** and seized power on October 24–25 (Old Style), November 6–7 (New Style).

Octobrists (Little Octobrists)—Youth organization for children ages 7 to 10.

Old Bolsheviks—Prerevolutionary members of the Communist Party; many were Lenin's comrades, activists, and highly placed in the Soviet government and Party. During the Great Terror of the 1930s, Stalin destroyed virtually all the Old Bolsheviks, along with many of their relatives and associates, as well as millions of others.

Old Style—See **New Style.**

ordinary psychiatric hospitals (OPH)—Hospitals for treatment of the nonviolent mentally ill and sometimes for incarceration of political prisoners.

orgburo (Organizational Bureau)—A subcommittee, from 1919 to 1952, of the Central Committee of the CPSU, subordinate to the Politburo.

Orthodox Church—See **Russian Orthodox Church.**

otkhodnik—A person who left his or her collective farm.

Paleo-Asiatic peoples—People whose native tongues are based on ancient languages of northeastern Asia.

peasant *(krest'ianin)*—A farmer; a villager. As a class, peasants were at the bottom of society.

pech'—A stove; in particular, the traditional rural Russian tiled or brick stove used for both heating and cooking, big enough to sleep on for warmth in winter.

perestroika—Word used by Mikhail Gorbachev to signify his policy of "reconstruction" of the Soviet economy, Party, and society.

pogrom—Attack, often deadly, against Jews.

Politburo—See **Central Committee.**

proletarians (proletariat)—Factory and other blue-collar workers.

propiska—A document conferring official permission to live in a city; a residence permit.

Provisional Government—Governing body, formed after the February Revolution, that grew out of the imperial legislature (Duma). The Bolsheviks overthrew the Provisional Government and seized power on October 24–25 (Old Style; November 6–7 New Style).

Presidium of the Supreme Soviet (pre-1936, the Central Executive Committee)—The Supreme Soviet's executive committee, it was the main lawmaking body between sessions of the Supreme Soviet. It also elected the Council of Ministers. The Chairman of the Presidium was the official head of state but was not as powerful as the Party's General Secretary.

rabfak—Acronym for workers' school. Founded in 1919, *rabfaki* (pl.) provided basic remedial education for workers. The last such school closed in 1941.

raspredelenie—The government's postgraduate job assignment program.

Red Army—The name of the Soviet army, 1918–1945.

Reds—Bolsheviks and their supporters.

right—A conservative political group.

ruble—Russian currency; the currency of the Soviet Union.

Russian Federation/RSFSR/Russian Republic/Russia—The largest of the 15 republics of the USSR.

Russian Orthodox Church—Under the tsars the Russian Orthodox Church was the official state church. After the Revolution, the Russian Orthodox Church, though persecuted, continued to have more followers than any other religious institution in the Soviet Union. The Russian Orthodox Church has links with other Orthodox churches.

Russian Social Democratic Workers' Party (RSDWP or SDs)—Russian Marxist party (established in 1898) that emerged out of the Populist movement following its breakup in 1879 and that underwent a split between the Bolsheviks under Vladimir Lenin (1870–1924) and the Mensheviks under Yuly Martov (1873–1923) in 1903.

rynok—Marketplace where peasants sell their produce and handcrafted items.

samizdat—Self-published, the word signifies illegal writing copied and circulated by readers from hand to hand.

samogon—Illegal homemade alcoholic drinks, particularly vodka.

secret police (security police)—This organization underwent name changes over the years, but its basic mission remained the same: to prevent any sort of political nonconformity, to spy on citizens and foreigners at home and abroad, to prevent unauthorized contact with foreigners, to run the gulag camps, and when called upon, to be the agents of terror. The various abbreviations and acronyms for the secret police were Cheka (1917–1922); GPU, later OGPU (1922–1934); NKVD (1934–1946); MGB (1946–1953); and KGB (1954–1991).

serf—An unfree laborer. In Russia before their emancipation by Tsar Alexander II in 1861, about half of Russian peasants were serfs who belonged to private owners. Part and parcel of the land they lived and worked on, serfs were obligated to toil for the landowner for half of their total work days.

shabashnik—A person who privately supplied services, repairs, or manual labor, full-time or on the side; such work usually occupied a gray area between legal and illegal.

shaman (shamanism)—A healer-priest who claims to be able to communicate with gods and the spirit world; religious practice centering on a shaman's rituals.

shchi—Cabbage soup.

Shia (Shiite)—A member of the smaller of the two largest branches of Islam. Shiites believe that descendants of Ali, the fourth caliph after Mohammed's death, are divinely ordained to be caliph, the spiritual and civic leader of the Islamic world.

socialism—Public ownership of the means of production. State socialism defines Soviet society since full communism was not achieved.

Socialist Realism—First proposed by Stalin, in conference with various writers, in 1932; announced publicly by Stalin's cultural spokesman, and "chief witch hunter," Andrei Zhdanov, as the officially approved artistic style for literature in 1934. Socialist Realism conveyed a romantic, idealized, easily understood, optimistic picture of Soviet life and the Soviet future. Although originally formulated for literature, Socialist Realism soon was mandatory for all officially approved art, including painting, sculpture, film, theater, music, and dance, until the end of the Soviet Union.

Socialist Revolutionary Party (SRs)—Established 1901–1902. Like their Populist forebears, SRs continued to see themselves as the peasants' champions. SRs won a majority of seats in the Constitutional Assembly in the November 1917 election. Lenin shut the assembly down on January 19, 1918, after its first and only meeting.

soviet—Council.

Soviet republics—The major administrative subdivisions of the USSR, which numbered 15 when the Soviet Union was dissolved.

sovkhoz—See **state farm.**

special psychiatric hospitals (SPH)—Mental hospitals for incarcerating political prisoners and the criminally insane.

state farm (*sovkhoz;* acronym for state farm)—A government owned and managed enterprise whose workers (*sovkhozniki*), in contrast to early collective-farm workers, had defined cash salaries and benefits, including vacation time and pensions.

Sunni—A member of the larger of the two biggest divisions of the Muslim religion. Sunnis believe that the first four caliphs were the legitimate successors to Mohammed. They adhere to the *sunna:* Islamic practices based on Mohammed's words and actions. In 1989 Sunnis were the great majority of the Soviet Union's Muslims. In contrast to Shiite Muslims, who believe caliphs are divinely ordained, Sunnis support an elected caliph (the title of Mohammed's successors as heads of Islam).

Supreme Soviet—Soviet parliament, the USSR's highest legislative body; composed of two houses, Soviet of the Union and Soviet of Nationalities.

Symbolists—A group of mystical, romantic poets, painters, and writers who flourished between the 1890s and World War I in Russia and other

European countries. They tried to express their mystical yearnings through the use of flowery language and muted blue, green, and gray color schemes. They believed that nothing is as it seems: behind every word or object lies its true meaning or essence, which connects with all other deeper realities in the universe. The Russian Symbolist movement was distinguished from other European Symbolist art by its strong religious element. By trying to uncover, through art, the essential reality behind appearances, some Russian Symbolists, such as Alexander Blok, hoped to experience a brief oneness with Christ.

tamizdat—"Published over there," *tamizdat* writings are those that were smuggled and illegally published outside the USSR.

The Thaw—The title of Ilya Ehrenburg's 1954 novel, used to describe post-Stalin (relative) relaxation of censorship and terror.

trudoden'—See **labor-day**.

Uniate Church—Established 1596, recognizes the Roman Catholic pope as head of the church while preserving most Orthodox rituals.

USSR—Union of Soviet Socialist Republics; proclaimed in 1922 as the official name of the Soviet Union.

virgin land; virgin land campaign—Land that has never been farmed. First Secretary Nikita Khrushchev's campaign to raise crops in virgin land areas of the Kazakh Republic and some neighboring parts of the Russian Republic. The undertaking was unsuccessful.

War Communism—Name the Bolsheviks gave to their economic policy during the Civil War, a policy that included forced requisitioning of grain.

Whites—Various forces that fought against the Bolsheviks and their supporters in the Civil War.

Winter War—War in 1939–1940 against Finland, motivated by the USSR's desire to grab territory from that country. The Finns put up a heroic resistance but were so vastly outnumbered they finally were forced to cede over 16,000 square miles containing 420,000 people.

Young Pioneers—Youth organization for children ages 10 to 16.

zakuski—Appetizers.

Zionism—An international movement formerly for the reestablishment (later support) of the state of Israel.

for further reading

Many more possibilities for further reading can be found in the endnotes to each chapter.

NONFICTION

Amalrik, Andrei. *Involuntary Journey to Siberia.* New York: Harcourt Brace Jovanovich, 1970.

Applebaum, Anne. *Gulag.* New York: Doubleday, 2003.

Bonner, Elena. *Mothers and Daughters.* New York: Alfred A. Knopf, 1992.

Cerf, Christopher, and Marina Albee, eds. *Small Fires: Letters from the Soviet People to Ogonyok Magazine 1987–1990,* trans. Hans Fenstermacher. New York: Summit Books, 1990.

Eaton, Katherine Bliss, ed. *Enemies of the People: The Destruction of Literary, Theater, and Film Arts in the Soviet Union in the 1930s.* Evanston, IL: Northwestern University Press, 2002.

Edelman, Robert. *Serious Fun: A History of Spectator Sports in the USSR.* New York: Oxford University Press, 1993.

Ermolaev, Herman. *Censorship in Soviet Literature: 1917–1991.* New York: Rowman and Littlefield, 1997.

Fitzpatrick, Sheila. *Everyday Stalinism: Ordinary Life in Extraordinary Times: Soviet Russia in the 1930s.* New York: Oxford University Press, 1999.

Garrard, John G., and Carol Garrard. *Inside the Soviet Writers' Union.* New York: Free Press, 1990.

Ginzburg, Eugenia. *Journey into the Whirlwind.* Translated by Paul Stevens and Max Hayward. New York: Harcourt, Brace, and World, 1967.

———. *Within the Whirlwind.* Translated by Ian Boland. San Diego: Harcourt Brace Jovanovich, 1981.

Hochschild, Adam. *The Unquiet Ghost: Russians Remember Stalin.* New York: Viking Penguin, 1995.

Kaiser, Robert G. *Russia: The People and the Power.* New York: Pocket Books, 1977.

Kaminskaya, Dina. *Final Judgement.* Translated by Michael Glenny. New York: Simon and Schuster, 1982.

King, David. *The Commissar Vanishes: The Falsification of Photographs and Art in Stalin's Russia.* New York: Metropolitan Books, 1997.

Kosterina, Nina. *The Diary of Nina Kosterina.* Translated by Mirra Ginsburg. New York: Crown, 1968.

Lee, Andrea. *Russian Journal.* New York: Vintage Books, 1984.

Loza, Dmitrii. *Fighting for the Soviet Motherland: Recollections from the Eastern Front.* Edited and translated by James E. Gebhardt. Lincoln: University of Nebraska Press, 1998.

Mandelstam, Nadezhda. *Hope Against Hope.* Translated by Max Hayward. New York: Modern Library, 1999. (The first volume of her memoir.)

———. *Hope Abandoned.* Translated by Max Hayward. New York: Atheneum, 1974. (The second volume of her memoir.)

Medvedev, Zhores A., and Roy A. Medvedev. *A Question of Madness.* Translated by Ellen de Kadt. New York: W. W. Norton, 1979.

Merridale, Catherine. *Night of Stone: Death and Memory in Twentieth Century Russia.* New York: Viking Penguin, 2001.

Millar, James R. *The ABCs of Soviet Socialism.* Urbana: University of Illinois Press, 1981.

Reese, Roger R. *The Soviet Military Experience: A History of the Soviet Army, 1917–1991.* London: Routledge, 2000.

Remnick, David. *Lenin's Tomb: The Last Days of the Soviet Empire.* New York: Vintage Books, 1994.

Riordan, Jim, ed. *Soviet Youth Culture.* Bloomington: Indiana University Press, 1989.

Shipler, David K. *Russia: Broken Idols, Solemn Dreams.* New York: Times Books, 1983.

Smith, Hedrick. *The Russians.* Revised edition. New York: Ballantine Books, 1984.

———. *The New Russians.* New York: Random House, 1991.

Stites, Richard. *Russian Popular Culture: Entertainment and Society since 1900.* New York: Cambridge University Press, 1992.

Willis, David. *Klass: How Russians Really Live.* New York: Avon Books, 1987.

Zickel, Raymond E., ed. *Soviet Union: A Country Study.* 2nd ed. Washington, DC: Library of Congress. Federal Research Division, 1991. Also available at http://lcweb2.loc.gov/frd/cs/sutoc.html.

FICTION

Babel, Isaac. "Early Stories," "The Odessa Stories," "The Red Cavalry Stories," and "Stories 1925–1938." In *The Complete Works of Isaac Babel* Edited by Nathalie Babel, translated by Peter Constantine. New York: W. W. Norton, 2001.

Baranskaya, Natalya. "A Week Like Any Other." In *A Week Like Any Other: Novellas and Stories.* Translated by Pieta Monk. Seattle: Seal Press, 1990.

Grekova, I. "Ladies' Hairdresser" and "The Hotel Manager." In *Russian Women: Two Stories*. Translated by Michel Petrov. San Diego: Harcourt, Brace, Jovanovich, 1983.

Grossman, Vasily. *Life and Fate*. Translated by Robert Chandler. New York: Perennial Library, 1987.

Pasternak, Boris. *Doctor Zhivago*. New York: Pantheon, 1958.

Rybakov, Anatoli. *Children of the Arbat*. Translated by Harold Shukman. New York: Dell, 1988.

———. *Heavy Sand*. Translated by Harold Shukman. Middlesex, England: Penguin Books, 1981.

Shalamov, Varlam. *Kolyma Tales*. Translated by John Glad. Middlesex, England: Penguin Books, 1994.

Solzhenitsyn, Aleksandr. *Cancer Ward*. Translated by Nicholas Bethell and David Burg. New York: Bantam Books, 1969.

———. *The First Circle*. Translated by Thomas P. Whitney. New York: Harper and Row, 1968. Available in a dramatized version: *First Circle*, 3 1/2 hours on three cassettes, PBS Home Video.

———. *Matryona's House*. In *"We Never Make Mistakes," Two Short Novels by Alexander Solzhenitsyn*. 2nd ed. Translated by Paul W. Blackstock. Columbia: University of South Carolina Press, 1971.

———. *One Day in the Life of Ivan Denisovich*. Translated by Max Hayward and Ronald Hingley. New York: Bantam Books, 1963.

Voinovich, Vladimir. *The Life and Extraordinary Adventures of Private Ivan Chonkin*. Translated by Richard Lourie. New York: Farrar, Straus, and Giroux, 1977.

POETRY

Akhmatova, Anna. "Requiem." In *The Complete Poems of Anna Akhmatova*. Translated by Judith Hemschemeyer. Brookline, MA: Zephyr Press, 1990.

Mandelstam, Osip. Selected poems in Victor Terras, "Death of a Poet: Osip Mandelshtam." In *Enemies of the People: The Destruction of Literary, Theater, and Film Arts in the 1930s*. Edited by Katherine B. Eaton. Evanston, IL: Northwestern University Press, 2002.

DOCUMENTARIES

East Side Story. Directed by Dana Ranga, 1997. Color, 78 min. Kino International Corp. In various languages, with English subtitles. Excerpts from seven Soviet and various Eastern bloc Hollywood-style musicals.

"How Good Is Soviet Science?" Episode of *Nova* (TV program). Directed by Martin Smith, 1987. Color and B&W, in English, 58 min. In association with WGBH Boston and NDR Hamburg.

If the People Will Lead. Directed by Paul Bonesteel, 1992. Color, in English, 58 min. Oakland, California, Video Project. Reviews the events of the three days in 1991 leading up to the collapse of the Communist Party government and the role of the Soviet people in securing their freedom.

Russian Trinity. Color, 90 min. In English. PBS Home Video. Explores the interconnections among the Kremlin, the secret police, and the Bolshoi Theater.

Russia's War: Blood upon the Snow. In English, on multiple tapes, approx. 10 hours. IBP Films Distribution, London; Victory Series, Moscow; PBS Home Video. Covers Stalin's regime, 1924–1953; the German invasion; the 900-day siege of Leningrad; and the Soviet Union's ultimate victory.

Uncle Chatzkel. Directed by Rob Freedman, 1999. Color, 52 min.; English with some (subtitled) Russian, Yiddish, and Lithuanian. First Run/Icarus Films. A 93-year-old Lithuanian Jew who survived the Russian Revolution, two World Wars, the Holocaust, the Communist regime, and Lithuania's transition to an independent state tells his life story.

FEATURE FILMS

Ballad of a Soldier. Directed by Grigory Chukhray, 1958. B&W, 89 min. Russian with English subtitles. Connoisseur Video Collection. The adventures of a young soldier, who, briefly furloughed as a reward for bravery, is on his way home from the front to visit his mother.

The Cranes Are Flying. Directed by Mikhail Kolotozov, 1957. B&W, 94 min. Russian with English subtitles. Criterion Collection. A young couple in love are separated when he has to go to war.

East/West. Directed by Régis Wargnier, 2000. Color, 115 minutes. In Russian and French with English or French subtitles. Rated PG; Oscar nominee. Columbia TriStar Home Video. A young couple and their son are among the thousands of Russian émigré families who shortly after the Second World War were invited to return to the USSR to help rebuild. Those who returned were, at best, condemned to a miserable existence with little hope of escape. *New York Times* critic A.O. Scott commented that the film "uses the resources of melodrama to shed light on forgotten history."

Freeze, Die, Come to Life. Directed by Vitaly Kanevski, 1989. B&W, 105 min. Russian dialogue, English subtitles. Fox Lorber Home Video. The story of two children growing up in a grubby post–World War II mining community/gulag zone, in the Soviet Far East. Based on the director's own boyhood experiences.

The Inner Circle. Directed by Andrey Konchalovsky, 1991. Color, 134 min. Rated PG-13. In English. The terror of the Stalin years revealed through the eyes of Stalin's film projectionist.

Little Vera. Directed by Vasily Pichul, 1988. Color, 110 min. Russian with English subtitles. Lumivision/Water Bearer Films. Winner, Best Film and Best Actress, Chicago Film Festival. Depicts life and boredom in a drab industrial town; the first Soviet film with an explicitly sexual episode.

One Day in the Life of Ivan Denisovich. Directed by Casper Wrede, 1971. Color, 105 min. In English. Sony Video Software. A masterful dramatization of Solzhenitsyn's classic novel of a prisoner in one of Stalin's slave labor camps.

INTERNET RESOURCE

The University of Illinois's Russian and East European Center has a very useful Web site with many links for teachers and students: http://www.reec. uiuc.edu.

index

About the Author

KATHERINE B. EATON was for many years professor of English at Tarrant County College in Forth Worth, Texas. She has twice been a Fulbright Lecturer in Iasi, Romania. She is the author of *The Theater of Meyerhold and Brecht* and the editor of *Enemies of the People: The Destruction of Soviet Literary, Theater, and Film Arts in the 1930s.* Dr. Eaton has also written journal and encyclopedia articles and book reviews on the subject of Soviet theater.